Wisdom, Worship, and Poetry

Wisdom, Worship, and Poetry

FORTRESS COMMENTARY ON THE BIBLE
STUDY EDITION

Gale A. Yee

Hugh R. Page Jr.

Matthew J. M. Coomber

Editors

Fortress Press

Minneapolis

WISDOM, WORSHIP, AND POETRY
Fortress Commentary on the Bible Study Edition

Unless otherwise noted, Scripture quotations are from New Revised Standard Version Bible, copyright © 1989 by the Division of Education of the National Council of Churches of Christ in the United States of America.

Excerpted from the *Fortress Commentary on the Bible: The Old Testament and Apocrypha*
(Minneapolis: Fortress Press, 2014); Gale A. Yee, Hugh R. Page Jr., and Matthew J. M. Coomber, volume editors.

Fortress Press Publication Staff:
Neil Elliott and Scott Tunseth, Project Editors
Marissa Wold, Production Manager
Laurie Ingram, Cover Design.

Copyeditor: Jeffrey A. Reimer

Typesetter: PerfecType, Nashville, TN

Proofreader: David Cottingham

Library of Congress Cataloging-in-Publication data is available

ISBN: 978-1-5064-1583-3

eISBN: 978-1-5064-1584-0

CONTENTS

Publisher's Note about Fortress Commentary on the Bible Study Editions — vii

Abbreviations — ix

Series Introduction — 1

Reading the Old Testament in Ancient and Contemporary Contexts
  Matthew J. M. Coomber — 5

The People of God and the Peoples of the Earth
  Hugh R. Page Jr. — 31

Reading the Christian Old Testament in the Contemporary World
  Daniel L. Smith-Christopher — 43

Themes and Perspectives in the Poetic Writings   Timothy J. Sandoval — 495
  Job   *Alissa Jones Nelson* — 519
  Psalms   *W. Derek Suderman* — 547
  Proverbs   *Carole R. Fontaine* — 601
  Ecclesiastes   *Micah D. Kiel* — 627
  Song of Songs   *Hugh R. Page Jr.* — 643

PUBLISHER'S NOTE

About the Fortress Commentary on the Bible Study Editions

In 2014 Fortress Press released the two-volume *Fortress Commentary on the Bible*. See the Series Introduction (pp. 1–3) for a look inside the creation and design of the Old Testament/Apocrypha and New Testament volumes. While each comprehensive commentary volume can easily be used in classroom settings, we also recognized that dividing the larger commentaries into smaller volumes featuring key sections of Scripture may be especially helpful for use in corresponding biblical studies courses. To help facilitate such classroom use, we have broken the two-volume commentary into eight study editions.

Please note that in this study edition the page numbers match the page numbers of the larger Fortress Commentary on the Bible volume in which it first appeared. We have intentionally retained the same page numbering to facilitate use of the study editions and larger volumes side by side.

Wisdom, Worship, and Poetry was first published in Fortress Commentary on the Bible: The Old Testament and Apocrypha.

ABBREVIATIONS

General

AT	Alpha Text (of the Greek text of Esther)
BOI	Book of Isaiah
Chr	Chronicler
DH	Deuteronomistic History
DI	Deutero-Isaiah
Dtr	Deuteronomist
Gk.	Greek
H	Holiness Code
Heb.	Hebrew
JPS	Jewish Publication Society
LXX	The Septuagint
LXX B	Vaticanus Text of the Septuagint
MP	Mode of production
MT	Masoretic Text
NIV	New International Version
NRSV	New Revised Standard Version
OAN	Oracles against Nations (in Jeremiah)
P.	papyrus/papyri
P	Priestly source
PE	Pastoral Epistles
RSV	Revised Standard Version
TI	Trito-Isaiah

Books of the Bible (NT, OT, Apocrypha)

Old Testament/Hebrew Bible

Gen.	Genesis
Exod.	Exodus
Lev.	Leviticus
Num.	Numbers
Deut.	Deuteronomy

Josh.	Joshua
Judg.	Judges
Ruth	Ruth
1 Sam.	1 Samuel
2 Sam.	2 Samuel
1 Kgs.	1 Kings
2 Kgs.	2 Kings
1 Chron.	1 Chronicles
2 Chron.	2 Chronicles
Ezra	Ezra
Neh.	Nehemiah
Esther	Esther
Job	Job
Ps. (Pss.)	Psalms
Prov.	Proverbs
Eccles.	Ecclesiastes
Song.	Song of Songs
Isa.	Isaiah
Jer.	Jeremiah
Lam.	Lamentations
Ezek.	Ezekiel
Dan.	Daniel
Hosea	Hosea
Joel	Joel
Amos	Amos
Obad.	Obadiah
Jon.	Jonah
Mic.	Micah
Nah.	Nahum
Hab.	Habakkuk
Zeph.	Zephaniah
Hag.	Haggai
Zech.	Zechariah
Mal.	Malachi

Apocrypha

Tob.	Tobit
Jth.	Judith
Gk. Esther	Greek Additions to Esther
Sir.	Sirach (Ecclesiasticus)

Bar.   Baruch
Let. Jer.   Letter of Jeremiah
Add Dan.   Additions to Daniel
Pr. Azar.   Prayer of Azariah
Sg. Three.   Song of the Three Young Men (or Three Jews)
Sus.   Susanna
Bel   Bel and the Dragon
1 Macc.   1 Maccabees
2 Macc.   2 Maccabees
1 Esd.   1 Esdras
Pr. of Man.   Prayer of Manasseh
2 Esd.   2 Esdras
Wis.   Wisdom of Solomon
3 Macc.   3 Maccabees
4 Macc.   4 Maccabees

New Testament

Matt.   Matthew
Mark   Mark
Luke   Luke
John   John
Acts   Acts of the Apostles
Rom.   Romans
1 Cor.   1 Corinthians
2 Cor.   2 Corinthians
Gal.   Galatians
Eph.   Ephesians
Phil.   Philippians
Col.   Colossians
1 Thess.   1 Thessalonians
2 Thess.   2 Thessalonians
1 Tim.   1 Timothy
2 Tim.   2 Timothy
Titus   Titus
Philem.   Philemon
Heb.   Hebrews
James   James
1 Pet.   1 Peter
2 Pet.   2 Peter
1 John   1 John

2 John	2 John
3 John	3 John
Jude	Jude
Rev.	Revelation (Apocalypse)

Journals, Series, Reference Works

ABD	*Anchor Bible Dictionary*. Edited by David Noel Freedman. 6 vols. New York: Doubleday, 1992.
ACNT	Augsburg Commentaries on the New Testament
AJA	*American Journal of Archaeology*
AJT	*Asia Journal of Theology*
ANET	*Ancient Near Eastern Texts Relating to the Old Testament*. Edited by J. B. Pritchard. 3rd ed. Princeton: Princeton University Press, 1969.
ANF	*The Ante-Nicene Fathers*. Edited by Alexander Roberts and James Donaldson. 1885–1887. 10 vols. Repr., Peabody, MA: Hendrickson, 1994.
ANRW	*Aufstieg und Niedergang der römischen Welt: Geschichte und Kultur Roms im Spiegel der neueren Forschung*. Edited by Hildegard Temporini and Wolfgang Haase. Berlin: de Gruyter, 1972–.
ANTC	Abingdon New Testament Commentaries
AOAT	Alter Orient und Altes Testament
AbOTC	Abingdon Old Testament Commentary
AOTC	Apollos Old Testament Commentary
A(Y)B	Anchor (Yale) Bible
BA	*Biblical Archaeologist*
BAR	*Biblical Archaeology Review*
BDAG	Bauer, W., F. W. Danker, W. F. Arndt, and F. W. Gingrich. *Greek-English Lexicon of the New Testament and Other Early Christian Literature*. 3rd ed. Chicago: University of Chicago Press, 1999.
BEATAJ	Beiträge zur Erforschung des Alten Testaments und des Antiken Judentum
Bib	*Biblica*
BibInt	*Biblical Interpretation*
BJRL	*Bulletin of the John Rylands University Library of Manchester*
BJS	Brown Judaic Studies
BNTC	Black's New Testament Commentaries
BR	*Biblical Research*
BRev	*Bible Review*
BSac	*Bibliotheca sacra*
BTB	*Biblical Theology Bulletin*
BZAW	Beihefte zur Zeitschrift für die alttestamentliche Wissenschaft
CAT	Commentaire de l'Ancien Testament

CBC	Cambridge Bible Commentary
CBQMS	Catholic Biblical Quarterly Monograph Series
CC	Continental Commentaries
CH	*Church History*
CHJ	*Cambridge History of Judaism*. Edited by W. D. Davies and Louis Finkelstein. Cambridge: Cambridge University Press, 1984–.
ConBNT	Coniectanea biblica: New Testament Series
ConBOT	Coniectanea biblica: Old Testament Series
CS	Cistercian Studies
CTAED	*Canaanite Toponyms in Ancient Egyptian Documents*. S. Ahituv. Jerusalem: Magnes, 1984.
CTQ	*Concordia Theological Quarterly*
CurTM	*Currents in Theology and Mission*
ExpTim	*Expository Times*
ETL	*Ephemerides Theologicae Lovanienses*
ExAud	*Ex auditu*
FAT	Forschungen zum Alten Testament
FC	Fathers of the Church
FRLANT	Forschungen zur Religion und Literatur des Alten und Neuen Testaments
HAT	Handbuch zum Alten Testament
HBT	*Horizons in Biblical Theology*
HNTC	Harper's New Testament Commentaries
HR	*History of Religions*
HSM	Harvard Semitic Monographs
HTKAT	Herders Theologischer Kommentar zum Alten Testament
HTR	*Harvard Theological Review*
HTS	Harvard Theological Studies
HUCA	*Hebrew Union College Annual*
HUCM	Monographs of the Hebrew Union College
HUT	Hermeneutische Untersuchungen zur Theologie
IBC	Interpretation: A Bible Commentary for Teaching and Preaching
ICC	International Critical Commentary
Int	*Interpretation*
JAAR	*Journal of the American Academy of Religion*
JAOS	*Journal of the American Oriental Society*
JBL	*Journal of Biblical Literature*
JBQ	*Jewish Bible Quarterly*
JECS	*Journal of Early Christian Studies*
JJS	*Journal of Jewish Studies*
JNES	*Journal of Near Eastern Studies*

JNSL	*Journal of Northwest Semitic Languages*
JQR	*Jewish Quarterly Review*
JRS	*Journal of Roman Studies*
JSem	*Journal of Semitics*
JSJ	*Journal for the Study of Judaism in the Persian, Hellenistic, and Roman Periods*
JSNT	*Journal for the Study of the New Testament*
JSOT	*Journal for the Study of the Old Testament*
JSOTSup	Journal for the Study of the Old Testament Supplement Series
JSQ	*Jewish Studies Quarterly*
JSS	*Journal of Semitic Studies*
JTI	*Journal of Theological Interpretation*
JTS	*Journal of Theological Studies*
JTSA	*Journal of Theology for Southern Africa*
KTU	*Die keilalphabetischen Texte aus Ugarit.* Edited by M. Dietrich, O. Loretz, and J. Sanmartín. AOAT 24/1. Neukirchen-Vluyn: Neukirchener, 1976.
LCC	Loeb Classical Library
LEC	Library of Early Christianity
LHB/OTS	Library of the Hebrew Bible/Old Testament Studies
LW	*Luther's Works.* Edited by Jaroslav Pelikan and Helmut T. Lehmann. 55 vols. St. Louis: Concordia; Philadelphia: Fortress Press, 1958–1986.
NAC	New American Commentary
NCB	New Century Bible
NCBC	New Cambridge Bible Commentary
NedTT	*Nederlands theologisch tijdschrift*
Neot	*Neotestamentica*
NICNT	New International Commentary on the New Testament
NICOT	New International Commentary on the Old Testament
NIGTC	New International Greek Testament Commentary
NovT	*Novum Testamentum*
NPNF[1]	*The Nicene and Post-Nicene Fathers,* Series 1. Edited by Philip Schaff. 14 vols. 1886–1889. Repr., Grand Rapids: Eerdmans, 1956.
NTL	New Testament Library
NTS	*New Testament Studies*
OBT	Overtures to Biblical Theology
OTE	*Old Testament Essays*
OTG	Old Testament Guides
OTL	Old Testament Library
OTM	Old Testament Message
PEQ	*Palestine Exploration Quarterly*
PG	Patrologia graeca [= Patrologiae cursus completus: Series graeca]. Edited by J.-P. Migne. 162 vols. Paris, 1857–1886.

PL	John Milton, *Paradise Lost*
PL	Patrologia latina [= Patrologiae cursus completus: Series latina]. Edited by J.-P. Migne. 217 vols. Paris, 1844–1864.
PRSt	*Perspectives in Religious Studies*
QR	*Quarterly Review*
RevExp	*Review and Expositor*
RevQ	*Revue de Qumran*
SBLABS	Society of Biblical Literature Archaeology and Biblical Studies
SBLAIL	Society of Biblical Literature Ancient Israel and Its Literature
SBLDS	Society of Biblical Literature Dissertation Series
SBLEJL	Society of Biblical Literature Early Judaism and Its Literature
SBLMS	Society of Biblical Literature Monograph Series
SBLRBS	Society of Biblical Literature Resources for Biblical Study
SBLSCS	Society of Biblical Literature Septuagint and Cognate Studies
SBLSP	*Society of Biblical Literature Seminar Papers*
SBLSymS	Society of Biblical Literature Symposium Series
SBLWAW	SBL Writings from the Ancient World
SemeiaSt	Semeia Studies
SJT	*Scottish Journal of Theology*
SNTSMS	Society for New Testament Studies Monograph Series
SO	Symbolae osloenses
SR	*Studies in Religion*
ST	*Studia Theologica*
StABH	Studies in American Biblical Hermeneutics
TD	*Theology Digest*
TAD	*Textbook of Aramaic Documents from Ancient Egypt.* Vol. 1: *Letters.* Bezalel Porten and Ada Yardeni. Winona Lake, IN: Eisenbrauns, 1986.
TDOT	*Theological Dictionary of the Old Testament.* 15 vols. Edited by G. Johannes Botterweck, Helmer Ringgren, and Heinz-Josef Fabry. Translated by David E. Green and Douglas W. Stott. Grand Rapids: Eerdmans, 1974–1995.
TJT	*Toronto Journal of Theology*
TNTC	Tyndale New Testament Commentaries
TOTC	Tyndale Old Testament Commentaries
TS	*Theological Studies*
TZ	*Theologische Zeitschrift*
VE	*Vox evangelica*
VT	*Vetus Testamentum*
VTSup	Supplements to Vetus Testamentum
WBC	Word Biblical Commentary
WSA	Works of St. Augustine: A Translation for the Twenty-First Century
WUANT	Wissenschaftliche Untersuchungen zum Alten und Neuen Testament

WUNT   Wissenschaftliche Untersuchungen zum Neuen Testament
WW   *Word and World*
ZAW   *Zeitschrift für die alttestamentliche Wissenschaft*
ZBK   Zürcher Bibelkommentare
ZNW   *Zeitschrift für die neutestamentliche Wissenschaft und die Kunde der älteren Kirche*

Ancient Authors and Texts

1 Clem.   *1 Clement*
2 Clem.   *2 Clement*
1 En.   *1 Enoch*
2 Bar.   *2 Baruch*
Abot R. Nat.   *Abot de Rabbi Nathan*
Ambrose
    Paen.   *De paenitentia*
Aristotle
    Ath. Pol.   *Athēnaīn politeia*
    Nic. Eth.   *Nicomachean Ethics*
    Pol.   *Politics*
    Rhet.   *Rhetoric*
Augustine
    FC 79   *Tractates on the Gospel of John, 11–27.* Translated by John W. Rettig. Fathers of the Church 79. Washington, DC: Catholic University of America Press, 1988.
    Tract. Ev. Jo.   *In Evangelium Johannis tractatus*
Bede, Venerable
    CS 117   *Commentary on the Acts of the Apostles.* Translated by Lawrence T. Martin. Cistercian Studies 117. Kalamazoo, MI: Cistercian Publications, 1989.
Barn.   *Barnabas*
CD   Cairo Genizah copy of the Damascus Document
Cicero
    De or.   *De oratore*
    Tusc.   *Tusculanae disputationes*
Clement of Alexandria
    Paed.   *Paedogogus*
    Strom.   *Stromata*
Cyril of Jerusalem
    Cat. Lect.   *Catechetical Lectures*
Dio Cassius
    Hist.   *Roman History*

Dio Chrysostom
  Or.   *Orations*
Diog. Diognetus
Dionysius of Halicarnassus
  Thuc.   *De Thucydide*
Epictetus
  Diatr.   *Diatribai (Dissertationes)*
  Ench.   *Enchiridion*
Epiphanius
  Pan.   *Panarion (Adversus Haereses)*
Eusebius of Caesarea
  Hist. eccl.   *Historia ecclesiastica*
Gos. Thom.   *Gospel of Thomas*
Herodotus
  Hist.   *Historiae*
Hermas, *Shepherd*
  Mand.   *Mandates*
  Sim.   *Similitudes*
Homer
  Il.   *Iliad*
  Od.   *Odyssey*
Ignatius of Antioch
  Eph.   *To the Ephesians*
  Smyr.   *To the Smyrnaeans*
Irenaeus
  Adv. haer.   *Adversus haereses*
Jerome
  Vir. ill.   *De viris illustribus*
John Chrysostom
  Hom. 1 Cor.   *Homiliae in epistulam i ad Corinthios*
  Hom. Act.   *Homiliae in Acta apostolorum*
  Hom. Heb.   *Homiliae in epistulam ad Hebraeos*
Josephus
  Ant.   *Jewish Antiquities*
  Ag. Ap.   *Against Apion*
  J.W.   *Jewish War*
Jub.   *Jubilees*
Justin Martyr
  Dial.   *Dialogue with Trypho*
  1 Apol.   *First Apology*

L.A.E.	*Life of Adam and Eve*
Liv. Pro.	*Lives of the Prophets*
Lucian	
Alex.	*Alexander (Pseudomantis)*
Phal.	*Phalaris*
Mart. Pol.	*Martyrdom of Polycarp*
Novatian	
Trin.	*De trinitate*
Origen	
C. Cels.	*Contra Celsum*
Comm. Jo.	*Commentarii in evangelium Joannis*
De princ.	*De principiis*
Hom. Exod.	*Homiliae in Exodum*
Hom. Jer.	*Homiliae in Jeremiam*
Hom. Josh.	*Homilies on Joshua*
Pausanias	
Descr.	*Description of Greece*
Philo	
Cher.	*De cherubim*
Decal.	*De decalogo*
Dreams	*On Dreams*
Embassy	*On the Embassy to Gaius (= Legat.)*
Fug.	*De fuga et inventione*
Leg.	*Legum allegoriae*
Legat.	*Legatio ad Gaium*
Migr.	*De migratione Abrahami*
Mos.	*De vita Mosis*
Opif.	*De opificio mundi*
Post.	*De posteritate Caini*
Prob.	*Quod omnis probus liber sit*
QE	*Quaestiones et solutiones in Exodum*
QG	*Quaestiones et solutiones in Genesin*
Spec. Laws	*On the Special Laws*
Plato	
Gorg.	*Gorgias*
Plutarch	
Mor.	*Moralia*
Mulier. virt.	*Mulierum virtutes*
Polycarp	
Phil.	*To the Philippians*

Ps.-Clem. Rec.	*Pseudo-Clementine Recognitions*
Pss. Sol.	*Psalms of Solomon*
Pseudo-Philo	
L.A.B.	*Liber antiquitatum biblicarum*
Seneca	
Ben.	*De beneficiis*
Strabo	
Geog.	*Geographica*
Tatian	
Ad gr.	*Oratio ad Graecos*
Tertullian	
Praescr.	*De praescriptione haereticorum*
Prax.	*Adversus Praxean*
Bapt.	*De baptismo*
De an.	*De anima*
Pud.	*De pudicitia*
Virg.	*De virginibus velandis*
Virgil	
Aen.	*Aeneid*
Xenophon	
Oec.	*Oeconomicus*

Mishnah, Talmud, Targum

b. B. Bat.	*Babylonian Talmudic tractate Baba Batra*
b. Ber.	*Babylonian Talmudic tractate Berakhot*
b Erub.	*Babylonian Talmudic tractate Erubim*
b. Ketub.	*Babylonian Talmudic tractate Ketubbot*
b. Mak.	*Babylonian Talmudic tractate Makkot*
b. Meg.	*Babylonian Talmudic tractate Megillah*
b. Ned.	*Babylonian Talmudic tractate Nedarim*
b. Naz.	*Babylonian Talmudic tractate Nazir*
b. Sanh.	*Babylonian Talmudic tractate Sanhedrin*
b. Shab.	*Babylonian Talmudic tractate Shabbat*
b. Sotah	*Babylonian Talmudic tractate Sotah*
b. Ta'an.	*Babylonian Talmudic tractate Ta'anit*
b. Yev.	*Babylonian Talmudic tractate Yevamot*
b. Yoma	*Babylonian Talmudic tractate Yoma*
Eccl. Rab.	*Ecclesiastes Rabbah*
Exod. Rab.	*Exodus Rabbah*
Gen. Rab.	*Genesis Rabbah*

Lam. Rab.	*Lamentations Rabbah*
Lev. R(ab).	*Leviticus Rabbah*
m. Abot	*Mishnah tractate Abot*
m. Bik.	*Mishnah tractate Bikkurim*
m. Demai	*Mishnah tractate Demai*
m. ʿEd.	*Mishnah tractate ʿEduyyot*
m. Git.	*Mishnah tractate Gittin*
m. Pesaḥ	*Mishnah tractate Pesaḥim*
m. Šeqal.	*Mishnah tractate Šeqalim (Shekalim)*
m. Shab.	*Mishnah tractate Shabbat*
m. Sotah	*Mishnah tractate Sotah*
m. Taʿan.	*Mishnah tractate Taʿanit*
m. Tamid	*Mishnah tractate Tamid*
m. Yad.	*Mishnah tractate Yadayim*
m. Yebam.	*Mishnah tractate Yebamot*
m. Yoma	*Mishnah tractate Yoma*
Num. Rab.	*Numbers Rabbah*
Pesiq. Rab.	*Pesiqta Rabbati*
Pesiq. Rab Kah.	*Pesiqta Rab Kahana*
S. ʿOlam Rab.	*Seder ʿOlam Rabbah*
Song Rab.	*Song of Songs Rabbah*
t. Hul.	*Tosefta tractate Hullin*
Tg. Onq.	*Targum Onqelos*
Tg. Jer.	*Targum Jeremiah*
y. Hag.	*Jerusalem Talmudic tractate Hagiga*
y. Pesaḥ	*Jerusalem Talmudic tractate Pesaḥim*
y. Sanh.	*Jerusalem Talmudic tractate Sanhedrin*

Dead Sea Scrolls

1QapGen	*Genesis apocryphon* (Excavated frags. from cave)
1QM	*War Scroll*
1QpHab	*Pesher Habakkuk*
1QS	*Rule of the Community*
1QSb	*Rule of the Blessings* (Appendix b to 1QS)
1Q21	*T. Levi*, aramaic
4Q184	Wiles of the Wicked Woman
4Q214	Levi[d] ar (*olim* part of Levi[b])
4Q214b	Levi[f] ar (*olim* part of Levi[b])
4Q226	psJub[b] (4Q *pseudo-Jubilees*)
4Q274	Tohorot A

4Q277	Tohorot B^b (*olim* B^c)
4Q525	*Beatitudes*
4QMMT	*Miqsat Ma'aśê ha-Torah*
4QpNah/4Q169	4Q Pesher Nahum
4Q82	*The Greek Minor Prophets Scroll*

Old Testament Pseudepigrapha

1 En.	*1 Enoch*
2 En.	*2 Enoch*
Odes Sol.	*Odes of Solomon*
Syr. Men.	*Sentences of the Syriac Menander*
T. Levi	*Testament of Levi*
T. Mos.	*Testament of Moses*
T. Sim.	*Testament of Simeon*

INTRODUCTION

The *Fortress Commentary on the Bible*, presented in two volumes, seeks to invite study and conversation about an ancient text that is both complex and compelling. As biblical scholars, we wish students of the Bible to gain a respect for the antiquity and cultural remoteness of the biblical texts and to grapple for themselves with the variety of their possible meanings; to fathom a long history of interpretation in which the Bible has been wielded for causes both beneficial and harmful; and to develop their own skills and voices as responsible interpreters, aware of their own social locations in relationships of privilege and power. With this in mind, the *Fortress Commentary on the Bible* offers general readers an informed and accessible resource for understanding the biblical writings in their ancient contexts; for recognizing how the texts have come down to us through the mediation of different interpretive traditions; and for engaging current discussion of the Bible's sometimes perplexing, sometimes ambivalent, but always influential legacy in the contemporary world. The commentary is designed not only to inform but also to invite and empower readers as active interpreters of the Bible in their own right.

The editors and contributors to these volumes are scholars and teachers who are committed to helping students engage the Bible in the classroom. Many also work as leaders, both lay and ordained, in religious communities, and wish this commentary to prove useful for informing congregational life in clear, meaningful, and respectful ways. We also understand the work of biblical interpretation as a responsibility far wider than the bounds of any religious community. In this regard, we participate in many and diverse identities and social locations, yet we all are conscious of reading, studying, and hearing the Bible today as citizens of a complex and interconnected world. We recognize in the Bible one of the most important legacies of human culture; its historical and literary interpretation is of profound interest to religious and nonreligious peoples alike.

Often, the academic interpretation of the Bible has moved from close study of the remote ancient world to the rarefied controversy of scholarly debate, with only occasional attention to the ways biblical texts are actually heard and lived out in the world around us. The commentary seeks to provide students with diverse materials on the ways in which these texts have been interpreted through the course of history, as well as helping students understand the texts' relevance for today's globalized world. It recognizes the complexities that are involved with being an engaged reader of the Bible, providing a powerful tool for exploring the Bible's multilayered meanings in both their ancient and modern contexts. The commentary seeks to address contemporary issues that are raised by biblical passages. It aspires to be keenly aware of how the contemporary world and its issues and perspectives influence the interpretation of the Bible. Many of the most important insights of contemporary biblical scholarship not only have come from expertise in the world of antiquity but have also been forged in modern struggles for dignity, for equality, for sheer survival, and out of respect for those who have died without seeing justice done. Gaining familiarity with the original contexts in which the biblical writings were produced is essential, but not sufficient, for encouraging competent and discerning interpretation of the Bible's themes today.

Inside the Commentary

Both volumes of *The Fortress Commentary on the Bible* are organized in a similar way. In the beginning of each volume, **Topical Articles** set the stage on which interpretation takes place, naming the issues and concerns that have shaped historical and theological scholarship down to the present. Articles in the *Fortress Commentary on the Old Testament* attend, for example, to the issues that arise when two different religious communities claim the same body of writings as their Scripture, though interpreting those writings quite differently. Articles in the *Fortress Commentary on the New Testament* address the consequences of Christianity's historic claim to appropriate Jewish Scripture and to supplement it with a second collection of writings, the experience of rootlessness and diaspora, and the legacy of apocalypticism. Articles in both volumes reflect on the historical intertwining of Christianity with imperial and colonial power and with indexes of racial and socioeconomic privilege.

Section Introductions in the Old Testament volume provide background to the writings included in the Torah, Historical Writings, Wisdom, Prophetic Writings, and a general introduction to the Apocrypha. The New Testament volume includes articles introducing the Gospels, Acts, the letters associated with Paul, and Hebrews, the General Epistles and Revelation. These articles will address the literary and historical matters, as well as theological themes, that the books in these collections hold in common.

Commentary Entries present accessible and judicious discussion of each biblical book, beginning with an introduction to current thinking regarding the writing's original context and its significance in different reading communities down to the present day. A three-level commentary then follows for each sense division of the book. In some cases, these follow the chapter divisions of a biblical book, but more often, contributors have discerned other outlines, depending on matters of genre, movement, or argument.

The three levels of commentary are the most distinctive organizational feature of these volumes. The first level, "The Text in Its Ancient Context," addresses relevant lexical, exegetical, and literary aspects of the text, along with cultural and archaeological information that may provide additional insight into the historical context. This level of the commentary describes consensus views where these exist in current scholarship and introduces issues of debate clearly and fairly. Our intent here is to convey some sense of the historical and cultural distance between the text's original context and the contemporary reader.

The second level, "The Text in the Interpretive Tradition," discusses themes including Jewish and Christian tradition as well as other religious, literary, and artistic traditions where the biblical texts have attracted interest. This level is shaped by our conviction that we do not apprehend these texts immediately or innocently; rather, even the plain meaning we may regard as self-evident may have been shaped by centuries of appropriation and argument to which we are heirs.

The third level, "The Text in Contemporary Discussion," follows the history of interpretation into the present, drawing brief attention to a range of issues. Our aim here is not to deliver a single answer—"what the text means"—to the contemporary reader, but to highlight unique challenges and interpretive questions. We pay special attention to occasions of dissonance: aspects of the text or of its interpretation that have become questionable, injurious, or even intolerable to some readers today. Our goal is not to provoke a referendum on the value of the text but to stimulate reflection and discussion and, in this way, to empower the reader to reach his or her own judgments about the text.

The approach of this commentary articulates a particular understanding of the work of responsible biblical interpretation. We seek through this commentary to promote intelligent and mature engagement with the Bible, in religious communities and in academic classrooms alike, among pastors, theologians, and ethicists, but also and especially among nonspecialists. Our work together has given us a new appreciation for the vocation of the biblical scholar, as custodians of a treasure of accumulated wisdom from our predecessors; as stewards at a table to which an ever-expanding circle is invited; as neighbors and fellow citizens called to common cause, regardless of our different professions of faith. If the result of our work here is increased curiosity about the Bible, new questions about its import, and new occasions for mutual understanding among its readers, our work will be a success.

Fortress Commentary on the Old Testament

Gale A. Yee
Episcopal Divinity School

Hugh R. Page Jr.
University of Notre Dame

Matthew J. M. Coomber
St. Ambrose University

Fortress Commentary on the New Testament

Margaret Aymer
Interdenominational Theological Center

Cynthia Briggs Kittredge
Seminary of the Southwest

David A. Sánchez
Loyola Marymount University

READING THE OLD TESTAMENT IN ANCIENT AND CONTEMPORARY CONTEXTS

Matthew J. M. Coomber

As students file into their desks on the first day of my "Introduction to the Old Testament" course, they are greeted with a PowerPoint slide that simply states, in bold red letters, "Caution: Dangerous Texts Ahead!" The students often respond with the mixture of chuckles and uneasy looks that I intend to provoke. To some extent, the slide is offered tongue in cheek, but not entirely. As with any wry statement, the cautionary slide holds an element of truth. The Old Testament contains powerful teachings and radical ideas that have moved the hearts and minds of both adherents and skeptics for millennia.

While the texts of the Old Testament have had a profound effect on societies and cultures for a long span of time, their texts often take a back seat to the Gospels and the Pauline Letters in popular Christian religion. Even though they constitute well over half of the content of Christian Bibles, very few of my students claim to have read much—if any—of the Old Testament or Apocrypha, despite the fact that I teach at a Roman Catholic university in which the vast majority of the students are Christian. In fact, only a handful of my students claim to have been exposed to the stories of the Old Testament outside of either Sunday school or in episodes of the popular cartoon series *Veggie Tales*. Due to this lack of exposure to the Old Testament, I feel compelled to give them fair warning about what they have gotten themselves into by signing up for what may seem like an innocuous required course. I take it as a professional responsibility to alert them to the fact that a keen examination of the ancient Near Eastern library that sits on their desks has the power to change their lives and forever alter the ways in which they experience the world.

Any collection of books containing calls to wage wars of conquest, to resist the temptation to fight while under threat, thoughts on God's role in governance, and meditations on what it means to live *the good life* has the potential to change lives and even inspire revolutions. To assume that the Bible is harmless is both foolish and irresponsible. After all, the Old Testament's contents have been used by some to support slavery and genocide while inspiring others to engage in such dangerous pursuits as enduring imprisonment, torture, and death in attempts to liberate the oppressed. And just as with using any powerful instrument, be it a car or a surgical blade, reading the Old Testament demands care, responsibility, and substantial consideration from those who put it to use.

Books that promote powerful ideas are complex tools that often belong to the readers as much as—if not more than—their authors. The level of consideration required to read, interpret, and actualize such books is magnified when approaching ancient texts such as those found in the Old Testament. These biblical books bridge multiple theological, cultural, and linguistic worlds, which demand multiple levels of understanding and interpretation. Readers must inhabit three worlds (contexts) when reading any of the books of the Old Testament or Apocrypha, from Genesis to 4 Maccabees: (1) the ancient contexts in which they were written, (2) the modern contexts into which the text is being received, and (3) all of those contexts in between wherein interpreters in each generation have shaped the reading of the texts for their own time and place. *The Fortress Commentary on the Bible: The Old Testament and Apocrypha* approaches these ancient texts with due reverence to this complexity. The purpose of this introduction is to explore a few of the many considerations that are required in reading this ancient Near Eastern scriptural library in its ancient and modern contexts.

A Few Considerations on Receiving Ancient Texts with Modern Minds

The word *context*, whether pertaining to events or a book, looks deceptively singular. A student trying to uncover the context of the US civil rights movement will find many contextual viewing points: those of African Americans who rose up against institutionalized oppression, those of segregationists who tried to maintain the status quo, those within the Johnson administration who worked to find a way forward without losing the Democrats' white voters in the South, and the list goes on.

Challenge of Finding an Ancient or Modern Context

The words *ancient context* and *modern context*, when applied to the Old Testament, also need to be considered in the plural. Considering the ancient context, the books of the Old Testament contain the theologies of diverse communities who lived, wrote, argued, and worked to understand their relationship with the divine under a wide variety of circumstances. An attempt to find a single context for the book of Isaiah, for example, is as complex as finding a single sociohistorical setting of the United States, from the colonial period to the present; it cannot be done. The same is true with the modern context. As these religious texts are received in Chicago or Mumbai, on Wall Street or on skid row, they flow into and take on very different meanings and contexts.

Differing Expectations and Intents of Ancient and Modern Histories

Readers in the age of science have certain expectations when reading a history, and these expectations inform how histories—whether written before or after this age—are received. Modern readers want to know, with scientific precision, when, why, and where events happened. Great value is placed on reconstructions of events that are backed up by reliable sources and with as little interpretive bias as possible. A *good* history of the Battle of the Bulge should include not only dates and locations but also eyewitness accounts of allied forces, Wehrmacht and SS divisions, and civilians. Expectations of accuracy and value in objectivity are a service both to the study of the past and to understanding how these events helped to shape the present. However, when dealing with the Old Testament it is easy to project our appreciation for accuracy and disdain for bias onto the ancient texts, which ultimately is not a fair way to approach these ancient texts.

Long before there was even a concept of "Bible," many of the texts of the Old Testament were passed down through oral tradition, only to be written down and finally canonized centuries later; this is evidenced in the repetitive Torah narratives, such as the creation refrain in Gen. 1:1—2:4a and the lyrical hymn of Deborah in Judges 5. To imagine the original texts as printed, bound, copyrighted, and collected works, as we hold them today, is both inaccurate and misleading. Moreover, assuming the intents and expectations of the oral historian to be akin to those of modern historians is misleading, and focusing on accuracy can limit the scope of a passage's message when the intent of the passage rests in the ideas it promotes. Cultures that employ oral tradition do not make dates, places, or accuracy a priority; rather, they are interested in the telling and retelling of a story to develop an understanding or identity that can answer the questions of the times into which they are received. Take the account of King Solomon's wealth in 2 Chron. 9:22-24, for example.

> King Solomon surpassed all the kings of the earth in wealth and wisdom. All the kings of the earth came to pay homage to Solomon and to listen to the wisdom with which God had endowed him. Each brought his tribute—silver and gold objects, robes, weapons, and spices, horses and mules—in the amount due each year (JPS).

Such an account served a purpose to the ancient author and his audience, but the account was certainly not accurate. Putting aside the issue of transoceanic travel for contemporary rulers in the Americas or the South Pacific, Israel held no such wealth in the tenth century BCE, and such superpowers as Egypt and Assyria would never have been compelled to offer tribute. While questions surrounding the reality of Solomon's wealth are not a center of contentious debate in the public sphere, questions pertaining to the creation of the universe are highly controversial; the front lines of this debate can be seen at the doors of the Creation Museum in Petersburg, Kentucky.

Founded by Ken Ham and Answers in Genesis (AiG), a Christian apologetics organization, the Creation Museum is a prime example of how scientific-age expectations are frequently placed on the ancient texts of the Old Testament. With the motto "Prepare to Believe," the museum promotes Gen. 1:1—2:4a as a scientific explanation for the creation of the cosmos, an event that is said to have occurred around 4,000 BCE, as determined through James Ussher's seventeenth-century-CE biblically based calculations. It is important to consider that the questions the Creation Museum seeks to answer do not likely match the agenda of the authors of Gen. 1:1—2:4a, which is connected to the Babylonian myth the *Enuma Elish* and/or the battle between the Canaanite god Baal and Yam, each of which centers on order's conquest of chaos. It also does not take into consideration that those who canonized the Torah followed this story with another creation story (Gen. 2:4b-25), which is juxtaposed with the first, making it unlikely that the ancient intent was to give a *scientific* account of our origins. Furthermore, the authors of the texts believed that the sky was a firmament that held back a great sky-ocean (Gen. 1:6-8), from which precipitation came when its doors were opened, and that the moon was self-illuminating (Gen. 1:14-18). A key danger in treating Old Testament books with modern historical and scientific expectations is not only receiving inaccurate messages about our past but also failing to realize the intent of the authors and the depth of meaning behind the messages they conveyed.

Projecting Modern Contexts onto the Ancient Past

The oft-repeated notion that only the winners write history is not entirely true, for readers rewrite the histories they receive by projecting their own personal and cultural perspectives onto them. The medievalist Norman Cantor stresses how individuals tend to project their own worldviews and experiences onto the past, thereby reinventing the past in their own image (156–58). Whereas Cantor dealt with issues of secular history, biblical history appears to follow suit, as found in such art pieces as Dutch painter Gerard van Honthorst's piece *King David Playing the Harp*. In the painting van Honthorst depicts the king with European-style attire and instrument. In contextually ambiguous passages, such as the land seizures in Mic. 2:1-4, we find scholars filling in the blanks with characters that make more sense in our time than in the ancient past, such as the mafia (Alfaro, 25). It is difficult for a reader not to project his or her own time and culture onto the text, for that is the reader's primary reference point; to escape doing so is likely not possible. But just as complete objectivity is not attainable, an awareness of its hazards can help readers exercise some degree of control regarding how much they project their present onto the past.

Bringing One's Ideology to the Text

Just as readers bring their notions of history to the Old Testament, so also they bring their ideologies. While attempts to view Old Testament texts through the biblical authors' eyes may be made, one's perceptions can never be entirely freed from one's own experiences, which help shape how a particular idea or story is read. This challenge is a double-edged sword. On one side of the sword, the ideology and experiences of the reader may cloud the text's original meaning and intent, causing unintended—and sometimes intentional—misreadings of a passage. When this occurs, the resulting interpretation often tells us more about the social or ideological location of the reader than the biblical characters who are being interpreted. Albert Schweitzer found that nineteenth-century biographies on the life of the "historical Jesus" turned out to be autobiographies of their authors; romantics uncovered an idealist Jesus, political radicals found a revolutionary, and so on (Schweitzer). On the other side of the sword, one finds an advantage shared by oral tradition. Reading a text through one's own experiences can breathe new life into the text and allow it to speak to current circumstances, as found in postcolonial, feminist, and queer interpretations. Since readers cannot fully remove themselves from their own ideological locations, it is important to acknowledge that a reader's ideas and biases are brought to the text and that much is to be learned by considering various interpretations.

Because ideology plays a role in interpretation, it should be noted that history—and biblical histories, in particular—do not exist in the past, but are very much alive and active in the present. YHWH's granting of land to Abraham's dependents, for example, plays a prominent role in the Israel-Palestine conflict. This is addressed by Keith Whitelam and James Crossley, who find the biblical text shaping modern perceptions of land via cartography. A post-1967 war edition of *The Macmillan Bible Atlas* contains a map of Israel with borders that look remarkably similar to the modern-day border with Gaza—despite great uncertainty surrounding ancient Israel's borders— and that is inscribed with Gen. 13:14-15: "The Lord said to Abram . . . 'Lift up your eyes, and look from the place where you are, northward and southward and eastward and westward; for all the land which you see I will give to you and to your descendants forever'" (RSV; see Whitelam 61–62; Crossley 176). Whether one sees this connection in a positive or negative light, clear political implications of the biblical past can be seen.

Differing Views on the Old Testament's History

Another factor to be considered, which is also highly political, is the lack of consensus pertaining to the historicity of biblical narratives and the state of ancient Israel, ranging from the exodus narrative to the Davidic monarchy. The degree to which these events and histories are *real histories* or *cultural memory* has been the subject of much debate and polemic within the academy. Many scholars agree that the story of the Hebrew exodus out of Egypt is cultural memory, with varying degrees of historical truth, ranging from seeing the Hebrews as an invading force to an indigenous movement within Canaan that rose up against exploitative rulers. But one of the most heated debates in the history of ancient Israel has revolved around the dating of the monarchy and the rise of Judah as a powerful state.

The traditional view, often referred to as the *maximalist* perspective, gives greater credence to the Bible's account of the monarchy's history. Scholars of this persuasion accept, to varying degrees, the Old Testament's stories of the rise of Israel beginning with King Saul and continuing on through the destruction of Israel and Judah. So-called *minimalists* give less credence to biblical accounts, relying more on archaeological and extrabiblical sources to develop their views of the monarchy and the presence of a powerful state, for which they find little evidence. While largely unnoticed outside the academy, the debate has caused great animosity within. Maximalist scholars have been accused of burdening archaeology with the task of upholding the biblical narratives (Davies), while minimalists have been accused of attempting to erase ancient Israel from world history (Halpern).

The purpose of addressing the maximalist/minimalist debate in this introduction is to emphasize that biblical scholarship contains diverse voices and points of view on the Bible's history, which will be seen in the commentaries of this volume. It is good that these different perspectives are aired. When approaching an area of history that is of such great importance to so many, yet with so little definitive information available, it is important to articulate and compare different ideas so as to produce and refine the historical possibilities of the Bible's contexts. In this way we see how differing views of biblical interpretation can work as a dance, where partners can complement each other's work, even if tempers can flare sometimes when partners step on one another's toes.

Reading the Old Testament in Its Ancient Context

It is apparent that contemplating the ancient contexts of the Old Testament requires several areas of consideration. While there is no end to the complexities involved with pursuing a greater understating of the world(s) out of which the books of the Old Testament developed, this section is intended to draw the reader's attention to some of the Old Testament's physical environments, political climates, and theological diversity.

Physical Environments of the Old Testament

The geography and ecology of ancient Palestine can easily be overlooked, but their value for understanding the Old Testament should not be underestimated. While the Old Testament represents diverse social settings that span hundreds of years, all of its authors lived in agrarian societies where land, climate, economics, and religion are inseparable. Due to agrarian societies' dire need to ensure successful and regular harvests—whether for survival or with the additional aspiration of building empire—farming practices become incorporated into religious rituals that end up dictating planting, harvesting, and land management. This strong connection between faith and farming led to rituals that served as an interface between spirituality and socioeconomic activities, effectively erasing the lines between religious and economic practice (Coomber 2013). In the end, the ritualization of agrarian economics helps shape perceptions of the deity or deities to which the rituals are connected: the Feast of Unleavened Bread (Exod. 23:14-17), the barley harvest festival incorporated in the Passover feast (Exodus 12; cf. John 19:29, the wheat-harvest Feast of Weeks, also known as Pentecost (Lev. 23:15-21; cf. Acts 2:1), and the fruit-harvest Feast of Booths (Lev. 23:33-36). Thus geography and ecology affected not only the way ancient Hebrews farmed but also how they came to understand God. Moreover, the geographical regions in which many of them farmed influenced these understandings.

Regions of Ancient Israel

Ancient Israel can be divided into a number of geographical areas, each of which presents its own unique environment. Furthest to the west is the *coastal plain*, which held great economic importance in the way of trade. This is especially visible in the development of manufacturing and shipping cities such as Ekron and Ashkelon. Due to the region's trade potential, it was usually controlled by foreign powers and is not frequently mentioned in the Old Testament (e.g., Judges 16; 2 Kings 16; Jer. 25:20; Amos 1:8; Zeph. 2:4).

The lowland *Shephelah* and the *highlands* are just east of the coastal plain, forming an important region of Israel, which is at the center of most of the Old Testament's stories. This fertile land, composed of low hills and valleys, is good for animal husbandry and the cultivation of grains, cereals, nuts, olives, and grapes. These areas were valuable for both subsistence farming and the production of trade goods, in which surrounding empires could engage. The agrarian potential of this area also made Shephelah and the highlands a target for foreign invasion. This region's political influence was heightened by the cities of Jerusalem, Samaria, and Lachish.

The *Jordan Valley*, east of the highlands, contains the lowest natural surface in the world and is part of a fault that extends into Africa. The valley follows the Jordan River from the city of Dan through the city of Hazor and the Sea of Galilee before flowing into the Dead Sea. Aside from the important role that the Jordan Valley plays in Ezekiel's vision of water flowing out of the temple to bring life to the Dead Sea (Ezekiel 47), the region is rarely mentioned.

To the east of the Jordan Valley is the *Transjordan highlands*, which is often referred to as "beyond the Jordan" (e.g., Josh. 12:1). Extending from the Dead Sea's altitude of 650-feet below sea level to the 9,230-foot peak of Mt. Hermon, this region contains a diverse range of topography and climates that allow for the cultivation of diverse agricultural goods, including grains, fruits, timber, and livestock. The agrarian potential of the area attracted a number of peoples, including the Moabites, the Ammonites, and the Edomites.

Whether valued for their sustaining, trade, or defensive capabilities, the topography of ancient Israel and its surrounding lands influenced its inhabitants' ability or inability to find sustenance and pursue their own interests. When empires such as Assyria and Babylon were on the rise, this region attracted their rulers who sought the earning potential of the land, and these events—or the cultural memories they inspired—influenced the Old Testament authors' stories of defeat and are reflected in their perceptions of God's attitudes toward them.

Climatic Challenges

While the land in and around Israel was some of the most sought after in the ancient Near East, its inhabitants endured serious meteorological challenges. The ancient Israelites lived at the crossroads of subtropical and temperate atmospheric patterns—producing rainy winter seasons and dry summers—and the effects of these patterns shaped the ways in which the Hebrews lived: the resulting erratic precipitation patterns result in a 30 percent chance of insufficient rainfall (Karmon, 27). The unpredictability of each growing season's weather pattern meant that the rainfall of a given season could play out in any number of ways, each demanding specific farming strategies for which farmers had little foresight or room for error. Subsequent failed seasons that diminished surpluses could lead to debt and the selling of family members into slavery or even the extinction of a family line.

Everything in society—from the interests of the poorest farmer to the king—depended on successful harvests and access to their crops, and the strong desire for divine assistance is reflected in Old Testament narratives that emphasize fidelity to YHWH. The seriousness placed on securing favorable rainfall and accessing harvests is clear in warnings against following other deities, such as the weather god Baal (e.g., Judg. 2:11; 2 Kings 3:2; Ps. 106:28; Hosea 9:10), God-given visions that foretell rainfall (Genesis 41), and the granting and withholding of rain as reward or punishment (Deut. 11:11-14; cf. 1 Kings 17–18). Additionally, there are strict rules to protect land access (Leviticus 25) and condemnation against abuses (1 Kings 21; Isa. 5:8-10; Mic. 2:1-4).

The physical environments of the Old Testament authors are an important consideration, because they not only affected the way the authors lived but also helped to shape their views of God and the world around them. From the development of the ancient Hebrews' religious rituals to finding either God's favor or wrath in agrarian events (see Zech. 10:1; 1 Kings 17–18), the topography and climatic environments that affected cultivation played key roles in how the biblical authors perceived and interacted with the divine.

Sociopolitical Contexts of the Old Testament

In addition to the challenges presented by Israel's geographic and climatic setting, its strategic location between the empires of Mesopotamia and northern Africa presented a recurring threat. As these empires invaded the lands of ancient Israel for military and economic reasons, the biblical authors and redactors received and transmitted these events into their religious narratives: foreign invasion was often perceived as divine punishment—with the notable exception of the Persians—and the defeat of foreign forces was perceived as a result of divine favor. Before addressing foreign influences on the Old Testament's ancient contexts, a brief overview of Israel's domestic structures should be considered.

Israel's Domestic Sociopolitical Contexts

While ancient Palestine's Mesopotamian neighbors developed cities and urban economies in the Early Bronze Age (3300–2100 bce), Palestine largely remained a patchwork of scattered settlements that functioned as a peripheral economy, engaging in trade activity as neighboring empires made it lucrative, and receding into highland agriculture when those powers waned (Coomber 2010, 81–92). Adapting to the demands of waxing and waning empires—rather than taking significant steps toward powerful urban economies of its own—resulted in a marked reliance on subsistence strategies on into the seventh century bce (Coote and Whitelam).

Biblical accounts of Hebrew societal structures present a patronage system that had its roots in small family units called the *bet av* ("father's house"), which together formed a *mishpahah* ("family" or "clan"), which expanded up to the tribe, or *shevet*. When the monarchy was established, the *malkut* ("kingdom") became the top rung. While the *malkut* and *shevet* held the top two tiers, the phrase "all politics is local" applies to ancient Israel: loyalty structures were strongest at the bottom.

Philip Davies and John Rogerson note that the *bet av*, "father's house," likely had a double meaning (32). While it indicated a family unit that included extended lineage and slaves—excluding daughters who left the family at marriage—it likely also denoted the descendants of a common ancestor, who may not have lived under a single roof (e.g., Gen. 24:38). While the *bet avim* grew through the births of sons and the accumulation of wives and slaves, the danger of collapse due to disease, war, and a lack of birth of sons presented a constant threat. Debt was also a threat to a *bet av*, inspiring legal texts that protected its access to arable land (Leviticus 25; Deut. 25:5). It was the patriarch's responsibility to care for the family's economic well-being, as well as to pass on traditions, the history of the nation, and the laws of God (Deut. 6:7; 11:8-9; 32:46-47). The *bet av* also had power over such judicial matters as those of marriage and slave ownership.

Mishpahah denotes a level of organization based on a recognizable kinship (Numbers 1; 26). It had territorial significance, as seen in tribal border lists of Joshua 13–19, and was responsible for dividing the land. While *mishpahah* is difficult to translate, Norman Gottwald offers the useful definition, "protective association of extended families" (Gottwald 1999, 257). If the immediate or extended families of a citizen who had to sell himself to an alien could not redeem him, the *mishpahah* became the last line of protection from perpetual servitude (Lev. 25:48-49).

Shevet refers to the largest group and unit of territorial organization, which was primarily bound together by residence. Military allegiances appear to have belonged to this level, against both foreign and domestic threats—as seen in the Benjamite battles of Judges 12 and 20–21. Gottwald sees the *shevet* as more of a geographic designation pertaining to clusters of villages and/or clans that gathered for protective purposes rather than as representative bodies within a political system (Gottwald 2001, 35).

The *malkut,* or kingdom, is a source of continued contention in the so-called minimalist/maximalist debate mentioned above. The Old Testament account claims that the kingdom of Israel was founded when Saul became king over the Israelite tribes (1 Samuel 9) and continued through the line of David, after Saul fell out of favor with God. Israel's united monarchy is reported to have spanned 1030 to 930 BCE, when King Rehoboam was rejected by the northern Israelites (1 Kgs. 12:1-20; 2 Chron. 10:1-19), leading to the period of the divided monarchy, with Israel in the north and Judah in the south. These two kingdoms existed side by side until Israel was destroyed by Assyria (734–721 BCE). Judah entered into Assyrian vassalage in the 720s and was destroyed by the Babylonians around 586 BCE. Those who give less credence to the biblical account take note that there is little extrabiblical evidence of a monarchy prior to King Omri, aside from the Tel Dan Stele, which refers to "the House of David," which may refer to a king.

While Israel's domestic organizational landscape played a major role in the development of biblical law and narrative, the biblical authors' interactions with surrounding peoples had profound effects on the stories they told. The main imperial influences, from the premonarchical period to the fall of the Hasmonean Dynasty, were Egypt, Philistine, Assyria, Babylon, Persia, the Greeks, and the Romans.

Israel's Foreign Sociopolitical Contexts

The Egyptian Empire played an important role in the development of the Torah, as seen in the stories of Abram and Sarai (Genesis 12), Joseph (Genesis 37–50), and throughout the entire exodus narrative, interwoven into many areas of the Old Testament. The authors of Exodus used the backdrop of Egypt's powerful *New Kingdom* (1549–1069 BCE) to display their faith in YHWH's power, and other books draw on this narrative as a recurring reminder of the Israelites' debt and obligations toward their god (e.g. Deut. 5:15, 24:17-22, 23:7-8; Ps. 106:21; Ezekiel 20; Amos 2:10; Mic. 6:4), and as a vehicle of praise (Psalms 78; 81; 135; 136). The Jewish holiday of Passover, which is referred to throughout the Old Testament, has its roots in this anti-Egyptian epic. A later and weaker Egypt returns to play a role in the story of Judah's lengthy downfall: King Hezekiah (d. 680s) enters into a failed anti-Assyrian alliance with Egypt (Isaiah 30–31; 36:6-9), and King Zedekiah (d. 580s) enters into a failed anti-Babylonian alliance with Pharaoh Hophra (Ezek. 17:15; Jer. 2:36).

While their point of origins are in dispute (Amos 9:7 puts their origin at Caphtor), the Philistines tried to invade Egypt in 1190 BCE, but were repelled by Ramses III, who settled them in the coastal towns of Gaza, Ashkelon, and Ashdod (Deut. 2:23). From there, they continued their incursions along the coastal plain and perhaps even drove out their Egyptian rulers, under the reign of Ramses IV (d. 1149 BCE). They play a key adversarial role in the book of Judges, as found in the stories of Shamgar (Judg. 3:31) and Samson (Judges 13–16). Their military competencies are reflected in the story of their capture of the ark of the covenant in 1 Sam. 4:1—7:2. Fear of the Philistine threat helped influence the people's decision to choose a king to unite the tribes (1 Sam. 8–9). The biblical authors continued to portray the Philistines as a threat to the Israelites, but Philistine influence in the highlands faded as the power of Assyria grew.

Assyria's fearsome power and influence in the region gave them a villain's role in the Old Testament. The biblical authors perceived Assyria's incursions into Israel and Judah as YHWH's punishment for such transgressions as idolatry and social injustice. While archaeological evidence of Philistine-Israelite interaction is scant, there is plenty of archaeological and extrabiblical evidence of Assyria's impact on Israel and Judah.

From the start of its ninth-century conquests, Assyria was feared for its ruthless force. The psychological impact of Assyria's powerful conscripted forces, iron chariots, siege engines, and public mutilations surface in the writings of the Old Testament authors. The Assyrians enforced submission through power and fear, deporting conquered rulers to prevent uprisings (2 Kings 17:6, 24, 28; 18:11). When uprisings occurred, Assyrian troops were deployed from strategically positioned garrisons to flay, impale, and burn the perpetrators, as portrayed in Assyrian palace-reliefs.

In the late eighth century, both Israel and Judah felt the full weight of Assyria's might. The northern kingdom of Israel was destroyed in 721 BCE after joining an alliance of vassals that stopped paying tribute to Assyria. At the end of the century, King Hezekiah entered Judah into a similar alliance with Egypt (Isaiah 30–31), which resulted in the invasion of his kingdom and the siege of Jerusalem. According to 2 Kgs. 18:13-16, the siege was broken when Hezekiah sent a message of repentance to the Assyrian king, Sennacherib, at Lachish, promising to resume his tribute obligations. Other texts in 2 Kings suggest that Sennacherib abandoned the siege to deal with political unrest at home (19:7, 37) or a plague (19:35-36). Despite his efforts to subvert Sennacherib's dominance of Judah, Hezekiah and his successors continued to rule as vassals.

Under the rule of King Nebuchadnezzar, the Babylonian Empire captured Nineveh in 612, destroyed the Egyptians at the battle of Carchemish in 605, and captured Jerusalem in 597, deporting many inhabitants. After a rebellion by King Zedekiah in 586, the Babylonians destroyed Jerusalem and the temple and deported a significant portion of Judah's population (2 Kings 24; 2 Chronicles 36). The prophets Ezekiel, Jeremiah, and Habakkuk saw Nebuchadnezzar's conquest as YHWH's punishment for the sins of the Judean state (Ezekiel 8–11; Jer. 25:1-14; Hab. 1:6-10). The events of the Babylonian conquest are largely supported by archaeology and extrabiblical literature (Grabbe, 210–13).

Biblical claims of the removal of all Judeans but the poorest "people of the land" (2 Kgs. 24:14-16; 25:12; Jer. 52:16, 28-30) are reflected in the archaeological record, which indicates that inhabited sites decreased by two-thirds, from 116 to 41, and surviving sites shrank from 4.4 to 1.4 hectares, suggesting a population collapse of 85 to 90 percent (Liverani, 195). Such a massive exile plays a formidable role in the Old Testament, as described in the stories of significant characters such as Ezekiel and Daniel. Rage associated with this event is found in Psalm 137, which recounts the horrors of the exile and ends with the chilling words "a blessing on him who seizes your [Babylonian] babies and dashes them against the rocks!" (137:9 JPS). The exiled Hebrews who returned to Palestine after the Persians conquered the Babylonians returned to a destroyed Jerusalem that no longer enjoyed the security of a defensive wall. Some of the returnees helped to reshape Judaism with a flourishing priesthood and the composition of scholarly works and biblical texts. While exile is portrayed in negative terms, many Jews remained in the lands to which they had been deported; this had the effect of spreading Judaism outside the confines of Palestine.

After overthrowing his grandfather King Astyages of the Medes in 553 BCE, Cyrus of Persia (d. 530) rapidly expanded his empire, moving westward into Armenia and Asia Minor and east toward India, and defeated Babylon in 539. But unlike previous conquests, the Old Testament treats Persian dominance as a time of hope. As successor to the Babylonian Empire, King Cyrus instituted a policy of allowing victims of Babylonian exile to return to their homelands, where he sponsored their local religions. To the biblical authors, this policy was met with celebration and as a sign of YHWH's love for his people. The authors of 2 Chron. 36:23 and Ezra 1:2 portray King Cyrus as crediting YHWH with his victories and with the mandate to rebuild the temple in Jerusalem; Ezra 1:7 even portrays the Persian king personally returning the vessels that Nebuchadnezzar had seized from the temple four decades before. While the Bible treats Cyrus's policy of return as inspired by YHWH, Davies and Rogerson note that the practice was neither new nor disinterested, as it served to restore the national culture of a large and culturally varied empire (59). It is important to note the great shift in how the biblical authors treated King Cyrus of Persia, as opposed to the kings of the Assyrians and Babylonians, whom they disdained. In Isaiah 40–50, Cyrus is championed as the great savior of the Judean deportees and of the rebuilding of Jerusalem. In fact, while oracles against foreign nations are a key theme in prophetic oracles, none are directed against Persia. Even when their rulers are compliant with the murder of Jews, they are portrayed as either acting against their own desires or out of ignorance (Daniel 6; Esther).

Like the exile, itself, the return from exile plays an important role in the politics and religion of the Old Testament. Accounts of these events are found in the books of Ezra and Nehemiah. While the Bible presents the return as a blessing from God and a time of joy, it does not seem to have been without its hardships. It can be deduced from Ezra and Nehemiah that resettlement involved various tensions; in Ezra 3:3, those who had remained in Judah during the exile, along with other neighboring peoples, take the Canaanites' role in the book of Joshua: "an evil influence which will, unless strenuously rejected, corrupt the 'people of God'" (Davies and Rogerson, 88). It was during the Persian period that the Jerusalem temple was rebuilt and the priesthood gained power and influence.

The long march of succeeding empires continued with the rise of Alexander the Great, who seized control of the Greek city-states in 336 BCE and conquered the Persian Empire before his death in 323. Unlike previous empires that might make their subjects worship a particular deity or relocate to a different region, the Greek ideal of *Hellenism* posed a particular cultural threat. Hellenism promoted a view in which people were not citizens of a particular region, but of the world, enabling the integration of Greek and regional cultures, thus breaking down barriers that separated local peoples from their foreign rulers. Within a hundred years, Koine Greek had become the lingua franca, and Greek philosophy, educational systems, art and attire, politics, and religion permeated the empire. The consequences of Hellenization had profound linguistic, political, and theological effects on the biblical authors who lived and wrote during this period. Jews who lived outside of Israel became more familiar with the Greek language than Hebrew. By the second century CE, Greek had become so widely spoken among the Jewish community in Alexandria, Egypt, that the Hebrew Bible was translated into Koine Greek, which came to be called the Septuagint.

Greek rule eventually led to the severe oppression of the Jewish people at the hands of the usurper king Antiochus IV (d. 164 BCE), who sought to weed out cultural diversity in the Seleucid Empire. King Antiochus, who called himself *Epiphanes* ("god made manifest"), was known for his erratic character, which manifested itself in his brutal hatred of the Jews. Even his allies referred to him by the nickname *Epimanes*—a play on Epiphanes—meaning "the crazy one." He is known for looting the Jerusalem temple to fund his battles against the Ptolemies and for forbidding the Jewish rite of circumcision and sacred dietary laws.

King Antiochus was also known for instigating treachery among the Jewish leadership, giving Jason—of the pro-Greek Onias family—the high priesthood in return for complying with Antiochus's plans to Hellenize Jerusalem by building a gymnasium and enrolling its people as citizens of Antioch (2 Macc. 4:7). Further strife erupted when Menelaus, another aspirant for the high priesthood, offered Antiochus even greater gifts for the office. The rivalry of Jason and Menelaus led to the sacking of Jerusalem, slaughtering of its citizens, and the looting of its temple (2 Macc. 5:11-23; Josephus 12.5.3 §§246–47). The horrors of life under King Antiochus IV are reflected in the horn that emerges from the fourth beast in the apocalyptic vision of Dan. 7:7-8, and is then slain by the "Ancient One" (7:11).

From stripping the temple to pay for his wars to setting up an altar for Zeus in the temple, King Antiochus IV's brutality against the Jews led to a revolt that started in the Judean village of Modein in 167 BCE and spread rapidly throughout the region—as chronicled in 1 and 2 Maccabees and in Josephus's *Antiquities of the Jews* (c. 100 CE). A guerrilla warfare campaign that was led by Judas Maccabeus eventually liberated and purified the temple—an event celebrated today in the Jewish festival of Hanukkah. The Maccabean revolt drove out the Greeks and expanded the borders to include Galilee. While the revolt was successful in ushering in a period of self-rule, the resulting Hasmonean Dynasty fell prey to the lust for power. As civil conflict broke out between two rival claims to the throne, the Roman general Pompey invaded Judea in 63 BCE, seizing control of the region for his empire. In 40 BCE, the Roman Senate appointed an Edomite convert to Judaism, *Herod the Great*, as king of Judea. Despised by his people, the puppet king had to take Jerusalem by force, from where he ruled harshly.

Each of these empires, vying for control over the Southern Levant, brought with them challenges that helped to shape the Hebrew people by influencing the ways they viewed themselves, their God, and their religious practices.

Religious Contexts of the Old Testament

Despite common perceptions of the Bible as a univocal work, the Old Testament represents diverse theologies of communities that spanned centuries and were influenced by the religious systems of their contemporaries. Babylonian and Canaanite musings over the power of order over chaos, as found in the *Enuma Elish* and Baal narratives, are present in Gen. 1:1—2:4a and referenced in Ps. 74:12-17. The authors of the Bible's Wisdom literature exchanged ideas with their foreign neighbors, as found in parallels between the Babylonian story I Will Praise the Lord of Wisdom and the book of Job, and passages from Proverbs that mirror the words of the Egyptian thinkers Ptah-Hotep and Amen-em-opet (e.g., Prov. 22:4; 22:17—24:22). Understanding the diversity of theological perspectives in the Old Testament can aid both exegesis and hermeneutics by giving the reader greater insight into the biblical authors' ideas of God and uncovering layers of meaning that might otherwise go unnoticed.

Monotheism and Henotheism

It should not be assumed that all Old Testament authors were monotheists: many were *henotheists*. Henotheism promotes a multi-god/dess universe in which the adherent gives allegiance to a supreme primary deity. Elements of this outlook appear to be found in God's decision to create humanity "in our image, after our likeness" (Gen. 1:26 RSV), and in YHWH's anxiety over the man that he created becoming "like one of us" in Gen. 3:22. YHWH also expresses his disgust in that the *sons of God* mated with human women, resulting in the birth of the nephilim (Gen. 6:2-4). In the *Song of Moses*, Moses poses the rhetorical question, "who is like you, O Lord, among the gods?" (Exod. 15:11). The writer of Ps. 95:3 proclaims, "YHWH is a great God, the king of all divine beings," while 97:9 asserts that YHWH is "exalted high above all divine beings." These examples pose a number of questions about the biblical authors' views on the divine. Two that will be briefly addressed here concern the identity of God and the role of the other deities being inferred. The supreme deity of the ancient Hebrews is given several names and titles, representing different personality traits and theological views.

Elohim

The name or title *Elohim*, which is usually translated from the Hebrew into English as "God," makes its first appearance in Genesis 1. The name Elohim is used to identify the Hebrews' supreme deity in several Old Testament texts, including those found in the books of Genesis, Exodus, Psalms, and Job. As in the Bible's priestly creation story (Gen. 1:1—2:4a), Elohim is portrayed as an all-powerful, confident, commanding, and somewhat distant deity, whose supremacy and majesty are emphasized.

YHWH

YHWH is an anthropomorphic god who exhibits tendencies toward both kindness and severity and is self-described as a jealous god who, unlike other ancient Near Eastern gods, demands the exclusive allegiance of his followers. The name YHWH, which is often translated into English as "the LORD"—from the Hebrew *adonay*—makes its first appearance in the second creation story (Gen. 2:4b). The name YHWH carries a sense of mystery. Derived from the Hebrew verb *hawah*, meaning "to be," YHWH is difficult to translate, but means something like "he who is" or "he who causes what is." Some believe that YHWH's origins can be traced to the god YHW, who was worshiped in the northwestern region of the Arabian Peninsula known as Midian: this is where Moses first encounters YHWH (Exodus 3).

YHWH has strong associations with Canaanite culture, which highlights discrepancies between biblical directions for the deity's worship and how the deity was worshiped in popular religion. Whereas the biblical authors convey strict messages that YHWH should be worshiped alone, the remains of Israelite homes reveal that other gods and goddesses, such as Asherah—whom the author(s) of Jeremiah refers to as *the queen of heaven*—were worshiped alongside YHWH (Dever, 176–89). Jeremiah 44 appears to give a glimpse into the popular polytheistic or henotheistic religion of sixth-century-BCE Judah. After YHWH threatens the people for worshiping other gods, the women say that they will not listen but will continue the traditions of their ancestors and give offerings to the queen of heaven, who protected them well (Jer. 44:16-17). Further biblical evidence of Asherah's popularity is found in the biblical authors' continual condemnation of her worship, often symbolized through the presence of pillars and poles, as they worked to direct the people toward monotheism (Deut. 7:5; Judg. 3:7-8; 1 Kgs. 14:15, 23; Jer. 17:17-18).

El

The name or title *El* appears around two hundred times in the Old Testament, with frequent use in the ancestor stories of Genesis and surfacing throughout the Old Testament. Its presence poses some interesting questions.

On one level, El is a common Semitic title for "divine being," and can be read as an appellative for "divinity," often compounded with other words such as *el-shadday* ("God Almighty" [Gen. 17:1; Exod. 6:3; Ezek. 10:5]) and *el-elyon* ("God Most High" [Gen. 14:22; Deut. 32:8-9; Ps. 78:35]). In addition to a title referring to God, El is also the name of the chief god of the Canaanite pantheon. Often portrayed as a bearded king on his throne, and referred to as the "Ancient One," El was worshiped in Canaan and Syria both before and after the emergence of Israel. The frequent use of El for God—and the Canaanite god's prominence in Israel—has led many to conclude that El developed into YHWH. Mark Smith asserts, "The original god of Israel was El. . . . Isra*el* is not a Yahwistic name with the divine element of Yahweh, but an El name" (Smith, 32; emphasis on *el* in "Israel" is mine). A cross-pollination of Canaanite and Hebrew religion is found in the use of Canaanite El imagery to describe the "Ancient One" in Dan. 7:9-10 who sits on a throne with white garments and hair as pure as wool. Furthermore, the description of "one like a human being coming with the clouds of heaven," who "came to the Ancient One and was presented before him" (Dan. 7:13), dovetails with images of the Canaanite god Baal coming before El. Whether or not the authors of Daniel 7 envisioned El, the imprint of Canaanite religion appears to have been stamped on ideas of God and passed down through the generations. While not accepted by biblical authors, popular religion in ancient Israel appears to have had a complex network of deities that fulfilled various roles in daily life. (For a helpful overview on differences between "popular" and "official" religion in ancient Israel, see Stavrakopoulou.)

The idea that El was absorbed into YHWH is also supported by the fact that the chief god of the Canaanite pantheon is never condemned in the Old Testament, but his son Baal, consort Asherah, and other gods face vicious condemnation (Num. 25:2; Deut. 4:3; Judg. 6:30; 1 Kgs. 16:31—18:40). Why would the biblical authors attack lesser Canaanite deities but leave the head god unscathed? One possible answer is that El had become synonymous with YHWH; both share a compassionate disposition toward humanity (Exod. 34:6; Ps. 86:15), use dreams to communicate (Gen. 31:24; 37:5; 1 Kgs. 3:5-15), and have healing powers (cf. *KTU* 1:16.v–vi with Gen. 20:17; Num. 12:13; Ps. 107:20 [Smith, 39]).

The Divine Council

As El served as chief of the Canaanite pantheon, YHWH was head of the *divine council*, whose members were often referred to as "the sons of gods." In Gen. 28:12; 33:1-2; Pss. 29:1 and 89:6-9, we find YHWH at the head of subordinate divine beings who are collectively referred to as the "council of Lord" (Jer. 23:18 and the "congregation of El" (Ps. 82:1). In Psalm 82, God attacks the congregants for their oppressive acts against humanity, for which they are doomed to die like mortals (vv. 5-7). In Job 1:6-7, Job's troubles begin when the divine council convenes with YHWH, and God asks "the satan" where he has been. The satan also appears on the divine council in Zechariah, where YHWH delivers judgment between two members of his entourage. The clearest depiction of the divine council's function is in 1 Kgs. 22:19-22, where YHWH seeks guidance and direction from the council, the members of which confer in open discussion before one spirit approaches YHWH with a proposal. Following a common motif in ancient Mediterranean literature, humans are sometimes transported before God and the divine council, as found in a party feasting with Elohim in Exod. 24:9-11 and Isaiah's commission as prophet in Isaiah 6 (Niditch 2010, 14–17).

Concluding Words on the Complexities of the Ancient Context

Reading the Old Testament in its ancient contexts requires a variety of considerations and an understanding that there are divergent views on these contexts. But this complexity should not discourage readers of the Bible from contemplating the origins of the Old Testament books, because a better understanding of their origins results in a broader understanding of their meanings and potential applications to our modern contexts. The authors of this volume's commentaries have worked to give the reader the best possible overview of the sociohistorical contexts that underlie the books of the Old Testament, opening its texts in new ways so that new meanings can be derived. While this section has highlighted some of the many considerations that need to be addressed when reading the "Very Dangerous Texts Ahead," the variety of contexts out of which the Old

Testament's books emerged is paralleled by the diversity of cultures, faiths, and societies into which they have been received.

Reading the Old Testament in Its Contemporary Contexts

Actively engaging the Old Testament in both its ancient and modern contexts enables readers to discover new levels of meaning that would otherwise go unnoticed. Through acknowledging an Old Testament text's historical setting, exploring how it has been interpreted through the millennia, and noticing the questions and challenges that it raises for our contemporary settings, engaged readers are better able to receive multiple levels of meaning that aid the reader in better understanding the biblical authors' intentions and discerning the passage's potential relevance to conversations that are unfolding today.

The Challenge of Bringing Ancient Context in Line with Modern Contexts

To participate in this process, however, is not a simple task. Beyond working to discern the various levels of meaning within the Old Testament, it is of paramount importance for readers to also acknowledge the preconceptions and biases they bring with them as they work to connect the ancient writings to their own world—an issue that is explored at length below.

As humorously demonstrated in A. J. Jacobs's book *The Year of Living Biblically*, it is important to remember that the texts of the Old Testament were not written for twenty-first-century audiences, but for citizens of the ancient world. As he recounts in his book, Jacobs tried to live as literally as possible according to the laws of the Hebrew Bible for one year. His experiment revealed that to live by the rules of the Hebrew Bible is to live as an outlaw in much of the modern world, whether because the Hebrew Bible calls for the execution of people who wear mixed fibers or because it mandates sacrificing animals in urban centers. This clash of ancient and modern cultures occurred in a very serious way in the tragic murder of Murray Seidman. Mr. Seidman's killer referenced Lev. 20:13 as his motivation for stoning the elderly and mentally disabled man (Masterson).

Conversely, some people, like Charlie Fuqua, assert that engaging with the Old Testament's historical contexts is not required. During the 2012 United States election, Fuqua ran for a seat on the Arkansas state legislature and released a book titled *God's Law: The Only Political Solution*. In his book, Fuqua calls for the creation of legal channels that will facilitate the execution of disobedient children, as commanded in Deut. 21:18-21 (2012, 179). While Fuqua's views represent a fringe group of theomonists that include such Christian reconstructionists as Cornelius Van Til and Rousas John Rushdoony, his example illustrates the importance of contemplating the important differences that exist between the biblical authors' societies and those into which their writings are received today. One must ask questions such as, Did the authors of Deut. 21:18-21 actually seek the execution of disobedient children, or did they pose an extreme example to illustrate a point on child rearing? Another important question to consider is, Did Deut. 21:18-21 originate at a time when resources were so scarce and the production of food so difficult that a child who didn't contribute to—but rather threatened——the common good posed a threat to the community's survival? Growing and cultivating food could certainly be a matter of life and death. Fuqua's failure to engage Deut. 21:18-21, choosing instead to blindly subscribe to the text at face value, is a very serious and dangerous matter, especially considering his aspirations for political office. But while vast differences separate the cultures and societies of the Old Testament authors and the world that we inhabit today, a surprising number of connections do exist.

Whether a Judean farmer or an American physician, we all share such aspects of the universal human experience as love, hate, trust, betrayal, fear, and hope—all of which are reflected both in the Old Testament and in our daily lives. Such themes as women working to find justice in societies that offer little, the quest for love along with its dangers and rewards, and people's struggle to understand their relationships with power, whether personal or political, are all found in the stories of the Old Testament and are still highly relevant to us today.

It should be pointed out, however, that earnestly engaging the Old Testament in its ancient and modern contexts is difficult, even hazardous. Several key considerations that help in an engaged reading of the books of the Old Testament are included here, including issues of biblical ownership, methods of interpretation, and approaches to the reception of its texts.

Whose Bible Is It, Anyway?

While the texts of the Old Testament are commonly used with an air of authority and ownership, their ownership is open to question. So, to whom do they belong? Now that their authors are long dead—and their works have passed through generations and around the world—who is the heir of these works? To which community would they turn and say, "The keys are yours"? One problem with answering this question is that the Old Testament's authors and editors did not represent a unified tradition through which a unified voice could be offered. Furthermore, the faiths and cultures of the twenty-first century CE are so far removed from the ancient authors' that they would most likely be utterly unrecognizable to them. On one level, it is a moot question. Those authors are dead, and they do not get a say regarding who uses their works, or how. Be that as it may, it is an important question to consider, for recognizing that the Old Testament has a number of spiritual heirs with divergent views of the divine underscores the vast interpretive possibilities these texts contain. While many faith traditions draw on the books of the Old Testament, the three largest—in order of appearance—are Judaism, Christianity, and Islam.

The Hebrew Bible (the *Tanakh*) of Judaism is composed of twenty-four books, which are divided into the Torah (Law), the Nebiim (Prophets), and the Ketubim (Writings). The Torah gives accounts of the creation, the establishment of the Hebrew people, and their movement out of captivity in Egypt toward the land that was promised to their ancestors. The public reading of the Torah is a religious ritual that culminates with the annual holiday of *Simchat Torah*, which celebrates its completion. Although the Tanakh forms the whole of Jewish biblical literature, it is supplemented by other interpretive collections.

The Christian *Old Testament*, sometimes referred to as the *First Testament*, sets the books of the Tanakh in a different order and serves as the first section of the *Christian Bible*, as a whole. Canonization of the Old Testament varies among different Christian traditions. Roman Catholicism,

Eastern Orthodoxy, and some Protestant groups include the seven additional books in their canon, as well as additions to the books of Esther and Daniel; these additions are called the *deuterocanon* ("second canon") or *Apocrypha* ("hidden"). Many of the books of the Old Testament are popularly seen as a precursor to the coming of Jesus and his perceived fulfillment of the law.

Islam incorporates many of the figures of the Old Testament into its sacred writings, the Holy Qur'an. Giving particular reverence to the Torah and the Psalms, the Qur'an honors Abraham, Isaac, and Moses as prophetic predecessors to the faith's final and greatest prophet, Muhammad (d. 632 CE).

While each of these traditions draws deep meaning and conviction from the Hebrew Scriptures, they also use them in different ways to reflect their own unique spiritual paths and theologies. The question of which group is the rightful heir of the biblical authors is impossible to answer definitively, since each claims to be in fact the rightful heir. The fact that such a diverse pool of people turns to these texts as sacred Scripture amplifies the many possibilities for Old Testament interpretation.

Evolving Views of the Old Testament and Its Interpretation

Whether or not it is done consciously, all readers of the Old Testament are engaged in some level of interpretation; there are no passive readers of the Bible. When people read the books of the Old Testament, they do so actively, bringing their own presuppositions, experiences, and cultural norms to a text. In essence, readers of the Old Testament bridge the ancient to the modern by way of exegesis and hermeneutics.

Exegesis looks at the texts in their ancient contexts, while hermeneutics works to discern how they relate to a modern reader's situation. Biblical scholars and readers have developed a number of methods for bringing the ancient and the modern together, often with specific objectives and theological motives in mind.

Biblical Literalism

Biblical literalism—which asserts that the Bible is the inerrant word of God, unaltered and untainted by human agency during its transmission from God to humanity—is a prevalent form of interpretation in the United States, practiced commonly within fundamentalist and some evangelical communities. The literal meanings of individual biblical texts were long considered alongside allegorical, moral, and mystical interpretations; it was not until the Reformation's second wave, in the seventeenth century, that literalism became a way to approach the Bible as a whole.

Protestant Christians who broke from the authority of Roman Catholicism found a strong sense of liberation in the idea of gaining access to God's direct word through the Scriptures. If an adherent could access God directly through a Bible, what need did they have for such individual or institutional arbitrators as priests, popes, or the Roman Church? Whereas early Reformers like Martin Luther and John Calvin viewed Scripture as being inspired by God with human involvement in its transmission, some of the second wave of Reformers, such as Amandus Polanus (d. 1610) and Abraham Calov (d. 1686), placed even greater emphasis on the Bible's inerrancy. The movement known as Protestant Scholasticism promoted the idea that any human involvement in the creation of the Bible was strictly mechanical; those who wrote the words were merely tools used by God. This was the first time that the idea of the inerrancy of Scripture as a literal interpretive approach was applied to the Bible—as a whole.

Despite the many developments in biblical interpretation that have occurred between the seventeenth and twenty-first centuries CE, many North American Christians still self-identify as biblical literalists. However, almost nobody practices biblical literalism in the strictest sense, for it would be an almost untenable position. The various contributions by the different religious communities that went into the writing of our biblical texts have resulted in contradicting versions of similar content (cf. Exod. 21:2-8 with Deut. 15:12-13). Given these challenges, how could A. J. Jacobs's experiment in living in strict accord with biblical law have any hope of being tenable, or even legal?

Historical Criticism

The influence of the Enlightenment—with its emphases on reason and searching for facts—gave rise to *the historical-critical movement*, which works to reconstruct the ancient contexts of the Bible. Baruch Spinoza (d. 1677) argued that the same scientific principles that were being applied to other areas of knowledge should be applied to the Bible as well. The results, which are still highly influential on how biblical scholarship is conducted today, have challenged such traditionally held Old Testament notions as the Genesis account(s) of the creation, Moses' composition of the Torah, and the historical validity of the Hebrew exodus out of Egypt, to name a few. Scrutinizing a particular text's origins through asking such questions as, Who wrote the text? For what purpose? and, Under what circumstances? Historical critics work to better understand what lies beneath the text.

Historical criticism's influence on biblical scholarship has shaped the way that many theologians read the Bible by adding to our understanding of the ancient contexts behind biblical texts. *Religionsgeschichte* ("history of religions") is a tool of historical criticism that reads biblical texts in their ancient religious contexts. Another historical-critical tool is *form criticism*, which has gleaned new meaning from such passages as the Song of Deborah (Judges 5) by considering their oral prehistory, reconstructing the *Sitz im Leben* ("original setting"), and analyzing their literary genres.

Social-Scientific Criticism

In the late 1970s—with the publication of Norman Gottwald's *The Tribes of Yahweh*—biblical scholars began to look at the books of the Old Testament through the lens of their sociological settings. Since then, numerous scholars have used societal patterns both to fill in many of the hidden contexts that are simply not addressed in the texts themselves and to better understand the societal motivations behind the Old Testament authors' messages.

One advantage to the social-scientific method of interpretation is its ability to inform hermeneutics (again, the application of biblical texts to modern circumstances). Social-scientific models have proven to be of particular use in shedding light on the contexts and motivations behind biblical texts while opening new ways of understanding how those texts might relate to the modern world (Chaney; Coomber 2011). A tempting misuse of social-scientific models of interpretation, however, is to treat the findings gained through social-scientific models as hard evidence that can stand on its own. Social-scientific models that deal with tribalism, urban development, religious-political interactions, or economic cycles can provide insight into how humans—and their systems—are expected to behave; they do not, however, prove how humans and systems did behave. It is for this reason that social-scientific approaches should be used in tandem with all available data, be it archaeological or literary.

Commenting on the great value of using social-scientific models in the interpretation of biblical texts, Philip Esler writes that their use "fires the social-scientific imagination to ask new questions of data, to which only the data can provide the answers" (Esler, 3). In other words, these models are useful for the interpretation of evidence, not as evidence in and of themselves. Social-scientific criticism has proven especially useful in the development of contextual readings of the Old Testament, which address issues ranging from political interpretations of the Bible to interpretations within such minority groups as LGBT (lesbian, gay, bisexual, and transgender) and disabled communities.

Contextual and Reception Readings and Criticisms

Contextual readings of the Old Testament provide excellent examples of how the ancient stories and ideas of the Old Testament can speak to the modern contexts of diverse communities. These forms of criticism, like social-scientific or literary criticism, often take on an interdisciplinary nature. While a plethora of contextual topics have been covered biblically, those that address issues of empire, gender, and race are briefly covered here.

Empire

Just as issues of empire were integral in the formation of the Old Testament, as addressed in the "Reading the Old Testament in Its Ancient Contexts" section above, Old Testament texts continue to influence the ways people approach issues of empire today. On the one hand, the imagery that celebrates conquest in the invasion of Canaan (Joshua) and the glory of Solomon's kingdom (e.g., 1 Kings 4) could be used to support the building of empire. On the other hand, those who challenge the rise or expansion of empires can draw on anti-imperial readings that condemn the conduct of royals and their exploitation of the citizenry (e.g., Micah 3), and legislation against economic injustice in the Torah, Writings, and Prophets.

Pro-imperial readings of the Old Testament can be seen in the building and expansion of US influence, such as the idea of *Manifest Destiny*, which portrays the Christian European settlement of the United States as God's divine will. Manifest destiny involved a reimagining of the Pilgrims—and later European settlers—as the new Hebrews, pushing aside the Native American peoples—who took on the role of Canaanites—in order to create a new Israel. The Rev. Josiah Strong's publication *Our Country* echoes this sentiment in its assertion that God was charging European Christianity "to dispossess the many weaker races, assimilate others, and mold the remainder" (Strong, 178). Reverberations of the Old Testament–rooted Manifest Destiny still surface in aspects of American exceptionalism, which influences the US political spectrum and can be seen in such approaches to foreign policy as "the Bush Doctrine," which works to spread American-style democracy as a path to lasting peace.

Just as the Old Testament has been used for empire building, it has also been used to challenge empire and its institutions. While the exodus narrative helped to shape the idea of Manifest Destiny, it also became a powerful abolitionist force in attacking the institutions of slavery and segregation. During the abolitionist movement, the powerful imagery of the exodus story gave hope and power to free African Americans and slaves alike. The power of the story was harnessed again in the mid-twentieth century, giving strength to those who struggled for racial equality (Coomber 2012, 123–36). Recent biblical scholarship has also turned to the Old Testament to address various issues of modern-day economic exploitation and neoimperialism (e.g., Gottwald 2011; Boer, ed.; West 2010).

A highly influential outcome of the crossing of Bible and empire has been *postcolonial interpretation*. As European empires spread throughout the world, they brought the Bible and Christianity with them. With the twentieth-century waning of European imperialism, colonized and previously colonized peoples have found their own voices in the Bible, resulting in a variety of new interpretations and new approaches to major Old Testament themes. Postcolonial interpretation has enriched the field from Mercedes García Bachmann's use of Isaiah 58 to address issues of "unwanted fasting" (105–12) to raising questions about whether the Christian canon should be reopened to include the folk stories and traditions of colonized Christian communities that feel unrepresented by the current Bible (Pui Lan).

Gender

Studies in gender have also revealed a wide range of interpretive possibilities and have come to the forefront of biblical scholarship during the past four decades. While often treated as the sex of the body, the word *gender* is a complicated term that addresses a variety of factors of embodiment, including mental and behavioral characteristics. *Masculinity* and *femininity*, for example, take on different attributes and expectations depending on the society or culture in which they exist. While gender is an area of study that is continually developing into various branches, both within and outside of biblical studies, one of its most predominant manifestations in biblical studies is found in *feminist criticism.*

Women have been longtime readers and commentators on biblical texts, even though their work has rarely been given the same consideration as their male counterparts, who have long served as the vanguard of the academy. Hildegard of Bingen (d. 1179) authored a commentary on Genesis 1–2 (Young, 262); R. Roberts (d. 1788) composed numerous sermons on a range of texts for a clergyman acquaintance (Knowles, 418–19); and abolitionist Elizabeth Cady Stanton (d. 1902) helped to publish *The Woman's Bible.* These three women serve as but a few examples of women who have made important contributions to biblical studies, though their work is unknown to many.

Feminist criticism continues to be a very effective mode for recovering women's insights, perspectives, knowledge, and the feminine principle in biblical texts, often rescuing those voices and interpretations from centuries of marginalization by patriarchal and even misogynistic interpretation. Elisabeth Schüssler Fiorenza claims that, unlike many other forms of biblical criticism, feminist biblical studies does not owe its existence to the academy but to social movements for change, and also to a desire for the ongoing pursuit of equal participation and equal rights, which have in practice been restricted to a small group of elite men (Schüssler Fiorenza, 8–9). Schüssler Fiorenza argues that since the Bible has most often been used in these struggles for either "legitimating the status quo of the kyriarchal order of domination *or* for challenging dehumanization, feminist biblical interpretation is best articulated as an integral part of wo/men's struggles for authority and self-determination" (9). Like so many forms of contextual and received readings, feminist criticism can serve as a liberating force by revealing perspectives within the Bible's texts that have otherwise gone unnoticed.

An example of recovering the woman's perspective in the Old Testament is found in feminist commentaries on such texts as Isa. 42:14, in which God says,

> For a long time I have held my peace,
>> I have kept still and restrained myself;
> now I will cry out like a woman in labor,
>> I will gasp and pant.

Patricia Tull has highlighted the way in which YHWH adopts the power of a woman in labor to emphasize God's own divine power of creation (Tull, 263). Another example of uncovering women's voices to find justice in patriarchal cultures—which work to subvert women's voices and rights—is found in Sharon Pace Jeansonne's treatment of Tamar as a woman who seizes power to find justice in a society that is set up to stop her from doing so (Jeansonne, 98–106).

Feminist criticism—as with most any other form of biblical criticism—is polyvocal, with a broad spectrum of biblical views, including those who have argued that the Bible might be best left alone (Bal, 14). Male scholars have also engaged with feminist-focused readings of Old Testament texts. Daniel Cohen's midrash on Genesis 3, for example, addresses misogynistic interpretations of the Garden of Eden story (Cohen 141–48).

Similar to some of feminist criticism's attempts to reclaim the women's voice in the Bible and address misogynistic interpretation, *queer criticism* works to uncover LGBT perspectives in the Old Testament and messages that are of importance to LGBT communities. Queer interpretation has addressed a number of such topics, including K. Renato Lings's work on homophobic critiques of the destruction of Sodom in Genesis 19—a text often used to condemn homosexuality—in which he argues that attaching homosexuality to the sin of Sodom was a later interpretive development, unrecognized by biblical authors (Lings, 183–207). Others have shed new light on the ways in which biblical texts are interpreted to affect modern-day political decisions, such as the issue of same-sex marriage (see Stahlberg).

Conclusion

To be an engaged reader of the Old Testament involves simultaneously navigating the worlds of the biblical authors and redactors, as well as all those who have interpreted its texts. It is through approaching a biblical text or idea through these multiple angles that the multilayered meanings of the Old Testament books can be unlocked, not only in regard to the authors' intentions, but also in ways that the biblical writers may have never been able to foresee. These multiple intersections with the biblical text help people to have meaningful conversation and debate on topics ranging from climate change, to same-sex marriage, to the international banking crisis, and more. Naturally, being an engaged reader requires considerable effort, but it is through deliberating on biblical texts in all of their complexity that deeper meaning can be found, and more honest—or at least informed— readings of the Bible's contents can be gleaned.

In this volume, the contributors' commentaries provide a tool through which people can develop their engagement with the books of the Old Testament and Apocrypha. Whether approaching this volume as a researcher, educator, member of the clergy, or student, it is the intent of the *Fortress Commentary on the Old Testament* to inform readers about the Old Testament books' historical contexts, interpretive histories, and the modern contexts with which they engage, while also serving as an opening through which the conversation can be expanded.

Works Cited

Alfaro, Juan I. 1989. *Justice and Loyalty: A Commentary on the Book of Micah*. Grand Rapids: Eerdmans.

Bachmann, Mercedes L. García. 2009. "True Fasting and Unwilling Hunger (Isaiah 58)." In *The Bible and the Hermeneutics of Liberation*, edited by A. F. Botta and P. R. Andiñach, 113–31. Atlanta: SBL.

Bal, Mieke. 1989. *Anti-Covenant: Counter-Reading Women's Lives in the Hebrew Bible*. Sheffield: Almond.

Boer, Roland, ed. 2013. *Postcolonialism and the Hebrew Bible: The Next Step*. SemeiaSt 70. Atlanta: SBL.

Cantor, Norman F. 1992. *Inventing the Middle Ages: The Lives, Works, and Ideas of the Great Medievalists of the Twentieth Century*. Cambridge: Lutterworth.

Chaney, Marvin L. 1999. "Whose Sour Grapes? The Addressees of Isaiah 5:1–7 in the Light of Political Economy." In *The Social World of the Hebrew Bible: Twenty-Five Years of the Social Sciences in the Academy*, edited by Ronald A. Simkins and Stephen L. Cook. *Semeia* 87:105–22.

Cohen, Daniel. 2007. "Taste and See: A Midrash on Genesis 3:6 and 3:12." In *Patriarchs, Prophets and Other Villains*, edited by Lisa Isherwood, 141–48. London: Equinox Publishing.

Coomber, Matthew J. M. 2010. *Re-Reading the Prophets through Corporate Globalization: A Cultural-Evolutionary Approach to Understanding Economic Injustice in the Hebrew Bible*. Piscataway, NJ: Gorgias.

———. 2011. "Caught in the Crossfire? Economic Injustice and Prophetic Motivation in Eighth-Century Judah." *BibInt* 19, nos. 4–5:396–432.

———. 2012. "Before Crossing the Jordan: The Telling and Retelling of the Exodus Narrative in African American History." In *Exodus and Deuteronomy: Texts @ Contexts*, edited by Athalya Brenner and Gale A. Yee, 123–36. Minneapolis: Fortress Press.

———. 2013. "Debt as Weapon: Manufacturing Poverty from Judah to Today." *Diaconia: Journal for the Study of Christian Social Practice* 4, no. 2:141–55.

Coote, Robert B., and Keith W. Whitelam. 1987. *The Emergence of Early Israel in Historical Perspective*. Sheffield: Almond.

Crossley, James G. 2008. *Jesus in an Age of Terror: Scholarly Projects for a New American Century*. London: Equinox.

Davies, Philip. 2000. "What Separates a Minimalist from a Maximalist? Not Much." *BAR* 26, no. 2:24–27, 72–73.

Davies, Philip, and John Rogerson. 2005. *The Old Testament World*. 2nd ed. Louisville: Westminster John Knox.

Dever, William G. 2008. *Did God Have a Wife? Archaeology and Folk Religion in Ancient Israel*. Grand Rapids: Eerdmans.

Esler, Philip F. 2005. "Social-Scientific Models in Biblical Interpretation." In *Ancient Israel: The Old Testament in Its Social Context*, edited by Philip Esler, 3–14. London: SCM.

Fuqua, Charles R. 2012. *God's Law: The Only Political Solution*. Salt Lake City: American Book Publishing.

Gottwald, Norman. 1999. *The Tribes of Yahweh: A Sociology of the Religion of Liberated Israel, 1250–1050* BCE. Sheffield: Sheffield Academic Press.

———. 2001. *The Politics of Ancient Israel*. Louisville: Westminster John Knox.

Grabbe, Lester L. 2007. *Ancient Israel: What Do We Know and How Do We Know It?* London: T&T Clark.

Halpern, Baruch. 1995. "Erasing History: The Minimalist Assault on Ancient Israel." *BRev* 11: 26–35, 47.

Jacobs, A. J. 2007. *The Year of Living Biblically: One Man's Humble Quest to Follow the Bible as Literally as Possible*. New York: Simon & Schuster.

Jeansonne, Sharon Pace. 1990. *The Women of Genesis: From Sarah to Potiphar's Wife*. Minneapolis: Fortress Press.

Josephus, Flavius. 1854. *The Works of Flavius Josephus: Comprising the Antiquities of the Jews, a History of the Jewish Wars, and Life of Flavius Josephus, Written by Himself*. Translated by William Whiston. Philadelphia: Jas. B. Smith.

Karmon, Yehuda. 1971. *Israel: A Regional Geography*. London: Wiley-Interscience.

Knapp, A. Bernard. 1988. "Copper Production and Eastern Mediterranean Trade: The Rise of Complex Society in Cyprus." In *State and Society: The Emergence and Development of Social Hierarchy and Political Centralization*, edited by J. Gledhill, B. Bender, and M. T. Larsen, 149–72. London: Unwin Hyman.

Knowles, Michael P. 2012. "Roberts, R. (ca. 1728–88)." In *Handbook of Women Biblical Interpreters*, edited by M. A. Taylor and A. Choi, 418–20. Grand Rapids: Baker Academic.

Kwok Pui-lan. 2003. "Discovering the Bible in the Non-Biblical World." In *Searching the Scriptures: A Feminist Introduction*, edited by Elisabeth Schüssler Fiorenza, 276–88. New York: Crossroad.

Lings, K. Renato. 2007. "Culture Clash in Sodom: Patriarchal Tales of Heroes, Villains, and Manipulation." In *Patriarchs, Prophets and Other Villains*, edited by Lisa Isherwood, 183–207. London: Equinox.

Liverani, Mario. 2007. *Israel's History and the History of Israel*. Translated by Chiara Peri and Philip Davies. London: Equinox.

Masterson, Teresa. 2011. "Man, 70, Stoned to Death for Being Gay." *NBC10 Philadelphia*. Accessed October 14, 2013. http://www.nbcphiladelphia.com/news/local/Man-70-Stoned-to-Death-for-Homosexuality-Police-118243719.html.

Niditch, Susan. 2010. "Experiencing the Divine: Heavenly Visits, Earthly Encounters and the Land of the Dead." In *Religious Diversity in Ancient Israel and Judah*, edited by Francesca Stavrakopoulou and John Barton, 11–22. London: T&T Clark.

Schüssler Fiorenza, Elisabeth. 2013. *Changing Horizons: Explorations in Feminist Interpretation*. Minneapolis: Fortress Press.

Schweitzer, Albert. 1968. *The Quest of the Historical Jesus: A Critical Study of Its Progress from Reimarus to Wrede*. New York: Macmillan.

Smith, Mark S. 2002. *The Early History of God: Yahweh and the Other Deities in Ancient Israel*. Grand Rapids: Eerdmans.

Stahlberg, Lesleigh Cushing. 2008. "Modern Day Moabites: The Bible and the Debate About Same-Sex Marriage." *BibInt* 16:422–75.

Stavrakopoulou, Francesca. 2010. "'Popular' Religion and 'Official' Religion: Practice, Perception, Portrayal." In *Religious Diversity in Ancient Israel and Judah*, edited by Francesca Stavrakopoulou and John Barton, 37–58. New York: T&T Clark.

Strong, Josiah. 1885. *Our Country: Its Possible Future and Its Present Crisis*. New York: The American Home Missionary Society.

Tull, Patricia K. 2012. "Isaiah." In *Women's Bible Commentary: Twentieth-Anniversary Edition*, edited by C. A. Newsom, S. H. Ringe, and J. E. Lapsley, 255–66. Louisville: Westminster John Knox.

West, Gerald. 2010. "The Legacy of Liberation Theologies in South Africa, with an Emphasis on Biblical Hermeneutics." *Studia Historiae Ecclesiasticae* 36, Supplement: 157–83.

Whitelam, Keith W. 2007. "Lines of Power: Mapping Ancient Israel." In *To Break Every Yoke: Essays in Honour of Marvin L. Chaney*, edited by R. B. Coote and N. K. Gottwald, 40–79. Sheffield: Sheffield Phoenix Press.

Young, Abigail. 2012. "Hildegard of Bingen (1098–1179)." In *Handbook of Women Biblical Interpreters*, edited by M. A. Taylor and A. Choi, 259–64. Grand Rapids: Baker Academic.

THE PEOPLE OF GOD AND THE PEOPLES OF THE EARTH

Hugh R. Page Jr.

The Bible Is Just the Beginning

The Bible is preeminently a book about people. That may strike some as a rather odd assertion given the stature enjoyed by the Bible as sacred text containing, in many faith traditions, everything one needs to know about God and salvation. Nonetheless, some of the more important foci of the Old and New Testaments have to do with the saga of the human family and the women and men that are dramatis personae in this unfolding drama. In the twenty-first century CE, our appreciation of how Scripture narrates that story is much more nuanced than it was perhaps a generation or two ago. We are much more aware of the processes by which traditions are shaped and preserved. We have a deeper understanding of the myriad stages through which the inspired words of prophets, poets, and sages proceed before being canonized: as well as of the place the Bible occupies in the global ecology of sacred texts. Moreover, we recognize that many of the world's sacred texts have important things to say about the human condition. Thus perspectives on what it means to be "people of God," women and men in a special relationship with a transcendent being, or members of a large and diverse human family sharing a common terrestrial abode vary widely. Moreover, in today's world, scholarship in fields such as genetics and anthropology is changing the way we think about human origins and notions of personhood.

It is because of new ideas about humanity and its origins that responsible readers of the Bible must, therefore, examine biblical conceptions of personhood, while keeping in mind the ways in which both the human family in general and those individuals called into special relationship with the God of Israel are construed. In so doing, they must also look at how such ideas have shaped, and continue to influence, notions about the world and its inhabitants today; are related to comparable ideas about personhood in other faith traditions; relate to what scientific evidence reveals about the human family; have been complicit in the exploitation of colonized peoples; and stand in relationship to those ideas about the human family articulated in documents such as the United Nations Declaration of Human Rights and the Declaration on the Rights of Indigenous Peoples. Such a task is necessary if we are to enhance the extent to which the Bible can be deployed as a resource in building a more just and equitable global community. Failure to do so may limit the extent to which members of faith communities for which the Bible is authoritative are able to join in meaningful dialogue about the future of our global community and the institutions that support it. It may also inadvertently lend credence to the idea that religious texts and traditions have no place in conversations about those ideals on which a cosmopolitan global community should be based in the future.

The Earth and Its Peoples—A View from the Ethnographic Record

Science has revealed that modern human beings are the result of a remarkable evolutionary process. We share common African ancestry, and our diversity at this point in time bears witness to an array of migratory, climatic, and genetic adaptations that span hundreds of thousands of years. Our cultural landscape is vast and remarkable in its variation. For example, the comprehensive cultural database maintained by Human Relations Area Files at Yale University (see http://www.yale.edu/hraf/collections.htm) contains information on several hundred cultures.

The *Ethnographic Atlas*, a massive project undertaken by George Peter Murdock (1969) and ultimately brought to full fruition in the 1970s, contains information on more than one thousand distinct groups. As an ethnologist, Murdock was particularly interested in both the comparative study of cultures and the identification of behavioral traits that manifest locally, regionally, and internationally (see especially Murdock 1981, 3). His work calls attention to the breadth of lifeways characteristic of peoples around the world. Scholarship continuing in the vein of Murdock's has led to the identification of some 3,500 cultures on which published data are readily available (see, e.g., Price, 10). Such studies have also resulted in the development of templates for comparing social organization, religious beliefs, and other information about the world's disparate peoples (see Ember and Ember; and Murdock et al.). Needless to say, the vision of the human family derived from this research is remarkable. Social scientists see this diverse collage of languages, customs, and religious traditions as the end result of developmental forces that have been operational for *aeons*. It is also for them a mystery to be probed using the critical tools at their disposal. Ethnographic investigations and theory testing have laid bare and will continue to reveal its undiscovered truths. However, humankind has not revealed, and is not likely to yield, the sum total of its secrets to even the most dogged of investigators. Like the stories of primordial reality we encounter in the biblical book of Genesis, such research offers a place from which to begin pondering what it means to be human.

Human life is, of course, dynamic. New social and religious groups are born constantly. The first two decades of the current millennium have even witnessed the dissolution of geopolitical boundaries, the creation of new nation states, and the birth of new religious movements. Thus notions of culture and personhood in our era are anything but static. Our human family continues to grow and with each passing day becomes more diverse and increasingly complex. Research in the social sciences has increased our understanding of how culture and identity evolve. We know more today than ever before about the ways language, physical environment, and other factors contribute to ideas about what it means to be a fully actualized self and to be in relationship with those other selves that are one's family members, friends, and neighbors. It has also shed light on the role that the collection and preservation of religious lore play in this process. Sacred traditions and texts serve as the repositories for stories about how people and the groups in which they are embedded came to be. They also function as points of reference for the nurture of persons and the communities in which they live.

The challenge we face in an era when such traditions are often read narrowly or uncritically—without an eye toward their implicit limitations—is to create charitable and inclusive approaches that allow us to engage and appropriate them. Such strategies necessitate that we become well versed in the ways that stories, both ancient and modern, shape our identities, beliefs, and relationships with one another. Whether one has in mind venerable tales such as the Babylonian *Enuma Elish* and the so-called Priestly account of creation (Gen. 1:1—2:4a), or modern cinematic myths like the *Matrix* or *Prometheus* sagas, narratives of one kind or another provide a context for understanding who we are and how we choose to live. Returning to the Bible itself, it is arguable that one of its central aims is to inform us of what it means to be finite beings that are threads in a sacred cosmic fabric woven, as it were, by a divine and ineffable artisan.

Ancient Near Eastern Lore and Conceptions of Personhood

In the late nineteenth and early twentieth centuries, scholars such as James Frazer and Stith Thompson began looking seriously at cultural practices and folklore from various parts of the world. The results were remarkable, though not without some degree of controversy. Frazer's efforts included his Victorian-era classic *The Golden Bough* (Frazer 1981) and an equally important, if less celebrated, three-volume work titled *Folk-Lore in the Old Testament* (Frazer 1918a; 1918b; 1918c); and Thompson's work on folklore motifs was pioneering insofar as it laid important groundwork for the comparison of tales from around the world. Although questions remain about the aims and theoretical presuppositions of these early works, their efforts, and those of the scholars following in their immediate footsteps, set the stage for much of the social-scientific research we have seen in the twentieth and twenty-first centuries, even in the field of biblical studies.

Among biblical scholars, the pioneers of form criticism and the so-called myth and ritual school found in this body of information—and other information gathered from ancient Near Eastern sources—a treasure trove useful for contextualizing and interpreting key portions of the Old Testament. Among form critics, Hermann Gunkel must be noted. His collection of essays in *What Remains of the Old Testament* and topical studies of literary *Gattungen* ("forms") as such pertain to the Bible in *The Legends of Genesis* and *The Folktale in the Old Testament* repay—even today—careful reading

(1928; 1964; 1987). Among myth and ritual adherents, Sigmund Mowinckel's work deserves pride of place, especially his *Psalmenstudien* (1966). These pioneers' use of ethnological resources in the study of Scripture were paralleled by those of Johannes Pedersen in his two-volume study of ancient Israelite culture (1926–1940) and extended in subsequent generations by Theodor Gaster's efforts to reclaim and expand the work of Frazer (1950; 1959; 1969); Mary Douglas's exploration of the body as social map (1966); Bruce Malina's use of a circum-Mediterranean paradigm to understand the roles of women and men in the Bible (1989); and others whose work has explored the intersections of Jewish, Christian, Mediterranean, and other cultural traditions both ancient and modern.

Several lessons can be gleaned from this body of research. The first is that people are in some ways "hardwired" to create and tell stories. These stories help in making sense of life crises such as birth, maturation, and death. They are also pivotal in defining the self and the social networks into which individual selves are embedded. A second lesson is that one particular genre, creation stories—whether they focus on the birth of deities (theogonies), the universe (cosmogonies), humanity, tribal confederations, monarchies, or all of the aforementioned—have a direct impact on the ways people understand their place in the world. Creation stories define social and ethnic boundaries, reify social and political hierarchies, and ascribe status based on age, gender, and other ontological and ascribed markers. These two factors should inform the ways information about individuals and groups embedded in poetry, rituals, royal inscriptions, and other texts is understood. A few examples from the ancient Near East are particularly illustrative.

The Mesopotamian flood tradition encountered in the Atrahasis myth has, among its more important purposes, articulation of a basic theological anthropology—one that is based on an understanding of the mutable and immutable dimensions of an, at times, capricious cosmos. Human beings are oddly situated in this power-filled and unstable environment. They are remarkable for three reasons. The first is because they are made of the flesh and blood of a divine insurgent and sacrificed because he led a rebellion against the harsh labor imposed on a subset of deities in the pantheon.

> When the gods themselves were men,
> They did the work. They endured the toil.
> The labor was onerous.
> Massive was the effort. The distress was exceedingly great. (Lambert and Millard, 42
>   [tablet 1.1.1–4], translation my own)

> Let them sacrifice the divine leader.
> Let the gods purify themselves by immersion.
> With his essence—flesh and blood—let Nintu mix the clay,
> So that divinity and humanity may be thoroughly
> Blended in the amalgam.
> For all time let us hear the drumbeat.
> In the flesh of the god let the ghost remain.
> Let her [Nintu] inform him [the slain god] of his token.
> So that there will be no forgetting,
> The spirit will remain. (Lambert and Millard, 58 [tablet 1.4.208–17], translation my own)

The human heartbeat is the "drum" reminding women and men for all time of the immortal lineage that is uniquely their own. The second reason that people are special is due to their being extended kin, as it were, of Atrahasis, the "exceedingly wise one," who managed to survive the great deluge by which all of humanity was destroyed. To them belongs the empowering, yet dangerous, model of this *liminal* ancestor. As William Moran noted more than four decades ago: "The Atrahasis Epic is an assertion of man's importance in the final order of things. It is also a strong criticism of the gods" (Moran, 59).

Humans are also special (see Moran, 60–61) for a third reason: because they are living proof of the imprudence of the gods and goddesses they serve. Created to assume the day-to-day labor deemed too difficult for immortals to bear, the din of their daily existence proved far too disruptive of their divine patrons' and matrons' sleep. Their death was decreed because they were, in a word, "noisy" (Lambert and Millard, 66 [tablet 1.7.354–59]). It is only through the quick-witted intervention of Enki, his personal god, that Atrahasis and his family are able to escape the inundation. Atrahasis is a powerful symbol of what can happen when human perseverance and divine subterfuge are allied.

The Atrahasis myth suggests that people are made of supernatural "stuff" and are heirs to a distinctive lineage. It also emphasizes that in a world filled with danger, the gods who are in control of the fates of women and men do not always have the best interest of the human family in mind. Although all mortals are in a sense beings belonging to and dependent on the gods, the implication of the sobering reality revealed in this myth is that in order to survive, women and men would do well to leverage their inner resources while at the same time relying, should all else fail, on timely divine intervention by those deities with whom they have a special relationship. Such assertions are, of course, in conversation with anthropologies articulated in other lore across a wide spectrum of genres. For example, Gilgamesh—particularly the Old Babylonian version of this Akkadian classic—focuses attention on the unique challenges confronted by one species of individual: monarchs. Of particular interest in this epic are their socialization, capacity to form friendships, quest for lasting renown, and insecurities about death. royal inscriptions, of which exemplars are too numerous to mention, continue in this vein and further define the traits of kings and those subject to their authority. Suzerainty treaties can be said to function in a comparable manner by defining the relationships of sociopolitical aggregates to one another. Sets of laws, like those found in the Code of Hammurabi, reify social status through taxonomies that identify insiders (e.g., king, free men, and those acquitted of offenses) and outsiders (e.g., criminals, widows, and orphans).

Another story, that of the travails of the god Ba'lu from the ancient city of Ugarit, offers a slightly different perspective on human life—this time from West Semitic lore. Unlike the story of Atrahasis, the Ba'lu myth is concerned primarily with how the enigmatic god of the fructifying rains—mainstays of human life—secures his place as head of the pantheon. Although the primary concern of this tale is Ba'lu's contest with rivals for ascendancy to the throne, it lifts the veil concealing the ongoing cosmic struggle between two such forces that inscribe the parameters for human existence: that is, life/fertility, represented by Ba'lu as numen of the storm, and Môtu, the embodiment of death and dissolution. At one point in this saga, he voluntarily submits himself to the authority and power of Môtu. His death, emblematic of nature's cyclic periods of aridity, leads his father 'Ilu, head of the pantheon, and his sister 'Anatu, to bewail its impact on the world. Both give voice to a lament intended, no doubt, to sum up the anguish of all affected by the storm god's departure.

> Ba'lu has died. What is to become of humanity?
> Dagan's child is no more. What will happen to earth's teeming masses? (CAT 1.5.6.23–24;
>   1.6.1.6–7)

The world and its inhabitants are part of the background landscape against which this divine drama unfolds. Nonetheless, as the narrative progresses, one realizes that each episode has a profound, if at times only partially articulated, impact on the peoples of the earth. Ba'lu returns to life, largely through the intervention of his sister 'Anatu. Eventually, he and Môtu have a fateful encounter that reveals, in no uncertain terms, that they are—and shall remain—in an interminable struggle.

> They fight each other like heroes
> Môtu is strong, as is Ba'lu
> Like raging bulls, they go head to head
> Môtu is strong, as is Ba'lu
> They bite one another like serpents
> Môtu is strong, as is Ba'lu
> Like animals, they beat each other to a pulp
> Môtu falls, Ba'lu collapses. (CAT 1.6.6.16–22)

The two battle to a virtual draw: an indication that the struggle between life and death is ongoing. The hope for "earth's teeming masses" is that the forces of life are able—at the very least—to withstand Death's furious and unrelenting onslaught. To be engaged nobly in the struggle is, therefore, to participate heroically in an age-old struggle that unites every member of the human family as kin. The warp and weft of day-to-day existence finds its ultimate significance in this ongoing cosmic battle. We see a stunning reflex of this mythology in the biblical Song of Songs, where the protagonists are anthropomorphized hypostases of Love (*'ahăbâ*) and Death (*māwet*).

> Seal me to your heart.
> Brand me on your arm.
> Love is equal to Death in its strength.
> Passion rivals Sheol in its ferocity.
> Its flames are a blazing fire.
> It is an eternal inferno. (Song of Songs 8:6, author's own translation)

Additional textual examples from Egypt and Anatolia could be cited, but the above suffice to show how implicit and explicit messaging about people—their nature, connection to one another, and relationship to the divine forces responsible for their creation and support—is conveyed in expressive culture.

The Hebrew Bible, Personhood, and Identity

Biblical references to the earth and its peoples are very much in conversation with these ancient Near Eastern traditions. The opening chapter of the Hebrew Bible contains a remarkable assertion in what scholars have traditionally designated the Priestly account of creation (Gen. 1:1—2:4a): that the world and everything in it is "good." It uses the Hebrew word *ṭôb* to describe its fundamental essence, a word whose semantic range connotes something sweet and pleasurable. Human beings are an important part of the created order. Made on the sixth day, they are distinguished only by gender: male and female. Neither ethnic nor regional markers are noted. All are made according to the divine "form" (*ṣelem*) and "pattern" (*dĕmût*)—that is, God's "image and likeness" according to the NRSV. Theirs are the tasks of reproducing and exercising control of the earth (1:26–28). The word used to describe what will be involved to reach this desired outcome (*kābaš*) connotes a process requiring forceful effort (Oswalt, 430). Also implied here is the idea that this is a laborious enterprise that is both collective and collaborative.

Following this masterful cosmogonic hymn, readers encounter in the remainder of Genesis a "mixed bag" of traditions about the earth's populace representing several sources: fragments of archaic poetry (2:23; 3:14-19; 4:23-24; 49); a descanting creation narrative (2:4b-24); etiological tales (11:1-9); ethnohistorical musings about the origins of particular peoples (4:17-22); an epic about the peregrinations of Israel's ancestors (11:31—36:43); and an extensive novella dealing with a key figure in the national saga: Joseph (37–50). While these materials can be read—as scholarly literature attests—from a variety of perspectives, one thing is very clear: together they tell the story of the God of Israel's relationship with the world and its peoples, some of whom—namely, Abraham, Sarah, and their descendants—are called to take on special responsibilities for the entirety of the human family (12:1-3). In fact, it could be argued that a significant portion of the Genesis tradition (1:1—11:32) has been intended as a creative "riff" on, or response to, Sumero-Akkadian lore (like that found in Atrahasis) about the origins of humanity.

One of the unifying threads holding together the narrative tapestry of Genesis and the remaining books of the Torah/Pentateuch is the story of how the world is affected by the shifting, strained, at times tumultuous, dynamic, and constantly evolving relationships among those who are the offspring of the primordial family. While highlighting theological themes such as *calling* (Exod. 3:1-15); *covenant* (Exod. 6:1-8; 20:1-17); *sin and redemption* (Exod. 32:1-35); *divine immanence and transcendence* (Exod. 25:1—31:18); *holiness* (Lev. 10:3; 20:26); *significant individuals* (Exod. 2:10; 15:20; 2:21; 3:1); *groups* (Exod. 3:8; 6:19); and *events* (Exodus 15; Num. 3:14-16; 9:15-16); these books also articulate a gestalt ("general sketch") for comprehending what it means to be part of a human family. This can entail struggling both to recognize its connectedness and to honor its diversity. It can also involve wrestling with the challenge of managing intergroup crises that influence the welfare of peoples living in proximity; competing for limited resources; and dealing with those changing geopolitical realities that generate population shifts, form new social movements, and give rise to diasporas. It is for this reason that one of the foci of these books, and the sources used therein, is the establishment of social, religious, and other boundaries that determine personhood, group affiliation, and status. For example, the Priestly creation story (Gen. 1—2:4a) can be said to inscribe broad and inclusive parameters for personhood. Since all human beings bear the imprint of the creator's "form" and "pattern," they can be said to belong to a single unified group, for which gender is the only subclassification (1:26-27). The implication of this is that everyone created *by* God belongs *to* God and is therefore part of the "people of God."

Genealogical tables, such as that found in Genesis 10, offer a more nuanced view of group identity based on location, language, and kin group (e.g., 10:5). The story of the Tower of Babel goes a step further in its linkage of linguistic heterogeneity to human hubris and a divine response to quell it (Gen. 11:5-7). Although it can be read simply as an entertaining etiology accounting for the diversity and spread of languages, it does contain a polemical strain resistant to linguistic solidarity, centralized government, and the conscription of resources needed to build monumental structures and to maintain the places—that is, cities—where they are most likely to be found in antiquity. Thus the story seems to be suggesting, on one level, that diversity and difference are preferable to a homogeneity whose consequences, intended or unintended, are to transgress the boundary separating mortals from God.

The block of material inclusive of the ancestral epic and the story of Joseph's rise to Egyptian prominence offers an even more complex picture of the "people of God." On the one hand, the "yes" given by Abram/Abraham to the call of YHWH (Gen. 12:1-3), and the covenant made with him (Gen. 15:18; 17:1-27) by YHWH, serve to distinguish him and his descendants among the "people of God"—that is, as a conduit of blessing to the entirety of the human family (Gen. 12:3). On the other hand, an inversion of status—from "temporary sojourner" to "inheritor" of Canaan (17:6-8)—is also promised, one that sets the stage for what is later described in Joshua and Judges. The story of Joseph's tensions with his brothers, as well as that of the peculiar circumstances leading Jacob and his kin to go to Egypt, set the stage for further musing on several issues. The first is how the kin group through whom all of the "people of God" are to be blessed understands its internal subdivisions (Genesis 49; Deuteronomy 32–33). The second has to do with how the kin group's liberation, covenant at Sinai, sojourn in the wilderness, and occupation of Canaan (Exod. 4:1—20:21; 32:1—35:29; Num. 1:1—36:13; Joshua; and Judges) are construed, particularly in terms of how these sources present Israel's relationship to its neighbors, both as stewards of a unique revelatory experience and part of a larger family of divine offspring. The third concerns the final book of the Pentateuch—Deuteronomy—that serves as the transitional bridge to the Former Prophets. From a literary standpoint, it is a rearticulation and expansion of core precepts first articulated in Exod. 20:1-17. It inscribes very narrow parameters for Israel's self-understanding and relationship to its neighbors. "When you come into the land that the Lord your God is giving you, you must not learn to imitate the abhorrent practices of those nations" (Deut. 18:9).

The book of Deuteronomy has very strict stipulations for the centralization of worship (12:1-28), prophetic practice (18:15-22), the conduct of war (20:1-20), and the care of those without material support (24:14-15, 17-18). All of these grow out of a particular self-understanding, stated most succinctly in what Gerhard von Rad long ago identified as a short creedal statement.

> A wandering Aramean was my ancestor; he went down into Egypt and lived there as an alien,
> few in number, and there he became a great nation, mighty and populous. When the Egyptians
> treated us harshly and afflicted us, by imposing hard labor on us, we cried to the LORD, the God
> of our ancestors; the LORD heard our voice and saw our affliction, our toil, and our oppression.
> The LORD brought us out of Egypt with a mighty hand and an outstretched arm, with a terrifying
> display of power, and with signs and wonders; and he brought us into this place and gave us this
> land, a land flowing with milk and honey. (Deut. 26:5-9)

Israel's identity as an "alien" subject to "hard labor" and "oppression," now liberated by YHWH, is
the backdrop against which Deuteronomy's exclusive covenantal obligations are formulated. The
jealousy of YHWH (Deut. 4:24) establishes impermeable cultural and ethical borders separating
Israel from its neighbors. Deuteronomy and the historical narrative of the occupation of Canaan
and the flowering of the monarchy are written in accordance with its principles. This so-called
Deuteronomistic History (abbreviated Dtr by some scholars) consists of Joshua, Judges, the books
of Samuel, and 1 and 2 Kings. It offers a far more complex, yet ultimately less inclusive, vision of
the "people of God."

For example, we encounter the technical designation *'am yhwh* ("YHWH's people") in the Pentateuch's oldest strata (e.g., Judg. 5:11, 13—an ancient Hebrew poem; and Num. 11:29; 16:41).
Here it refers to either the members of Israel's tribal confederation (Judges) or the Israelite community on the march through the wilderness following its flight from Egypt (Numbers). It is present
much more frequently in Dtr, where it denotes those faithful bound by the Deuteronomic covenant
(Deut. 27:9—*lĕ'am layhwh*); Israel before the establishment of the monarchy (1 Sam. 2:24); the
fallen military contingent that supported Jonathan and Saul (2 Sam. 1:12); and as an *ethnonym* for
those under the reign of David (2 Sam. 6:21), Jehu (2 Kgs. 9:6), and Jehoida (2 Kgs. 11:17). We also
find the terms *'am hā'ĕlōhîm* or *'am 'ĕlōhîm* ("people of God") used in reference to the Israelite tribal
contingent armed for battle (Judg. 20:2) and to those under David's sovereign rule (2 Sam. 14:13).
Beyond these references, we encounter the term "YHWH's people" in 2 Chron. 23:16 (paralleling
2 Kgs. 11:17). Another enigmatic reference—to "the God of Abraham's people"—is found in Ps.
47:9, a poem asserting the universal kingship of *'ĕlōhîm* ("God").

Although references to "Yahweh's people" and "people of God" do not appear in the Latter
Prophets (Isaiah, Jeremiah, Ezekiel, and the Book of the Twelve) or the Writings (outside of the
Chronicler), we can certainly detect a keen interest in the world's peoples in many of these books.
In some instances, the focus is decidedly polemical. The pointed critique of Israel's neighbors in
prophetic oracles is an excellent example (e.g., Isaiah 14–19; Ezekiel 26–30). The bimodal subdi-
vision of humanity in Proverbs (between those who heed Wisdom's voice and others who do not
in Proverbs 8–9). A third case in point is the distinction made between "those who lead many to
righteousness" in Dan. 12:3) and their opponents. In others, there is an affirmation of the God of
Israel's keen interest in building an inclusive eschatological community (e.g., Isa. 66:18-21) and
questioning a culture of entitlement and condemnatory rhetoric among Israelite prophets (Jon.
4:9-11). In Jewish apocryphal literature, we also see an interest expressed in the relationship among
peoples. In the Greek Addition F to Esther, an editor has called attention to the different "lots" God

has assigned to "the people of God" and to "all the nations" (10:10). The author of the Wisdom of Solomon takes a slightly different tack. While adopting a rhetoric that accentuates the difference between the "righteous" and the "ungodly" (Wisdom), it also calls attention to the common ancestry of humanity:

> there is for all one entrance into life, and one way out. (Wis. 18:9)

What we have, therefore, in the Hebrew Bible are multiple visions of what it means to be "people of God" and "peoples of the earth." Some are narrow. Others are selectively inclusive. All must be read with an eye toward genre, the setting in which the text was produced, and the social, political, and religious circumstances it seeks to address.

It goes almost without saying that biblical writers and their initial audiences were concerned with theological issues such as Israel's election and the implications such issues have on the community's holiness and distinctiveness when compared to its neighbors. In light of this special calling, as it were, boundaries—their creation, maintenance, and occasional erasure—take on particular significance. Maintenance is a sign of covenantal fidelity (Deut. 7:1-6) and purity (Lev. 10:1-3). Periodic transgression is, at least in some instances, a necessary survival strategy. Judges is an excellent case in point (see Page). We see evidence in this book of the crossing of bodily, cultural, and other borders as part of what characterizes Israelite life during that bittersweet epoch when "there was no king in Israel" and "people did what was right in their own eyes" (Judg. 21:25). Israel's identity as a people with a unique identity, mission, and teleological objective is, thus, variously articulated in the Hebrew Bible. These overlapping, competing, and complementary ideas of what it means to be a "people of God" among "the earth's peoples" require attentiveness to the religious objectives, political aims, and eschatological foci of the books in which they are found. Therefore, any attempt to fully reconcile all aspects of these disparate conceptions is likely to meet with frustration. Instead, it is perhaps better to recognize that the Hebrew Bible does not speak with a single voice on the issue of what it means to be part of the human family.

Looking beyond the Bible

One could argue that this absence of uniformity in the Hebrew Bible is an invitation not simply to read, but also to query and "talk back to" its books. Among the questions we should ask is what sources—in addition to Scripture—we ought to consult in making sense of who we are, what our relationship should be to one another, and what our place is in the universe. This process is far more involved than turning to Genesis or some other biblical book for a "proof text" (the practice of using a specific text as the final authoritative word on a given issue). Instead, it requires taking into consideration modern geopolitical realities such as globalization and what the pure, applied, and social sciences are telling us about our biological origins, diversity, and connectedness.

It also makes it incumbent on Bible readers to be aware of how documents such as the United Nations Declaration on Human Rights (1948) and the United Nations Declaration on the Rights of Indigenous Peoples (2007) influence how we think about our rights and responsibilities as people of faith and citizens of the world. For example, article 1 of the former states that "all human beings are born free and equal in dignity and rights. They are endowed with reason and conscience and should act towards one another in a spirit of brotherhood" (United Nations General Assembly 2000, 326). An affirmation of this kind shapes the way one thinks about religious texts and traditions that qualify human freedom, equality, dignity, or rights endowed at birth. Furthermore, according to article 18 of the Declaration, "Everyone has the right to freedom of thought, conscience, and religion; this right includes freedom to change his religion or belief, and freedom either alone or in community with others and in public or private, to manifest his religion or belief in teaching, practice, worship, and observance" (United Nations General Assembly 2000, 327). Such texts can't help but influence our reading and deployment of those parts of the Bible that affirm behaviors that affirm or disagree with these statements and the ideals they represent. In the case of those that run counter, a hermeneutic inclusive of exegesis and critical engagement is warranted. Article 7 section 2 of the United Nations Declaration on the Rights of Indigenous Peoples states that "indigenous peoples have the collective right to live in freedom, peace and security as distinct peoples and shall not be subjected to any act of genocide or any other act of violence, including forcibly removing children of the group to another group" (United Nations General Assembly 2007, 5). Moreover, article 8 section 1 affirms that "indigenous peoples and individuals have the right not to be subjected to forced assimilation or destruction of their culture" (United Nations General Assembly 2007, 5). The reading or deployment of biblical passages that appear to celebrate or support behaviors of this kind can be neither ignored nor interpreted in a way that treats lightly the ways they have been used to justify policies that abrogate the rights of indigenous peoples around the world.

Thus, in our current era, perhaps the Bible should be seen less as the single authoritative source from which the final word on what it means to be "people of God" and "people of the earth" is to be found, and more as one of several interlocutors—including lived experience—informing our consideration of what is an unfolding *mystery* about the larger human experience that we are invited to prayerfully ponder.

Works Cited

Douglas, Mary. 1966. *Purity and Danger*. London: ARK.

Eilberg-Schwartz, Howard. 1990. *The Savage in Judaism: Anthropology of Israelite Religion and Ancient Judaism*. Bloomington: Indiana University Press.

Ember, Melvin, and Carol R. Ember, eds. 1999. *Cultures of the World: Selections from the Ten-Volume Encyclopedia of World Cultures*. New York: Macmillan Library Reference USA.

Frazer, James. 1981. *The Golden Bough*. 1890. Reprint, New York: Grammercy.

———. 1918a. *Folk-Lore in the Old Testament*. Vol. 1. London: Macmillan.

———. 1918b. *Folk-Lore in the Old Testament*. Vol. 2. London: Macmillan.

———. 1918c. *Folk-Lore in the Old Testament*. Vol. 3. London: Macmillan.

Gaster, Theodor H. 1950. *Thespis: Ritual, Myth, and Drama in the Ancient Near East*. New York: Harper & Row.

———, ed. 1959. *The New Golden Bough*. New York: Criterion.

———. 1969. *Myth, Legend and Custom in the Old Testament.* New York: Harper & Row.

Gunkel, Hermann. 1928. *What Remains of the Old Testament and Other Essays.* Translated by A. K. Dallas. New York: Macmillan.

———. 1964. *The Legends of Genesis: The Biblical Saga and History.* Translated by W. H. Carruth. Reprint of the introduction to the author's 1901 *Commentary on Genesis.* New York: Schocken.

———. 1987. *The Folktale in the Old Testament.* Translated by M. D. Rutter. Translation of the 1917 ed. Sheffield: Almond.

Lambert, W. G., and A. R. Millard, eds. 1999. *Atra-Hasis: The Babylonian Story of the Flood.* 1969. Reprint, Winona Lake, IN: Eisenbrauns.

Malina, Bruce. 1989. "Dealing with Biblical (Mediterranean) Characters: A Guide for U.S. Consumers." *BTB* 19:127–41.

Moran, William L. 1971. "Atrahasis: The Babylonian Story of the Flood." *Bib* 52:51–61.

Mowinckel, Sigmund. 1966. *Psalmenstudien: 1921–1924.* Amsterdam: Grüner.

Murdock, George Peter. 1969. *Ethnographic Atlas.* 3rd ed. Pittsburgh: University of Pittsburgh Press.

———. 1981. *Atlas of World Cultures.* Pittsburgh: University of Pittsburgh Press.

Murdock, George Peter, C. S. Ford, A. E. Hudson, R. Kennedy, L. W. Simmons, and J. W. M. Whiting. 1987. *Outline of Cultural Materials.* 5th ed. New Haven: Human Relations Area Files.

Oswalt, J. N. 1980. "Kabash." In *Theological Wordbook of the Old Testament,* edited by R. Laird Harris, Gleason L. Archer, and Bruce K. Waltke, 1:430. Chicago: Moody Press.

Page, Hugh R., Jr. 1999. "The Marking of Social, Political, Religious, and Other Boundaries in Biblical Literature—A Case Study Using the Book of Judges." *Research in the Social Scientific Study of Religion* 10:37–55.

Pedersen, Johannes. 1926–1940. *Israel: Its Life and Culture.* 4 vols. London: Oxford University Press.

Price, David H. 2004. *Atlas of World Cultures: A Geographical Guide to Ethnographic Literature.* 1989. Reprint, Caldwell, NJ: Blackburn.

Rad, Gerhard von. 1966. *The Problem of the Hexateuch and Other Essays.* London: SCM.

Thompson, Stith. 2001. *Motif-index of Folk-Literature: A Classification of Narrative Elements in Folk-tales, Ballads, Myths, Fables, Mediaeval Romances, Exempla, Fabliaux, Jest-Books.* Rev. ed. 6 vols. Bloomington: University of Indiana Press.

United Nations General Assembly. 2000. "Universal Declaration of Human Rights (1948)." In *Sourcebook of the World's Religions: An Interfaith Guide to Religion and Spirituality,* edited by J. Beversluis, 325–28. Novato, CA: New World Library.

———. 2007. *United Nations Declaration on the Rights of Indigenous Peoples.* http://www.un.org/esa/socdev/unpfii/documents/DRIPS_en.pdf.

READING THE CHRISTIAN OLD TESTAMENT IN THE CONTEMPORARY WORLD

Daniel L. Smith-Christopher

In nineteenth-century Charleston, South Carolina, the Old Testament seemed to assure Episcopal clergyman Frederick Dalcho that slavery was consistent with Christian faith. The same Old Testament, however, particularly Josh. 6:21, just as powerfully inspired fellow Charleston resident and former slave Denmark Vesey to plan a slave revolt. Those involved in the slave revolt felt assured that God would help them "utterly destroy all in the city, both men and women, young and old, with the edge of the sword" (Edgerton 1999, 101–25). In 2010, Steven Hayward, at that time F. K. Weyerhaeuser Fellow at the American Enterprise Institute, published an essay in which he read the story of Joseph in Egypt as a dire warning against government intervention, and suggested that his reading of these texts from Genesis served as a defense of a free-market, private-property economic system. Also in 2010, John Rogerson, professor of Scripture at Sheffield University, began his book on Old Testament theology, written because he, too, believed that the "Old Testament has something to say to today's world(s)," by stating that he wrote as "an Anglican priest . . . a humanist and a socialist" (Rogerson, 11). Dr. James Edwards, of the Center for Immigration Studies, reads some of the Mosaic laws of the Old Testament as defending firm national borders, low tolerance for immigration rights, and concerns for cultural corruption by outsiders (Edwards 2009 n.p., online), while Dr. Lai Ling Elizabeth Ngan of Baylor University, an Asian American scholar, finds that the Old Testament story about God's listening to the prayers of the "foreign woman," namely Hagar, "redefines boundaries that others have inscribed for her"; the story suggests that modern Christians should uphold the dignity of all peoples and resist denigrating people because of physical or racial differences (Ngan 2006, 83).

These are six Christians, all reading their Old Testament in the contemporary world. The fact that not all of these voices are biblical scholars, however, only serves to highlight the fact that reading the Christian Old Testament in the contemporary world is a complex mixture of the scholarly as well as the popular, stereotyped traditional views as well as innovative new insights, and that reading the Old Testament often strikingly divides readers into quite seriously opposing social and political views. Does this mean that reading the Christian Bible (Old or New Testament) in the modern world is a parade example of Cole Porter's 1934 song "Anything Goes"? Is it a matter of some disappointment that we can still agree with Leo Perdue's 1994 observation that "no commanding contemporary theology has yet appeared to form a consensus" (Perdue 1994, 8)?

I would argue that there is no cause for despair. Quite to the contrary! One of the most fascinating aspects of reading the Christian Old Testament in the contemporary world is not simply that there is unprecedented enthusiasm and diversity among scholars and viewpoints in the field but also that *this diversity itself is part of an ongoing debate and discussion.* At the outset, however, we should clarify that we are interested in thinking about serious readings of the Christian Old Testament, and not merely social or political propaganda that lightly seasons its rhetoric with a few Bible verses.

Marketplaces vs. Museums

Biblical scholarship is separated from religious propaganda not only by the fact that biblical scholarship presumes a basic orientation in the relevant historical contexts of the ancient world, familiarity with a diversity of texts both ancient and modern, and the ability to recognize a good argument supported by credible evidence or reasonable suggestions. These are all essential, of course. What really separates biblical scholarship from propaganda is the fact that biblical scholarship in the contemporary world is part of an ongoing discussion—a discussion that knows *and listens* to the challenges of others and seeks to contribute one's own insights *as part of the discussion.* As in all fields of discovery and intellectual endeavor, the success of biblical scholarship is not to be measured by the achievement of some dominant unanimity, but rather is judged by the quality and results of the participation in the scholarly tasks at hand and the *shared perception* that progress is taking place. We are seeing and understanding biblical texts in ever more profound and provocative ways. However, one of the most striking aspects of the rise of simplistic or propagandist use of the Bible is precisely its refusal to engage in dialogue, self-correction, or even acknowledgment of rival views, beyond the occasional ad hominem dismissal of arguments based solely on their association with groups identified by politicized generalizations—for example, "those liberals."

What we are suggesting is that there is an essential *dialogue* in modern, serious reading of the Bible. So, if this essay on reading the Christian Old Testament is not to be a rehearsal of some of the grand theories generally agreed on, now and forever (like a quiet museum tour of accomplishments), it is time for a new guiding image. I am intrigued by suggestions of the Cuban American New Testament scholar Fernando Segovia, who celebrates diversity in dialogue over the Scriptures. Segovia has famously suggested the "marketplace of ideas," rather like Wole Soyinka's discussion of the Silk Road market town Samarkand, as an image of modern sharing and exchanging of multicultural ideas and friendships (see Segovia and Tolbert; Segovia; Soyinka). An introduction to reading the Christian Old Testament in the contemporary world does not need to provide a historical survey of the "great ideas" that led to the present. Good surveys already exist, if European-dominated ideas are one's particular interest (e.g., Ollenburger; Rogerson 1984; Hayes and Prussner). Marketplaces can be elusive, however. They exist within the totality of the lives of people from everywhere, people who set up stalls and shop. Like the night markets of Auckland, New Zealand, or Darwin, Australia, they appear at designated places, at the designated hours, but otherwise there is only quiet. In short, the image of the marketplace suggests that we need a guidebook.

Laura Pulido, Laura Barraclough, and Wendy Cheng have recently published a marvelous, politically informed tour guide titled *A People's Guide to Los Angeles* (2012). The introduction itself is worth the price of admission. In these preliminary observations, the authors reflect on guidebooks and Los Angeles itself.

> *A People's Guide to Los Angeles* is a deliberate political disruption of the way Los Angeles is commonly known and experienced. . . . Guidebooks select sites, put them on a map, and interpret them in terms of their historical and contemporary significance. All such representations are political, because they highlight some perspectives while overlooking others. Struggles over who and what counts as "historic" and worthy of a visit involve decisions about who belongs and who doesn't, who is worth remembering and who can be forgotten, who we have been and who we are becoming.

They continue,

> Mainstream guidebooks typically describe and interpret their sites through the story of one person—almost always a man, and usually the capitalist who invested in a place, or its architect or designer. In doing so, they reinforce an individualized and masculinist way of thinking about history. Meanwhile, the collectives of people who actually created, built, or used the space remain nameless.

It would be difficult to think of a better series of thoughts to begin an essay on reading the Christian Old Testament in the contemporary world, because biblical analysis is rarely, if ever, written without some contemporary concerns in mind. Modern biblical theologies, for example, now usually identify the perspective of the author in the contemporary world (e.g., Brueggemann 1997; Rogerson 2010). Thus I am quite certain that part of the reason I agree with this need for a new image is that I write as a Christian who was born into, and very self-consciously remain informed by, the Quaker tradition. I also learned a great deal of biblical history, language, and theology from my fellow Christian sectarians the Mennonites, and I was first inspired to think seriously about biblical theology in high school by reading Vernard Eller, a theologian from yet another of my sister sectarian movements, the Church of the Brethren (informally known as the Dunkers). This means that I write as a Christian raised on "counterhistories" of the Christian movement—George Fox on Pendle Hill, Margaret Fell at Swarthmore, Conrad Grebel in Zurich, and Alexander Mack in Philadelphia—in addition to the canonical events of Christian history, such as the councils, the division between Rome and the Eastern Orthodox, Calvin, Luther, Wesley, and so on. I am thus well aware that texts, like towns, are susceptible to decisions about which locations are worthy of a visit, and which locations ought to be "memorialized" as deeply important. We could visit the old, established halls memorializing conquest or power—or we can find the marketplaces where we can encounter new ideas, argue with the "stall keepers" (the authors), make offers and listen to the counteroffers. In short, Christian biblical scholarship is tolerant of a variety of particular views of biblical texts, grammar, history, or theological interpretation. It is quite properly intolerant of the refusal to participate in dialogue with others. One of the hallmarks of propagandist abuses of the Bible in the modern world is the virtual absence of dialogue with other serious students of the Bible—a refusal to appear in the marketplace where ideas are examined and challenged.

It might seem that all this "marketplace" talk runs the risk of privileging process rather than results, and thus avoiding the hard work of evaluating whether ideas are good or bad, and then promoting the good. It is a uniquely contemporary heresy, however, to privilege solitary ideas or accomplishments while overlooking the long processes that often lead to any achievements worthy of celebration. Furthermore, to celebrate dialogue in the development of Christian thought about the Bible has sometimes been thought to be a uniquely modern phenomenon. That is already a mistake. What constitutes the "Old Testament," and even whether to have one, have both been matters of serious debate in Christian history.

The Christian Old Testament as a Product of Dialogue

Let us begin with a deceptively simple question: What constitutes the Old Testament? Christians do not even agree on this! Before the early Christian movement that historians now routinely refer to as "orthodox" arose victorious, the determination of what would be the authorized and foundational writings for Christian faith was a lively debate. The so-called *Festal Letter* 39 of Athanasius, which includes the earliest authoritative "list" of a canon of the Christian Bible, is dated to (a surprisingly late) 367 CE. Before then, debates about texts clearly ranged widely, and this does not even address the interesting continued use of noncanonical lore in popular, pre-Reformation medieval theater in the streets and churches of Europe (see Muir).

Furthermore, Athanasius's fourth-century declaration did not really settle the matter. Protestant, Catholic, and Orthodox Christians have each determined to authorize slightly different Old Testaments. Catholics, staying with the collection of Jewish writings that appeared in some of the old Greek translations known as the Septuagint (LXX), have included a series of books in the Old Testament that Protestants do not recognize, which Catholics call "deuterocanonical," and the Orthodox have chosen to include even a few more of these later Jewish (but still pre-Christian) writings. Protestants usually refer to these works as "the Apocrypha." Having said this, however, the difference between Christian canons has fewer implications for biblical scholarship than one might suspect at first. This is primarily because academic biblical studies, including biblical theological work, now tends to overlook specific church doctrines regarding the categories of "canonical," "deuterocanonical," and "noncanonical" writings. In the biblical studies marketplace, no text, artifact, ancient translation, or geographical context is "off limits" to research, comment, and consideration.

Canonical works obviously get the most attention—but it is hardly exclusive—and commentaries and critical analysis of *noncanonical* writing often make significant contributions to the further understanding of the canonical work as well. But we aren't finished with dialogue in relation to the existence of the Old Testament.

In fact, Christianity was marked by diversity in dialogue from the very beginning, as any sober reading of the arguments discussed in the book of Acts clearly reveals. One reason that dialogue is such an important context for thinking about the Old Testament is the fact that *the very existence of a "Christian Old Testament" was not a matter of widespread agreement in the earliest history of Christianity*. The early Christian convert Marcion (c. 85–160) famously proposed that true Christianity ought to discard any connection whatsoever to Judaism and the Jewish tradition; he embraced only a limited number of writings to represent this clean break between Jesus and the Jewish tradition (he proposed only a version of Luke, and ten Pauline epistles). However, the reaction was furious and widespread. W. H. C. Frend argues that Marcion holds the distinction of being "one of the very few opponents of orthodoxy whom Greek and Latin theologians united in damning. For nearly a century after his death . . . he was the arch-heretic" (212). Clearly, not every idea in the marketplace survives. We can stop cynically humming Porter's "Anything Goes" now.

The first Christian centuries, therefore, bequeath a task to all subsequent generations of readers of the "Christian Old Testament," namely, to take these writings into serious consideration when determining the nature of Christian faith. Furthermore, the vast majority of modern Christian communities (Protestant, Catholic, and Orthodox) have agreed with the church fathers and mothers of the first centuries that Christianity does indeed have a "canon," and that the Hebrew writings are part of it. Is this a settled issue, then? Hardly. Before we can speak of ways the Christian Old Testament is being read in the contemporary world, it is important to acknowledge, however briefly, that there are still ways it is *not* being read, and that it is even effectively ignored, in Christian faith and practice. Marcion still haunts us.

Tourism vs. Engagement: Ignoring the Marketplace?

As Aidan Nichols has recently acknowledged for the Catholic Church (2007), and as many others have suggested for other churches (Jenkins 2006, 42–47), a serious tendency remains among many Christian traditions in the modern world to overlook the larger part of their Bible before the Gospel of Matthew begins. Effectively ignoring the witness of the Old Testament for modern Christian faith and practice has sometimes been referred to as "Neo-Marcionism" (Nichols, 81). Even though few modern Christians would explicitly admit to it, the lack of effective education or preaching in Old Testament/Hebrew Bible studies is an alarming prospect for Christian faith and practice. A Christian theology cannot be true to the historic legacy of the faith tradition if it perpetuates such a neo-Marcionite subordination of these texts. This can happen in a number of ways, but it is more typical of popular and/or propagandist readings of the Bible than in biblical scholarship. In fact, some ways of "reading the Christian Old Testament" are simply ways to avoid it!

For example, there is a huge market for "Bible prophecy" books in the United States. One of the most significant criticisms of this popular literature is not only its total neglect of serious biblical scholarship on the prophetic books of the Old Testament but also its exclusive interest in how the books of the Bible may be "decoded" so that they can be understood to refer to contemporary events—as if the eighth-century-BCE book of Amos were actually speaking about twentieth-century Russia, or second-century-BCE portions of the book of Daniel were actually speaking about the twentieth-century ayatollahs of Iran. This "decoding" process usually neglects the historical content of the Old Testament book at hand in favor of what it is "understood" to be saying about modern times. In short, the actual content is merely a code. Its decoded meaning has nothing to do with what is actually written, when it was written, or who may have written it. One effective way of entirely ignoring a biblical book, then, is to completely reconstruct it without regard to its actual content as a historical work. This may not be Marcion's original idea, but he would clearly approve. This radical transformation of the work has little to do with actual study of it, nor is this part of the serious dialogue taking place about how the books of the Old Testament ought to inform contemporary Christian faith and practice.

This case of wildly popular literature on Bible prophecy in the modern world is particularly ironic. While some Christians frequently fault biblical scholars for not accepting the "plain sense" of the biblical text, it is astounding how carefully the various approaches to Bible prophecy omit any engagement with the most straightforward, or "plain," messages of the prophets of ancient Israel, namely, God's concern for the poor and the judgment threatened against the rich and powerful, those who, in the unforgettable images of Amos and Isaiah,

> trample the head of the poor into the dust of the earth,
>> and push the afflicted out of the way (Amos 2:7)

or who

> join house to house,
>> who add field to field,
> until there is room for no one but you,
>> and you are left to live alone
>> in the midst of the land! (Isa. 5:8)

No decoding seems necessary here. Radically altering the Old Testament texts beyond any credible historical or theological contexts in the process is clearly to do violence to those texts.

Another even more problematic way to virtually ignore the Old Testament in the Christian tradition is the Christian idea that the Old Testament is "old" and therefore largely replaced by the New Testament. Jesus is thus understood to have so reformed Jewish thought, very much as in Marcion's original proposal, that very little of the Old Testament is left of any real importance for Christian theology (save, perhaps, for the Ten Commandments). The dangers of such a "de-Semiticized" Jesus are legion, beginning with the problem of failing to understand Jesus' own faith tradition. For example, the event universally known as the "cleansing of the temple" is incomprehensible apart from recognizing that Jesus cites two Hebrew prophets in the act (Jer. 7:11 and Isa. 56:7). The reactions to Jesus' famous "reading" in his home synagogue in Luke 4 are equally incomprehensible apart from carefully noting the Old Testament references therein. Such examples can be multiplied throughout the New Testament.

Finally, the Hebrew tradition in both its historic and contemporary expressions is revered by a living people. Contemporary Christian scholarship is increasingly open to dialogue with Jewish biblical scholarship. Even though all Christians share most of the books of the Jewish canon with Judaism, there has been historically a significant difference in Jewish study of the Bible as opposed to Christian study (see summaries in Sommer 2012). One of the important characteristics of modern Christian readings of the Old Testament is that Jewish, Roman Catholic, Orthodox, and Protestant Scripture scholars are all in dialogue and discussion with each other in biblical studies on levels unprecedented before the twentieth century, and these dialogues continue in a variety of academic contexts in the twenty-first century.

Exorcising the ghost of Marcion from contemporary Christian scholarship of the Old Testament properly insists that taking the Old Testament seriously for Christian faith and practice involves a consideration of what Old Testament writings can say to the Christian tradition, not vice versa; Christian tradition should not use the Old Testament to buttress predetermined doctrinal ideas derived from the New Testament. Dictating terms to the Old Testament will never allow it to speak to Christian faith and practice in new and challenging ways. That isn't the way a marketplace works, after all, and trying to fix prices and control commodities only leads to other marketplaces.

The Role of Historical Events in the Old Testament for Christian Faith and Practice

We have already determined that the adjective *Christian* in our title means that we are interested in how the Old Testament speaks to Christian faith and practice, and therefore we are interested in discussing the role of "biblical theology." Here we encounter one of the loudest sectors of our marketplace. There are contemporary scholars (see Barr) who maintain an older tradition that suggests Old Testament scholarship should never be primarily "religious" or "theological," but rather historical, examining texts and other ancient evidence and then handing the results over to the theologians. Thus some scholars believe that biblical theology seeks to identify an exclusively *historical* expression of *past* belief (e.g., What did the ancient Israelites believe?). Indeed, the famous inaugural lecture of Johann Gabler in 1787, considered by some to be the "founding document" of this understanding of biblical theology (Gabler, 497), argued quite forcefully for maintaining a clear separation between biblical theology, defined as an exclusively historical enterprise, on the one hand, and systematic ("dogmatic") theology on the other.

It should be acknowledged that many modern biblical scholars would insist on this same separation between the historical and the theological approaches to Old Testament study and firmly place themselves in the "historical questions only" camp. Some scholars, again citing the late James Barr, have no objection to doing Christian theology based on biblical ideas, but believe that the formulation of these religious ideas ought to be a separate task from the exclusively historical task of Old Testament study. There are others who have doubts about religious belief in general or about the viability or validity of the specific religious traditions that make religious use of these writings. Some biblical scholars self-identify as atheists, for example, and there are even contemporary biblical scholars who openly condemn the very notion of a viable contemporary belief informed by the Bible (e.g., Avalos).

Both versions of the "historical analysis only" argument would maintain that it is not only possible but also necessary for a scholar of biblical texts to refrain from allowing contemporary interests or commitments (religious or otherwise) to "bias" or "interfere" with the task of historical analysis. This proposed form of historical analysis is represented as an activity that seeks to emulate scientific methodology as much as possible. The goal of this approach is thus described as "objective knowledge," or at least a close approximation of objective knowledge, even if these scholars were to acknowledge that certain influences or limitations of a time period certainly apply, such as the state of historical, archaeological, and textual studies at the time. In either case, the result is similar: a form of biblical studies that would be understood entirely as an aspect of historical investigation, no different in kind from determining what Shakespeare or Isaac Newton may have "believed," on religious (or any other) questions. Thus, while some may think or hope that their work could contribute to Christian faith and practice, they would carefully leave that task to others.

Interest-Free Biblical Analysis?

Recent debates, however, forcefully challenge many of the methodological assumptions that a bias-free analysis of historical texts is even a possible, much less laudable, goal. The term *postmodernism* is normally assigned to such challenges. Especially since the work of Thomas Kuhn (who gave us the concept of a "paradigm shift," 1996) and Paul Feyerabend (who calls for an "anarchist theory of knowledge," 2010), even the notion of an "objective" *scientific* analysis (science being the purported, even if largely self-appointed, model of objective analysis for all fields of inquiry) has been largely abandoned as both claim and goal. Motivations or interests do not necessarily poison results, but in the postmodern age, we are always vigilant about their influence, and thus the tendency in postmodernism is to declare such "interests" in the work itself. Does this preclude the possibility of doing biblical theology for modern Christian faith and practice? I contend that the postmodern criticism of a "bias-free" analysis of the Bible not only allows an enterprise of biblical theology but also positively encourages it.

The endless debates about the precise meaning of postmodernism need not distract us from a useful insight associated with this term: *all knowledge is contingent.* What we "know" usually depends on what we seek to know, and thus the questions we think to ask. Furthermore, what we investigate is influenced by own concerns, and we also sort out and determine which of our results are the most important. This is all part of the dialogue of diversity and, in twenty-first-century study of the Christian Old Testament, is now a widely acknowledged working assumption. Few would deny the importance of not only the identification of one's own working interests and assumptions in thinking about how the Christian Old Testament can speak to the modern age but also the retrospective work of placing older Old Testament theological writings in important social and historical contexts in ways that deepen our appreciation of their achievements and limitations (Rogerson 1984).

Is There a "Collapse of History" in Christian Old Testament Study?

There is an interesting debate going on in another sector of the marketplace. In his recent important monographs on the problems of Old Testament biblical theology, Leo Perdue refers to a "collapse of history" in recent biblical studies. One of the ways he formulates this point is to ask: Can these predominantly religious texts really help us reconstruct historical events in ancient Israel? If not, how can it be said that Israel's experience is important for contemporary readers who are seeking to read these texts as a guide to events that inform contemporary faith and practice? Perdue alludes to an important ongoing debate that began in the late twentieth century, a debate about our ability to know much actual history from what is available to us both in the Old Testament texts and in the relevant archaeological work (both ancient texts and artifacts) that supplements the study of biblical texts.

Especially after the publication of Thomas L. Thompson's widely cited monograph *The Historicity of the Patriarchal Narratives* (1974), fiery debates ensued between scholars who were divided (often unfairly) into "camps" called "minimalists" and "maximalists." These terms referred to those who despaired of the ability to be confident about historical events at all (thus "minimalists") and those who thought there was actually a great deal more evidence for biblical history than was often acknowledged (so Dever 2001; 2003). An interesting summary view of some of the historical debates is provided by Grabbe.

However, as some contemporary scholars have pointed out (see Brueggemann), these debates about historical events and biblical narratives mask the importance of answering a previous question, namely, whether *establishing that an event happened—or precisely how it happened—automatically dictates a corresponding religious significance to that event.* Clearly, it does not. Even if I can be convinced, for example, that the measurements of the temple provided in Ezekiel 40–48 are precise, accurate dimensions of the Jerusalem temple during the first millennium BCE, this does not strike me as having monumental importance for Christian faith and practice. It may have quite fascinating historical interest, but *theological* significance? This can also apply to less obscure issues. For example, determining that the texts in the opening chapters of the book of Exodus give us a more or less "historically reliable" report of the actual events of Israelites departing from Egypt does not thereby answer the question: Of what significance is the departure from Egypt *for contemporary Christian faith and practice?* Simply agreeing on the *historical* reliability of a biblical passage leaves considerable ground to cover on questions of *significance.* Simply agreeing on the historical details of the exodus, for example, does not thereby make one a liberation theologian. In fact, precious little of the powerful writings of liberation theology, beginning with the 1968 gathering of bishops in Medellín, Colombia (CELAM), actually debated the historical details of the book of Exodus. It is not that the historical story is insignificant, but rather its historical significance, if any, needs to be *part* of the theological argument, and not the entire task.

What happens when different perspectives can no longer be united on a particular reading of biblical events, especially on the accompanying significance of those events? Dominant and influential Old Testament theologies of the past depended on accepting an assigned weight to particular passages or biblical events that were considered central or guiding concepts, and thus critically important for modern theology. For example, Walter Eichrodt proposed that the idea of God's establishing agreements or "covenants" with God's people represents the central notion of the entire Hebrew Bible (Eichrodt 1961; 1967; the original German volumes were published in 1933 and 1935). Gerhard von Rad's equally influential Old Testament theology (Rad 1962; 1965; German 1957 and 1960) argued for the central importance of certain narratives of faith that Israelites allegedly repeated (he used the term "creeds") as indications of their faith, and thus suggested that Israelites were people who identified with such narratives. There is little doubt that such theological arguments, based on readings of the Old Testament, exerted a powerful influence on Christian theological education throughout the Western world in the twentieth century.

However, what if differing perspectives on the part of modern readers of the Bible—especially influenced by differing life situations (ethnicity, gender, etc.)—suggest to some modern readers that different biblical "events" in the Old Testament (whether unquestionably historical or not) are more important than others? Examples are not difficult to cite. On the one hand, after 1968, Latin American biblical scholars (especially Roman Catholic scholars) determined that the Moses and Exodus stories had a powerful message for them in their modern-day circumstances of economic poverty. On the other hand, Native American (Osage) professor of American studies Robert Allan Warrior famously challenged biblical theologians who celebrated the exodus and the entry to a "promised land" by noting that Native Americans frankly had more in common with the beleaguered Canaanites, reminding us that indigenous peoples continue to have an ambiguous relationship with the legacy of the book of Joshua (see Warrior). Nineteenth-century African American slaves also determined that the Jonah and Daniel stories had powerful messages for them in their circumstances of oppression and suppression (Levine; Cone 1992). Finally, recent suggestions view the conquest of Jerusalem in 587 and the subsequent exile of thousands of Judeans (Albertz; Ahn) as a biblical event with serious theological implications (Brueggemann; Smith-Christopher 2002). Nineteenth-century Maori Christians in New Zealand determined that the prophets were powerful examples of a new form of pantribal leadership that had new potential to unite previously fragmented tribal peoples in opposition to growing European settlement, and some even looked to the Davidic monarchy as a model for a new and culturally unprecedented Maori king, and thus an answer to the power and authority of the British Crown (Elsmore 1985; 1989). Is all this also a "collapse of history"? Or is it really the collapse of *dominant readings* of history in the face of alternative decisions about central ideas, events, and themes?

There is little doubt that some Christian biblical scholars and theologians lament the absence of the dominant Old Testament readings. Such a view arguably represents a kind of wistfulness for the "good old days" when a dominant perspective seemed to influence writing and doing (and teaching!) Old Testament theology in Christian institutions of higher learning. Not only does this "hoped-for dominant" perspective do violence to those who were never part of the "dominant perspective" (because they were either gender or cultural minorities, e.g., women, African American,

Asian American, Latino/Latina, or theological minorities such as Anabaptists, Quakers, or Pentecostals), but it is also arguably built on a largely discredited model of intellectual progress that mimics seventeenth- to twentieth-century Western imperial politics and social values—namely, the (intellectual) goal of domination and the vanquishing of opposition.

Surely an alternative to dominance or conquest is concord, dialogue, and cooperation in common causes. If we are to read the Christian Old Testament, and consider it theologically significant, then that theological significance will have to extend to the entire world. The *emerging* Christian world is now based in the Southern Hemisphere (Jenkins 2002). Reading the Christian Old Testament is thus by necessity a global enterprise. The modern marketplace is diverse indeed, and there are a number of ways to recognize this diversity.

Contemporary Worlds in Dialogue

We have seen that Segovia's "marketplace of ideas" does not so much despair of speaking of the past at all, much less signal a "collapse of history." The issue is not whether history can be written any longer. Rather, the issue is how different histories, and different texts, can be understood to matter in differing contexts. Marketplaces can resist organization. Nevertheless, there are perhaps two general ways of sorting the diversity in view. One way is to focus on the identities of the participants themselves, especially in those cases when they consciously and explicitly draw on these identities in their reading of the Bible. The other is to focus on challenges to the human enterprise in local or global contexts. Many of these challenges will require that we marshal our collective wisdom in order to survive as a species, and there are hardly more urgent reasons for biblical scholars to make their contribution to the ideological, spiritual, and political will of people to act in positive ways.

Text and Experience: The Feminist Pioneering of New Questions

New Testament scholar Elisabeth Schüssler Fiorenza points out that it was early feminist critical studies that largely opened up critical readings of both the New and Old Testaments from a perspective informed by particular "interests" (see Schüssler Fiorenza). One of first of these interests was reviewing the long-presumed subordination of women in the narratives of the Bible. It is interesting to see how this work progressed in a variety of different directions, all inspired by gender-related questions. For some feminist readers of the Bible, restating the often unacknowledged positive and powerful roles of women in the Bible is an important corrective to assumptions about the exclusive biblical focus on men (Gafney; Meyers 1988/2013). Phyllis Trible, on the other hand, pioneered the role of an unvarnished focus on destructive texts featuring violence against women, calling them "texts of terror" and thus highlighting dangerous tendencies within historical biblical cultures themselves (see Trible). Renita Weems, similarly, opened a line of investigation on the prophetic use of violent language associated with feminized subjects and objects that also betrayed violent attitudes (e.g., "Lady Jerusalem," Weems 1995). Kathleen O'Connor, Elizabeth Boase, and Carleen Mandolfo have taken this conversation further, suggesting that there is evidence of an ongoing dialogue with "Lady Jerusalem" that began with the violent imagery noted by

Weems in Hosea and Ezekiel, but then continued to Lamentations and Deutero-Isaiah, suggesting that there is acknowledgment of and even repentance for this violence (see O'Connor; Boase; Mandolfo). There are many other directions that studies can go, many of which explicitly identify as feminist, or gender-interested, analysis (see, e.g., Yee 2003).

The feminist approach, far from being a limiting perspective, has moved methodologically from an interest in one formulation of a "minority" perspective—namely, the role of women—to a comparative interest in how this critical approach relates to other issues of "gendering" and "embodiment" in the Bible (homosexuality, prostitution, especially the vexed question of temple prostitution, foreign wives of mixed marriages, gender in relation to slavery, etc.). This approach can also move beyond questions of gender. These early feminist perspectives quite logically moved toward an interest in those who are considered "marginalized" in Hebrew texts—for example, Edomites, Egyptians, Moabites, those lumped together as "aliens" in the Mosaic laws, foreign workers—for other reasons. Interesting work indeed. But what does it have to do with Christian faith and practice?

While not all feminist analysis of the Bible is done with the hope that it will contribute to a more equitable and egalitarian Christian movement in the contemporary world, a considerable amount is.

Cultural Identities and Social Situations in the Marketplace

Feminism is not the only "contemporary interest" that has driven new questions in Christian biblical analysis. Especially those who hope biblical analysis will affect Christian faith and practice have made significant contributions. Already in narratives of freed slaves in North America, African American readers of the Bible were reflecting on their own insights, especially as a countertheology to the European preachers who constantly preached obedience and subservience (see Raboteau; Hopkins and Cummings). In fact, it is possible to trace a twentieth-century flowering of these early readings, some of which began by reexamining the role of explicitly identified Africans in biblical history (see Felder) in a manner similar to those who reexamined the Old Testament stories explicitly about women. One clear goal was to highlight African presence in the Bible that had been neglected in the face of racial prejudice in the modern world against those of African descent. However, in the wake of important calls for a more assertive black theology in the twentieth century (Cone 1970), this project then expanded in different directions in ways very similar to the expansion of gender-related questions (and often intersecting with gender questions, e.g., in "womanist" analysis; see Weems 1991). In the African American context, the appearance of the groundbreaking work *Stony the Road We Trod* (Felder) was a major contribution to the maturing of contemporary, consciously African American biblical scholarship. Included in this collection were essays that dealt not only with historical-critical analysis of the Bible from an African American perspective, but with the use of the Bible in the history of African American interpretation. Further work on African American history of interpretation (Callahan; Wimbush) continues to make important contributions to unique insights into both the later use of Scripture, but also arguments contributing to historical understanding of the texts themselves. Not only is the role of the Bible in African American history itself the subject of important analysis, but African American biblical analysis is also interested in examining texts that have been used historically to suppress both those of explicitly African descent (for example, to defend slavery) and many non-European peoples. A convergence in methods, and sometimes goals, began to emerge that sought to forge alliances across explicitly named cultural or ethnic categories.

So, even though it has followed a different trajectory than African American scholarship, Latino/ Latina literature now also holds an important place in the context of the United States. For example, Justo González, Jean-Paul Ruiz, and Miguel De La Torre (2002; 2007) have published monographs and commentaries on Old Testament themes. Interestingly, however, De La Torre has taken a somewhat pessimistic attitude as to whether cross-cultural analysis of the text will influence the general discipline. De La Torre is clear—Euro-Americans are largely not to be trusted for biblical analysis, because "Euroamerican Christians, either from the fundamentalist right or the far liberal left, probably have more in common with each other and understand each other better than they do Christians on the other side of the racial and ethnic divide" (De La Torre 2007, 125). Nevertheless, serious contributions continue to challenge biblical scholars to take seriously the contributions of those who write Old Testament analysis from an openly acknowledged perspective. Gregory Lee Cuéllar, for example, compares passages of Isaiah to the Mexican and Mexican American folk music style known as the *Corrido*, not only to suggest ways that the biblical texts can be understood in contemporary Mexican American communities, but also to propose potential new readings for the book of Isaiah itself (Cuéllar 2008).

While there have been a number of important works from Asian American biblical scholars in the late twentieth century that consciously draw on Asian themes and identity, a significant milestone was the publication in 2006 of the collected volume *Ways of Being, Ways of Reading*. This volume was comparable in many ways to the impact of the 1991 work *Stony the Road We Trod* in the African American scholarly context. It includes retrospective and survey essays, even very personal reflections on academic work (e.g., Yee 2006), as well as examples of contemporary work of some of the most prominent American scholars using cross-cultural approaches.

Finally, in terms of the American context, it is notable that Randall Bailey, Tat-siong Benny Liew, and Fernando Segovia have initiated a dialogue between Latino/a American, Asian American, and African American scholarship, hoping to find common ground in "minority" analysis of the Bible (Bailey, Liew, and Segovia), suggesting the possibilities of a convergence and maturing of methods of analysis, even as they reject any sort of false consensus on similarity of cultural contexts.

Although it is fair to say that readings explicitly related to specific cultural and ethnic identities and traditions continue in the century, attention has tended to turn toward social, political, and economic locations as another significant source of issues that influence the reading of Scripture. In the last quarter of the twentieth century, a number of Old Testament scholars consciously incorporated sociological and anthropological analysis in their ancient historiography of the Bible (Gottwald; Overholt 1992, 2003), and this dialogue with social sciences certainly continues (Chalcraft). Exegetical issues of the most recent writing in Old Testament studies soon converged on a series of questions closely associated with the influence of Edward Said's classic work *Orientalism*, which further built on the early social theories and the observations of the postcolonial theorists Frantz Fanon and Albert Memmi. Once this dialogue with Said's influence was articulated powerfully in the many works of R. S. Sugirtharajah, the rise of postcolonial approaches to Scripture became a significant movement in the early twenty-first century. Sugirtharajah's now classic compendium *Voices from the Margin* signaled a new energy in "interested perspectives" in the reading of the Bible.

The Rise of Postcolonial Biblical Analysis

We have already noted that Christianity—and its Bible—is seeing profound growth in the Southern Hemisphere in the twenty-first century. Twentieth-century Christians in developing societies, especially India, South America, and Africa, began to assert their own perspectives in the analysis of the Bible. After Said's influential work, they began to identify ways in which previous European scholarship contained certain social and cultural assumptions about Western superiority. They then began readings of the Bible within their past experiences of European colonial presence. In the process of reasserting a cultural and/or national identity, however, they soon realized that a reconstruction of cultural identity in the new world could never go back to a purified "precolonial" state, but must always be in dialogue with the social, political, and philosophical realities of having been deeply affected by Western thought and practice. Although in the context of religion and the Bible, one might better speak of "post-Western-missionaryism," the discussions in biblical studies borrowed a term from social and cultural theory to identify their new reviews of the Bible in their own contexts: *postcolonialism*. Postcolonial biblical exegesis provided special tools for Christians in formerly colonized states (or among indigenous peoples in Western European settled lands, North and South America, Australia, and New Zealand). The questions whether, and to what extent, largely imported biblical scholarship was (and is) tainted by imperial goals of control and economic expansion raised serious concerns about those readings of Scripture that seemed deeply involved in that imperial process (De le Torre 2002). A prime example of attempting to counter Western domination was the Latin American assertion that the exodus is the prime event of the Old Testament—and thus liberation is the prime theological theme. However, it is important to note that these questions were being raised largely by Christian Bible scholars. Not all criticism of colonial and missionary policies rejected Christianity and the Bible as an unwanted imposition (see Roberts); sometimes it rather engaged in the more creative task of rereading the texts.

If "postcolonial" contexts include minorities living in multicultural nations, then Fernando Segovia's "Diasporic" approach to reading Scripture becomes especially suggestive. In the American context, this obviously can include African American, Asian American, and Mexican American readings of particular texts that resonate with themes, motifs, or elements of minority existence such that they lead to expositions of Old Testament texts that are suggestive for all readers of the Bible—and not only to fellow members of particular ethnic or cultural groups.

Ethnic and culturally informed readings challenge the notion that European scholarship has a privileged position in biblical scholarship generally, and in the construction of Christian theologies built from Old Testament texts particularly. What we have learned about diversity in dialogue is that the Christian reading of the Old Testament in the contemporary world will be richer, more learned, and more convincing in both textual and historical analysis only if our marketplace grows in its resemblance to the actual diversity of our worlds. What new insights into particular Old

Testament texts await the future BA, MA, or PhD theses and papers written by young Tibetan, Chinese, Navajo, Roma, or Aboriginal Australian students and scholars? What will they see that the rest of us have too quickly dismissed or completely overlooked? In the twenty-first century, we are likely to benefit from an increase of book titles like that of Senegalese American biblical scholar Aliou Niang: *Faith and Freedom in Galatia and Senegal: The Apostle Paul, Colonies, and Sending Gods.*

Let us reaffirm that diversity ought always to lead to dialogue. Agreements, shared insights, and common convictions that we are all learning from the dialogue ought to deliver even the most cynical from the simplistic hope that we Bible scholars would just please get to "the bottom line." Marketplaces don't have a bottom line! Dialogue and haggling over texts is simply the reality. The invitation, therefore, is to listen and learn. Incidentally, lest Christians think that all this is somehow radically new, those familiar with classic rabbinic dialogue and argumentation over religious texts are aware that dialogue with God and with each other is at the heart of theology.

Issues Driving Contemporary Biblical Analysis

Questions from identities and cultural experiences are not, however, the only major and significant sources of urgency in reading and rereading the Christian Old Testament. A number of contemporary global crises have inspired a renewed examination of the ways in which the Bible can be reread. The modern interest in trauma as the psychosocial reality of a world in crisis has recently gained ground in biblical analysis (see O'Connor; Janzen; Kelle). The millions of humans who flee wars and crises as international refugees have also influenced biblical analysis on ancient exile and deportation (see Ahn). The potential list of pressing issues is depressingly long, of course, but it is possible to examine a few examples to illustrate how this section of the marketplace can be organized. In fact, we can move from an example that is already very old but critically ongoing, war and peace in the Old Testament; to an issue that arguably has its roots in the twentieth century, environmentalism; and finally note the signs of a rising issue so new that it has barely begun to generate serious thought among biblical scholars: evolutionary philosophy, transhumanism, and the nature of the person.

War, Peace, and Violence and the Old Testament

Since the fourth century CE, the Christian church has been faced with direct responsibility for violence. The monarchical descendants of the Roman emperor Constantine made Christianity the official religion of the empire, leading into the Byzantine Empire. Biblical study was now intimately connected to the foreign policy of a powerful military machine, and would continue to have foreign policy implications from that time to the present. The continued relevance of the Bible to issues of war and peace is not difficult to discern in the writings of the Christian warriors and their chaplains on the one hand, and the Christian peacemakers and their communities on the other, throughout Western history especially. A clear majority in this debate has supported more violent interpretations, however regretfully they are sometimes offered.

The Jesus who said, "Love your enemies and pray for those who persecute you" (Matt. 5:44), and the Paul who exhorted, "live peaceably with all" (Rom. 12:18), were effectively trumped in Christian faith and practice very early on by an uncritical admiration for the genocidal Joshua and the conquering David (see Davies). There have been a variety of ways in which Christians have responded to the use of the Old Testament as a moral trump over the pacifist Jesus. Once again, the similarities to the methods of feminist biblical analysis are instructive.

For example, especially since the churches in twentieth-century Europe began to mobilize an opposition to the Cold War threats in their own backyards, innumerable monographs have attempted to reexamine the actual practices of Old Testament violence and warfare, either with explicit admiration (so, famously, Yadin), or appropriate levels of horror (Craigie; Niditch; Collins). In modern Old Testament study, then, one is hopefully exposed to the potential dangers of a casual and unguarded use of biblical texts that are so clearly contrary to contemporary moral judgments and international standards of justice.

Finally, similar to those who sought to lift up exemplary moments previously overlooked, there are those who seek to highlight strongly peaceful passages in the Bible that may even have been in critical dialogue with more violent episodes in the canon and thus reveal an internal dialogue or debate that reveals stronger peace voices among the canonical choir (Enz; Smith-Christopher 2007). This approach articulates how a certain form of Hebrew nonviolence would have been a logical expression of theological tendencies that had their roots in the Servant Songs of Second Isaiah and the universalism of the book of Jonah, where we find openness to the repentance of national enemies like the Assyrians, who are portrayed as repenting ". . . of the violence of their hands." Further developments can affirm the wisdom ethic of peacefulness—an ethic that frequently contrasts self-control over against brute force and earnestly recommends a sober, wise consideration of counsel and diplomacy (Prov. 16:7, 32; 17:27; 24:5-6). In fact, the Wisdom tradition may itself represent precisely a staging place for international discussion, given that wisdom values are as universal in the ancient Near East as any literary themes can be. Ancient Egyptian wisdom, Mesopotamian wisdom, and Greek wisdom all compare quite favorably to ancient Israelite forms.

Texts that reflect an Israelite "exilic" lifestyle, lived in "active nonconformity to the world" (as the famous 1955 Mennonite Church statement puts it), would also build on biblical protests against narrow ethnocentrism (e.g., the book of Ruth, Jacob's apology to Esau, Isaiah 56 and 66, and the striking affirmation in Zechariah 9 of a mixed-race people of God). In fact, there is evidence of a rising protest against violence and narrow self-centeredness (e.g., Ezekiel 40–48) that can be seen to affirm the Deuteronomic critique of the monarchy, and especially the condemnation of the monarchy in the penitential prayers of Ezra 9, Nehemiah 9, and Daniel 9. Thus the fact that there are passages where God is alleged to have called for the massacre of foreign cities does not necessarily cancel out or trump the fact that there are more hopeful passages on this subject as well, texts that openly question whether the stance of the Hebrews toward foreign peoples should be hostile and that envision a different and more peaceful reality (Isaiah 2; 19; Micah 4).

Regrettably, offering a more peaceful reading of the Old Testament will not likely bring about world peace. But if the late Colonel Harry Summers of the Army War College is correct that "it is the passions of the people that are the engines of war" (Summers, 75–76), then perhaps careful biblical analysis will remove at least one major ideological prop and provocation that has certainly been used in the past to excuse quite reprehensible behavior among those who honor the Scriptures (see Trimm).

Environmentalism

Biblical analysis that is driven by ecological concerns can be clearly dated to responses to the famous 1967 article in *Science* by Lynn White, accusing Christianity for providing the "roots" of the ecological crisis in God's injunction to the first couple in Gen. 1:28 to "subdue" and "have dominion" over nature. The late twentieth century then saw an increase of literature that highlighted ways that the Hebrew Bible/Old Testament affirmed a spirituality of care and responsibility for the earth as God's creation. Much of this work owes a great deal to the early writings of Australian biblical scholar Norman Habel (see also Hallman; so now Craven and Kaska; Deane-Drummond). The often-cited "this-worldly" emphasis of much Old Testament ethical discussion, and even the imagery of deep fascination with and appreciation of the created world (Job 38–41; Psalm 147–48), however, continues to inspire further development in pioneering biblical theologies. Genesis portrays God involving Adam in the naming of other creatures (Gen. 2:19) and further records God's intention to "re-create" the world in the Hebrew version of the flood narrative, the basic outlines of which were clearly known to the Jewish people by the time of the Babylonian captivity, and most likely borrowed from Mesopotamian traditions.

A related development is in the direction of animal rights. Concern for animal welfare is not absent from Hebrew law or narrative (Deut. 25:4; Numbers 22). The flood story, of course, involves the considerable responsibility of Noah to preserve animals. The Old Testament strikingly expresses certain visions of peace by referring to changes in the animal kingdom (Isa. 11:6: the wolf living with the lamb) and even hinting that in their first created state, humans were vegetarian (before Gen. 9:4, where eating meat is first explicitly mentioned). Psalm 148 portrays the created animals of the world praising God, and Job famously portrays God's careful attention and knowledge of the details of the animal kingdom (Job 39; on animal rights work, see Linzey 1995; 2009; Miller).

Work in environmentalism more generally, and animal rights specifically, have been parts of a move to appreciate biblical themes that buttress a more responsible care for the earth (Toly and Block). There are, however, some serious economic and even political issues at stake here. On the issue of environmentalism particularly, there has been a serious backlash from those with business interests who see strong environmentalist movements as potential threats to their expansion of industry. Not unexpectedly, then, this reaction has motivated more conservative Christian scholars to reassert a strongly pragmatic and typically short-term ethic of consumption unmitigated by strong concerns for conserving resources in the long term. Christians in this tradition, rarely biblical scholars themselves, are clearly not impressed with nuanced arguments about responsibility for species and their survival. Nor are they likely to be impressed by arguments based largely on Old Testament passages, especially if that concern is perceived as requiring economic sacrifices. An interesting example of this reaction is the work of Steven Hayward, from the conservative think tank the American Enterprise Institute. In a published essay titled "Mere Environmentalism" (the title itself is an homage to evangelical hero C. S. Lewis) and subtitled "A Biblical Perspective on Humans and the Natural World," Hayward suggests that the Genesis narratives promote the hierarchy of creation with humanity at the top. He therefore construes a biblical mandate, not for preservation of the environment, but for a "stewardship" that promotes responsible use of resources and a free-market-driven effort to conquer the "untamed wilderness," and furthermore as free of government intervention as possible. Indeed, Hayward further argues that the story of Joseph in Pharaoh's household is a warning against centralized state control, because Joseph's centralization of resources for the Pharaoh leads directly to the enslavement of the Hebrews. Environmental degradation, therefore, may be a matter calling for repentance, but definitely not for government regulation (33). Finally, Noah offers sacrifice of animals after the flood, Hayward notes, so this story provides no basis for simple preservation, and certainly suggests that animals were to be used for human benefit.

The twenty-first century is likely to see more, rather than less, of this polemical exchange in biblical scholarship. Although more propagandistic approaches have tended to avoid participation in scholarly organizations like the Society of Biblical Literature, we are likely to see more direct engagement over the use, and abuse, of Scripture on various issues of social, and especially economic, importance.

The Nature of the Person: The Rise of Evolutionary Social Science and Philosophy

Finally, it is important in the context of this essay to speculate about issues that may well emerge more fully as the twenty-first century develops. In the wake of Daniel Dennett's polemical 1996 assertion of atheist scientism, titled "Darwin's Dangerous Idea," there is a rise of perspectives represented by the following: "If you believe in a traditional concept of the soul, you should know that there is little doubt that a fuller appreciation of the implications of evolutionary theory . . . is going to destroy that concept"; and, "we must openly acknowledge . . . the collapse of a worldview that has sustained human energies for centuries" (Stanovich, 3). Will biblical studies also be challenged by evolutionary thought? If so, in what way?

In Christian theology and biblical studies, the classic beginning point for discussion of the nature of the human person is the concept of the *imago Dei*, the creation of humanity in the image and likeness of God (Gen. 1:26-27). J. Richard Middleton, for example, seeks to rethink the *imago Dei* debates in a modern context, noting that older Christian theological uses of Genesis 1 were rather strained, and usually presumed that the significance of "the image" and "likeness" of God was precisely human *reason*. Recent discussion has emphasized the royal context of these terms, suggesting that humans are portrayed as royally deputized representations of divine authority and responsibility in the world. Middleton even suggests that the *imago Dei* is, in fact, a politically sophisticated as well as theologically loaded term in Genesis, because here we find the textual staging ground for a narrative culture war against Mesopotamian hegemonic narratives of conquest and subservience. These Mesopotamian narratives were weapons in a philosophical/ideological war that accompanied the invading and conquering armies that conquered both the northern kingdom (722 BCE) and Jerusalem and Judah (597/587).

While it is quite possible to celebrate the theological importance of all humanity from an explicitly evolutionary view of the emergence of *homo sapiens*, it is also clear that some interpretations of human evolution threaten to radically debase and reduce humanity to a mere "sack of genes," with little inherent worth, whose values, art, and faith are mere "spandrels" (that is, accidental and irrelevant by-products) that accompany the real work of genetic reproduction. The value of life is thus no longer inherent in creation, but purely instrumental, as some humans serve as sexual slaves, soldiers, and workers for the shrinking and increasingly ruthless elite. The masses are already once again being pacified by the modern equivalent of bread and circus: ever smaller and more inexpensive sources of digital pornography, graphic violence, and (contra Kant's imperative) the view of fellow humans as means rather than ends.

In this context, religious faith (including, of course, the Bible) is strongly dismissed as "nothing but" the result of evolutionary mechanisms for survival. We perceive deities only because of our ancient and genetically honed "agency detection devices" (instincts that perceive potential threats in the environment). Others suggest that religion was merely a part of a sophisticated social "mate selection" mechanism whereby mates with trustworthy values could be quickly identified. In short, religion is a neural response pattern.

The interesting question is no longer, "Can a biblical scholar believe in evolution and teach Genesis"? Of course they can, and do. What is new is the rising insistence of a form of evolutionary social thought that would dismiss all religious speculation as irrelevant. Such a radically reductionist anthropology seeks to replace the "Eden myth" with an equally implausible and comprehensive "African Savannah myth" that subsumes all humanity into categories of neural survival mechanisms driven by reproductive genes. Does the Old Testament have anything to say in this decidedly modern discussion?

The resources of Wisdom literature and its emphasis on sober assessments of God's moral patterns in the created world provide a foundation beyond Genesis for seeking dialogue with naturalists and biologists. But the issues will continue to press, and will no longer be simply the leisure-time, science-fiction reading of those whose day jobs are in biblical studies. Seeking biblical guidance on the nature of the human person will become increasingly pressing in this century in the light of (1) increased emphasis in the human sciences on "transhumanism," according to which humans can be enhanced by further evolutionary merging with technology; (2) manipulation of genetic information to favor certain human traits (already taking place passively by rejecting human eggs in artificial insemination processes that bear indications of undesired genetic traits); (3) progress in artificial intelligence such that ethical questions are becoming increasingly prominent (when does turning off a machine consist of killing a living being? etc.); (4) further work in cloning; and (5) the location and identification of personhood as directly (and some would say: *only*) a function of neural brain activity, thus raising the possibility of "downloading" human persons into hardware.

Are these exclusively theological issues? Do they have any implications for biblical analysis? Will a biblical analysis arise, for example, driven in part by the prescience of the science fiction writer Philip K. Dick, who anticipated many ethical issues dealing with modern technology? It is possible that biblical scholars will simply suggest that radically new technologies are not the business of textual analysis. However, when those technologies raise serious questions about the nature and value of the human person, it is hard to resist the notion that biblical analysis has something to say to this issue.

Return to the Beginning: Does the Marketplace Matter? Are There Any Real People There?

Finally, we can pick up on a discussion that was left aside at the very beginning of this essay. What about the clashes among various readings of the Old Testament? Is biblical studies hopelessly mired in disagreements such that, in the end, an individual must simply hum along with Porter's "Anything Goes"?

Appearances, especially in the contemporary world, can be deceiving. The reality of extensive and exciting discussion and debate in biblical studies does not mean that the field is wandering aimlessly. Furthermore, the impressive level of publication and discussion does not mean that there is no consensus of methods or results among biblical scholars. Biblical scholars, like professionals in other fields such as medicine, engineering, or astronomy, certainly stay in touch with each other's work, and through international organizations (the largest being the Society of Biblical Literature) continue to pursue common interests, projects, and even enjoy continued debates and disagreements. It is hardly the case, as philosopher Alvin Plantinga somewhat sourly suggests, that biblical scholars can never agree on anything, explaining (for Plantinga, presumably) why Christians usually do not take their work seriously.

Plantinga may be surprised, however. The influence of biblical scholarship on wider Christian practices might be slow in manifesting itself, but it is absolutely clear. Plantinga should be impressed with the articulate, profound, and serious assessment of the importance of biblical analysis in the 1994 document of the Pontifical Biblical Commission titled "The Interpretation of the Bible in the Church." Calling the historical-critical method of biblical analysis "indispensable for the scientific study of the meaning of ancient texts," the document critically assesses, both positively and negatively, many current approaches to biblical analysis common in universities and biblical scholarship, and recommends much of modern biblical scholarship to the Catholic world more widely. Furthermore, the document famously refers to fundamentalist readings of Scripture as "intellectual suicide." Unimpressed with official declarations by hierarchies? One need only examine the textbooks for Catholic *high school* students, including those explicitly recommended by the bishops, to see the profound impact of biblical scholarship on questions of multiple authorship, historicity, the dangers of literalism, and so on.

Only the most conservative Christians today believe that the only way to treasure the significance of the narratives of Genesis is to take them literally, or believe that Moses wrote every word of the Pentateuch. Only the most fundamentalist Christians today would think that the book of Jonah is about surviving in the gullet of a marine animal, or that nearly one-fifth of the entire population of ancient Egypt left with Moses in the thirteenth century BCE. Furthermore, what many Christians in the church pews and Sunday schools *do* know is that a profound Christian faith can be enriched by learning that an unnamed second prophet we call "Second Isaiah" likely reapplied some of the thought of the eighth-century Isaiah of Jerusalem, but also proclaimed radically new thoughts in the late sixth-century BCE when the Persian emperor Cyrus lived. Furthermore, Christians today know much more about the horrific tragedy of the destruction of Jerusalem in 587, and how Lamentations is a powerful poetic response to that tragedy, and how Psalms contains religious poetry from long after the time of David. None of these ideas are shocking to Christians in the churches any more, and none of them are destructive of anything but the most simplistic of readings of the Old Testament.

Finally, what Christians in the churches surely know is that the Bible invites—indeed nearly demands—the careful attention of many different cultures, genders, ages, and contexts who are brought into dialogue as they listen, read, discuss, and debate the meanings and importance of these texts of the Old Testament. There is important historical information we can know, but there is so much more to ask. For those who love only quiet museum tours of "certainties" enclosed in glass cases so that the masses can be enlightened, biblical studies in the contemporary world is not for them. The marketplace is teaming, ebullient, and alive.

Works Cited

Ahn, John. 2010. *Exile as Forced Migrations: A Sociological, Literary, and Theological Approach on the Displacement and Resettlement of the Southern Kingdom of Judah*. Berlin: de Gruyter.

Albertz, Rainer. 2003. *Israel in Exile: The History and Literature of the Sixth Century B.C.E.* Atlanta: Society of Biblical Literature.

Avalos, Hector. 2007. *The End of Biblical Studies*. New York: Prometheus.

Bailey, Randall, Tat-siong Benny Liew, and Fernando F. Segovia, eds. 2009. *They Were All Together in One Place? Toward Minority Biblical Criticism*. Atlanta: Society of Biblical Literature.

Barr, James. 2000. *History and Ideology in the Old Testament: Biblical Studies at the End of a Millennium*. Oxford: Oxford University Press.

Boase, Elizabeth. 2006. *The Fulfillment of Doom? The Dialogic Interaction between the Book of Lamentations and the Pre-Exilic/Early Exilic Prophetic Literature*. London: T&T Clark.

Brueggemann, Walter. 1997. *Theology of the Old Testament: Testimony, Dispute, Advocacy*. Minneapolis: Fortress Press.

Callahan, Allen Dwight. 2006. *The Talking Book: African Americans and the Bible*. New Haven: Yale University Press.

Chalcraft, David. 2006. *Social-Scientific Old Testament Criticism*. London: T&T Clark.

Collins, John J. 2004. *Does the Bible Justify Violence?* Minneapolis: Fortress Press.

Cone, James H. 1970. *A Black Theology of Liberation*. Maryknoll, NY: Orbis.

———. 1992. *The Spirituals and the Blues: An Interpretation*. Maryknoll, NY: Orbis Books.

Craigie, Peter. 1979. *The Problem of War in the Old Testament*. Grand Rapids: Eerdmans.

Craven, Toni, and Mary Jo Kaska. 2011. "The Legacy of Creation in the Hebrew Bible and Apocryphal/Deuterocanonical Books." In *Spirit and Nature: The Study of Christian Spirituality in a Time of Ecological Urgency*, edited by Timothy Hessel-Robinson and Ray Maria McNamara, RSM, 16–48. Eugene, OR: Pickwick.

Cuellar, Gregory L. 2008. *Voices of Marginality: Exile and Return in Second Isaiah 40-55 and the Mexican Immigrant Experience*. New York: Peter Lang.

Davies, Eryl. 2010. *The Immoral Bible: Approaches to Biblical Ethics*. London: T&T Clark.

Deane-Drummond, Celia. 2008. *Eco-Theology*. London: Darton, Longman & Todd.

De La Torre, Miguel. 2002. *Reading the Bible from the Margins*. Maryknoll, NY: Orbis.

———. 2007. *Liberating Jonah: Forming an Ethic of Reconciliation*. Maryknoll, NY: Orbis.

Dennett, Daniel. 1996. *Darwin's Dangerous Idea*. New York: Simon & Schuster.

Dever, William G. 2001. *What Did the Biblical Writers Know and When Did They Know It?* Grand Rapids: Eerdmans.

———. 2003. *Who Were the Early Israelites and Where Did They Come From?* Grand Rapids: Eerdmans.

Edwards, James. 2009. *A Biblical Perspective on Immigration Policy*. Washington, DC: Center for Immigration Studies. http://www.cis.org/ImmigrationBible

Egerton, Douglas R. 1999. *He shall go out free : The lives of Denmark Vesey*. Madison, WI: Madison House, 1999

Eichrodt, Walter. 1961. *Theology of the Old Testament*. Translated by J. A. Baker. Vol. 1. London: SCM.

———. 1967. *Theology of the Old Testament*. Translated by J. A. Baker. Vol. 2. London: SCM.

Elsmore, Bronwyn. 1985. *Like Them That Dream: The Maori and the Old Testament*. Wellington, New Zealand: Tauranga Moana Press.

———. 1989. *Mana from Heaven*. Auckland: Reed.

Enz, Jacob. 2001. *The Christian and Warfare: The Roots of Pacifism in the Old Testament*. Eugene, OR: Wipf & Stock (reprint).

Fanon, Frantz. 1963. *The Wretched of the Earth*. New York: Grove.

Felder, Cain Hope, ed. 1991. *Stony the Road We Trod*. Minneapolis: Fortress Press.

Feyerabend, Paul. 2010. *Against Method*. New York: Verso.

Foskett, Mary F., and Jeffrey Kah-jin Kuan, eds. 2006. *Ways of Being, Ways of Reading: Asian American Biblical Interpretation*. St. Louis: Chalice.

Frend, W. H. C. 1984. *The Rise of Christianity*. Minneapolis: Fortress Press.

Gabler, Johann P. "An Oration on the Proper Distinction between Biblical and Dogmatic Theology and the Specific Objectives of Each." In Ollenburger, *Old Testament Theology*, 497–506.

Gafney, Wilda C. 2008. *Daughters of Miriam: Women Prophets in Ancient Israel*. Minneapolis: Fortress Press.

González, Justo L. 1996. *Santa Biblia: The Bible through Hispanic Eyes*. Nashville: Abingdon.

Gottwald, Norman. 1979. *The Tribes of Yahweh*. Maryknoll, NY: Orbis.

Grabbe, Lester. 2007. *Ancient Israel: What Do We Know and How Do We Know It?* New York: T&T Clark.

Habel, Norman. 1993. *The Land Is Mine: Six Biblical Land Ideologies*. Minneapolis: Fortress Press.

Hallman, David G. 1994. *Ecotheology: Voices from South and North*. Maryknoll, NY: Orbis.

Hayes, John H., and Frederick Prussner. 1984. *Old Testament Theology: Its History and Development*. Atlanta: John Knox.

Hopkins, Dwight N., and George C. L. Cummings, eds. 2003. *Cut Loose Your Stammering Tongue: Black Theology in the Slave Narratives*. Louisville: Westminster John Knox.

Janzen, David. 2012. *The Violent Gift: Trauma's Subversion of the Deuteronomistic History's Narrative*. LHB/OTS 561. London: T&T Clark.

Jenkins, Philip. 2002. *The Next Christendom: The Coming of Global Christianity*. New York: Oxford University Press.

———. 2006. *The New Faces of Christianity: Believing the Bible in the Global South*. New York: Oxford University Press.

Kelle, Brad. 2013. *Ezekiel*. New Beacon Bible Commentary. Kansas City: Beacon Hill.

Kuhn, Thomas. 1996. *The Structure of Scientific Revolutions*. 3rd ed. Chicago: University of Chicago Press.

Levine, Lawrence. 1977. *Black Culture and Black Consciousness.* New York: Oxford University Press.

Linzey, Andrew. 1995. *Animal Theology.* Urbana: University of Illinois Press.

———. 2009. *Creatures of the Same God.* New York: Lantern.

Mandolfo, Carleen. 2007. *Daughter Zion Talks Back to the Prophets.* Atlanta: Society of Biblical Literature.

Meyers, Carol. 1988/2013. *Rediscovering Eve: Ancient Israelite Women in Context.* Oxford: Oxford University Press.

Middleton, J. Richard. 2005. *The Liberating Image: The Imago Dei in Genesis 1.* Grand Rapids: Brazos.

Miller, David. 2011. *Animal Ethics and Theology.* New York: Routledge.

Muir, Lynette R. 1995. *The Biblical Drama of Medieval Europe.* Cambridge: Cambridge University Press.

Niang, Aliou. 2009. *Faith and Freedom in Galatia and Senegal.* Leiden: Brill.

Nichols, Aiden. 2007. *Lovely Like Jerusalem: The Fulfillment of the Old Testament in Christ and the Church.* San Francisco: Ignatius.

Niditch, Susan. 1993. *War and the Hebrew Bible: A Study in the Ethics of Violence.* Oxford: Oxford University Press.

Ngan, Lai Ling Elizabeth. 2006. "Neither Here nor There: Boundary and Identity in the Hagar Story." In Foskett and Kuan, *Ways of Being,* 70–83.

O'Connor, Kathleen. 2002. *Lamentations and the Tears of the World.* Maryknoll, NY: Orbis.

Ollenburger, Ben, ed. 2004. *Old Testament Theology: Flowering and Future, Sources for Biblical and Theological Study.* Winona Lake, IN: Eisenbrauns.

Overholt, Thomas. 1992. *Cultural Anthropology and the Old Testament.* Minneapolis: Fortress Press.

———. 2003. *Channels of Prophecy: The Social Dynamics of Prophetic Activity.* Eugene, OR: Wipf and Stock.

Perdue, Leo. 1994. *The Collapse of History: Reconstructing Old Testament Theology.* Minneapolis: Fortress Press.

Plantinga, Alvin. 2009. "Two (or More) Kings of Scripture Scholarship." In *Oxford Readings in Philosophical Theology,* vol. 2, *Providence, Scripture, and Resurrection,* ed. Michael C. Rea, 266–301. Oxford: Oxford University Press.

Pulido, Laura, Laura Barraclough, and Wendy Cheng, eds. 2012. *A People's Guide to Los Angeles.* Berkeley: University of California Press.

Raboteau, Albert J. 1978. *Slave Religion: The Invisible Institution in the Antebellum South.* New York: Oxford University Press.

Rogerson, John. 1984. *Old Testament Criticism in the Nineteenth Century: England and Germany.* London: SPCK.

———. 2010. *A Theology of the Old Testament.* Minneapolis: Fortress Press.

Roberts, Nathaniel. 2012. "Is Conversion a 'Colonization of Consciousness'?" *Anthropological Theory* 12:271–94.

Ruiz, Jean-Pierre. 2011. *Readings from the Edges: The Bible and People on the Move.* Maryknoll, NY: Orbis.

Said, Edward W. 1979. *Orientalism.* New York: Vintage.

Schüssler Fiorenza, Elisabeth. 2009. *Democratizing Biblical Studies.* Louisville: Westminster John Knox.

Segovia, Fernando F. 2000. *Decolonizing Biblical Studies: A View from the Margins.* Maryknoll, NY: Orbis.

Segovia, Fernando F., and Mary Ann Tolbert, eds. 1985. *Reading from this Place,* vol. 1, *Social Location and Biblical Interpretation in the United States.* Minneapolis: Fortress Press.

Smith-Christopher, Daniel. 2002. *A Biblical Theology of Exile.* Minneapolis: Fortress Press.

———. 2007. *Jonah, Jesus, and Other Good Coyotes: Speaking Peace to Power in the Bible.* Nashville: Abingdon.

Sommer, Benjamin, ed. 2012. *Jewish Concepts of Scripture: A Comparative Introduction.* New York: New York University Press.

Soyinka, Wole. 2003. *Samarkand and Other Markets I Have Known.* New York: Methuen.

Stanovich, Keith. 2004. *The Robot's Rebellion.* Chicago: University of Chicago Press.

Sugirtharajah, R. S., ed. 2006. *Voices from the Margin: Interpreting the Bible in the Third World.* 3rd ed. Maryknoll, NY: Orbis.

Summers, Harry G. 1984. "What Is War?" *Harper's,* May, 75–78.

Toly, Noah J., and Daniel I. Block, eds. 2010. *Keeping God's Earth: The Global Environment in Biblical Perspective.* Downers Grove, IL: IVP Academic.

Thompson, Thomas L. 1974. *The Historicity of the Patriarchal Narratives: The Quest for the Historical Abraham.* Berlin: de Gruyter.

Trible, Phyllis. 1984. *Texts of Terror: Literary-Feminist Readings of Biblical Narratives.* Minneapolis: Fortress Press.

Trimm, Charles. 2012. "Recent Research on Warfare in the Old Testament." *Currents in Biblical Research* 10:171–216.

Rad, Gerhard von. 1962. *Theology of the Old Testament.* Vol. 1. New York: Harper & Row.

———. 1965. *Theology of the Old Testament.* Vol. 2. New York: Harper & Row.

Warrior, Robert Allen. 1996. "Canaanites, Cowboys, and Indians." In *Native and Christian: Indigenous Voices on Religious Identity in the United States and Canada*, edited by James Treat, 93–104. New York: Routledge.

Weems, Renita J. 1991. "Reading Her Way through the Struggle: African American Women and the Bible." In Felder, *Stony the Road We Trod,* 57–77.

———. 1995. *Battered Love: Marriage, Sex, and Violence in the Hebrew Prophets.* Minneapolis: Fortress Press.

White, Lynn, Jr. 1967. "The Historical Roots of Our Ecological Crisis." *Science* 155:1203–7.

Wimbush, Vincent L., ed. 2000. *African Americans and the Bible: Sacred Texts and Social Textures.* New York: Continuum.

Yadin, Yigael. 1963. *The Art of Warfare in Biblical Lands.* London: Weidenfield & Nicolson.

Yee, Gale A. 2003. *Poor Banished Children of Eve: Woman as Evil in the Hebrew Bible.* Minneapolis: Fortress Press.

———. 2006. "Yin/Yang Is Not Me: An Exploration into an Asian-American Biblical Hermeneutics." In Foskett and Kuan, *Ways of Being,* 152–63.

Introduction to Wisdom and Worship: Themes and Perspectives in the Poetic Writings

Timothy J. Sandoval

Introduction

This article provides a general introduction to the poetic writings of the Hebrew Bible. It describes features of biblical poetry in general, then discusses the two major "genres" constituting the poetic writings: first, the biblical Wisdom literature (Proverbs, Job, Ecclesiastes) as well as the Song of Songs; and second, those texts related to worship in ancient Israel, especially the Psalms. This article also describes the important role of scribes—and others—in the production and transmission of biblical wisdom and worship texts, and concludes with brief reflections as to the challenges and possibilities that individuals and communities face when appropriating the Bible's poetic books today.

Biblical Poetry

"All which is not prose is verse; and all which is not verse is prose," Moliere once quipped. Biblical scholars, however, seldom settle for such blunt, and in this case tongue-in-cheek, distinctions. Some have written entire books cataloging the array of tropes, literary features, and strategies that when present in a text might be said to distinguish "biblical poetry" from prosaic narrative compositions (Watson 1984; 1995). Others have called into question the very possibility of distinguishing adequately between prose and poetry in the Bible, preferring to understand prose and poetry as standing on different ends of a continuum of biblical literary style (Kugel). As Luis Alonso Schökel has contended, it is impossible to "distinguish strictly between prose vocabulary and poetic vocabulary" or to "distinguish techniques which are exclusively poetic" (19).

Even as scholars debate the distinctions between biblical poetry and prose, several literary features or characteristics are widely recognized as signaling whether a biblical text might be regarded as poetry. The most ubiquitous of these characteristics, and certainly the most commonly acknowledged feature, is the presence of parallelism, or a correspondence of the second half of a line of Scripture with its first half. Although not completely unrecognized prior to the modern period, Anglican bishop Robert Lowth in his *De sacra poesi Hebraeorum* (1753) most famously described this characteristic of biblical poetry. Lowth described three major types of parallelism: synonymous, antithetic, and synthetic. In synonymous parallelism, the second half of a line essentially repeats the thought of the first half using a similar or related terminology ("An evildoer listens to wicked lips; / and a liar gives heed to a mischievous tongue," Prov. 17:4). With antithetic parallelism, the second half of the line presents the same or related message as the first half by using contrasting terms ("A wise child makes a glad father, / but a foolish child is a mother's grief," Prov. 10:1). Synthetic parallelism is the most elastic of Lowth's categories. With this sort of parallelism, the second half of the verse in some sense expands or builds on the first half to complete it ("Haughty eyes and a proud heart— / the lamp of the wicked—are sin," Prov. 21:4).

Lowth's description of biblical parallelism has proven to be "extraordinarily tenacious" and is still widely cited even as scholars have made important refinements to his analysis and categorization of different types of parallelism (Kugel, 15). Most importantly, the parallelism between two parts of a poetic line of Scripture is not a simple correspondence in meaning, as Lowth's term "synonymous" might suggest; nor need there be a direct correspondence between terms in each line as the designations "antithetic" or "synthetic" could imply. As Adele Berlin writes, parallelism "involves many types of linguistic repetition or equivalences—grammatical structures, semantic terms, words, and sounds" (309). For Kugel, it is the sequencing within a poetic line that is most important. The second part of the line expands on the first part, "carrying it further, echoing it, defining it, restating it, contrasting with it," and "it is this, more than any aesthetic of symmetry or paralleling, which is at the heart of biblical parallelism" (51).

Although the significance of parallelism as one indicator of biblical poetry cannot be denied, scholars have also sought to correct a one-sided view of its preeminence as the primary sign that a biblical text is poetry. Most scholars, like Wilfred G. E. Watson, who offers a taxonomy of features and tropes in biblical poetry, rightly view parallelism as only one characteristic of a poetic text. It is not "*the* characteristic of Hebrew poetry" (Watson 1995, 118, emphasis mine). In fact, parallelism is also sometimes a technique of biblical prose, and some poetic lines do not employ parallelism (Kugel, 70; Berlin, 304).

Hence, scholars have cataloged other important characteristics of biblical poetry besides parallelism. In the poetic tradition of some languages, rhyming and meter—a fixed and regular rhythmic pattern (e.g., iambic pentameter)—are important features of poetry. Although rhyming words can be found in biblical poetry, some scholars suggest it is not a prominent device of biblical poetry (Berlin, 310). By contrast, many students of the Bible have long contended that meter is in fact a feature of biblical poetry and have attempted to count syllables, thought units, and analyze accent patterns to demonstrate this. The nature, and even the existence, of meter in biblical poetry, however, has been increasingly contested. Although certainly biblical poetry at different points makes use of specific, identifiable, and recurring patterns of sound, which is rightly called rhythm (Berlin, 308), most scholars would concede that meter—a regular and relatively inflexible pattern of sounds—is not present in the same way that it is, for instance, in certain traditions of English or classical Greek poetry. As Michael Patrick O'Connor writes, "no consensus has ever been reached in the matter of Hebrew meter because there is none" (O'Connor, 138, cited by Peterson and Richards 1992, 42).

Besides identifying parallelism and the rhythmic patterns of syllables or accents, scholars also point to other aspects of biblical texts that suggest their poetic quality. As Berlin has noted, biblical poetry deploys a host of rhetorical strategies: hyperbole, merismus, personification, rhetorical questions, and so forth. Alliteration, plays on words, and paronomasia, as well as repetitions and refrains, also can be discovered in the poetic books of the Bible. A high density of literary tropes or metaphorical and symbolic language, which for some theorists is the most important indicator that a text is poetic, is also present in biblical poetry (Berlin, 311–13). However, like parallelism, such rhetorical or literary features are not unique to biblical poetry.

Biblical Wisdom Literature

If deciding what constitutes biblical poetry is a somewhat complicated task, discerning which of these biblical poetic texts should be described as "Wisdom literature" is likewise not self-evident. Scholars generally do agree that Proverbs, Job, and Ecclesiastes constitute the three Wisdom books of the Hebrew Scriptures. Likewise, a good number of psalms, such as Psalms 1; 36; 37; 49; 73; 119; 127; 128; 133 have been called "wisdom psalms." The wisdom psalm designation, however, is not precise, and scholars debate which psalms are best said to be related to the wisdom tradition. Some also reckon the Song of Songs as a wisdom composition, but it shares few significant characteristics with indisputable wisdom compositions. Outside of the Hebrew canon, the deuterocanonical (or apocryphal) books of Ben Sira (Sirach) and Wisdom of Solomon are also regularly reckoned as Wisdom books, while examples of wisdom works can also be found among the Dead Sea Scrolls (for example, 4QInstruction) and throughout the literature of the ancient Near East, especially ancient Egypt.

So just what *does* constitute Wisdom literature? How is it, for instance, that three texts as remarkably distinct as (1) Proverbs, with its poetic instructions (1–9) and lists of short sayings (10–29); and (2) Job, with its exploration of the possibility of disinterested piety (1:9), its extended "dialogue" between Job and his "friends" (3–27), and its divine speeches "from the whirlwind" (38–41); and (3) Ecclesiastes, with its skeptical (or joyful?) evaluation of limited human possibilities in the face of inevitable death, all come to be understood as part of the same literary, intellectual, and moral tradition that is called wisdom? How is that certain other texts, including some psalms, likewise are said to share in this tradition? And why is it that most psalms and the Song of Songs are often *not* regarded as wisdom texts? The answer to these questions, of course, is that despite important differences, Proverbs, Job, Ecclesiastes, and a number of other texts not only share much in common but also share *more* with each other than they do with other sorts of biblical literature, including most psalms and Song of Songs. Indeed, Proverbs, Job, Ecclesiastes, and the other wisdom texts noted above share what might be called a set of "family resemblances," as Michael V. Fox and others have similarly put it (Fox, 17).

Vocabulary

One family resemblance that Proverbs, Job, and Ecclesiastes share is a common vocabulary or terminology. Terms derived from the Hebrew words for wisdom, knowledge, understanding, folly, and so forth are prominent in these texts.

> Folly is a joy to one who has no sense,
>> but a person of understanding walks straight ahead. (Prov. 15:21)

> So I turned to consider wisdom and madness and folly . . ." (Eccles. 2:12)

> Who is this that darkens counsel by words without knowledge? (Job 38:2)

This wisdom characteristic can also be found in some wisdom psalms (e.g., Ps. 49). However, it is not prominent in most Psalms, or in the Song of Songs.

A cluster of moral terms related to the Hebrew words for justice, righteousness, wickedness, and so forth are also widely represented in Proverbs, Job, and Ecclesiastes:

> the same fate comes to all, to the righteous and the wicked, to the good and to the evil. (Eccles. 9:2)
> The house of the wicked is destroyed,
>> but the tent of the upright flourishes. (Prov. 14:11)
> See, God will not reject a blameless person,
>> nor take the hand of evildoers. (Job 8:20)

Certain wisdom psalms also make use of this moral vocabulary ("The wicked borrow, and do not pay back, / but the righteous are generous and keep giving," Ps. 37:21), although such rhetoric is of course common to other psalms as well. Song of Songs, however, again does not share this wisdom family trait and makes little use of the moral language common to wisdom books.

Teaching

A further easily discernible characteristic that most biblical works that belong to the wisdom family share is a rhetorical emphasis on teaching. This is particularly evident in Proverbs, especially in chapters 1–9, which explicitly sought to teach its ancient readers or hearers what it meant to be wise and just, as its scribal authors and redactors understood wisdom and justice:

> Hear, my child, your father's instruction,
>> and do not reject your mother's teaching. (Prov. 1:8; cf., e.g., Prov.1: 2-6; 2:1; and see
>> sections "Wisdom's Morality" and "Israel's Worship" below)

Although the mode of teaching present in Job and Ecclesiastes is not as obvious as in Proverbs, an instructional emphasis can be discerned in the pages of these books as well. Early on in Job, for example, the satan figure prominently announces one of the questions this book self-consciously explores—the possibility of disinterested piety: "Does Job serve God for nothing?" (1:9). Later, the dialogues between Job and his friends attempt to reckon with the related questions of why Job suffers and why the wicked prosper (see Job 21). In exploring these and other concerns, the text is not merely engaging in an intellectual exercise of moral philosophy but also instructing the reader or hearer in what the scribes who produced Job regarded as key questions emerging from the moral rhetoric of Wisdom literature. These questions seem related to the retributive, or cause-and-effect, rhetoric of traditional, didactic wisdom texts like Proverbs (see section "Israel's Worship" below).

In Ecclesiastes, the voice of Qohelet (or "the Teacher," perhaps the historical author or a literary invention of the scribal authors) asks, "What do people gain from their toil?" (1:3) and explores the fundamental moral question of what is "good for mortals to do" (2:3). Qohelet's famous refrain—which is also a conclusion of his investigations—that there is nothing better than to eat and drink and enjoy what one can (e.g., 2:24; 3:13) is also a form of instruction. As Eccles. 12:9 explicitly puts it, "Besides being wise, the Teacher also *taught* the people knowledge, weighing and studying and arranging many proverbs." Yet for humans who inevitably face death and who witness or experience injustice (e.g., 2:12-19; 9:1-10), Qohelet's instruction is also a vehicle for a deeper sort of critical reflection on the value of traditional wisdom teaching like that encountered in Proverbs.

The teaching emphasis of other biblical books sometimes designated as wisdom works is also not as direct as in Proverbs. Most of the psalms, for instance, are not directly concerned with instruction, but with other matters (offering praise [Psalm 150], structuring lament [Psalm 3]; celebrating torah [Psalm 119]). Even those psalms that are regularly designated as wisdom psalms are sometimes only indirectly instructional. For instance, rather than offering the hearer much specific moral teaching via a rhetoric of wisdom, knowledge, and folly, Psalm 37 appears most concerned to motivate the reader or hearer to remain steadfast in righteousness in the face of persecution and the prospering of the wicked. Similarly, unless the Song of Songs is understood in allegorical terms as revealing the love of the divine for Israel (or of Christ for the church), the erotic poetry of that book can likewise be viewed as instructional only in very broad rhetorical terms.

Solomon

King Solomon is the great patron of wisdom in ancient Israel and in ancient Judaism. Much as Moses was identified with the giving of torah and David with the composition of the Psalms, Solomon is the Israelite ancestor associated with Wisdom literature. A connection with King Solomon is thus a further family trait that can suggest a text belongs to the biblical wisdom tradition.

Solomon's legendary wisdom is recounted in the early chapters of 1 Kings. In 1 Kings 3, rather than petition the divine for "long life, or riches, or for the life of your enemies" (v. 11), Solomon requests the ability to govern well and "to discern between good and evil" (v. 9). He subsequently receives from the divine "a wise and discerning mind" unrivaled among humans before or after him

(v. 12). First Kings 4:29-34 reiterates the fact that Solomon possessed "very great wisdom" and notes his composition of 3,000 proverbs and 3,005 songs, while in 1 Kgs. 10:1-10 the queen of Sheba marvels at Solomon's legendary wisdom and verses 23-25 recall in summary fashion both his great wisdom and wealth.

Several of the collections that make up the book of Proverbs are directly or indirectly related to Solomon (1:1; 10:1; 25:1). Ecclesiastes does not explicitly name Solomon but does allude to Qohelet (or "the Teacher") as "the son of David, king in Jerusalem" (1:1; cf. 1:12). The presentation of the royal figure in 1:12—2:26 likewise seems at least in part designed to evoke memories of King Solomon. Job is not attributed or related to Solomon, but its status as Wisdom literature is never questioned, being secured by the other wisdom family traits the book demonstrates. By contrast, Psalm 72 is directly related to Solomon but is usually classed as a "royal psalm" and not Wisdom literature. The erotic poetry of the Song of Songs, of course, likewise alludes directly to Solomon (1:1, 5; 3:7-11; 8:11-12), but this connection with the legendary king is essentially the book's only wisdom characteristic.

International Influence, Universal Perspective

Although King Solomon is the great patron of wisdom in ancient Israel, the biblical wisdom texts also belong to a broader ancient Near Eastern literary tradition and share many family traits, including a kind of universal moral perspective, with a range of texts from Egypt and Mesopotamia. Because of its affinity with this international tradition, the Israelite wisdom books have sometimes been said to represent a foreign or non-Israelite element in biblical literature. In the past, for instance, some scholars argued that verses in Proverbs that invoke Israel's deity, YHWH, are late or secondary reworkings of a literature that is basically non-Israelite.

Sections of Proverbs are, of course, attributed to non-Israelites. A certain Agur speaks at 30:1, and the mother of Lemuel is the author of the instruction at 31:1-9. What's more, Prov. 22:17—23:11 (or 24:22) is also almost certainly influenced by the Egyptian Instruction of Amenemope. The character of Job, though not necessarily the book's author, is also a non-Israelite. But claims about biblical wisdom's foreignness are overstated. The Bible's Wisdom literature certainly shows affinities to other ancient Near Eastern works, but so do other parts of the Bible (cf. biblical and ancient Near Eastern creation stories, flood stories, covenant texts, and so forth). The Wisdom literature, like the rest of the Bible, belongs to a broader ancient Near Eastern cultural milieu and is largely the product of scribes, at least some of whom would have been multilingual and engaged in managing international relations for the Israelite and Judahite (and later Judean) political and economic elite. It is thus to be expected that the work of these comparatively cosmopolitan Israelite and Judahite (and later Judean) scribes would reflect their intimate knowledge of the scribal wisdom works of neighboring peoples.

However, it is true that Israelite wisdom books appear, on the one hand, less concerned with certain themes prominent in other parts of the Bible that scholars have sometimes regarded as central to Israelite identity and, on the other hand, more concerned with broader, universal questions of ethics or morality. Proverbs, Job, and Ecclesiastes do not, for instance, much mention torah, the cult, the Sinai covenant, or the exodus. Rather, the book of Proverbs emphasizes a general and broad moral instruction and the formation of character through the attainment of virtues and values that the ancient sages believed were necessary to produce good and flourishing human lives (see "Wisdom's Virtues" below). More critical or self-consciously reflective wisdom books like Job and Ecclesiastes likewise explore issues that other ancient Near Eastern texts also address. Job's wrestling with the suffering of the righteous, for instance, finds parallels in a text such as the Babylonian Theodicy. Likewise, the famous call in Ecclesiastes to eat, drink, and enjoy life in the face of inevitable death is a perspective echoed in works such as the Mesopotamian Epic of Gilgamesh and the Egyptian Harpers' Songs.

Genre and Forms

Texts that belong to the Wisdom literature family also often participate in the same genres and share certain literary forms. Michael V. Fox suggests there are two main wisdom genres from the ancient Near East: "didactic Wisdom and critical (or speculative) Wisdom" (17). Didactic wisdom regularly takes the form of a wisdom "instruction," the teaching of traditional values and virtues passed down usually from a father to a son. In biblical Wisdom literature, the instruction form is primarily evident in the poems of Proverbs 1–9, where the parental voice—identified as both male and female at the outset in 1:8 (see also 4:3; 6:20; 10:1; 15:20; 23: 22; 28: 7; 29:3, 15, 17; 30:17), but as male in 4:3—is closely identified with the words spoken by personified Woman Wisdom, who also instructs the book's addressee. The instruction form is also evident at 22:17—23:11 (24:22), a passage that is likely dependent on the Egyptian Instruction of Amenemope, and at 31:1-9, where the voice of another female teacher, the mother of Lemuel, instructs her son. Didactic wisdom books, however, can also incorporate forms besides the instruction (see below).

According to Fox, critical wisdom books "reflect and comment *on* doctrines and values" that didactic Wisdom literature seeks to directly inculcate in its hearers (17, italics original). This genre is represented by texts such as Job and Psalms 49, 73, and 88. Fox does not regard Qohelet as a species of critical wisdom—though others surely would. For him, although "Qohelet contains much critical or reflective material . . . it presents itself as a teaching about how to live one's life and is to be classed as didactic" (17–18). Most psalms and the Song of Songs, however, belong to neither the genre of didactic wisdom or critical wisdom. The genres of the psalms are diverse (see "Worship and the Psalms" below), and Song of Songs is best described as ancient erotic poetry, though there is a long tradition in both Judaism and Christianity of interpreting the book as an allegory of God's love for Israel or Christ's love for the church.

Besides the "instruction," the literary form perhaps most commonly associated with biblical Wisdom literature is the *mashal*, regularly translated as "proverb" in English. The short, usually two-line proverb, or *mashal*, is prevalent in Proverbs 10–29 and is common to wisdom books obviously dependent on Proverbs (such as Sirach). Ecclesiastes also includes relatively long sections of short proverbs (see 7:1-13 and aspects of 5:1-12 and 9:17—11:6), even if these proverbs seem sometimes to be more intentionally arranged and deliberately ironic and provocative than most of the sayings in Proverbs—for example:

A good name is better than precious ointment,
   and the day of death, than the day of birth. (7:1)

Sorrow is better than laughter,
   for by sadness of countenance the heart is made glad. (7:3)

The *mashal* is a form not regularly associated with non-wisdom psalms or Song of Songs, although like Job, the poetry in these books is often presented in couplets that regularly deploy parallelism, as do most *meshalim*.

Some biblical scholars have sought to understand biblical proverbs in light of the study of the short, pithy, usually one-line folk saying easily identifiable in a host of cultures (e.g., "A stitch in time saves nine"; "One who chases two rats will kill nothing," a Yoruba proverb cited by Pachocinski, 292). For these commentators, the short sayings that make up much of the book of Proverbs (especially chs. 10–29) likely find their origin in the oral, folk wisdom of the Israelite peasant population. Others, however, have emphasized the literary as opposed to oral quality of the two-line *mashal* in the Bible and have identified the royal court, the temple, or some sort of formal educational institution as the most likely social setting for the development of the *meshalim* of Proverbs and for the origins of Wisdom literature more generally.

However, the term *mashal* does not denote only the kind of short saying (or proverb) that is common in Proverbs 10–29. The prophetic allegories in Ezekiel 17 and 24, for instance, are each represented as a *mashal*. What's more, in Prov. 1:6, the term is paralleled to "figure" and "riddles," which suggests that the word can also refer to some sort of deflected discourse in need of interpretation. As Fox concludes, the *mashal* can be broadly understood as a "trope" or some sort of symbolic language, or more narrowly as a short saying or a proverb (54–55).

Both didactic wisdom and critical wisdom literature, of course, deploy other identifiable forms besides the instruction or the *mashal*. Another ancient form adapted by Ecclesiastes, for example, is the royal testament (1:12—2:11) whereby a king recounts his own greatness and exploits. Job too contains a multitude of forms. The book, for instance, opens and closes with a prose tale that frames an extended wisdom dialogue between Job and his friends (Job 3–27), while the words attributed to Elihu later in the book (Job 32–37) are related to Israel's hymn tradition. Other easily identifiable forms taken up by wisdom texts include an acrostic poem (Prov. 31:10-31), the macarism or beatitude (e.g., Ps. 1:1; Prov. 3:13; Eccles. 10:17), and numerical sayings (e.g., Prov. 6:16-19; 30:18-31).

Wisdom Morality: Virtues and Their Value

If "teaching" in the tradition of Solomon is a characteristic of Wisdom literature and the "instruction" and the *mashal* are among the prominent literary forms used to present wisdom lessons, what exactly does Wisdom literature teach or instruct one in? What are the universal moral perspectives and questions that the texts address with their vocabulary of wisdom and righteousness, wickedness, and folly?

Wisdom's Virtues

Several scholars (such as Brown) have pointed to the prologue of Proverbs (1:2-7) as key to understanding that book's moral goals, which are themselves foundational to the moral vision of the wisdom tradition in ancient Israel. After the superscription of 1:1, which gives the book its name—*Mishle* (Hebrew), or Proverbs—the prologue highlights the book's moral purposes largely, though not simply, through a series of infinitive constructions. The text seeks to instill three types of virtues: intellectual virtues ("wisdom," "insight," v. 2), social virtues ("justice, righteousness, and equity"; v. 3), and practical virtues ("shrewdness," "prudence," i.e., "cunning," v. 4). The design of the poem, not usually evident in English translations, literarily suggests that the book's authors especially prized the social virtues of verse 3, which stands at the pinnacle of the prologue's structure (see Brown, 23–30).

Both simple youth and advanced sages (see 1:4-5) can be instructed in the virtues that constitute the way or path of wisdom, a metaphorical complex important to Wisdom literature's moral discourse, especially in Proverbs 1–9. In wisdom thinking, there are only two moral options: the way of wisdom and righteousness, which leads to life, and the path of folly and wickedness, which leads to death. All who proceed in wisdom's way will increase in wisdom, or as Prov. 1:5-6 puts it, "gain in learning" and "acquire skill" to understand wisdom's moral teaching. The one who follows wisdom's way will learn to comprehend a "proverb" (or trope), a "figure," and "riddles." These words might designate specific genres that Proverbs deploys, although genuine riddles do not seem to be present in the book. By contrast, all of the terms individually, and when paired, connote some sort of figurative discourse or a discourse in need of interpretation. Thus, rather than naming specific forms of speech that might be found in Proverbs, they more probably together describe the character of the book's moral discourse and the project of acquiring and advancing in wisdom more generally. Following wisdom's way will produce intellectual, social, and practical virtue, as Prov. 1:2-4 claims. But wholly following the "way" of this teaching is not a simple activity. To travel wisdom's path fully will demand some hard interpretive work, like the unraveling of a riddle or the exploration of a trope.

The final verse of Proverbs' prologue introduces a further important concept for biblical Wisdom literature: the fear of the Lord (e.g., 1:7; 8:13; 9:10; Job 1:1; 28:28; Eccles. 12:13). The fear of the Lord is a much-discussed concept. As Fox recognizes, it can refer to a certain awe and respect of the holy Other. However, the notion of the fear of the Lord also retains traces of literal fear of a powerful deity, a fear that can motivate adherence to wisdom's way, as do the promises of rewards and punishment in Proverbs and elsewhere in Wisdom literature (Fox, 69–71). The emphasis on fear of the Lord as the beginning of wisdom (or knowledge) at the end of the Proverbs prologue places the intellectual, social, and practical virtues of wisdom's way (see 1:2-4) in intimate connection with a fundamental religious virtue, although ancient writers and readers would not have distinguished moral and religious virtues, or presuppose a religious-secular split in the way many contemporary people do. All the virtues belong to wisdom, which itself is intimately related to YHWH and YHWH's creation (see Prov. 8:22-31).

The prologue of Proverbs thus points toward key aspects of wisdom discourse, especially in didactic wisdom literature, which sages in different books build on, reflect on, and sometimes, as with the critical impulses of Job and Ecclesiastes, interrogate. Much of the content of the virtues and values that didactic wisdom offers are introduced early in Proverbs (chs. 1–9). The antisocial behavior of violent, greedy people is clearly denounced (1:10-19), and one should not withhold good from, or plan harm to, a neighbor (3:27-29). Chapter 6 warns against standing surety (vv. 1-5), laziness (vv. 6-11), deceptive behavior (vv. 12-15), arrogance, false testimony, and sewing "discord" (vv. 16-19), the last being a topic also taken up in 3:30-35. All of these practices or vices can contribute to social conflict and so highlight the premium the sages placed on social virtue noted above (1:3). Wisdom's concern with social stability, albeit in a clearly patriarchal vein, is also evident in the energy Proverbs invests in warning a male addressee of the "strange" or "foreign" woman, who on the literal level of the text is another man's wife with whom he might commit adultery (see Prov. 2:16-19; 5:3-20; 6:24-35; 7:1-27; 22:14; cf. Fox, 134–41, and below). Wise persons will know how to employ practical virtues—shrewdness and cunning—to promote and maintain social virtue and avoid vice, although the wisdom tradition knows such practical "wisdom" can often be used for ill rather than good. Wisdom literature's prizing of intellectual virtue is evidenced in Proverbs 8, which informs the hearer of Woman Wisdom's divine origins and her intimate relationship to the structure of the cosmos (see 3:19-20).

The virtues of wisdom's way introduced in Proverbs 1–9 are reiterated and expanded in the proverb collections of 10–29 (31). The short sayings in these chapters promote the virtues of diligence and hard work (10:4; 21:5), honesty in speech (16:13) and business dealings (11:1; 16:11), avoidance of adultery or the strange woman (22:14), kindness and generosity to the poor (14:31; 19:17) and social justice (21:3), as well as humility and fear of the Lord (11:2; 22:4). The sayings also acknowledge the efficacy of intellectual and practical virtues, but subordinate these to the divine will (16:1, 9; cf. 2:7).

Most of wisdom's virtues as presented in Proverbs are highlighted in one way or another in Job as well. In his self-defense, for example, Job claims to be one who embodied wisdom's virtues, especially social virtue: "I put on righteousness, and it clothed me; my justice was like a robe and a turban" (29:14). Job claims to have "delivered the poor" and the "orphan who had no helper" and to have made the "widow's heart sing"; he was "a father to the needy" and championed the cause of the "stranger" (29:12-16; cf. 30:24-25; 31:13-21). He likewise was sexually virtuous (31:1, 9), feared god (31:23; cf. 1:1), understood the limited value of wealth as opposed to wisdom (31:24-25; see also "Wisdom's Desirability" below), and was honest in speech and his dealings (31:30, 38-40). The poem treating wisdom's great value and inaccessibility (ch. 28), and the divine speeches (chs. 38–41), which highlight the mystery of creation, likewise point to this wisdom book's interest in esoteric intellectual matters.

Despite Ecclesiastes' more ambiguous instructional intentions, its author—whether Qohelet or a circle of scribes—likewise knows of wisdom's central social virtues, even if the text recognizes they are too often absent in society (3:16-17; 4:1-6). The book's intellectual curiosity is evident in its fundamental question about the "good" in human life and the Teacher's investigations into human strivings (e.g., 1:3-11; 2:1, 12). At Eccles. 7:16-17, wisdom's emphasis on practical virtue is also recognizable in Qohelet's famous exhortation: "Do not be too righteous, and do not act too wise; why should you destroy yourself? Do not be too wicked and do not be a fool; why should you die before your time?"

Wisdom's Desirability

Besides introducing virtues and values important to wisdom's way, Proverbs 1–9 also functions fundamentally to underscore for its addressee the *value* of wise instruction and the *worth* of following wisdom's way and acquiring wisdom's virtues. Most important to this rhetorical work of valuing wisdom's way are economic and erotic discourses, but they are not the only sorts of images the text deploys to describe wisdom's worth or desirability. Woman Wisdom, for example, does not merely cry out (1:20-33) like a prophet (cf. Jeremiah 7) to be heard and followed but also insists that wisdom, insight, and understanding should be passionately pursued as one might search for precious silver and treasure (2:4). Those who find wisdom are said to be "happy," and wisdom is described as more valuable than "silver," "gold," and "jewels" since "nothing you desire can compare with her." Wisdom's ways are "pleasantness" and "peace" (3:13-18), and wisdom affords security amid uncertainty in life (3:21-26).

The personification of wisdom as a woman is one of the most significant aspects of Israelite Wisdom literature (see esp. Prov. 1:20-33; 8:22-36; Sirach 24; Wis. 6:12-20; 7:22-28; cf. Job 28). Historical-critical scholarship has sought the origin of this figure in a number of ways. Some have understood her as simply a literary personification. Others suggest she is a hypostatization of YHWH's wisdom, while others underscore the influence of ancient goddess figures in her depictions, for example, Egyptian Ma'at, or more likely, Isis. Yet, whatever her provenance, the figure of Wisdom is also part of the effort of the ancient patriarchal authors to describe for a male audience the desirability or worth of their moral perspectives, their way of wisdom. Wisdom is not only valuable like material wealth. She is also presented in terms of a desirable, marriageable woman. In Prov. 4:5-8, the addressee is encouraged to "acquire" (cf. Boaz's marriage, or "acquisition," of Ruth in Ruth 4:10) and to "love" Wisdom, to "not forsake" her, and to "embrace her." If the addressee does these things, if he attains to wisdom's virtues, Woman Wisdom will not only "keep" and "guard" him but also bring him "honor," as might the ideal wife of the ancient patriarchal imagination. As Prov. 4:9 promises the addressee, Wisdom will "place on your head a fair garland" and "bestow on you a beautiful crown," images that many scholars (though not all) associate with ancient marriage customs (cf. Song 3:6-11).

In binary fashion not uncommon to patriarchal discourse, in Proverbs 1–9 Woman Wisdom—a symbol of the right way of wisdom and righteousness—is regularly contrasted with the strange or foreign woman (see 2:16-19; 5:3-20; 6:24-35; 7:1-27; cf. Woman Folly in 9:13-18). Literally understood, the patriarchal text presents the strange woman as an illegitimate and dangerous sexual partner for its imagined young male addressee; she is another man's wife and the opposite of the addressee's (potentially) real wife (see 5:15-20). The addressee of Proverbs is urged to be content with his own real wife but also to seek Woman Wisdom, whose desirability is constructed in erotic terms associated with legitimate patriarchal marriage. The addressee's real wife, but especially Wisdom, whom he might acquire like a wife, can save him from the dangers of illicit sex with the strange, adulterous woman (2:16-19; 6:24) and more generally from the illicit "way" of folly and wickedness, for which the strange woman is also a trope.

The image of desirable, valuable wisdom is also present in Job, where "the price of wisdom is above pearls" (Job 28:18; cf. 28:15-19). Qohelet likewise knows that "wisdom excels folly as light excels darkness" (2:13), even if such a statement in Ecclesiastes is designed to relativize wisdom's worth. Images of desirable, personified Wisdom in the Hebrew Bible not surprisingly also influenced later Jewish reflection on wisdom, for example, in Philo and the New Testament (John 1; 1 Cor. 1:18-21; Col. 2:3). Woman Wisdom (or in Greek, *sophia*) has likewise proven an important, generative biblical-theological image for critical feminist theologians.

Wisdom's Moral Rhetoric

One of the oft-noted features of the moral discourse of especially didactic wisdom texts such as Proverbs, or the words of Job's friends in Job 3–27, is a cause-and-effect rhetoric.

> A slack hand causes poverty,
>> but the hand of the diligent makes rich. (Prov. 10:4)

> I have not seen the righteous forsaken,
>> or their children begging bread. (Ps. 37:25)

This act-consequence rhetoric of biblical Wisdom literature has been much discussed. Klaus Koch, for instance, famously argued that such rhetoric is evidence that some biblical texts (such as Proverbs) present an inherent relationship between deeds and their results so that any punishment or reward for wrongdoing or virtuous activity was essentially an automatic byproduct of the act itself; it did not necessarily require the divine to act as the agent of retribution to mete out punishments and rewards.

Koch's view regarding acts and consequences in the Bible has been criticized and refined by other scholars. Nonetheless, a strong retributive rhetoric is undeniably present in much Wisdom literature and the moral import of such rhetoric is important to grasp. Some readers understand the cause-and-effect rhetoric in books like Proverbs in strong, literal fashion as promising and threatening real material and social rewards and punishments: if one keeps wisdom, one will prosper, but if one strays to the way of folly, misfortune awaits. This simplistic ideology, then, is sometimes thought to stand in stark contrast to Job and Ecclesiastes, which are characterized as offering critical, more nuanced responses to traditional wisdom's act-consequence schema. These critical wisdom works understand that a simple retributive moral view of the cosmos does not accurately reflect reality, since sometimes the wicked prosper, the righteous suffer, and wisdom does not always secure a flourishing life for those who follow its way (see Crenshaw).

The retributive rhetoric of much Wisdom literature, however, should not be understood in overly literal terms or caricatured as fundamentally naive about the vagaries of human experience. Wisdom writers never understood their retributive rhetoric to represent the way the world actually and always operates. Even scholars who believe that traditional wisdom's cause-and-effect rhetoric implies a strong retributive principle to be at work in the real world have long noted that the sages recognized "exceptions" to their retributive rule. Others suggest that such retributive rhetoric may have formed part of a pedagogical strategy that would have proved effective for instructing young students (see Prov. 1:4; Crenshaw, 267).

Yet if the retributive rhetoric of wisdom texts like Proverbs is part of a pedagogical strategy and not merely a series of literal promises of reward and punishment, it is also more than this. Didactic wisdom literature in particular functions fundamentally as moral instruction that seeks to form the character of its hearers or addressees by promoting a range of values and virtues it regards as essential (though perhaps not sufficient) for attaining a good and flourishing life. Wisdom literature's retributive rhetoric is thus a piece of this tradition's larger discursive moral work. The certainty of its rhetorical structure—if this, then this—supports the ancient sages' broader certainty that wisdom is integrally related to the divine act of creation. Wisdom's virtues belong to the very structure of the cosmos that YHWH created (Prov. 8:22-31). A child or unreflective youth might initially follow wisdom's way out of a hope for the real rewards or fear of the real punishments articulated by wisdom's retributive rhetoric. But this is not the end of wisdom's way. More mature students who learn to understand wisdom's tropes and figures—its broader symbolic moral discourse—would come to do so not through any external motivation of rewards and punishment, but because the acquisition of wisdom's virtues—the aligning of oneself with the genuine moral structure of YHWH's created cosmos—has become its own reward.

Israel's Worship: A Brief Overview

Understanding the Bible's poetic (and other) texts that relate to worship in ancient Israel is just as challenging a task as reckoning with biblical poetry's wisdom texts. It can be instructive to first gain an overview of the particulars of worship in that milieu—the *where*, *what*, *when*, and *who* of worship in ancient Israel. Yet even this seemingly straightforward undertaking can be vexing, for the study of ancient Israel's worship must reckon with several core issues or questions, each of which are complicated topics in and of themselves, taking different shapes depending on how the biblical sources and the data from the material remains of the ancient Levant are construed and prioritized, as well as how they are correlated to different epochs in ancient Israelite history. Hence, only a few of the most significant aspects of Israel's worship as attested in the Bible and in the material remains can be offered here before considering the way Scripture's poetic books, especially the Psalms, reflect Israel's worship practices and theology.

The Hebrew Scriptures testify to the fact that Israel's worship—its practices and ideological and theological expressions of devotion to their deity or deities—originated and developed in the often tumultuous and conflicted spiritual, socioeconomic, and political struggles of Israelite and Judean individuals and communities. Israel's worship reflected the effort of these individuals and communities to understand their existence and construct meaning for themselves in light of the divine reality that they understood themselves to have encountered. Put otherwise, worship in ancient Israel, as attested in the Bible and by the material remains of the ancient Levant, cannot be construed as monolithic. To the contrary, it developed over the centuries, taking different forms at different times and places, and was often contested by social actors.

Sites of Worship

One of the central questions for understanding the Bible's world of worship has to do with *where* worship happened in ancient Israel. Much of biblical literature, especially the Deuteronomist school and texts allied to the Deuteronomistic perspective, identify the temple in Jerusalem on Mount Zion as the most important site of worship. This centralization of worship is often associated with the religious reforms instituted by King Josiah of Judah in the late seventh century BCE (2 Kings 23). Yet the biblical texts also reveal that worship at different moments in the history of ancient Israel and Judah was quite diverse and not confined to the Jerusalem temple. For example, in a text that purports to recount events early in Israel's history, a certain Elkanah worshiped and sacrificed at Shiloh, where Eli was priest (1 Samuel 1). The Bible also speaks of important shrines at Bethel and Dan that were sanctioned by the monarchs of the northern kingdom of Israel, where official communal worship practices would have been carried out (1 Kgs. 12:25-33). So too the texts allude to "high places" where devotees would have also worshiped the divine outside of central sites like Bethel, Dan, or Jerusalem (1 Kgs. 12:31).

Yet worship in ancient Israel was likely not limited to these more or less official sites. Patrick D. Miller (62–76), for instance, notes that together the Bible and archaeological data suggest that extended families or clans could be associated with particular shrines, while some domestic households were also sites of religious practices. Judges 6:11; 19-24; and 8:22-27, for example, appear to allude to the shrine associated with Gideon's clan, while Jer. 19:13 and 32:29 attest to (non-Yahwistic) domestic rooftop worship.

Content of Worship

Besides the "where" of worship at temples, high places, and in family settings, an important issue for understanding ancient Israel's worship is a consideration of *what* took place at temples, shrines, and other cultic sites. Central here are, of course, the prayers and songs of individuals or the gathered community to which the Psalms testify (see "Worship and the Psalms" section below). Yet just as important are Israel's system(s) of offerings and sacrifices, which themselves are related to particular sites of worship and conceptions of holiness and purity. The Bible mentions an array of offerings and sacrifices that formed part of ancient Israel's worship. Several of these can be mentioned here briefly.

Tithes and offerings of firstfruits were offered primarily in thanksgiving to the deity. In large part, they served to support priestly service (Num. 18:12-32; Deut. 14:27-29; 18:3-5; 26:12; Neh. 10:37-38; 13:10-12), but also could be consumed by worshipers (Deut. 14:22-26; Miller, 118–20). The "burnt offering" (*'olah*), however, was fully consumed on the sacrificial altar (Lev. 1:9). The *'olah* sacrifice may have served to elicit divine favor or to call the deity's attention to a worshiper's plight. It also at points seems to have served an expiatory function (Leviticus 1) and could be associated with occasions of celebration as well (Lev. 22:17-22; Num. 15:1-11; Miller, 107–9). In contrast to the *'olah*, only a small part of the *minhah*, or "grain offering," was consumed on the sacrificial altar, with the remainder going to the priests as their portion (Lev. 2:9-10).

In contrast to both the *'olah*, which was fully consumed by sacrificial fire, and the grain offering, which was primarily the priestly portion, the meat of a well-being sacrifice (*zevah shelamim*)—whether offered as thanksgiving, in payment of a vow, or as a general freewill offering—was to be primarily consumed by the worshiper (Leviticus 3; Miller, 113).

According to Leviticus, a further sacrifice, the *hatta't*, or "purification offering" (in the past, often called the "sin offering"), functioned to purify the holy sanctuary from uncleanness that may have attached to it either through ritual impurity or impurity caused by unintentional sin (Leviticus 4–5; see especially Milgrom, 253–93). The *hatta't* is also the central offering in the Yom Kippur, or Day of Atonement, sacrificial ritual (Leviticus 16). A further sacrifice, the *'asham* (Leviticus 5), or "reparation offering" (sometimes rendered as "guilt offering"), like the *hatta't*, was "expiatory in some sense," or was "intended to deal with particular kinds of sins and their effects or with violations of the sacred." It served "primarily to make reparation for an offense of which one is guilty" (Miller, 117).

Occasions of Worship

Closely related to the where and what, or the site and content, of Israel's worship, is the *when* of Israel's worship. Worship in ancient Israel was both prompted by the intermittent needs of individuals and the community and structured into a regular cycle of religious celebration.

The different genres of the Psalms are testimony to particular moments of individual or communal crisis (such as illness [6], military threat [46]), or celebration and thanksgiving (such as healing [30], military victory [18], or a royal marriage [45]), that might provoke worship and be structured in and through worship practices (see "Worship and the Psalms" section below). Alongside such occasional moments of worship, the Bible also attests to Israel's worship of the divine at regular, recurring moments. Leviticus 23 and Numbers 28–29, for instance, record versions of the Bible's cultic or worship calendar. The Tamid, or "daily offering," was a sacrifice offered in the morning and evening (Num. 28:1-8), while other offerings were associated with the Sabbath day (Num. 28:9-10) and the new moon (28:11-15). The superscription of Psalm 92 identifies this text as a song for the Sabbath-day worship.

The complex traditions of cultic celebrations in the Bible also record a number of communal festivals. Three of the communal pilgrimage festivals were particularly important: (1) The spring Festival of Passover (Pesach), which celebrated the Hebrews' escape from Egypt (and at some point in ancient Israel's history incorporated a distinct agricultural festival of unleavened bread); (2) The Festival of Weeks or Pentecost (Shavu'ot), which marked the end of the grain harvest seven weeks after Passover; and (3) Booths (Sukkot), the fall harvest festival. The Psalms of Ascent (120–34) are often thought to be associated with pilgrims' ascent to Jerusalem for the celebration of the communal feasts.

Functionaries of Worship

Most Israelite women, men, and children would have participated in ancient Israel's worship life in important ways, such as by taking part in sacrificial meals and pilgrimage festivals, by offering prayers, making vows, uttering blessings, and likely in household worship rituals (see Miller, 203). Yet in the ancient patriarchal context, official worship leadership in Yahwistic religion would have predominantly fallen to adult male members of the community.

The central institution of the priesthood was likely reserved exclusively for males, and the Bible suggests that priestly responsibilities lay in three main areas (so Miller, 165–71): (1) Divination, or the discerning of the divine will, by, for instance, the casting of the Urim and Thummim (Deut. 33:8); (2) teaching torah, especially as this pertains to rituals associated with sacrifice and questions of uncleanness and holiness (Leviticus 13); (3) offering sacrifices and manipulating the blood of sacrifices (Leviticus 1–7).

Despite clear roles for priests, the priesthood itself was a contested institution that evolved throughout biblical history in relation to the roles of various priestly families and in terms of the status of various religious shrines or sites of worship. For example, the Levites likely originally held full priestly rank (as in Deuteronomy), but were according to certain texts demoted to the status of cultic assistants in a later epoch (Num. 3:5-10; 1 Chron. 23:2-6; Ezek. 44:10-16; see Miller, 162–65, 171–74). Other biblical texts similarly attest to "priestly politics" in ancient Israel and to the rise of the Zadokite or Aaronide priesthood (see 1 Kgs. 1–2).

Yet besides priests and Levites and their roles in worship, the Bible also attests to the role of other nonpriestly functionaries in ancient Israel's worship life, both women and men. Male and female musicians, singers, and dancers, for example, appear to have played important roles in worship contexts. As Ps. 68:25-26 (English vv. 24-25) states:

> Your solemn processions are seen, O God,
>   the processions of my God, my King, into the sanctuary—
> the singers in front, the musicians last,
>   between them girls playing tambourines.

A number of sometimes-obscure references in the Psalms likewise appear to suggest a role for singers, instruments, and musicians in biblical worship, while the antiphonal structure of certain Psalms (Psalms 122; 133; 136) is often thought to suggest participation in worship by a gathered assembly and not merely cultic functionaries. Although there are no clear data, in the family context, elders—women and men—likely would have held leadership roles in worship.

Objects of Worship

In the Bible, worship is primarily directed toward YHWH, the principal deity of the Israelites and Judahites (and later Judeans). Yet the fact that the ancient Israelites and Judahites worshiped deities besides YHWH is also well attested in the Bible. This worship, however, is regularly censured as illegitimate especially by the Deuteronomistic redactors of the Bible, and other allied voices, which sought to present the exclusive worship of YHWH as normative. Although certain texts in the Hebrew Bible may reveal a monotheistic impulse (such as the later chapters of Isaiah), exclusive worship of YHWH in the Hebrew Bible cannot usually in the strict sense be called monotheism, the belief in the existence of only one deity. Rather, it is monolatry, the exclusive devotion to one god, without denying the existence of other deities.

Jeremiah 44 is only one rather full example of a passage that alludes to the worship of a deity outside the realm of official Yahwism, although again with a negative evaluation that reflects the influence of Deuteronomistic theology. The text indicates that some ancient Judahites, apparently with significant leadership of women, worshiped a female deity. In Jer. 44:17-19 (cf. 7:16-18), first Judahite men and women and then only women—all refugees in Egypt from the destruction of Jerusalem by the Babylonians in 586 BCE—proclaim:

> we will do everything that we have vowed, make offerings to the queen of heaven and pour out libations to her, just as we and our ancestors, our kings and our officials, used to do in the towns of Judah and in the streets of Jerusalem. . . . And the women said, "indeed we will go on making offerings to the queen of heaven and pouring out libations to her; do you think that we made cakes for her, marked with her image, and poured out libations to her without our husbands' being involved?"

Besides the Queen of Heaven (likely the Mesopotamian deity Ishtar), the Bible probably speaks of another female deity worshiped by some ancient Israelites and Judahites. Allusions to the "asherah" in the biblical texts usually seems to refer to what was likely a tree or wooden cult object. At other points, however, it is possible that the text understands Asherah to be a female deity (2 Kgs. 23:4), who was worshiped alongside YHWH and who was well-known in the ancient Levant. Two now-famous inscriptions from Israelite sites at Kuntillet 'Ajrud and Khirbet el Qom, dating from the eighth century BCE, which mention YHWH and his Asherah, are likely allusions to this Israelite goddess. Some scholars also note that the depiction of Woman Wisdom, who is intimately related to YHWH in texts like Prov. 8:22-31, is reminiscent of ancient Near Eastern goddess figures and may in fact preserve a memory of the veneration of a female deity in Israel as well.

Worship and the Psalms

Although historians of ancient Israel have long described how the Bible testifies to the origins and development of Israelite religion, the biblical texts themselves imagine the major institutions, practices, and theologies of Israelite worship in light of a larger story of the divine's interaction with the descendants of Sarah and Abraham as recounted in the Pentateuch. In this larger story, the people's rescue from Egypt by their deity YHWH is the most important event. In the biblical narrative, the Torah, including instructions regarding Israel's sacrificial system, the roles of priests and other functionaries, the pilgrimage festivals, and even the Deuteronomic insistence on a single (Jerusalem) temple as a site of exclusive worship of YHWH, are all directions given to the Israelites in light of their escape from Egyptian slavery.

Outside the Pentateuch, Israel's other great worship text—the Psalms—also acknowledges this broader story of salvation, and recognizes identification with this narrative as a meaningful framework for Israel's worship life (Pss. 22:4-5; 66:5-7; 80:8; 83:9-11; 135:8-9). Indeed, the Psalter itself has been shaped into "five books" that parallel the structure of the five books of Moses, which transmit the people's foundational story. Certain "historical psalms," such as Psalm 136, also liturgically recall the people's history with their God—"who struck Egypt through their firstborn . . . , and brought Israel out from among them . . . who divided the Red Sea in two . . . and made Israel pass through the midst of it . . . , but overthrew Pharaoh and his army in the Red Sea" (136:10-15).

Yet Israel did not understand the encounter of the divine as belonging only to the great salvific moments of history. Adherence to the instruction of torah formed a kind of present response to the deity's past salvific work on behalf of the people. Likewise the Psalms reflect the ongoing encounter of individuals and communities with the deity in the midst of the rhythms of daily life. Indeed, upon hearing the moments of the great salvation story recited publicly in Psalm 136 (above), gathered worshipers likely would have proclaimed in antiphonal fashion an ongoing present relationship with the divine rescuer with the words, "for his steadfast love endures forever." Indeed, Israel's response to the deity in worship can in part be traced via the genres or forms of speech deployed throughout the Psalter.

Scholars long ago reached a broad consensus regarding the genres of most of the psalms in the book of Psalms. These forms or genres suggest how individual psalms may have functioned in Israel's worship. Psalms of individual or communal lament, for example, reveal human voices yearning for relief from the realities of suffering and injustice (individual lament psalms might include 3; 5–7; 13; 17; 22; 25–28; 31; 38–40; 42; 43; 51; 54; 57; 69–71; 120; 139; 142; communal laments might include 9; 12; 44; 58; 60; 74; 79; 80; 94; 137). Songs of thanksgiving express human gratitude for divine responses to petitions—for rescue, provision, and justice (18; 30; 32; 34; 40; 65–67; 75; 92; 103; 107; 116; 118; 138). Hymns of praise orient humans in relation to an exalted deity. They recall not only the divine majesty that worshipers might experience but also reveal and call forth joyful aspects of worship (Psalms 8; 19; 66; 100; 104; 111; 114; 148; 145–150; see Pleins).

The forms or genres of other psalms likewise point to their place in Israelite worship. As was already noted, the Songs of Ascent (Psalms 120–134) may have been associated with the practice of pilgrims "going up" to Jerusalem for one or another of the great festivals. A number of other psalms focus on Zion (Psalms 46; 48; 76; 87; 125), or the king, who likely played an important role in the official cult and in maintaining the institutions of worship (Psalms 2; 24; 29; 45; 47; 72; 93; 95–99; 101; 110). Certain psalms also seem clearly composed with liturgical contexts in mind (Psalms 15; 24), while the antiphonal structure of others suggests a concrete usage in acts of worship (Psalms 123; 133; 136). Still other psalms, as already mentioned, celebrate torah (Psalms 1; 119) or deploy wisdom vocabulary and forms to, for instance, help worshipers reckon with the anomalous realities of evil befalling righteous persons and the prosperity of the wicked (Psalms 36; 37; 49; 73; 127; 128; 133).

Conclusion: The Wisdom and Worship of Scribes, Others, and Us

An important question remains: Exactly *whose* ideas of wisdom and *whose* vision and models of worship does a reader encounter in the Bible's poetic books? To describe the wisdom and worship of these texts as "biblical" or even as "Israelite," "Judahite," or "Judean" is not only tautology but also perhaps obscures as much as it reveals when asking about the figures behind the Bible's wisdom and worship texts. As with most other biblical literature, it is likely that the poetic books as we have them in their *final* form in the Hebrew Bible are the product of intellectually or educationally elite scribes or sages. These scribes would have been overwhelmingly male and socially well-placed individuals.

Ideological critics of the Bible have often, and rightly, demonstrated the hidden biases of biblical writers, especially in terms of gender and class identification. Critical readers of the Bible must not ignore how socially well-placed, most often male, writers shaped biblical perspectives. Given the high status the Bible has among people of faith, especially Christians, this work of ideological critique must continue so that the particular perspectives of these elite men of ancient Israel are not unduly universalized as adequate and obligatory for all peoples, everywhere, and in every historical moment. Only the most conservative understanding of the Bible as inspired Word of God permits such an identification between certain meanings of the words of the biblical texts (as presented by contemporary authoritative interpreters) and theological and ethical demands the texts place on contemporary people of faith.

Although the poetic books are in the end products of intellectually elite scribes, the interests and values of the sages who produced this literature should not be uncritically collapsed into the interests of the 1–2 percent of the population of ancient Israel that constituted the economic and political elite of that society. Just as surely, scribal interests should not be viewed as identical to the 80–90 percent of the population that made up the peasant agricultural population. Though the scribal "class" would have been socially distinct, marked by education and elevated literacy, it was likely also quite diverse. Certainly the Bible at points suggests some scribes held high positions in the political institutions of ancient Israel, and these individuals likely identified closely with the economic and political elite (2 Sam. 8:17; 20:25; 1 Kgs. 4:3). Yet some scribes also would have been occupied with mundane tasks—for example, the penning of economic records and marriage contracts—making such strong identification with rulers and aristocrats less likely. Still others would have been more ambiguously placed at different levels in the administration of religious, economic, and political institutions of the court and temple. In any case, these scribes and sages likely understood their work and social station as qualitatively distinct from other social actors, whether peasant agriculturalists, artisans, or social elites (Sir. 38:24—39:11). As Ben Sira puts it, if scribes were not occupied with agriculture or handcrafts, they were "concerned with prophecies" and preserving "the sayings of the famous" and "seeking out meanings of proverbs" and parables (Sir. 39:1-3; cf. Prov. 1:2-6).

Indeed, besides managing religious, political, and economic institutions, largely on behalf of the political and economic elite, some master scribes or sages in Israel and Judah (and later Judea) also produced, read, and taught literarily, ethically, and theologically sophisticated texts like Psalms, Job, Proverbs, Ecclesiastes, and Song of Songs. They were, in other words, the guardians (and in part the creators and authors) of ancient Israel's literary, ethical-theological, and historical traditions. This is important since, as David Carr has explained, ancient scribes were not trained to serve as mere bureaucrats and copyists. A scribe's education was not merely about learning to read and write, or how to document financial transactions. Rather, scribal education in ancient Israel likely was largely concerned with moral instruction and centered on the study of culturally significant texts—like the Bible's poetic books. Scribes learned these texts, however, not by simply or primarily copying them, but in large part by hearing them dictated and by memorizing them. By becoming intimately familiar with culturally significant texts, scribes came to internalize the virtues, values, and perspectives of the texts they learned. The traditions a scribe learned and wrote on skin or shard also came to be written "on the tablet of the [scribe's] heart" (Prov. 3:3; 7:3; Carr).

One important moral impulse that the scribal voices in the Bible's poetic writings articulate is a cry for social justice—a purview often more closely associated with the prophets. Psalm 72, for instance, recounts the role of the ideal king who was to "judge your people with righteousness and your poor with justice" (v. 2). Proverbs likewise seeks to instill social virtue—"justice, righteousness, and equity"—in its hearers (1:3) and praises the rule of monarchs who ensure justice is done in their realms (e.g., Prov. 16:10, 13; 20:26, 28; 29:4, 14). The text also insists on fair economic practices (Prov. 11:1; 16:11; 20:10, 23) and demands justice in the legal sphere for the poor and marginalized (Prov. 22:22-23). The wisdom patriarch Job too claims to have protected the poor, widow, orphan, and traveler (Job 29:12-17), while the royal, Solomon-like figure in Ecclesiastes laments the absence of justice in his context (Eccles. 3:16—4:3).

Of course, the Bible's social justice—the justice and righteousness that the sages and scribes who produced the Bible envisioned—is not necessarily what many people today imagine when reflecting on social justice. Biblical social justice, for the most part, lacks the egalitarian impulse of most contemporary versions of justice emerging from liberal, Enlightenment thought. It likewise is not essentially concerned to eliminate poverty, as are many contemporary expressions of yearning for social-economic justice. Rather, the Bible's social justice is in general paternalistic and patriarchal.

As was the case elsewhere in the ancient Near East, in the Bible the king and other social-political elites—rulers and patriarchs of the community—were to act as a "father" to the community and to care for those in their charge. Those at the pinnacle of the patriarchal order were ultimately responsible to ensure that those lower in the chain of social-economic being—the poor and the needy—were cared for. Special concern was also to be directed toward those with liminal social status due to their not being clearly or firmly associated with a patriarchal household—widows, the fatherless, and foreigners. Even the eighth-century prophets, it seems, do not offer a vision of an economic revolution. Intolerable to them was not the *existence* of the needy (and certainly not a system of patriarchal privilege), but the gross *oppression* of the poor by those who were to be responsible to care for them. The economically and socially vulnerable were supposed to be assisted and protected. Their status, however, was not necessarily to be fundamentally transformed.

Though rhetorically distinct and emerging from an educational and literary context that likely was not as morally urgent as prophetic demands for social justice, the Bible's poetic voice of justice was nonetheless, like prophetic preaching, also a form of rhetorical and ideological "social control" over the political and economic elite. The powerful social positions inhabited by the political and economic elite made them vulnerable to ethical failures precisely in the social and economic realms; it made them liable to oppress the poor and to take advantage of the marginalized. Sagacious scribes addressed this reality not through prophetic oracles or visions but by transmitting and promoting a social-justice ideology that acknowledged the legitimacy of political and economic elites only insofar as they were agents of social justice.

In a real sense, then, it is a patriarchal, paternalistic, scribal vision of wisdom and worship that we encounter in the poetic books of the Bible. The literary and ideological "fingerprints" of male sages are most visible on the literature. However, this fact should not be overstated. With just a bit of (sometimes knotty) detective work, one can also discover traces of the fingerprints of others.

Scholars have for some time debated the methodological challenges involved in recovering female and nonelite voices in the Bible. These challenges revolve around questions like a text's relationships to its author, the weight that should be given to comparable literature where other voices are in fact named, or the nature of speech acts and the manner in which language carries traces of the voices of social actors who have "already" addressed a topic of discourse. Despite such debates, it is certain that the intellectually elite, male scribes ultimately responsible for the Bible's poetic books did not live in an ideological vacuum. Nor did the literary tradition over which they were guardians develop in a social vacuum. Hence we can expect that the voices of women and nonelite others in the discourses that the scribes developed were not completely erased.

For example, although the patriarchal tradition has erased her name, Proverbs itself records the instruction of a queen mother to her son Lemuel (31:1-9). Comparative studies of instructional texts, however, has revealed that her voice belongs to a chorus of other socially and economically well-placed women throughout the ancient Near East who attained scribal training and mastered a sage's learning (Fontaine). It is also likely that the sages or scribes who produced Proverbs drew on the wisdom of the broader Israelite and Judean agricultural, folk population when crafting their collections of wise sayings, especially in Proverbs 10–29. Certainly Prov. 25:1, with its note that King Hezekiah's men "transmitted" the subsequent proverbs, reminds the reader of the elite scribal context of wisdom. Nonetheless, especially the first half of many of the lines in the sayings collected in Proverbs 25–29 might well be derived from folk sayings, to which women and other nonelites surely contributed. Likewise, the Song of Songs, a text that many believe includes a strong female voice, may be related to popular love songs, which in folkloric traditions are in fact sometimes composed by women (Fontaine). What's more, it is probable that many of the laments, praises, hymns of thanksgiving, and pilgrimage songs of the Psalms were formed out of the responses to the real-life situations of the entire worshiping community of ancient Israel and Judah, not merely that of the male scribal intelligentsia.

The Bible's vision of wisdom and worship is thus not merely that of elite male figures. It rather includes, even if in submerged and dialogical fashion, the voices of the entire community of YHWH. Yet the ability to hear nondominant voices in the Bible is not merely a question of finding the right method to excavate those voices. It is also related to hermeneutics and the role of interpreters in understanding biblical texts. Simply put, the social contexts and experiences—or subjectivity—of some contemporary readers provide them with a different lens through which to read biblical texts, or differently attuned ears with which to hear submerged voices. Some women readers may thus more aptly than many male interpreters ask about, identify, and describe female voices in biblical books and more deftly uncover the patriarchal assumptions of those texts. Likewise, readers from non-Western cultures, where folk proverbs remain much more common than in Western societies, may be better situated to hear the oral wisdom of the agricultural peasant population of ancient Israel in the midst of the written scribal texts that make up Wisdom literature. So too poor and marginalized readers in the contemporary world bring a knowledge of the brutal realities of different sorts of social and economic oppression that can "thicken"—and sometimes problematize—understandings of the Bible's persistent concern with the needy. Put otherwise, if the voices of the whole people of YHWH in the ancient biblical texts are going to be heard, what is needed is something like what Cheryl B. Anderson has called "inclusive biblical interpretation." Such an approach to biblical interpretation promotes diverse readings of the Bible by the whole diverse people of God today and not merely the analyses of ecclesial and academic experts.

Hearing a full range of voices in the biblical texts by "reading against the grain" of the biblical texts with interpreters whose concerns and perspectives are different from our own may initially prove difficult for some readers; it may even at times prove scandalous. To have one's charitable giving and deeds challenged through an analysis of how the Bible's paternalistic views of justice may not be sufficient to liberate the poor from poverty can be difficult. To acknowledge the Bible's celebration of sexuality and the erotic in the Song of Songs in the midst of communities where anxiety around such subjects—especially with young people and sexual minorities—runs high likewise can prove exceptionally challenging. To ascribe positive agency to the strange, adulterous woman of Proverbs 7, whose sexuality is depicted as dangerous for young men, may prove downright offensive—at least initially so. However, to read against the grain this way *with* the strange women and *with* some feminist interpreters would not be to glorify adultery or to sanction through the Bible the throwing off of all sexual norms, as some might fear. It would rather be to imagine this strange woman as an active subject who claims control over her own sexuality in the midst of a patriarchal culture that dictated her choice of sexual partners and valued her primarily in terms of her ability to mother sons (see Fontaine). It would be to ask how the Bible's wisdom and worship traditions can speak today in contexts where patriarchy and sexism are as entrenched as ever. This sort of reading, like other readings associated with the Song of Songs' celebration of the erotic, or Wisdom literature's paternalistic economic justice, can create space in which a faithful and prayerful community of Bible readers might discern together a divine word of good news for all of God's people today. Indeed, throughout history, Jews and Christians have attempted to discern the Bible's vision of wisdom and worship in order to achieve for themselves and their communities, in their own times and places, better wisdom for life and more faithful worship of their God. Contemporary readers of these books are invited to continue in this tradition.

Works Cited

Anderson, Cheryl B. 2009. *Ancient Laws and Contemporary Controversies: The Need for Inclusive Biblical Interpretation*. Oxford: Oxford University Press.

Berlin, Adele. 1996. "Introduction to Hebrew Poetry." In *The New Interpreter's Bible*. Vol. 4, *1 and 2 Maccabees, Introduction to Hebrew Poetry, Job, Psalms*, edited by Leander E. Keck, 301–14. Nashville: Abingdon.

Brown, William P. 1996. *Character in Crisis: A Fresh Approach to the Wisdom Literature of the Old Testament*. Grand Rapids: Eerdmans.

Carr, David M. 2005. *Writing on the Tablet of the Heart*. Oxford: Oxford University Press.

Crenshaw, James L. 1998. *Education in Ancient Israel: Across the Deadening Silence*. New York: Doubleday.

Fontaine, Carol R. 2002. *Smooth Words: Women, Proverbs and Performance in Biblical Wisdom*. London: Sheffield Academic.

Fox, Michael V. 2000. *Proverbs 1–9: A New Translation with Introduction and Commentary*. AB. New York: Doubleday.

Koch, Klaus. 1983 (1955). "Is There a Doctrine of Retribution in the Old Testament?" In *Theodicy in the Old Testament*, edited by J. L. Crenshaw, 57–87. Philadelphia: Fortress Press.

Kugel, James L. 1981. *The Idea of Biblical Poetry: Parallelism and Its History*. New Haven: Yale University Press.

Lowth, Robert. 1753. *De sacra poesi Hebraeorum*.

Milgrom, Jacob. 1991. *Leviticus 1–16: A New Translation with Introduction and Commentary*. AB. New York: Doubleday.

Miller, Patrick D. 2000. *The Religion of Ancient Israel*. Louisville: Westminster John Knox.

O'Connor, Michael Patrick. 1980. *Hebrew Verse Structure*. Winona Lake, IN: Eisenbrauns.

Pachocinski, Ryszard. 1996. *Proverbs of Africa: Human Nature in the Nigerian Oral Tradition*. St. Paul, MN: Professors World Peace Academy.

Peterson, David L., and Kent Harold Richards. 1992. *Interpreting Biblical Poetry*. Minneapolis: Fortress Press.

Pleins, J. David. 1993. *The Psalms: Songs of Tragedy, Hope, and Justice*. Maryknoll, NY: Orbis.

Sandoval, Timothy J. Forthcoming. "Education: Hebrew Bible." In *Oxford Encyclopedia of Bible and Gender Studies*. New York: Oxford University Press.

Schökel, Luis Alonso. 1988. *A Manual of Hebrew Poetics*. Rome: Editrice Pontificio Istituto Biblico.

Watson, Wilfred G. E. 1995. *Classical Hebrew Poetry: A Guide to Its Techniques*. 2nd ed. Sheffield: Sheffield Academic Press. [originally published by JSOT Press, 1984]

JOB

Alissa Jones Nelson

Introduction

Job is not a text that lends itself to simple resolution. The format of the book itself seems to kick against any barriers imposed by unified hermeneutical perspectives. It holds in tension multiple genres, characters, voices, time periods, perspectives, and perhaps authors. It is a complex and difficult book, but this very complexity is what has made the book of Job such a ubiquitous text across religious, philosophical, literary, and artistic traditions, from Barth to Gutiérrez, Kafka to Camus, Milton to MacLeish, Blake to the Coen brothers.

The complexity of Job begins with its language and structure. The Hebrew is notoriously difficult to translate, due to obscure or unintelligible words and phrases. The book is also difficult to date with any certainty. Scholars generally agree on a date somewhere between the seventh and second centuries BCE, which is admittedly far from precise. The setting for the narrative is clearly the patriarchal era, but there are notable parallels with the book of Jeremiah and the Suffering Servant in Second Isaiah (both of which are more reliably dated to the sixth century BCE), and the questions Job raises surrounding issues of retribution, YHWH's power and justice, and the expectation of future liberation also resonate with the Babylonian exile, although there are no direct allusions to this context in the text itself.

The earliest reference to Job as a figure is Ezek. 14:14, 20, but this may be a reference to an earlier prose narrative or to an oral tradition, not to the book as we have it. We cannot date the book based on its relationship to other biblical passages, because many of these related passages also have uncertain dates. While the text as we have it certainly resonates with exilic themes, it lacks references to important issues in later Second Temple wisdom literature, which seems to indicate a final date of composition between the Babylonian captivity and the Second Temple period (Perdue, 78–84). Similarities between Job and Babylonian wisdom texts and traditions (The Babylonian

Theodicy, The Just Sufferer, I Will Praise the Lord of Wisdom, The Dialogue between a Man and His God) also point to some connection with a Babylonian context. The structure of the text seems to indicate different stages of composition, which may also represent a range of time periods. Perhaps we can safely argue that the final form of the text dates to the exilic or postexilic period, while admitting that we are unsure when it began or precisely how it reached its present state.

The authorship of the book is another open question. Most scholars agree that the author was an Israelite. Some argue that a single author composed the entire book (Wilson; Hartley), perhaps pulling material from earlier written or oral traditions (e.g., the prose prologue and epilogue, the interlude on wisdom in Job 28); others identify internal "inconsistencies," which they argue may indicate multiple authors and redactions of the book (Clines 1989; Perdue). Scholars have speculated that the author may have been a member of the upper class of Judahite society who was exiled to Babylon, perhaps wealthy, perhaps an intellectual, perhaps a court official. The author was not only skilled in terms of eloquence and argumentation but also appears to have been well-educated and somewhat unorthodox.

Even the genre categorization of Job is open to debate. While the book has traditionally been identified as Wisdom literature, some scholars argue that other genres might be more appropriate designations. Gerhard von Rad (1966; 1972) is perhaps the most well-known proponent of the book as Wisdom literature. Timothy J. Johnson builds on von Rad's thesis that "apocalyptic literature is the child of wisdom" and identifies the book of Job as an apocalypse (von Rad 1972, 179). Alternative genre identifications include dramatic lament, Greek tragedy, drama, comedy, and parody.

David Clines succinctly summarizes efforts to resolve these interpretive dilemmas as "intelligent speculation" (1989, lvii). Some scholars suggest that portions of the book they have identified as additions or interpolations should be removed in order to aid interpretation. The issue, however, is that one's interpretive bias, the themes one identifies as the "main" themes of the text, and the potentially anachronistic criteria by which one determines what counts as "coherence," inevitably impinge on one's choice of what portions of the book to amend or excise. As Kenneth Ngwa notes (360), one's analytical beginning determines to a large extent where one ends in interpreting Job. I would argue that the nature of the text requires the reader to embrace and explore contradictions and complexities rather than attempting to uncover or create a more or less synthetic reconciliation. It is much more interesting to wrestle with what may seem to be strange twists and turns in the text, and the ways in which more or less distinct components function in the text as we currently have it. This is what the remainder of this chapter will attempt to do.

Job 1–2: Prologue—Calamity Befalls a Righteous Man

THE TEXT IN ITS ANCIENT CONTEXT

The book opens with the assertion that Job is a man from the land of Uz. There have been many debates over where exactly Uz is. Edom has been suggested, as per Gen. 36:28; Lam. 4:21; and 1 Chron. 1:42. Hauran, a location in northern Palestine, is also a candidate. The key point is that it is not in Israel; Job is not an Israelite. This attempt to give the story a universal, transnational appeal is consistent with Wisdom literature as a genre. The concept of a chosen people or a special covenant between God and Israel is not mentioned, although the name of God (YHWH) is used repeatedly. The relationship is intimate but not explicitly national. It is clear that this is the Israelite God, but God's special connection to Israel is not part of the narrative.

From the beginning, Job's wholeness (Heb. *tam*, which also has the connotation of "integrity") and uprightness (*yashar*) are particularly important. These personal qualities also extend to his wealth and his family; three daughters and seven sons, both numbers representative of wholeness or completeness in ancient Near Eastern (ANE) contexts, further emphasize Job's *tam*; seven thousand sheep and three thousand camels also emphasize not only his wealth but also his *tam*. Ten is another important number representing perfection, which is included here by association (ten children, one thousand oxen). These numbers are also a way to emphasize the staggering extent of Job's wealth, his completeness in a material sense.

Tam means whole or complete rather than without sin, but one must maintain right relationships with God and others in order to maintain this wholeness; Job's actions on behalf of his children illustrate this concern. *Yashar* in Hebrew, translated "upright," also has the sense of straightness, directness; with Job, what you see is what you get. The dialogues bear this out. These qualities are the core of Job's integrity, and the words themselves recur throughout the text to emphasize their centrality to the conflict between Job and his interlocutors. Job's blamelessness is integrity, not sinlessness. Job also feared God, which is identified as the source of wisdom (Job 28). Job trusts and relies on God, which is one more reason why his suffering is so devastating to him.

Job's accuser ("the satan") is an interesting conundrum. He appears among the children of God and seems not to be out of place there; he is God's functionary. God controls his actions, which is why the satan needs permission to afflict Job, and also why God is ultimately responsible for all of the calamities that befall Job.

The ash heap (2:7-8) represents mourning, social isolation, and poverty. Job's suffering is physical, emotional, social, and psychic; he has been afflicted in every possible sense. Gustavo Gutiérrez declares that Job is "a sick as well as a poor man" at this juncture (6).

The use of *barak* to mean both "bless" and "curse" is intriguing and problematic. We can infer from the surrounding text that Job's statement in 1:21 is indeed "blessed be the name of the Lord," since the very next verse assures us that Job did not sin by charging God with wrongdoing. Then again, perhaps this qualification indicates that Job may have sinned by cursing God in spite of acknowledging God's right to do what God has done, and the next verse is meant to reassure us that Job is still *tam* in spite of this slip. In either case, the ambiguity is interesting, both here and in his wife's statement in 2:9. In Job 1:5, where Job is concerned about his children's sin, and in 1:11 and 2:5, where the satan incites God against Job, *barak* certainly seems to carry a negative connotation, but again the potential ambiguity is intriguing.

When Job's friends finally arrive (Job 2:11-13), they engage in traditional mourning rituals, tearing their clothes, sprinkling dust on their heads, and sitting with Job on the ground. They are silent for seven days, which may refer both to the traditional period of mourning and to the seven days of creation, as creation becomes a theme in the dialogues that follow. The primary mourner must be the first to speak, and Job breaks the silence in a spectacular fashion in Job 3.

▊ THE TEXT IN THE INTERPRETIVE TRADITION

Other biblical texts (Ezek. 14:14, 20; James 5:11) emphasize the endurance of Job in his trials; many later interpretive traditions also emphasize aspects of the "patient" Job based on Job's responses to suffering in the prologue. These themes fit nicely with questions and issues that would have been current at the time of the Maccabean revolt (165 BCE) and the destruction of the temple (70 CE) as well as the persecution of early Christian communities. In both the Septuagint and the apocryphal *Testament of Job*, the iconoclastic Job of the dialogues is intentionally softened in favor of an example of patient endurance and the development of a theology of resurrection. This tradition of Job the Patient is then carried forward by Eusebius, Augustine, Jerome, and Gregory the Great into medieval Christian interpretation, and beyond that into the Renaissance by influential figures such as Francis Bacon and John Donne. The Qur'an and Islamic traditions around Job (Ayyub, in Arabic) also develop this saintly view of Job as a long-suffering prophet of God, an example of patience, fortitude, and wisdom. In early Christian literature as well as art and architecture, Job is most often depicted as the patient sufferer, or alternatively as an athlete or warrior battling the satan, who is equated in early Christianity with the figure of the devil. The first interpretation makes endurance primarily a passive task, while the latter emphasizes the active nature of Job's struggle, the idea of victory and a prize to be won (Ambrose). As we will see, these interpretations become problematic when compared to Job's lengthy dialogue with his friends and, ultimately, with God.

Job's wife and her enigmatic outburst in 2:9 are also a key focus in interpretive tradition. Rabbinic commentary, the Septuagint, the Targum, and the *Testament of Job* all seek to give a better explanation for her behavior than what we have in the Masoretic Text. In the biblical text, Job's wife is never given a name, a history, or a place of origin and is consequently a secondary character. She is not mentioned as an agent in her children's births or in mourning their deaths. Her outburst to Job in 2:9 is thus without explicit context, although the reception of her character in subsequent interpretive texts testifies to some common points of understanding. It is interesting that the only woman who speaks in Job is also the only person who speaks without a lengthy explanation. Her presence is implied in the epilogue, perhaps; many interpreters assume that she takes part in Job's "having" ten more children, although birth is not explicitly mentioned. Rabbinic midrash assigns Job a new wife in the epilogue, namely Dinah, Jacob's daughter. Job's (first) wife is only mentioned twice more, as a literary device to illustrate Job's suffering (19:17) or to support his oath of innocence (31:10). As we encounter her in Job 2:9, we are left to speculate about the cause of her enigmatic statement.

Her cryptic comments have invited exposition in the Qur'an and Islamic tradition as well as among interpreters from Augustine, Jerome, Gregory the Great, and Martin Luther to Ellen van Wolde, Sarojini Nadar, and F. Rachel Magdalene. It is interesting that both the Septuagint and the *Testament of Job* present a nuanced and mostly sympathetic picture of this woman and her involvement in Job's suffering while the patristic tradition and medieval and Reformation Christian communities largely portray her as a foolish woman at best and as an agent of the satan at worst. In many Islamic and Christian interpretive traditions, she is portrayed as gullible rather than evil; this is often identified as a problem for women generally (Thomas Aquinas; Luther). Modern and postmodern interpretations have again picked up the ambiguity of her character and have demonstrated a keen interest in fleshing out Job's wife, as we will see below.

The identity and function of the satan have also been issues in interpretive tradition. Second Temple Jewish tradition, and later Christian tradition, identified Satan as a proper name and an independent personality; in the text of Job, the satan seems to be an office, a function, a sort of prosecuting attorney (Hartley, 71–72) rather than a discrete character (Perdue, 84–85). Nevertheless, subsequent interpretations have often read the character of the satan in Job as synonymous with this later concept of Satan.

◼ The Text in Contemporary Discussion

A particularly interesting cluster of contemporary interpretations focuses on the character of Job's wife. In line with the expansions introduced by the Septuagint and the *Testament of Job*, as mentioned above, there seems to be a common desire across temporal and cultural contexts to flesh out this interaction and to allow her to explain herself, her relationship to her husband, and the suffering that leads to her outburst (Clines 1989; Gravett 2012; Hartley; Klein; Magdalene; Nadar; Ngwa; van Wolde 1995). This speaks to a wide variety of contemporary social and political issues, including the recovery of female characters in the biblical texts; an analysis of their portrayal and their agency (or lack thereof), which might be relevant for women in religious communities today; questions about the role of women in marriage relationships and religious leadership; and political issues related to gender (in)equality and to the disproportionate suffering of women in contexts of conflict (e.g., Afghanistan and Darfur) and disease (e.g., the HIV/AIDS pandemic), where they are marginalized as actors and yet often suffer more than their male counterparts. Job's wife in the Hebrew text stands as a reminder of the many women who are marginalized, denied agency, and even made scapegoats in their suffering. Efforts to give Job's wife a voice, to resolve the ambiguity of her involvement in Job's drama, and to assign her a role that underlines both her agency and her narrative marginalization testify to the ancient and contemporary recognition that this simplistic portrayal of an otherwise central female character is insufficient and unsatisfactory. In this sense, the reception of Job becomes a critique of patriarchy even, or perhaps especially, in patriarchal contexts.

Job 3: Job's First Monologue—Curse and Lament

◼ The Text in Its Ancient Context

The genre of this section involves both curse (Job 3:1-10) and lament (3:11-26); the first section focuses on Job's wish that his suffering would never have begun, and the second focuses on his questions about why he continues to suffer, as well as his implicit wish for death.

Sheol is a reference to the netherworld, and Job here expounds on the idea that it is a place of quiet and rest compared to the suffering of his present condition. It is the great leveler; thus the wicked and the righteous, kings and slaves are all alike there. Conceptions of Sheol in the ANE are many and varied, but what is important here is how Job constructs this place, as a final refuge from his suffering. This will be a theme he picks up again and again in the dialogues.

Whereas the satan had accused God of hedging Job in for his own protection (Job 1:10), Job sees this same hedging in (3:23) as obscuring his vision, preventing him from walking in the way of wisdom as he had previously done. It is yet another source of suffering.

▮ THE TEXT IN THE INTERPRETIVE TRADITION

Interpreters have variously understood this chapter as a structured and coded lament according to fixed criteria (Hartley; von Rad 1972) and as a passionate outburst intended to convey something that is fundamentally incommunicable (Gutiérrez; Tamez 1986, 2004). In either case, it is certainly a stunning expression of emotion, and we are afforded the opportunity to understand the depth of Job's suffering and consequent despair before being launched into the theological debates that follow.

The theme of creation recurs throughout this chapter. It has been interpreted as a new strand of wisdom theology in the exilic context, one that counters traditional structures and opposes another new strand, which emphasizes the formation of and obedience to torah. The creation theme is evident in Job's opposition of light and darkness, which calls to mind the original creation of the world. Job's longing for chaos may represent a longing to annihilate the entire order of creation (Clines 1989; Perdue) or simply to undo the day of his own birth (Wilson). If we accept the former interpretation, we could argue that this monologue is the primary thing God rejects in God's speeches. Job's assertion that the order of creation is not "good," as God declared it in Genesis, requires God to respond defensively and to explain its goodness in terms other than those Job attempts to impose.

▮ THE TEXT IN CONTEMPORARY DISCUSSION

The above-noted shift in terms and perspective is an important point for contemporary debates about theodicy; the book of Job asks readers to acknowledge that human understandings of what constitutes "justice" and what role God plays in the process of maintaining a just order in God's creation are fundamentally subjective and perhaps flawed. It is important in contexts such as these to be responsive to efforts to reframe the terms in which this debate takes place.

The purpose of Job's curse and lament is to set the stage for the increasingly acrimonious dialogues in the following chapters. Here we are reminded that the story of Job is fundamentally a drama; Job 3 forces us to confront the violence of Job's emotions, the depth of his suffering, and the human aspect of his suffering; as readers, we are reminded that we should not forgo compassion in favor of intellectual debate. For those interpreters who see the suffering of the innocent as a primary theme in the book of Job, this chapter is an essential part of the issue. The question of how a person of faith responds to suffering (Clines 2003; Gutiérrez) is not merely an intellectual or philosophical question. The first step, as in Job 3, is to sit in silence with the sufferer and listen to the outpouring of grief. What comes next, as we will see below, is more complex.

The issues raised here and carried forward as themes throughout the book resonate with contemporary questions of social justice. What is the purpose of suffering, if any? Why do the innocent suffer? Alternatively, if one subscribes to the doctrine of original sin, is there such a thing as innocent suffering? How do one's opinions on these matters influence one's approach to injustice and suffering in the world? Is the book of Job relevant to these questions? These are issues to be explored in the following sections.

Job 4–27: Dialogues—On Righteousness, Suffering, and Justice

▌The Text in Its Ancient Context

The dialogue between Job and his friends is not unique among comparable Wisdom literature in the ANE, but it is the only Israelite literature to develop this form. Scholars have speculated that the content of the dialogues, particularly the issues of retribution, righteous suffering, and God's justice, either reflect a contest or debate between two types of sages in exile or outline common questions the Israelites were posing in light of their experience of exile. In either case, the text reflects a debate in which tragic events were the impetus for some parties to defend traditional concepts of retribution and find comfort in authority based on received wisdom, while others questioned everything. These various responses to loss also raised questions about which groups and which theologies would shape the future of the Israelites in their radically new context (Perdue, 91).

Both Job and his opponents appeal to esoteric knowledge, to revelations and visions that cannot be substantiated, only asserted. Theological arguments on all sides of the issues are based on this kind of "mantic wisdom," which seems to become more mainstream in the context of exile. This could be the result of an encounter with another kind of wisdom practiced in the ANE, that of skilled ritual practitioners such as the priests of Babylon. This is also a basis for the growth of apocalyptic literature (Johnson). The traditional divisions between "seers" and "sages," between prophets and religious leaders or temple functionaries, seem to be blurring in the absence of a centralized religious practice based around the temple (Perdue, 91–92). Thus Job's challenges to his friends are also challenges to priestly theology and the primacy of the temple in mediating and effectuating God's relationship with the Israelites. Israelite Wisdom literature exhibits a tension between knowledge of God derived from torah and knowledge derived from creation; as a non-Israelite, Job develops the latter theme, which allows him more autonomy and gives more weight to individual experience as an arbiter of wisdom. This is not a new issue, but Job develops it more fully and drives it in new directions (Perdue).

Job also subverts traditional images of God as Israel's protector. He turns these metaphors around to cast God as a destroyer and himself as a person mistakenly identified as an enemy of God. God the Divine Warrior in Job 6 and 16 looses his arrows against Job. God the Creator, who sets limits on chaos to preserve his creation, in Job 7, 26, and 27 treats Job like one of the chaos monsters who must be subdued. A particularly poignant passage in the context of exile is 10:1-17, where Job laments that no one can rescue him from God's hand. In the creation narratives, God's hand fashions humankind, and Job evokes this metaphor as a personal interaction in 10:8-12. In the

Deuteronomistic history and in the Psalms, God's hand signifies a power that repeatedly saved the Israelites. In Job's case, being in God's hand is the problem rather than the solution. God's creative and sustaining power has turned destructive. This is particularly evocative and emotive in an exilic context; where God's hand was once seen as a source of deliverance, it is now seen at best as having failed to prevent disaster and at worst as having directly imposed it. In another moving passage, Job 27:2-3, Job insists that God has denied him justice at the same time as he acknowledges that he lives only by the spirit or breath of God. This again calls to mind the creation narrative, wherein God breathes his own breath into human beings to give them life. Job will not give up his complaint as long as he lives, but he knows that his life continues only because God wills it. The poignancy of Job's cognitive dissonance here reflects a larger context in which the Israelites are trying to decide how to proceed into a collective future.

Job first mentions the idea of an umpire, someone to intervene between him and God, in 9:33. In 13:6, he begins to use explicitly legal language (argument, plea), and in 13:13-23 he sets the terms God should abide by in court. In 16:18-22, Job laments the impossibility of any mediator intervening between him and God, but in 19:23-27 he reiterates his intense desire that such a thing were possible. In chapter 23, he begins to consider the details of a legal case against God. Job 23:6 is an explicit reference to the covenant; the Hebrew *yarib* is a legal accusation of a breach of an agreement or covenant. The problem is that Job does not know where to find God to subpoena him, but God clearly knows where to find Job, since he has afflicted Job so severely. Job laments his disadvantage here and wishes that he could hide from God just as God hides from Job. The difficulty in locating God might also be a reflection of an exilic context, as the temple, the place where YHWH has traditionally been found, is no longer an option. Job is confident in his ability to win his case but not in his ability to compel God to participate.

■ THE TEXT IN THE INTERPRETIVE TRADITION

It is interesting that in rabbinic interpretation, where the Hebrew text would have been the primary source, the interpretive tradition is much more varied than traditions of the saintly Job found in Christian and Islamic interpretation, as we saw above. Rabbinic tradition is far more likely to emphasize the iconoclastic Job and to debate issues such as when he lived, whether he was a Jew or a gentile, what the reason was for his suffering, and whether he worshiped God out of love or fear. One explanation for the greater diversity of rabbinic interpretations is that rabbinic tradition lacked the rigid theological structures that dominated early Christian and Islamic communities (Vicchio 2006a). It is also interesting to note, however, that the grief-stricken, angry Job of the dialogues survived in medieval Christian liturgy, particularly in the Office for the Dead, where Job's laments were quoted extensively for their pathos and the emotional catharsis they lent to the bereaved. The tradition of Job as an avenue for the expression of grief in the face of suffering, death, and persecution thus has an older, if less ubiquitous, history. The use of Job in laments over HIV/AIDS in South Africa is an example of the contemporary continuation of this tradition (West with Zengele; West).

Even in these darker interpretations, both ancient and contemporary, Job 19:23-27 is often included as a beacon of hope, a belief in the resurrection of the dead and a panacea for suffering.

At several points in the text, Job seems to explicitly deny the possibility of resurrection (14:7-12; 16:18-22). This has not prevented generations of interpreters from seeing in 19:23-27 a theology of resurrection or even a prefiguration of Christ. For example, whereas the Hebrew text presents 14:14 as a seemingly rhetorical question ("If a man dies, will he live again?"), the Septuagint renders the same verse as a positive assertion ("For though a man die, he will live again"). The iconoclastic Job of the Hebrew text is intentionally softened in the Greek text and subsequent interpretations in Greek-speaking communities, providing an example of patient hope in the face of persecution by promising justice in the afterlife. Interpreters who carry forward this theme and find in Job a doctrine of resurrection, both the concept of bodily resurrection and the idea of a soul/body dualism and concomitant ideas of the afterlife of the soul, include Clement, Origen, Jerome, Gregory, Aquinas, and Luther as well as contemporary interpreters such as Janzen.

There are solid arguments against this interpretation, including the idea that the Redeemer (Wilson suggests that a less theologically loaded translation of the Hebrew *go'el* would be "Vindicator"; Clines [1989] suggests "Kinsman" or "Champion") is a personification of Job's plea, his affidavit in the legal case he wants to bring against God (Clines 1989); the idea that the Champion is God because God can be both judge and vindicator (Gordis; Hartley; see Isaiah 39); and the idea that the Champion is some other heavenly being, a personal god or an angel, a counterpart to the satan, who will vindicate Job in the heavenly council where the satan had condemned him (Terrien; Pope; Habel). A key question related to the identity of the Vindicator is *when* Job hopes this vindication will take place. The question hinges on how one interprets *'akharon* ("later," "finally," "at the last"). Does this refer to the end of Job's suffering? The end of Job's life? Or does it have eschatological significance? Job's statement in 19:26 offers little help, as the phrase "after my flesh has been thus destroyed" could refer to the current destruction of boils and skin disease or to the final destruction of death. Gerald Wilson argues convincingly that Job is expressing an impossible desire (conveyed repeatedly in the rhetorical Hebrew phrase *mi yitten*, or "who will give?"). The key point here is not *who* or *when*, but *whether*, and ultimately the answer is no (Wilson, 209). This is consistent with Job 16:19-20, in which Job laments the impossibility of any mediator between himself and God, and which provides a key by which we may also read 19:23-27 (Clines 1989, 465–66).

Furthermore, Job has been hoping for public vindication; the publicness of the affirmation of his righteousness is particularly important to him. He does not want to be thought of as a sinful man who deserved what he got, and the communal and social aspects of his suffering are particularly galling to him (as we will see in Job 29–31). Thus it seems more likely that Job is here referring to restoration and vindication in this life. This is partly an argument from context, because a theology of resurrection in Israel had not been developed by the time of the exile, and partly an argument from the text itself, because a belief in eventual restoration after death would undermine the fear of death, which Job expresses throughout the remainder of the book. If the solution to Job's suffering is simply that he will be restored in the afterlife, then the discussion should end here, and Job should have no more cause for complaint (Saadiah 1988). The argument that Job is here referring to an individual resurrection or afterlife ignores the context of these verses in the overall trajectory of Job's argument and the book as a whole. Thus Job desires intensely that God will vindicate him before his death, but he believes that in fact God is his enemy and will soon kill him. The focus is Job's repeated demand for a face-to-face encounter with God in a legal dispute (Clines 1989, 455–56).

Later Christian interpretive traditions read the themes of the New Testament as presented in a coded form in the Old Testament; hence Job is often viewed as a prefiguration of Christ by the early church fathers, including Ambrose, Augustine, Jerome, and Gregory the Great. Job's patience and humility in the face of the satan's affliction is likened both to a retelling of the story of Adam and Eve, wherein this time the protagonist manages to resist the woman's and the satan's temptations (John Chrysostom), and to Jesus' resistance of temptation in the desert (Gregory the Great). In all these cases, Job's integrity and patient acceptance of undeserved suffering at the hand of God paves the way for a concept of innocent suffering that undergirds both the incarnation and the salvific function of Christ's atonement (Hartley; Wilson).

Early Christian interpretation also emphasizes the issue of original sin as both an explanation for Job's suffering and as a way of absolving God of responsibility. According to this theology, no human being is innocent; thus questions of innocent suffering become irrelevant. Clement of Rome saw in Job proof of this theology. Early church fathers, including Jerome and Augustine, as well as later Reformers, such as John Calvin, supported and developed this interpretation, based primarily on 9:1-2 and 14:4-5.

As we saw above, early traditions tend to polarize Job as either the saint or the iconoclast. In medieval Jewish interpretation, Saadiah is one of the first to merge these traditions. He takes the tension between these two portrayals seriously, as do Maimonides and Gershonides (see also Vicchio 2006b, 97–98). Saadiah also takes up the theme of innocent suffering, offering three possible resolutions for this dilemma: suffering builds character; suffering is purification; suffering is a test. Saadiah underlines God's responsibility for Job's suffering and refuses to ascribe to the idea of life after death as a solution. In Job's case, death is final; Job himself does not believe in life after death. In Saadiah's view, this proves Job's uprightness. If Job had believed in an afterlife, his endurance of suffering could not have been disinterested; the very fact that he thinks death is the end proves his righteousness and disinterested service of God.

Scholars have been frustrated by the fact that the neat tripartite structure (three dialogue cycles, in the first two of which the friends speak in an established order and each receives an individual response from Job) breaks down in the third cycle, wherein Bildad's speech is quite short, and Zophar does not speak at all. Many have tried to rearrange the text so that this structure is preserved. Verses in Job 24 are redistributed to Zophar (Clines 2006); verses in Job 27 are ascribed to Bildad (Hartley). Again, it seems to me that it is more interesting to address the themes of the text than to attempt to re-create a structure for the speeches based on a potentially anachronistic concept of "coherence," which may have been significantly less important to the author(s) of Job than it appears to be to the book's interpreters.

Job's friends have sometimes been interpreted as corporate personalities representing distinct priestly and theological traditions whose theology in the exilic context is under serious strain (Hartley). Job has also been interpreted as a corporate personality, perhaps an alternative option to the traditional Israelite identification with the corporate personality of Jacob (van Wolde 2002) or the representative of a more abstract group, the poor and marginalized (Dussel). It seems clear that this text is not simply the story of extraordinary events in the life of a unique individual, although it is certainly that as well. Efforts to universalize the story by placing Job and his friends outside the nation of Israel, setting the story in the patriarchal period, and incorporating wisdom traditions from other ANE societies make it clear that this is not simply the history of one extraordinary individual and his encounter with God. Nevertheless, the themes of the text and the use of Israel's personal name for God also create a close resonance with a particularly Israelite context.

The encounter with Job's pain inspires fear rather than compassion in his friends; they have to malign his integrity in order to retreat into a comforting theological world where such visions do not trouble them (Wilson). This is an understandable reaction to the horrors of conquest and exile. Job is challenging the basis of an established theological understanding of the world; he does so because to him it seems horrible, but the friends find his viewpoint even more disconcerting (Gutiérrez). These differing perspectives are both understandable reactions to suffering. Integrity and experience are most important to Job; stability, security, authority, and intellectual understanding are primary for his friends. Both Job and his friends are willing to sacrifice Job himself to prove their respective points. Job's repeated appeals to his friends for compassion, and his insistence that those who do not suffer cannot understand his plight except by falling back on retributive principles, is consistent with liberation theologies and their various interpretations of these dialogues as Job's progress toward a more empathic and nuanced understanding of the poor and marginalized through his own experience of suffering (Job 24; see Tamez [1986, 2004]; Dussel; Gutiérrez).

▌ THE TEXT IN CONTEMPORARY DISCUSSION

Each of Job's comforters affirms retributive principles in a distinct way, yet their arguments have the same ultimate results in terms of their views of God, their views of humanity in general, and their views of Job in particular. Job's challenge to the retributive principle is not only a challenge to his friends but also to a long tradition of Wisdom literature and the organizing principles of the Israelite covenant relationship with YHWH. Clines (2003) is arguably right when he asserts that the book has nothing to say about the meaning of suffering generally; but it certainly addresses one of the core principles of the Israelite conception of the organization of YHWH's creation, and as such it has wider implications.

Job raises key questions about the authority of tradition. Job's friends defend traditional wisdom principles and by implication traditional religious hierarchies. Job's challenge to authority begins with the friends and extends beyond them to the principles they espouse and ultimately to God as the governor of the created order. In this sense, Job not only undermines the traditional content of wisdom teaching but also explodes the context, the pedagogical method, of being instructed. He refuses to bow to authority in the sense that traditional wisdom teaching demands; his own experience is his authority. This has interesting implications for contemporary discussions about theological and interpretive authority. Job becomes a blueprint for a theological world in which the vernacular voice, the interpretive insight based on personal experience over intellectual investigations (if indeed the two things can be separated), has the same authoritative force as the academic voice. Tradition is no longer the arbiter of acceptable theology.

In this context, we see evidence of the emergence of a theological concern with the individual. The extraordinary experience of a unique individual is the basis for both the questions and the answers Job provides. Job makes experience his theological starting point, while the friends make theological ideas their starting point (Rayan; Pyeon; Nam; Wilson). Tradition is inadequate to address Job's unique situation. This is consistent with a historical context in which the community is concerned with shaping a new and challenging future. Thus experience has become a corrective to the conceptual. The impossibility of dissociating idea from experience, truth from life, is a key theme throughout the book. It is also a key theme in contemporary debates about the meaning of suffering. Such a debate can never be purely philosophical; to disregard the concrete experience of those who suffer is to contribute to their suffering.

Job believes that God perverts justice, a position his friends find abhorrent. In many contemporary contexts, God's responsibility for suffering is an explicit reason for loss or lack of faith; in Job's case, it is a catalyst for reorientation of faith. Job's early wish that he would simply be allowed to die is replaced first by a vain hope that he might encounter God in a court setting on equal footing and then by a serious legal challenge to the conditions of his suffering and to God as the party responsible for it. Where some interpretive traditions have found the answers to Job's questions in the idea of the afterlife, as we saw above, contemporary discussions question whether this is an adequate explanation. One of the central tenets of liberation theologies and religious social justice movements is the idea that suffering cannot be addressed simply by asserting that the injustices of this life will be set right in the next. In these contexts, the argument is that the impetus for action rests with human communities; it is the responsibility of people of faith to act on behalf of those who suffer, and arguments insisting that sufferers must deserve their suffering and that the appropriate response is patience and fortitude in the hope of a reward in the hereafter perpetuate and legitimize structural injustices and are therefore part of the problem rather than the solution.

Job's suffering leads him to recognize the link between poverty, despair, and hopelessness that goes hand in hand with the lack of any prospect for change (Wilson, 59–60; Gutiérrez). The purpose of human life according to the book of Job may indeed be to acquire wisdom, but wisdom is not simply the reiteration of traditional authority structures or the maintenance of consistent principles in the face of a chaotic reality. The purpose of human life is to come to terms with experience, as Job tries to do. If wisdom is indeed know-how, gaining "mastery in life that will lead to blessing, satisfaction, and even prosperity" (Wilson, 3), then Job makes a powerful argument that retributive theology will not help a person achieve this goal. Thus Job provides a counternarrative to the dominant Deuteronomic themes of the Old Testament and the retributive understanding of traditional Wisdom literature, undermining retributive perspectives and reflecting a new understanding of how to live in a strange new context.

The question of wisdom at stake in the book of Job is the question of how to react appropriately to suffering, whether one's own or that of others (Clines 2003; Gutiérrez). As we saw above, the first step Job advocates in chapter 3 is to empathize with grief and anger. The second step, as outlined in the dialogues, is to confront both the structural issues that contribute to suffering and the authority figures who legitimize them. Contemporary debates over social justice in religious contexts are also attempts to achieve this, and they, like Job, often face similar resistance from traditional theologies and hierarchical structures, whether religious, political, or social. Antonio Negri's neo-Marxist reading sees Job as an allegory for humanity as a whole, subject to immense suffering as traditional estimations of meaning and value are destroyed one after the other, but finally restored by recognizing themselves as possessors of divine power and wisdom, able to govern their own world justly according to new principles of freedom, equality, and a common fight against oppression. This reading also resonates with themes in a variety of liberation theologies, which see in Job various possibilities for a structural understanding of poverty and an empathy leading to advocacy for the oppressed and marginalized (Gutiérrez; Tamez 1986; 2004; Dussel; West).

Job 28: Interlude—On Wisdom

■ THE TEXT IN ITS ANCIENT CONTEXT

This chapter depicts a wide-ranging and eloquent search for wisdom. In Job 28:23, the Hebrew emphasizes "God himself," God alone. God alone knows the way to wisdom, because God not only sees everything but also created everything; in this process, he "saw," "declared," "established," and "searched out" wisdom (28:27). And wisdom, perhaps ironically considering the repeated trope that no one knows the way to it (28:1-22), turns out to be precisely what tradition said it was: to fear the Lord and turn away from evil (28:28). This is also precisely the behavior Job is praised for in 1:1, 8; and 2:3. To be sure, wisdom is not a matter of intellect; it could be argued that this is the fundamental mistake the friends are making, pressing the case for wisdom as an understanding and acceptance of principles such as retribution. Nevertheless, the idea that the fear of the Lord is the beginning of wisdom is not new or unique to Job (see Prov. 1:7; Eccles. 12:13).

■ THE TEXT IN THE INTERPRETIVE TRADITION

Most commentators argue that this is an interpolation with little connection to its context (Hartley; Terrien; Newsom; Habel). Clines (2006, 908–9) argues that unless it can be attributed to one of the speakers, it is an "aberration." He thinks Elihu is the most likely of all the characters to attempt to answer the question, "Where shall wisdom be found?" Thus he asserts that this chapter is properly placed as the final speech of Elihu, because its theme (wisdom is the fear of the Lord) is consistent with the last lines of Elihu's final speech in the text as we have it (888). Clines advocates reordering the text so chapter 27 is Zophar's final speech, the Elihu speeches (Job 32–37) come next, and Job 28 is properly identified as Elihu's final speech (Clines 2006, 908). This is an interesting proposal and seems to solve quite a few issues with the text, but it is not the only theory.

Wilson argues that the fact that Job 27 and 29 both begin with identical phrases, indicating that Job is still speaking ("And Job again took up his discourse and said . . ."), demonstrates that Job 28 is also Job's speech, because it is sandwiched between these introductions. However, one could just as easily argue that the absence of such a clause at the beginning of Job 28 indicates that it alone is not Job's speech. Whereas Clines sees Elihu as the most likely speaker, Wilson (299) argues that the theme is closest to Job's words. According to the theology of the friends, "the world works according to discoverable principles, and Job needs to submit to those principles in order to achieve and maintain a life of wisdom and blessing. . . . In Job's mouth, the words of Job 28 stand firmly against the common assumptions of the sages" (Wilson, 305; see also Jones).

Sophia Magallanes agrees that the poem in Job 28 is appropriately placed in Job's mouth as a precursor to his vow of innocence, and it aligns with God's eventual response to Job in arguing that one understands divine justice through mundane, earthly matters rather than through abstract theological principles. In contrast to Wilson, Magallanes argues that this chapter provides convincing evidence that the text of Job expounds rather than rejects the traditional wisdom of Proverbs; justice only "appears to be absent in the world when the way of the God-fearer is hidden" (Magallanes, 202). Thus it is both poetic allegory and essential context for Job's final speech.

Scott Jones argues that the poem is intended not as a hymn to wisdom but as a critique of the way people like Job's friends have traditionally sought wisdom. In Job 28, Job rejects the earthly realm as providing adequate assistance in his struggle; he is thus encouraged to continue his battle with his attention focused beyond his friends in particular and beyond the created order in general.

It is clear from the above discussion that Job 28 still represents an enigma in the interpretive tradition of the book of Job. There are many attempts to explain its inclusion and to identify its speaker, but none that achieves wide scholarly consensus.

▋ THE TEXT IN CONTEMPORARY DISCUSSION

Regardless of how one chooses to explain Job 28, the key question is why an unattributed speech is included and what wisdom has to do with the other themes we have identified in the text. The simplest answer to the first question seems to be Wilson's, that Job is the speaker and that Job 28 is simply part of the structure of Job's discourse, as identified in chapters 27 and 29. While acknowledging that the simplest answer is not necessarily the best one, I would also argue that attempts to relocate and redistribute this speech, while interesting, are not ultimately more convincing than Wilson's argument. Attempts to use thematic issues to determine which speaker is most likely to have uttered this poem depends to a great extent on the interpreter's subjective opinion. It is perhaps more enlightening to analyze the ways in which an interpreter's assignment of Job 28 affects her or his overall interpretation of the important themes in the book as a whole. If Job 28 is ascribed to Elihu, then whether wisdom does in fact constitute fear of the Lord, as the Israelite wisdom tradition advocates, is an open question. If the same speech is put in the mouth of Job, then we have a reiteration of this primary principle of Wisdom literature, because God eventually affirms Job as having spoken rightly. In the latter case, the fear of the Lord has a new face, as Job's harsh language throughout the dialogues is here assessed as being consistent with fearing God and living wisely.

These options are instructive for debates about appropriate ways to bring ancient faith traditions into contemporary life. Some religious communities advocate adhering to the ancient traditions as closely as possible; others advocate translations and interpretations of these traditions that are more or less radical in their reassignments; still others reject ancient traditions and attempt to embrace the principles and motivations behind them. Job potentially provides support for each of these approaches, but the book also seems to fall more heavily on the side of those who embrace ambiguity and tension and are open to reinterpreting tradition based on new experiences and perspectives. Hence we have interpretations of Job's suffering in Hindu communities (Sitaramayya), appropriation of Job's laments in contexts of HIV/AIDS in South Africa (West with Zengele), and challenges presented by liberation theologies (Tamez; Dussel; Gutiérrez), all of which use Job to challenge existing religious structures and indeed standard uses of the book of Job itself, particularly those advocating patience and endurance in the face of suffering.

Job 29–31: Job's Final Monologue—Statement of Righteousness

THE TEXT IN ITS ANCIENT CONTEXT

In Job's final speech, he looks backward and forward in a more integrated manner than he has done thus far. He seems to have reached the end of his tether but still manages to confidently assert his rights (Clines 2006, 1036). He also seems to turn his back on his friends and turn his full attention to God (Wilson). Job's speech in chapter 27 was a short oath. Job 29–31 is much more expansive. These chapters reflect a neat tripartite structure, with Job's nostalgic reflection on his past (29), lament over his present circumstances (30), and his final oath of innocence (31).

Job's reflection on his past, "when the Almighty was still with me" (29:5a), may indicate that the ruptured relationship with God is one of Job's primary concerns (Wilson, 313). Nevertheless, the loss of wealth and status also seem quite important to Job, and "when the Almighty was still with me" could equally refer to the blessings associated with this state as to any Christianized sense of direct relationship with God, especially given the fact that this lament is followed by 29:5b-10, which clearly indicate the association of the Almighty's presence with earthly blessing and respect. Job craves approval, but it is also true that he helped the poor, orphans, widows, the blind, the needy, and strangers (29:13-16); and it is clear that Job expected to be rewarded with ease in return for his righteousness (29:18-20). His longing for his formerly privileged place in society is the theme of 29:21-25. Again, this is consistent with the context of exile, wherein the issue is not only physical and psychological pain but also a loss of status, being shamed and reviled.

Job's suffering is particularly galling because it is both intense and public; it seems the two things are interrelated in key ways. Job 30:1-15 laments Job's humiliation and describes his tormentors in particularly harsh terms, as less than human (30:1, 6-7). Job laments the passing of his honor and prosperity (30:15b, c) before he describes the extreme physical and psychological pain that torments him (30:16-31). This is further complicated by the pain Job experiences because God does not answer when Job cries out to God; God is afflicting Job in a way that Job would not afflict a human being in need (30:25-26). The spirit of God that paradoxically keeps Job alive in previous sections is now being poured out (30:16). It is clear that Job believes the problem is not that God is unaware; God is paying close and careful attention (30:20), and in the context of defeat, exile, and Diaspora, this itself is the problem.

Job next makes a series of "disavowals" (Clines 2006, 1013). Job's oaths in this chapter are serious; in his context, one who makes an oath and fails to fulfill it is inviting unmitigated disaster. Of course, Job does not think he can be proven wrong, and it is hard to imagine what further disaster could possibly befall him. Job's affidavit considers themes that resonate with standard tropes in Old Testament literature: dishonesty, adultery, injustice and the proper treatment of slaves, unfair or unsympathetic treatment of the disenfranchised (the poor, widows, and orphans), greed, placing trust in wealth or idols (a key prohibition in the Old Testament and an ostensible reason for the exile), revenge or rejoicing in the downfall of enemies, a failure of hospitality (another key Old Testament theme, particularly in stories about the patriarchs), covering up sin, and mistreatment of the land and the tenant farmers who till it (also a common Old Testament theme, where the land has a corporate personality, is able to cry out and weep, and is a key component in the covenant). Job disavows all of these errors; in an Israelite context, he disavows any violation of torah.

Finally, in Job 31, Job gives a forceful account of his belief in his own innocence. He is so confident of being able to answer all claims against him that we would wear any accusation as a crown for all to see, thus making a public affirmation of his innocence, which, together with the cessation of his suffering, is the primary thing he has wished for throughout his dialogue. Here his words end, with the Hebrew verb *tammu*, the same root used to describe Job as blameless and upright, integrating Job's affidavit with the idea that his words, like himself, are blameless and whole. God will eventually confirm this.

■ THE TEXT IN THE INTERPRETIVE TRADITION

This section skillfully moves the reader away from Job as an object of pity and toward a view of the Job of previous days, a man of power, wealth, and a sense of entitlement. Some interpreters have found in these passages more cause to chastise Job than to praise him, although he himself clearly thinks the actions he describes are evidence of his worthiness and integrity. It is up to the reader whether to hold Job to the standards of his own time, in which case he is rather remarkable for his insistence on "the importance of motivation in ethics," or to judge him by the standards of contemporary ideals and to find him wanting, for example in his owning of slaves, his treatment of his wife as property, his brooking no dissent or disagreement, and his failure to challenge a system that privileged him and disadvantaged others (Clines 2006, 1038; Tamez, 1986, 2004; Gutiérrez).

■ THE TEXT IN CONTEMPORARY DISCUSSION

Job's failure to address the systematic injustices of his society, from which he certainly profited, provides the impetus for much contemporary discussion around the book, including assertions that Job didn't go far enough in addressing the question of suffering because he is primarily (Tamez 1986, 2004) or solely (Clines 2003, 2006) concerned with his own unique case. This can be read as evidence that the wealthy can never fully understand the plight of the poor (Clines 2003); it can also be a testament to the power of experience to overcome prejudice (Tamez 1986). I would argue that this aspect of the book should not be read anachronistically through a contemporary lens, which demands that Job must see things our way if he is to be a hero for the marginalized. However, I would also argue that in the context of the exile, many aspects of social structure were being questioned; the challenge for interpreters is to allow the book to address the questions that it meant to address and not import new questions, which the book perhaps could not have envisioned.

Arguably, the issue is not the social structure of ancient Israelite society; the issue is how one should respond to suffering, and what role God plays in the governance of the world. Of course, the question of how one should respond to suffering could equally be explored in the context of changes to the systematic ways in which social structures perpetuate it, but in this case the text seems to be focused on undeserved suffering, particularly in the context of covenant and exile. In relation to contemporary debates, however, the book as a whole provides ample interpretive fodder for arguments against passivity, quiescence, and apathy in the face of injustice, whether its perceived source is one's friends, one's God, or one's society at large.

Job 32-37: Elihu's Monologue—Theology of Retribution

▌ THE TEXT IN ITS ANCIENT CONTEXT

At the end of Job 24, Job challenges his friends to prove him wrong. Their dwindling speeches in Job 25 seem to indicate that they are unable to do so. Elihu's stated purpose in intervening is to prevent Job's words from being taken as wisdom merely because his three friends could no longer muster an argument against him. This is the textual basis on which this new voice is introduced, although many interpreters would argue that this is a later addition. Elihu's compulsion to speak (32:17-22) is part of the prophetic tradition and evidence of the spirit of God compelling him to speak, as in the case of Jeremiah. Job also depicts himself as compelled to speak by his suffering (7:11; 10:1). This is perhaps further evidence that the distinction between "seer" and "sage," discussed above, was blurring in the context of the exilic search for new religious authority.

Elihu represents a more nuanced but still ultimately traditional view of the principle of retribution. One particularly interesting passage in this context is Job 33:23-28: here Elihu develops the earlier theme of a mediator, envisioning an angel with the authority to declare a person *yashar* ("upright"). There is some tension between the angel's defense of the person's *yashar* and the person's own confession of sin and "perverting the right." It seems that Elihu is advocating a sort of middle ground between Job's position and that of the friends, arguing that Job should not abandon hope of a mediator, but that he should also be prepared to confess to having "perverted the right." This is perhaps a more palatable version of the principle of retribution, but in the larger context of the book as well as the larger context of the exile, it still falls short of a satisfactory explanation for the apparent chaos of events.

▌ THE TEXT IN THE INTERPRETIVE TRADITION

Many commentators loathe Elihu (Terrien; Gordis; Newsom; Habel), while a few defend his appeal as a passionate young man who argues from emotion as well as intellect (McKay). Most interpreters agree that this section is a later addition to the text, although some argue that it adds nothing new and should be lifted out entirely. Some think that Elihu merely sets the stage for God's arrival (Timmer); others think his function is more nuanced, an artistic development appropriate to the larger structure of the text (Saadiah; Wilson). They argue that this section heightens the drama of God's appearance in the whirlwind, anticipates "the rather bombastic character of the divine appearance," and prepares the reader for Job's ultimate restoration by indicating that things are not hopeless (Wilson, 359). We might also see in Elihu a response to Job's request in 31:35 that someone would hear him. Saadiah thinks Elihu's advice is sound; the fact that Job does not respond to him indicates that Elihu has won his argument with Job. Alternatively, Thomas Aquinas sees the divine speeches as a rebuttal of Elihu who, like Job, suffers from a lack of wisdom. In any case, these chapters illuminate one more response to Job's suffering, which can certainly be characterized as innovative but which does not fundamentally change either Job's complaint or God's response to it.

Several commentators use Elihu's speeches as a means to resolve the tension in Job. Rashi argues that Job is indeed pious but not perfect; Job's primary problem is hubris, and consequently his failure is an intellectual rather than a moral one. Elihu provides Job a way out of this dilemma by reminding him of the need for humility. Rashi argues that God's speeches confirm Elihu's advice to Job, and Job's response in 42:6 indicates his adoption of perfect humility. Job's suffering is caused by a lack of wisdom and is the price he must pay to acquire wisdom (Maimonides, Gershonides). Aquinas agrees that the major lesson of Job is the importance of acquiring wisdom and the concomitant importance of humility regarding one's own opinions and status. He also sees Job's lack of reverence as an issue that Elihu correctly identifies as problematic. Luther and Calvin pick up this theme. Luther argues that Job's suffering causes him to complain too much and to fail to demonstrate appropriate reverence for God. Job's friends accuse him of sinning before he suffered; Luther thinks Job sinned as a result of his suffering. Calvin takes this further. He is offended by Job's impudence far more than by the content of his speeches. Calvin supports Elihu's argument that suffering is instructive, but argues that Elihu's response is not enough for the impudent Job, which is the reason God must eventually speak to Job directly. Calvin ultimately returns to the theology of the three friends; human beings must simply submit to God's power.

According to Clines, Elihu goes beyond the theology of the other friends and has a more nuanced concept of the suffering of the righteous. God uses suffering to instruct the righteous, and they may choose to listen and experience restoration or they may resist and face death. Elihu challenges the polarization of the righteous and the wicked; one can fall into sin and still be righteous. Elihu also believes that God communicates through the workings of nature, an idea borne out in God's speeches. Ultimately, Clines argues, Elihu doesn't go far enough. He still views suffering as punishment for wrongdoing, even if the ultimate aim is different. Elihu is sympathetic to Job, and his view of the natural world is partly accurate but still implies that human beings are the center of everything. As we will see below, this anthropocentric view of creation proves to be particularly problematic.

With regard to the key passage in 33:23-28, Wilson suggests that Elihu considers himself the messenger; Habel sees this angel as a heavenly mediator, a counterpart to the satan in the prologue. According to Clines, we must assume that the angel is carrying out God's bidding rather than acting in opposition to God, because Elihu argues that God uses suffering for communicative and redemptive purposes. This theme is also present in Job 5:1 and 16:20; Clines sees the mediator here as a prophetic voice whose duty is to convey God's will to human beings, a task that is consistent with other angelic interventions in the Old Testament. Thus the mediator is not someone who intercedes for Job, but someone who proves to Job that God is in the right (Clines 2006). However, in 33:24, the angel does appear to ask God to spare the person from death; we cannot be sure what the ransom is, but the implication is that the word of the angel seems to provide some form of compensation for divine justice. The surprising thing is that deliverance appears to come before repentance; it is a divine act of pity. This is consistent with certain prophetic texts, wherein repentance is often depicted as an act of gratitude for forgiveness rather than a precondition for it. The notion that repentance precedes forgiveness is arguably a Christian anachronism. If we accept this premise, perhaps the ransom is not concrete at all but merely a poetic device (Clines 2006). Job 33:26 seems to imply a thanksgiving offering rather than an atoning sacrifice, which may also be an anticipation of Job's own restoration prior to the sacrifice in Job 42.

The Text in Contemporary Discussion

Elihu is not only young; the word for *young* he uses in Job 32:6 also indicates a lack of social standing. He affirms an initial respect for age and the tradition of wisdom, but the words that follow do not reflect this in practice. One of Elihu's innovations is to propose that the divine spirit gives life to human beings but also provides them with wisdom. In contrast to the idea that observation and experience are the source of wisdom, and therefore that greater age means more opportunities for observation and experience and hence more wisdom, Elihu says that the spirit of God can inspire anyone, including someone as young as he is. Thus Elihu underscores the challenge to authority, another recognized theme in the book.

In Job 33, Elihu seems to find Job's protestations of innocence less problematic than his demands that God answer his complaints. Elihu argues that God does not need to answer Job, and moreover that God speaks to human beings in visions and through suffering, which is meant to correct their behavior. In other words, Job's suffering *is* God's communication, and Job should expect nothing further. However, God is merciful and does sometimes redeem sinners and extend their lives. Retribution need not be final; it is a teaching tool, designed to initiate turning or returning to God. Elihu believes that suffering comes to all people as a means of identifying sin, encouraging repentance, and ultimately restoring the person; suffering is instructive. This is a consistent theme in Job's interpretive tradition, from patristic to medieval to Reformation Christian communities. It is also a theme in contemporary discussions about the reasons for suffering, from the parenting trope that "suffering builds character" to the Christian tradition that encourages the sufferer to identify the ways in which God uses suffering to instill spiritual principles or to test faith. The theology of divine providence becomes especially problematic in this aspect, that suffering must be explained as somehow beneficial to the sufferer. This concept certainly has precedence in the wisdom tradition, but is developed in Job with particular reference to exilic concerns.

Thus, in spite of a certain amount of innovation, Elihu is still basing his theology (if not his speech) on received wisdom rather than on experience. God is sovereign and cannot be swayed by human behavior; human initiative is limited to observation and response, and learning how best to do this constitutes the search for wisdom. The innovation of Job, and one of the great sources of Job's continued relevance in contemporary religious and nonreligious contexts alike, is to undermine this foundation and to base his theology (or lack thereof) on lived experience.

Job 38:1—42:6: Theophany—God Responds and Job Relents

▊ THE TEXT IN ITS ANCIENT CONTEXT

This section begins as God answers Job out of the storm, which is a common setting for a theophany (2 Kgs. 2:1, 11; Pss. 18:7-15; 50:3; Ezek. 1:4; Nah. 1:3; Zech. 9:14) and also calls to mind God's appearance to the Israelites on Mount Sinai at the time of the exodus (Exod. 19:16-20). This detail is particularly important at this juncture, as this is also the first time since the prologue (with the exception of Job 12:9) that the personal name YHWH rather than the generic term for God has been used. In the storm imagery and in the use of the name God revealed to Moses, readers are reminded that this is the God of the covenant, who initiated a special relationship with the Israelites. This lends another dimension of meaning to what follows, as God's redefinition of justice resonates with a wider redefinition of the terms of the covenant as gratuitous rather than retributive.

The speeches of YHWH make use of the ANE genre of onomasticon—lists of items presented to illustrate and embody a particular category. In this case, the purpose seems to be to indicate by extension that there is no part of the created world outside of God's authority; the lists cover wild and domesticated animals, wild and cultivated land, as well as the heights of the heavens, the depths of the sea, and even symbolic places such as Sheol and the "innermost parts" of human beings. The form of these chapters also develops the genre of disputation, demonstrating the knowledge of a wise master against that of a student.

The symbol of the waters, as well as the great beasts Behemoth and Leviathan, represent YHWH's control over chaos. In other ANE texts (such as the Epic of Gilgamesh, the *Enuma Elish*, and the Atrahasis Epic), the waters threatened to overwhelm the gods who originally unleashed them; in the case of YHWH, readers are meant to infer that his strength and control are incontestable.

Some commentators hypothesize that Behemoth may be a hippopotamus, and Leviathan either a whale or a crocodile. Behemoth and Leviathan may simply be ciphers for the strongest land and sea creatures imaginable, thus reinforcing YHWH's dominion over the entire earth. Alternatively, it has been suggested that both beasts represent mythical chaos monsters. Various ancient texts (Herodotus, *Hist.* 2.68–71) and Egyptian hieroglyphs (ceiling of the Ramesseum) depict hippopotami and crocodiles in conjunction or succession; hence their association here is not without precedent. In ancient Egypt, only the pharaohs or the gods could hunt the hippopotamus, and such a hunt was considered a battle against evil. Defeat of the great beast also confirmed the hunter's right to rule. The description of Leviathan is similar to that of Lotan in Ugaritic literature, a mythic sea creature that Baal defeats in order to prove his supremacy. In any case, the primary purpose here is to establish YHWH's control over the forces of chaos and disorder and thus his authority over the created world.

In the wider context of Wisdom literature, the mysteries of the world illustrated in YHWH's speeches are also the means by which human beings confront the mysteries of God. Whereas Job confronts YHWH directly in the whirlwind, Wisdom literature teaches that readers can also confront God in the world around them. Wisdom literature is itself a search for explanation(s) in the context of certain historical periods and events; in this case, it is a search for meaning after the wrenching events of exile. In Wisdom literature, knowledge is a function of relationship and trust; hence Job's relationship with YHWH takes primacy over his ability to answer the questions YHWH poses in these speeches. Experiential reality, not rational speculation, is the foundation of wisdom in this context.

YHWH's speeches shift the tenor of the book from dialogue to examination. YHWH questions Job and challenges Job to instruct him. The initial emphasis is on Job's lack of wisdom. However, emphasis gradually shifts from Job's ignorance to YHWH's power; this is particularly evident in the shift from "who" questions to YHWH's direct references to himself as "I," and then the emphasis on "can you" questions directed at Job beginning in 38:31. Additionally, the focus gradually shifts from Job personally to humanity generally. These shifts in the series of apparently unanswerable questions that YHWH poses to Job seem to be an effort to reorient Job's perspective to take in the wider purview of creation, to see his suffering as a small issue in the grand scheme of things.

The question remains: Are these speeches an effective response to Job's complaint? The key point is that Job appears to accept them as such. While the reasons behind the lack of retributive organizing principles in YHWH's created world are not clearly stated, the affirmation that they are in fact lacking is enough for Job to achieve one of his key goals, his own vindication in the eyes of his friends. It is an interesting compromise. Job still fears God for naught, since his righteousness has not yet been directly affirmed, thus confirming YHWH's victory in the original wager with the satan; nevertheless, the possibility of Job's righteousness exists, and Job appears to accept this as his answer. Job may in fact repent, or not; the ambiguity of Job's response (which we will address in the next section) seems to indicate that YHWH's confirmation of the bankruptcy of retributive theology, rather than Job's response to this confirmation, is the central issue here.

❚ THE TEXT IN THE INTERPRETIVE TRADITION

Job's ultimate response to God in 42:6 has been the subject of much exegetical debate, with many interpreters concluding that the philological ambiguity of the verse is deliberate and so subverts the possibility of closure at the end of the dialogues because these issues cannot be simply resolved. William Morrow identifies three major interpretive possibilities in the meaning of Job's final statement: "Wherefore I retract [or "I submit"] and I repent on [or "on account of"] dust and ashes"; "Wherefore I reject *it* [implied object in 42:5], and I am consoled for dust and ashes"; "Wherefore I reject and forswear dust and ashes" (Morrow, 211–12). Another possibility is presented by Leo Perdue (125–26), among others: "I protest, but feel sorry for dust and ashes." Morrow identifies the major themes of Job's response in accordance with each translation as repentance, consolation, and rejection, respectively. Perdue's translation could be termed the "ironic" or "defiant" response. These basic themes accurately categorize the majority of interpretations of this verse.

Like many other issues in the book of Job, the choice of translation of this verse among interpreters rests primarily on thematic rather than philological grounds. The overall theme(s) identified by an interpreter of Job will affect her or his translation of this ambiguous verse, and her or his translation of this verse will deeply affect the identification of overarching themes in the book.

Perhaps, as in the case of the use of *barak*, this ambiguity is a deliberate literary device designed to subvert simplistic resolution.

Some interpretations argue that the message of YHWH's speeches and Job's responses is that YHWH's justice is greater than human justice (Gutiérrez; von Rad 1972); others argue that the beauty of creation is itself consolation for suffering (Gordis); still others argue that the problem is not innocent suffering but proper conduct in the face of suffering (Clines 2006). While commentators disagree on the overall purpose behind the speeches as well as whether they are an effective response to Job, most agree that the speeches contain both confirmation of YHWH's control over creation and disavowal of retribution as the organizing principle behind YHWH's created world.

None of these interpreters is able to definitively overcome the challenges posed by the opposite perspective, but the very existence of these counterchallenges is what makes the book itself, and particularly the concluding sections, so endlessly compelling. If, as Clines argues, the book of Job was intended to subvert closure, then we are in agreement with von Rad that "truth can be opposed to truth" and that this dissonant opposition can be a positive rather than a negative factor in biblical interpretation (Clines 1990; von Rad 1972, 312).

◼ The Text in Contemporary Discussion

YHWH challenges Job to establish the retributive order he and his friends seem to desire, to reward the righteous and punish the wicked. YHWH's speeches emphasize the point that Job has neither the knowledge nor the power to accomplish this. YHWH has the power and yet does not use it solely to this end. Many interpreters (von Rad 1975; Gutiérrez; Tsevat) have made a leap here to say that the issue is one of grace; human beings are expected to trust God without any guarantee of reward, as Gutiérrez says, "gratuitously." Others (Clines 2003, 2011; Perdue) argue that the text does not clearly indicate this interpretation; its concern seems to be to establish that one cannot assume that those who suffer are wicked. This is an important message, both in the context of Israel's exile and in contemporary contexts of suffering.

YHWH's first speech uses vivid imagery and mythic symbols to establish his control over the world he created. If YHWH does not govern the world according to retribution, it is not because he cannot, but because he will not. YHWH binds the wicked as he binds the sea; the sea is still destructive and indicative of chaos, but within the limits of YHWH's control. The same principle applies to the wicked. Again, in the case of this long list of wild animals, YHWH's power over them and their simultaneous threat to humanity and civilization indicates YHWH's control over forces dangerous to humankind without the elimination of these dangers. YHWH sustains the wild ox and ass in spite of the fact that they are of no use to humankind, as their domesticated relatives are. Images of warhorses and carrion birds also call to mind human death, which is part of the scheme of things and not something to be avoided.

YHWH's second speech focuses more directly on the core of Job's challenge, the issue of justice and just governance of the world. Both speeches emphasize the fact that YHWH's concern is for creation as a whole, not humanity specifically. In contemporary environmental debates, this passage has been used to encourage the development of theologies of the environment as well as more generally to counteract a theology that sees human beings as the focus and pinnacle of creation. YHWH's speeches here support a more symbiotic view of creation, where human beings are part of a natural order rather than tasked with directing or controlling it. By implication, such interpretations also challenge economic principles of unlimited growth as well as the idea that the righteous have the right to material prosperity and protection from chaos (Stokes Musser).

Job 42:7-17: Epilogue—A Righteous Man Restored

■ THE TEXT IN ITS ANCIENT CONTEXT

The burnt offering God demands in Job 42:7-9 indicates that it is Job's friends who have sinned; burnt offerings are characterized as sin offerings. The friends are accused of folly, of rejecting God or refusing to follow the way of the righteous that leads to true wisdom. The implication is that Job has followed the way of true wisdom, in spite of the fact that he complained in Job 3 that this way was hidden from him.

The remainder of the chapter is devoted to a description of Job's restoration. The doubling of all of his possessions, with the exception of his children, is particularly interesting (Job 42:10-12). This is not merely an indication that Job was restored to his former status and then some. It is also evocative of the Israelite law that a thief should restore double what he has taken. In some sense, this seems to be an admission of guilt on God's part, an indication that God was wrong to inflict suffering on Job and therefore owes some form of restitution.

The restoration of Job's family structure is also a key issue in the epilogue (Job 42:13-15). Much is sometimes made of Job's decision to grant his daughters an inheritance along with his sons. However, as Clines points out, daughters were permitted to inherit in the case that a father had no sons, and this condition may simply be a reflection of Job's enormous wealth. Equally, the basis for the daughters' inheritance seems to be their beauty rather than any sense of equity or protofeminist impulse on Job's part (Clines 2011). Van Wolde (1997) thinks this aspect is proof that Job has accepted his lack of control over his own fate and that of his children, typified by his scrupulous offerings on their behalf in the prologue. Job has learned to let go and enjoy things, and this new-found hedonism is the source of his behavior toward his daughters. In any case, the primary point of the text seems to be that Job was ultimately restored, that he even lived double the length of years ascribed to the average mortal (42:16), and by implication that the Israelites could expect a similar restoration.

■ THE TEXT IN THE INTERPRETIVE TRADITION

Interpretive tradition raises two primary issues in the epilogue: What is it that Job has spoken which God identifies as "right," and does Job's material restoration undermine the idea that it is possible to serve God gratuitously?

On the first question, Daniel Timmer (302–3) argues that Job and the friends are praised and chastised respectively for speaking *to* God, not *of* God. The subject of God's approval is Job's repentance or turning, and the subject of his disapproval is the friends' apparent failure to respond in this way to God's appearance; this is illustrated by Job's sin offering on their behalf, as Job facilitates their repentance. He sees the book as an example of wisdom pedagogy, both in form and content. Speaking to God not only involves pious submission but also allows for willful rebellion as a means to achieving the ultimate end of reverence for and "attachment to" God, which both undergirds and surpasses the wisdom enterprise (Timmer, 305).

Other interpreters argue that these verses provide the context in which we learn what was really at stake in Job's struggle: not the understanding or accomplishment of justice, but the understanding and accomplishment of undeserved generosity, as manifested in Job's prayer for his friends, as well as the acknowledgment of undeserved suffering, in that God does not accuse Job of sin. In this sense, Job has spoken of God what is right (Merkur). Still others see in this affirmation a legitimation of anger and lament as responses to suffering that do not undermine integrity or continued relationship with God (West).

Nam translates Job 42:7 as an argument that Job has spoken of God "constructively." The issue for him is one of efficacy rather than one of truth. Job's speeches have afforded God the opportunity to speak in return, and it is this situation rather than the content of Job's speeches that God affirms.

On the second question, some interpreters evade the issue by arguing that the epilogue was originally a separate story, together with the prologue, and so is not meant to address the issues raised in the dialogues and God's subsequent speeches. This assumes, unfairly I think, that the author or editor who put the two stories together was not capable of integrating them properly. Other interpreters have proposed more interesting theories. Gutiérrez interprets Job's restoration as the author(s)'s desire "to give human and material expression of the deep spiritual joy that Job has experienced in his final encounter with God" (12). Clines (2011) argues that it may be the case that Job's restoration is contingent on his willingness to make the required offering on behalf of his friends. This selfless act is confirmation of Job's reorientation, and it is that which is the prerequisite of Job's restoration. Van Wolde (1997, 2002) thinks that Job's restoration is an argument for a type of righteous hedonism, learning to enjoy the blessings of God rather than being bound by legal structures that attempt to delimit and earn such blessings.

Dan Mathewson argues that the epilogue is evidence of Job's struggle with "desymbolization" and "resymbolization." Thus the epilogue is not as simple as it seems; we cannot interpret it in the same symbolic world Job previously inhabited, because the poetic dialogues have intervened between the two. A goal of the survivor of trauma is "symbolic wholeness" or, in Job's case, "resymbolization," yet the divine speeches indicate that there can be no stasis in a world where chaos is limited but not eliminated. Perhaps the book of Job indicates that symbolic wholeness itself is impossible; it is not simply the previous symbolic wholeness of Job's world that is rejected, but any symbolic wholeness at all. Like suffering itself, the book of Job can never be fully synthesized.

It is also significant that this restoration of Job's wealth and family would have been understood among his friends and detractors as evidence of God's favor. This public vindication is something that Job has been longing for since the third chapter, and perhaps this is less a material reward for Job than a confirmation of the "rightness" of his behavior, and consequently of the possibility that a sufferer can be righteous and that a mortal can contend with God.

◼ THE TEXT IN CONTEMPORARY DISCUSSION

At the end of the book, we are left with as many questions as we had at the beginning. Job accepts his restoration as compensation for his suffering, or at least we must assume he does, since we hear no more from him directly. Job's friends are castigated but ultimately forgiven, and the process of their expiation is itself evidence of Job's reorientation away from retribution and toward gratuitousness as an organizing principle of life in the world YHWH has created. In one sense, Job has certainly been right: he complained that YHWH does not govern the world according to the principle of retribution, and YHWH's speeches confirmed that this is so. Job's acceptance, whether we categorize it as repentance, consolation, rejection, or silent defiance, nevertheless confirms that retributive justice is not something human beings can expect from YHWH. Van Wolde (1997) argues that the possibility of disinterested belief comes after God's speeches reorient Job's perspective, not before. It is this transition, rather than Job's initial patience, that proves the outcome of the divine wager. Job is fundamentally a story of progress toward the possibility of gratuitousness. Thus the epilogue does not simply reinscribe the principle of retribution. It leaves open the possibility that restoration, blessing, and vindication are things Job, and perhaps the exiled Israelites and contemporary readers as well, may hope for, although not something that can be earned. Just as Job's faith is or has become disinterested, God's blessings are also disinterested, and a person should enjoy to the fullest those blessings God chooses to bestow.

All interpreters see something of themselves in Job. This is no less true for Augustine or Maimonides than it is for Gutiérrez or Clines. This is a primary reason why Job is considered one of the great works of ancient literature and has been influential well beyond the religious traditions for which it is considered Scripture; it shows each reader something of her- or himself, and in so doing, it also points to the truth that all interpretation is a subjective endeavor.

Works Cited

Calvin, John. 1952. *Sermons from Job*. Edited by L. Nixon. Grand Rapids: Eerdmans.

Clines, David J. A. 1989. *Job 1–20*. WBC 17. Dallas: Word.

———. 1990. "Deconstructing the Book of Job." In *The Bible as Rhetoric: Studies in Biblical Persuasion and Credibility*, ed. M. Warner. 65–80. London: Routledge.

———. 2003. "Does the Book of Job Suggest that Suffering Is Not a Problem?" In *Weisheit in Israel: Beiträge des Symposiums, "Das Alte Testament und die Kultur der Moderne,"* anlässlich des 100. Geburtstags Gerhard von Rads (1901-1971), Heidelberg, 18.-21. Oktober 2001, edited by David J. A. Clines, Hermann Lichtenberger, and Hans-Peter Müller, 93–110. Münster: LIT Verlag.

———. 2006. *Job 21–37*. WBC 18a. Nashville: Thomas Nelson.

———. 2011. *Job 38–42*. WBC 18b. Nashville: Thomas Nelson.

Dussel, Enrique. 1983. "The People of El Salvador: The Communal Sufferings of Job." *Concilium* 169:61–68.

Gershonides. 1946. *Commentary on Job*. Translated by Abraham Lassen. New York: Bloch.

Goodman, L. E. 1988. *The Book of Theodicy: Translation and Commentary on the Book of Job by Saadiah Ben Joseph Al-Fayyumi*. New Haven/London: Yale University Press.

Gordis, Robert. 1978. *The Book of God and Man: A Study of Job*. Chicago: University of Chicago Press.

Gravett, Emily O. 2012. "Biblical Responses: Past and Present Retellings of the Enigmatic Mrs. Job." *Biblical Interpretation* 20: 97–125.

Gregory the Great. 1850. *Morals on the Book of Job.* 4 Vols. Trans. Charles Marriott. Oxford: Parker.

Gutiérrez, Gustavo. 1987. *On Job: God-Talk and the Suffering of the Innocent.* Translated by Matthew J. O'Connell. Maryknoll, NY: Orbis.

Habel, Norman C. 2004. "The Verdict on/of God at the End of Job." *Concilium* 4:2–38.

Hartley, John E. 1988. *The Book of Job.* NICOT. Grand Rapids: Eerdmans.

Janzen, J. Gerald. 2009. *At the Scent of Water: The Ground of Hope in the Book of Job.* Grand Rapids: Eerdmans.

Johnson, Timothy Jay. 2009. *Now My Eye Sees You: Unveiling an Apocalyptic Job.* Sheffield: Sheffield Phoenix.

Jones, Scott C. 2009. *Rumors of Wisdom: Job 28 and Poetry.* Berlin: de Gruyter.

Klein, Lillian R. 1995. "Job and the Womb: Text about Men, Subtext about Women." In *A Feminist Companion to Wisdom Literature*, edited by Athalya Brenner, 186–200. Sheffield: Sheffield Academic.

Luther, Martin. 1960. *Preface to the Old Testament.* Vol. 35, *Luther's Works*, edited by Theodore Bachmann. Philadelphia: Muhlenberg.

Magallanes, Sophia. 2011. "Bringing Wisdom Back Down to Earth: A Wisdom Reading of Job 28." PhD diss., Azusa Pacific University.

Magdalene, F. Rachel. 2006. "Job's Wife as Hero: A Feminist-Forensic Reading of the Book of Job." *BibInt* 14, no. 3:209–58.

Maimonides, Moses. 1956. *Guide for the Perplexed.* Translated by M. Friedlander. New York: Dover.

Mathewson, Dan. 2006. *Death and Survival in the Book of Job: Desymbolization and Traumatic Experience.* New York: T&T Clark.

McKay, J. W. 1979. "Elihu—A Proto-Charismatic?" *ExpTim* 70:167–71.

Merkur, Dan. 2004. "Psychotherapeutic Change in the Book of Job." In *From Genesis to Apocalyptic Vision.* Vol. 2, *Psychology and the Bible: A New Way to Read the Scriptures*, edited by J. Harold Ellens and Wayne G. Rollins, 119–39. Westport, CT: Praeger.

Morrow, William S. 1986. "Consolation, Rejection, and Repentance in Job 42:6." *JBL* 105, no. 2:211–25.

Nadar, Sarojini. 2003. "Re-Reading Job in the Midst of Suffering in the HIV/AIDS Era: How Not to Talk of God." *OTE* n.s. 16, no. 2:343–57.

Nam, Duck-Woo. 2003. *Talking about God: Job 42:7-9 and the Nature of God in the Book of Job.* New York: Peter Lang.

Negri, Antonio. 2009. *The Labor of Job: The Biblical Text as a Parable of Human Labor.* Translated by Matteo Mandarini. Edited by Roland Boer. Durham, NC: Duke University Press.

Newsom, Carol A. 2003. *The Book of Job: A Contest of Moral Imaginations.* Oxford: Oxford University Press.

Ngwa, Kenneth. 2009. "Did Job Suffer for Nothing? The Ethics of Piety, Presumption and the Reception of Disaster in the Prologue of Job." *JSOT* 33, no. 3:359–80.

Perdue, Leo G. 2007. *Wisdom Literature: A Theological History.* Louisville: Westminster John Knox.

Pope, Marvin H. 1965. *Job.* AYB. New Haven: Yale University Press.

Pyeon, Yohan. 2003. *You Have Not Spoken What Is Right about Me: Intertextuality in the Book of Job.* New York: Peter Lang.

Rayan, Samuel. 2006. "Wrestling in the Night." In *Voices from the Margin: Interpreting the Bible in the Third World*, edited by R. S. Sugirtharajah, 407–28. 3rd ed. Maryknoll, NY: Orbis.

Sitaramayya, K. B. 2001. *The Marvel and Mystery of Pain: A New Interpretation of the Book of Job.* Bangalore: MCC.

Stokes Musser, Sarah. 2012. "Comfort in the Whirlwind? Job, Creation, and Environmental Degradation." *WW* 32, no. 3:286–93

Tam, Edman P. C. 2002. "Silence of God and God of Silence." *AJT* 16, no. 1:152–63.

Tamez, Elsa. 1986. "A Letter to Job." In *New Eyes for Reading: Biblical and Theological Reflections by Women from the Third World*, edited by John S. Pobee and Barbara Von Wartenburg-Potter, 50–52. Geneva: WCC.

———. 2004. "From Father of the Needy to Brother of Jackals and Companion of Ostriches: A Meditation on Job." *Concilium* 4:103–11.

Terrien, Samuel. 1957. *Job: Poet of Existence*. New York: Bobbs-Merrill.

Thomas Aquinas. 1989. *The Literal Exposition on Job: A Scriptural Commentary Concerning Providence*. Translated by Anthony Damico. Edited by Martin D. Yaffe. Atlanta: Scholars Press.

Timmer, Daniel. 2009. "God's Speeches, Job's Responses, and the Problem of Coherence in the Book of Job: Sapiential Pedagogy Revisited." *CBQ* 71:286–305.

Tsevat, Matitiahu. 1981. *The Meaning of the Book of Job and Other Biblical Studies*. New York: Ktav.

van Wolde, Ellen. 1995. "The Development of Job: Mrs. Job as Catalyst." In *A Feminist Companion to Wisdom Literature*, edited by Athalya Brenner, 201–21. Sheffield: Sheffield Academic.

———. 1997. *Mr. and Mrs. Job*. Translated by John Bowden. London: SCM.

———. 2002. "Different Perspectives on Faith and Justice: The God of Jacob and the God of Job." *Concilium* 1:17–23.

Vicchio, Stephen J. 2006a. *The Image of the Biblical Job: A History*. Vol. 1, *Job in the Ancient World*. Eugene, OR: Wipf & Stock.

———. 2006b. *The Image of the Biblical Job: A History*. Vol. 2, *Job in the Medieval World*. Eugene, OR: Wipf & Stock.

———. 2006c. *The Image of the Biblical Job: A History*. Vol. 3, *Job in the Modern World*. Eugene, OR: Wipf & Stock.

von Rad, Gerhard. 1966. "Job XXXVIII and Ancient Egyptian Wisdom." In *The Problem of the Hexateuch and Other Essays*, 281–91. Translated by E. W. Trueman Dicken. Edinburgh: Oliver & Boyd.

———. 1972. *Wisdom in Israel*. London: SCM.

———. 1975. *Old Testament Theology*. Vol. 1, *The Theology of Israel's Historical Traditions*. Translated by D. M. G. Stalker. London: SCM.

West, Gerald O. 2008. "The Poetry of Job as a Resource for the Articulation of Embodied Lament in the Context of HIV and AIDS in South Africa." In *Lamentations in Ancient and Contemporary Contexts*, edited by N. C. Lee and C. Mandolfo, 195–214. Atlanta: Society of Biblical Literature.

West, Gerald O., with Bongi Zengele. 2004. "Reading Job 'Positively' in the Context of HIV/AIDS in South Africa." *Concilium* 4:112–24.

Wilson, Gerald H. 2007. *Job*. New International Bible Commentary. Grand Rapids: Baker Books.

PSALMS

W. Derek Suderman

Introduction

The Psalms have long been a treasured part of Jewish and Christian Scripture, functioning as a songbook, devotional and liturgical resource, source of comfort, and basis for messianic hope, as well as a window into ancient worship and liturgy. With its range of emotions and evocative language, the Psalms continue to "speak" to and for people in a fresh and compelling way in the contemporary world. In the words of Dietrich Bonhoeffer: "Whenever the Psalter is abandoned, an incomparable treasure is lost to the Christian church. With its recovery will come unexpected power" (Bonhoeffer, 162).

The term *psalm*, from the Greek *psalmos*, is *mizmor* in the Hebrew, referring to song or instrumental music. The Hebrew title, *sepher tehillim*, or "book of praises," underscores its concluding emphasis. Within the threefold Jewish Scripture (*Tanakh*), the book of Psalms is the first book in the "Writings"; it also plays a vital role within Christian Scripture, given that New Testament writers cite the Psalms—and Isaiah—more than any other scrolls.

Far from homogenous, however, the book of Psalms represents an anthology with a long compositional history, including material emerging from early in the preexilic period to well after the postexilic return to the land. Just as a contemporary hymnal gathers material from previous ones, remnants of prior collections can also be found (see 72:20). A recurring blessing and "amen" formula divides the Psalms, in their current shape, into five "books"—see Pss. 41:13; 72:18-19; 89:52; 106:48—similar to the five books of Moses, Genesis–Deuteronomy (Mays, 42).

While lament dominates the first three books of the Psalms (1–89), the tone shifts to praise and thanksgiving in the final two (90–150). The Dead Sea Scrolls, dating from 250 BCE to 70 CE, suggest that books 1–3 were already stable by this point, while more variation in order and content appears in books 4–5 (Wilson, 120–21).

The Language and Genres of the Psalms

The Psalms employ poetic language, whose perhaps most striking feature is the consistent appearance of parallel lines. The psalmists employ "antithetical" parallelism, on the one hand, to make a stark contrast.

> for the LORD watches over the way of the righteous,
> but the way of the wicked will perish. (1:6)

"Synonymous" parallelism, on the other hand, seems to say the same thing twice.

> For I know my transgressions,
>   and my sin is ever before me. (51:3)

Even here, however, there is a slight difference between the two lines, and even an "intensification" from one line to the next. Reading the space between the two lines as "how much more so" allows the reader to explore the more subtle difference between transgressions and sin on one hand and "knowing" and having my sin constantly before me on the other (Alter, 11).

The Psalms also use metaphor and imagery to great effect; the enemies are lions and bears, God is a rock or a mother hen protecting her brood, and so on. In addition, the Psalms employ similar vocabulary and return to certain motifs again and again. Indeed, repeating the same or related words can be used to signal emphasis, organize a particular psalm, or make intertextual connections. For this reason, this commentary will draw attention to key terms and refer the reader to places with linguistic and thematic connections to the passage under consideration.

Finally, Hermann Gunkel's work in the early twentieth century was a watershed in studying psalms, since he initiated the systematic investigation of their patterned language and so identified various genres or types (see Gunkel 1967; 1998). Although the sequence and specific elements within psalms vary, characteristics can be identified for lament, thanksgiving, hymns, royal, wisdom, and torah psalms (see Gerstenberger 1988, 9–21).

Lament or prayer (*tefillah*) psalms speak persuasively to convince God and others to respond favorably to the psalmist. They generally include an invocation to YHWH, a description of distress, and an appeal for help (see Psalm 6). These psalms often contain imprecations that call on God to punish the enemy and usually conclude with a statement of confidence or affirmation that YHWH has heard. Approximately one-third of the Psalter consists of laments, far and away the most numerous genre in the book.

Thanksgiving (*todah*) psalms publicly acknowledge answered prayer before a social audience. They typically describe a past situation of distress, how the psalmist called out to God, and the deliverance experienced (see Psalm 116). Thanksgiving psalms often conclude with an invitation to the social audience to join the psalmist in recognizing God's deliverance.

Hymns or psalms of praise (*tehillim*) typically recount God's attributes, deeds, and steadfast love, whether for Zion, Israel, humanity generally, or the broader creation. At its most basic, the psalmist cries *halelu yah* ("Praise YHWH").

Royal psalms relate to the king but do not constitute a unique genre; rather, they build on others, including lament (Psalm 21), thanksgiving (Psalm 18), or hymns (Psalm 2). Though some royal psalms have been recognized as messianic within both the Jewish and Christian traditions (Psalm 2), others understood as messianic are not self-evidently "royal" (22).

Wisdom psalms contain distinctive vocabulary, forms, and even organizational features; Psalm 119 is structured as an elaborate acrostic. Some scholars have attributed these elements to individual study and see wisdom material as reflecting primarily written rather than oral language, while others attribute such elements to liturgical changes in a postexilic setting.

Like royal psalms, torah psalms can be identified by content but reflect a mixture of distinct genre types (wisdom in Psalms 1; 119; a hymn in Psalm 19). Despite their relatively small numbers, the strategic location of royal, wisdom, and torah psalms within the organization of the Psalter highlight their significance.

Determining the ancient settings for various genres has proven more difficult than describing their genre characteristics, in part because psalm material was modified and reused in different contexts over time. The setting of individual laments has proven particularly vexing, with proposals ranging from individuals in distress anywhere (Gunkel 1967, 19–20), spoken by the king in a national assembly (Mowinckel, 1:225–28), used in judicial proceedings in the temple (Schmidt), and spoken by individuals in small, liturgical gatherings (Gerstenberger 1988, 13–14). While the first and last of these options hold the most promise, certainty eludes us.

In any case, the implied rhetorical setting that permits the psalmist to address both God and a broader social audience proves most significant for the ancient and contemporary function of these psalms, whatever the precise ancient setting(s) from which they emerged.

"Voice(s)" in the Psalms

While psalms are often described as prayers and therefore considered direct communication between humans and God, they consistently reflect a social element. While at times psalmists call on different groups to respond (Ps. 118:1-4), even individual laments include the three components of God, the psalmist, and others (Westermann, 169).

While the psalmist's own voice is primary, he often quotes the hostile speech of adversaries or articulates the words of support he wants others to articulate. Even the voice of God appears periodically, which, in their ancient setting, would have been articulated by a cultic functionary on behalf of the divine. Within the psalms, we hear the voice of each of the parties Westermann identifies.

Thus it is helpful to think of psalms as *oral* speech, as Gunkel suggested, which is said out loud and so able to address both a divine and social audience. The psalms also represent *potential* speech not limited to ancient contexts but reembodied in the contemporary world. As will be seen repeatedly, both potential and danger lie in how these words are used; contemporary religious communities who claim the Psalms as part of their Scriptures play the essential role of discerning among competing and even contradictory claims (Suderman 2012, 214).

In contemporary use, people tend to monopolize the "voice" of the Psalms by consistently casting themselves individually or collectively as the speaking subject(s). While often appropriate, this can become particularly discordant when psalms call on God's vengeance to destroy the enemy, leading some readers to wonder why such material is in the Bible at all (see Psalms 69; 109; 137). Christian lectionaries commonly skip over offending verses or omit entire psalms (Holladay, 304–15), in part because it is not clear how these can legitimately represent *our* words.

A potential antidote to this tendency lies in recognizing the various social roles reflected in the Psalms beyond that of the speaking subject and then identifying with those who *hear* rather than speak these words. For instance, rather than functionally eliminating calls for God to destroy the enemy, we may fruitfully consider whose contemporary voice such words may represent, and even when they may be appropriately spoken about us. More than merely a window into ancient culture and liturgy, the Psalms also function as a mirror for looking at ourselves more deeply.

A second and related temptation lies in monopolizing the "voice" of legitimate interpretation. While the strength of Western scholarship has been its insistence on placing psalms in their ancient contexts, this focus has also insisted on a historical and cultural gap between the ancient world and our own. While helpful, this emphasis can also prompt less attention to the contemporary function of this material within religious communities and even a pejorative view of "precritical" or non-Western perspectives.

Instead, we do well to recognize insights from devotional and liturgical readings, the broader history of interpretation, as well as global and lay perspectives. Indeed, the way in which many continue to read the Psalms reflects a closer affinity to the broader history of interpretation than Western biblical scholarship. As we attend to the gains of Western scholarship, we should also consider its limitations and drawbacks.

David and the Psalms

The Psalms have traditionally been associated with David, the "sweet singer of Israel," based on his association with music and prominence in the headings of the Psalter. While several headings relate specific psalms to contexts within his life (see Psalms 3; 51), the psalms themselves provide few clues as to their historical settings. Several other figures appear within the Psalm headings, including the "sons of Korah," Asaph, Solomon (72; 127), and even Moses (90).

With the emergence of Western biblical criticism, scholars began to question and then largely reject the headings as accurate depictions of authorship, and so sought other authors and historical contexts. Gunkel and his followers shifted the focus of Psalms scholarship away from authorship to determining the genre and social settings of particular psalms. The discovery of ancient texts at Ugarit, written in a Canaanite dialect very similar to biblical Hebrew, provided direct parallels to vocabulary and grammatical structures in the Psalms.

In recent decades, "canonical criticism" has prompted interest in the shape and organization of the Psalms and has reinvigorated discussion of the role and significance of David vis-à-vis the Psalms. Where Brevard Childs described the Psalm headings as representing early "midrashic exegesis" (Childs 1971), Gerald Wilson noted that "orphan" psalms were increasingly linked to a biblical figure or setting, with the number of "David" psalms increasing from the Hebrew to the Septuagint, Qumran, and Syriac Psalters (Wilson, 155–56); in effect, the Psalms became *more* linked to David over time rather than less so. Indeed, the Hebrew phrase *ledavid*, usually rendered "of David," was understood as the dative "concerning" or "about David" in the Greek Septuagint.

Thus, rather than claims of authorship, these headings function in a later stage of composition to place the psalms within the broader context of other scriptural scrolls, where they function as ancient "cross-references" to orient the reader (Mays, 11–13). To claim this element as reflecting historical authorship on one hand or to dismiss it as "unoriginal" on the other fails to recognize the ancient function and contemporary potential of this element.

The "Ancient Context(s)" of the Psalms

The long and complex compositional history of the Psalms complicates what we refer to as their "ancient context(s)." For instance, "ancient context" could mean either the earliest level of material within the psalm, where and when it was written, or the social setting in which it was initially used. It could also refer to a specific psalm's broader cultural context, including its radical transformation from sun or Baal worship to celebrating torah or praising YHWH (Psalms 19; 29). Alternatively, "ancient context" could also refer to the enhanced function a psalm could take beyond its original intent by its location within the larger scroll, as when a preexilic royal enthronement psalm prompts messianic expectation after exile (Psalm 2).

Thus, for our purposes, "ancient context" has at least a dual meaning: the setting in which the psalm arose or was originally used (its ancient social setting and function) and the role of a particular psalm within the book of Psalms itself. As a cathedral can be constructed, modified, and continue to function over time, it may be best to recognize that psalms have the potential to pass through and function differently within multiple contexts.

Psalms 1–2: Introduction

■ THE TEXT IN ITS ANCIENT CONTEXT

Psalms 1–2 function as a joint introduction that orients the book to wisdom, torah, and messianic categories (Mays, 42–44).

The first psalm begins: "Happy is the one who does *not* walk . . . , stand . . . , or sit," before introducing its positive counterpoint as those who "delight in the law of YHWH [*torath yhwh*]." While the psalm primarily employs wisdom terminology (happy, advice, way), it thus also introduces the key phrase that introduces each of the Psalter's torah psalms (Pss. 1:2; 19:7; 119:1). The idyllic scene then builds on wordplay, where both trees and humans "prosper/flourish" (1:3), and the psalm ends with characteristic wisdom vocabulary, contrasting the "ways" and fates of the righteous and wicked. The psalmist's concluding confidence introduces a basic tension, since later laments reflect settings where the righteous do *not* prosper and the wicked appear to triumph (see Psalms 9–10; 73).

Psalm 2 is a royal psalm that portrays the opposition of rival kings to God and divine support for "his anointed" (*al meshiho*); while the righteous "meditate" on the law (1:2), the peoples "meditate" on emptiness (2:1). Divine first-person speech underscores God's connection with Zion and emphatically describes the king as "my son," language central to the Davidic covenant and common in the ancient Near East, but it is unique here in the Psalms (2:2; cf. 2 Sam. 7:14; Mays, 47). Scholars have proposed the initial setting for this material as an enthronement festival that celebrates the monarchy, similar to those found in other ancient Near Eastern sources. In any case, Psalm 2 depicts the king as a militaristic leader, which prompts a warning directly aimed at would-be rivals. The concluding "Happy is the one . . ." introduces the only wisdom element in this otherwise royal psalm, which both links back to the start of Psalm 1 (1:1) and introduces "refuge," a repeated motif in the book. Though initially a royal enthronement song, the fall of the monarchy combined with the Davidic covenant promising a descendant on the throne "forever" transformed it into a messianic one (Psalm 89; 2 Sam. 7:11-17).

■ The Text in the Interpretive Tradition

While Christian interpreters identify the "anointed" as Christ, they differ in how this is understood. Both Origen and Jerome saw Jesus speaking in Ps. 2:3, with the latter reading "chains" as "the heavy burden of the law." Luther, however, saw this Psalm as David speaking of Christ, with the "rod of iron" representing "the holy Gospel, which is Christ's royal scepter in his Church." Rather than reading it as directly about Christ, Calvin read Psalm 2 as David depicting his own rule, which then becomes a "type" for Christ (Holladay, 169–72, 193, 197).

While the church fathers' interpretations of the Psalms articulate a consistent polemic against the Jews that implies awareness of a Jewish audience, there is little corresponding material from [redundant?] rabbinic sources; though it contains some material reaching back to the third century, the *Midrash on the Psalms* (*Midrash Tehillim*) emerged in the thirteenth century (Gillingham, 45).

While Rashi articulates his own interpretation of Psalm 2, he also notes that rabbinic tradition read it in light of the Messiah (Holladay, 151). Thus the debate between the emerging Jewish and Christian traditions lay not in whether Psalm 2 was messianic, but rather in whether Jesus fulfilled this role. While Psalm 2 is a significant "messianic" psalm within the Christian tradition, it does not appear in Jewish liturgy (cf. Psalms 72; 110; Holladay, 144).

■ The Text in Contemporary Discussion

Messianic readings of the Bible have had long-standing effects. The biblical claim of YHWH's strong support for the king and expectation of dominion has been used to support the "divine right" of kings and the imperialistic aspirations of Christendom. Contemporary claims to national "exceptionalism" reflect a similar tendency to read one's own country as the rightful heir to the status of ancient Israel and thus claim divine sanction for military and socioeconomic domination (see Psalm 18).

The tendency to read into the first-century context later assumptions regarding the parting of the ways between Jews and (gentile) Christians can cloud the mutual understanding of contemporary members of both groups. For instance, on one hand it is problematic to treat first-century documents claiming Jesus to be the Messiah as "Christian," since Jesus' disciples and most (if not all) New Testament writers were Jews; on the other, it is also problematic to treat Jesus' fulfillment of messianic expectation as self-evident (see Psalm 22; Luke 24:13–35). Greater recognition of the diversity of Judaism(s) in the first century as well as the interpretive methods and assumptions of various groups hold promise for improving our understanding of both Jewish and Christian traditions.

Psalms 3–8: Refuge in the Midst of Enemies

◼ THE TEXT IN ITS ANCIENT CONTEXT

Psalms 3–8 are each identified as "of David," which both distinguishes them from the introduction and inaugurates the Davidic collection extending through books 1–2 of the Psalms (3–41; 42–72). In so doing, this section begins the lament that dominates the first three books of the Psalms (3–89) and also reflects the three subjects intrinsic to lament: God, the psalmist, and others (Westermann, 169).

Psalm 3 begins with the invocation "Oh YHWH" characteristic of lament psalms that, in a polytheistic context reflected in Babylonian parallels, immediately identifies the specific deity being addressed. In characteristic fashion, this invocation leads to a description of distress, in this case being surrounded by enemies, and a call for God to act or intervene (3:1-2, 7). This psalm also reflects the dynamic of shifting to address various audiences that appears repeatedly in the Psalms, speaking first *to* YHWH, then *about* God, and finally *to* the divine once again. The final verse reflects a shift in tone characteristic of lament, deriving confidence from articulating pain and being heard. Heard in light of the heading's setting of David's fleeing Absalom, David's grief at his son's death may highlight the relative restraint of the psalm (2 Sam. 18:33); "break the teeth" proves defensive and less strident than appeals to destroy the enemy elsewhere (cf. Psalms 109; 137). Psalm 4, which also complains of enemies, again reflects a shift in audience where the psalmist calls on his social audience to speak against his ostracized status (4:2-6). By exhorting listeners to "trust in YHWH," this section also introduces a significant motif in the Psalms.

Psalm 5 addresses God persistently, identifying slander and wicked speech as its key concern (5:9; cf. 3:2; 4:6). The psalmist calls on God to allow the rebellious enemies' schemes to fall on themselves, in contrast to those "who take refuge in you" (5:10-11; cf. 2:11). References to God as "king" and to the "holy temple" become significant motifs elsewhere (93, 99).

Psalm 6 again speaks of enemies, although the major concern here appears to be sickness (6:2); Psalm 30 gives thanks for deliverance from such a context. Where the previous addressed God saying "you hate all *evildoers*" (*po'ale 'aven*, 5:5), here the psalmist explicitly challenges his social adversaries: "Depart from me, all you *evildoers*" (6:8; cf. 4:2); the NRSV's rendering of the latter as "workers of evil" obscures this connection. The confidence that God has heard "my *prayer* [*tefillah*]" prompts the change in tone and concluding conviction that the enemies will be stopped (6:8-10).

Psalm 7 again claims refuge in YHWH amid enemies. In addition to characteristic calls for God to "rise up" and "awake," the psalmist's claim of innocence and integrity provides the basis for God's attention (7:3-5, 8; cf. Job 1:1; 9:20-22). The appeal to God as judge functions alongside the conviction that the wicked's own designs will entrap them (7:9). With no indication that the situation has changed, Psalms 3–7 each conclude with a shift in mood and a statement of confidence or affirmation. In their ancient setting, this change may have responded to a cultic official's "oracle of salvation" affirming the initial petition.

Psalm 8 reiterates divine sovereignty, linked to creation rather than the king (cf. Psalm 2). In language reminiscent of Genesis, the psalmist marvels that the creator of the universe "remembers" them. The transfer of royal attributes to humanity (glory, honor, crown, dominion) reflects God's care for human creatures despite hardship, challenging ancient conceptions of the human role as slaves at the whim of the gods, as reflected in the Babylonian creation account.

▮ THE TEXT IN THE INTERPRETIVE TRADITION

Psalm 8 has been employed repeatedly within both the Jewish and Christian traditions, but in divergent ways; what has served as a "hymn of creation" for Jews has been a messianic psalm for Christians. Translation emerged as a point of dispute from the beginning, particularly over *ben 'adam* ("son of man") in 8:4. This psalm has long prompted messianic interpretation within the Christian tradition, beginning already in the New Testament (see Ps. 8:2; Matt. 11:25; 21:16; Luke 10:21). Perhaps the most striking example appears in Ephesians 1, which claims "that the one who sits at the right hand of God (Ps. 110:1) is the one who has put all things in subjection under his feet (Ps. 8:6)" (Gillingham, 3–4, 22; Eph. 1:20-23).

Psalm 6 has also had particular significance as one of seven "penitential psalms" within the Christian tradition (cf. Psalm 51).

▮ THE TEXT IN CONTEMPORARY DISCUSSION

While psalms are often described as prayers to God (Brueggemann, 34), Psalms 3–7 prove characteristic of laments in that they consistently address a social as well as divine audience and so reflect multiple social roles that enhance their function as potential speech (Suderman 2010, 165–69).

Thus, while "evildoers" have been associated with magic workers in the ancient world (Mowinckel, 2:4–8), they can also be read as those who benefit from the social, economic, political, and military configuration of our globalized world. Beyond providing words to speak, laments also provide lessons in empathy for the voices of others and the opportunity to recognize where we may even have functioned as an "enemy" or been part of a system perpetrating such misdeeds (see Psalm 141). Thus the contemporary function of lament requires communities of discernment that do not identify exclusively with the speaker but are committed to attend to and evaluate the laments they hear (Suderman 2012, 212–17).

Finally, while the elevated status of humans in Psalm 8 represents good news for victims of abuse and those on the socioeconomic margins, overemphasis on human "dominion" can also provide ideological cover for minimizing the human impact on the environment. Biblical depictions of creation where humanity does *not* lie at the center may be particularly important in light of contemporary ecological concerns (see Psalm 104; Job 38–41).

Psalms 9–16: Confronting Hostile Speech

▮ THE TEXT IN ITS ANCIENT CONTEXT

Psalms 9–10, joined as one psalm in the Septuagint, reflect an acrostic poem (see Psalm 119) that has been disrupted by a middle section, calling into question the confidence of the outside frame (9:17—10:10; Gerstenberger 1988, 72–73). Psalm 9 begins with thanksgiving for past deliverance that underscores God's continuing role as king and, therefore, judge (9:4-16; cf. 89; 93–99). While Psalm 9 continues the confident tone of Psalm 8, God blots out the "memory" (*zikram*) of the wicked and "remembers" (*zakar*) them for judgment (9:5-6, 12; cf. 8:4).

The middle portion, however, articulates lament and abandonment. Here the way of the wicked endures (10:5), offering three quotations of the enemy reflecting "dismissals of God and assertions of self-sufficiency and autonomy" (Brueggemann, 225; see 10:6, 11, 13). The initial confidence that God will not "forget" (*shakach*; Ps. 9:12, 18) contrasts with the nations who "*forget* God" and the wicked who believe that "God has *forgotten*" (9:17; 10:11). While the psalmist reasserts God's commitment to the "cry of the afflicted," the success of the wicked prompts the call for YHWH to "rise up" and "not *forget*" (Ps. 10:12) and so exercise divine kingship by executing justice (10:15-18).

Psalm 11 builds on God's role as a judging king (11:1, 4-7), but addresses a plural, social "you" and never God directly. Psalm 12 returns to appeal directly to God for help from hurtful speech, again quoting the adversary (12:4). The voice of YHWH responds directly to the beginning of this psalm and the earlier call: "I will now *rise up*" (v. 5; cf. 9:19; 10:12). While salvation oracles generally lie outside of the psalms themselves (Gerstenberger 1988, 81), the divine "I" here counteracts the adversarial speech of the enemies.

Psalm 13, the shortest lament in the Psalter, provides a characteristic example of this genre and repeats its basic question four times: "How long . . . ?" This emphatic repetition underscores the sense that God has "forgotten" and "hidden your face" (Ps. 13:1-2; cf. 10:11). Psalm 14, virtually identical to Psalm 53 in the "Elohistic Psalter" (Psalms 42–83; see below), both quotes the apathy of the fool and directly challenges those seeking to "confound the plans of the poor" (14:1, 6; cf. 6:8), providing a scathing indictment of contemporaries (14:3-4). The last verse of Psalm 14 also employs language familiar from the prophets to directly address the despair of exile (Jer. 30:3; Amos 9:14; Gerstenberger 1988, 220).

Psalm 15 reflects an entrance liturgy centered on requirements to access the temple (cf. Psalm 24). Hope for "deliverance . . . from Zion" (Ps. 14:7) leads into questions by worshipers seeking to enter sacred space and the response of cultic functionaries (15:1-5). While emphasis on ethical requirements rather than ritual elements may reflect a later reinterpretation of an earlier liturgy (Gerstenberger 1988, 88), they also contrast directly with the wicked in previous psalms; those allowed access are right-doers (*po'el tsedeq*; cf. 5:5; 6:8; 14:4); speak truth (*'emeth*) "in his heart" (cf. Psalm 9); does not slander (cf. 12:4); and so on (15:2-5).

Finally, Psalm 16 reiterates confidence that again contrasts the psalmist with the wicked. Whereas others say "there is no God" (14:1), the psalmist "takes refuge," saying, "you are my Lord" (16:1-2). The psalmist, responding in part to the earlier frustration over the prosperity of the wicked (10:4), repeats that he has chosen YHWH, a choice that has prompted gladness, security, and recognition of "the path of life" (16:9-11).

■ The Text in the Interpretive Tradition

Where Origen generally sees enemies allegorically as "vices" and other "enemies of the moral and spiritual life," an increasingly gentile church also used this vocabulary against the Jews. Nonetheless, "while the church fathers were not slow to identify their enemies, they were usually reluctant to curse them or to establish precedents for other Christians to do so" (Thompson, 54–56).

In light of ongoing research into the early differentiation between emergent Judaism and early Christianity as well as the long-standing negative effects of such exegesis, we do well to heed Thompson's caution: "*The history of Christian anti-Jewish exegesis . . . ought to stand as an object lesson of what* not *to do with the Psalms*" (Thompson, 70).

■ THE TEXT IN CONTEMPORARY DISCUSSION

With social media and instant communication, contemporary culture knows the potential for both life-giving and damaging "speech." These psalms draw particular attention to malicious speech by repeatedly quoting hostile voices, witnessing to social isolation and estrangement. Such quotations also allow the psalmists to go beyond conventional limits and articulate "'unspeakable' complaints against God" (Jacobson, 49, 55).

The wicked's claim that "there is no God" (Ps. 10:4; 14:1) also proves striking given the rise of "new atheism." In contrast to contemporary debates, however, here this claim reflects a lack of accountability beyond oneself more than deductive reasoning or an abstract philosophical stance (Mays, 81–82); most significantly, suffering leads the psalmist *to* rather than *away from* God.

Psalms 17–22: Zion Theology and the Davidic King

■ THE TEXT IN ITS ANCIENT CONTEXT

Psalm 17, twice identified as a "prayer" (*tefillah*; heading, v. 1), calls for rescue from the wicked enemy. The psalmist contrasts his rightful speech with the arrogant speech of the wicked and again calls for YHWH to "Rise up!" (v. 13), a phrase initially linked to lifting the ark of the covenant to symbolize God's presence in battle (see Num. 10:34). While the psalmist's claims of innocence and righteousness frame the psalm (17:3-4, 15), God's sword and other military imagery link it to the following.

In Psalm 18, the king gives thanks for answered prayer through military success, with a parallel version appearing within the narrative of David (see 2 Sam. 22:1-51). The psalm describes divine support that provides the king with training and strength for battle (18:34, 39). The Hebrew root for "salvation/victory" (*yasha'*) appears five times in various forms, culminating with:

> . . . exalted be the God of my *salvation*,
>> the God who gave me vengeance
>>> and subdued peoples under me. (Ps. 18:46b-47)

While victory is related to the psalmist's righteousness and blamelessness (18:20-25), the psalm's Zion theology directly links God to the Davidic king or "his anointed" (*meshiho*, v. 50), who destroys the enemy with divine aid (cf. Psalm 89a).

Psalm 19, one of three torah psalms (cf. Psalms 1; 119), appears in the midst of this description of royal power. While initially describing the "glory of God" in the heavens in a manner similar to

Canaanite sun worship (19:1-6), the second section glowingly describes the "law" (*torah*) in six parallel lines, with the final verse again linking law to "meditation" (*hegyon*; cf. Ps. 1:2; Josh. 1:8). While the dramatic shift in vocabulary and theme has led many to treat it as combining two unrelated poems, Psalm 19 also holds together as it stands and even provides a "polemic" against sun worship (Sarna, 74). Its placement amid royal psalms both builds on references to legal vocabulary (Ps. 18:22, 30) and embodies the central role the law was to hold in the life of the Israelite king (Deut. 17:18-19). It also illustrates how the meaning of material can be transformed (cf. Psalm 29). Psalm 19 reflects the positive view of law (*torah*) assumed within the Old Testament (Exod. 20:1-3; Deut. 30:11-19), so that "Torah study is an act of worship" (Sarna, 95).

Psalm 20 reiterates divine protection for the king, initially addressing the monarch with a series of well-wishes ("May YHWH answer you . . .", 20:1-5 [author's translation]), moving to speak about the king and YHWH to a broader social audience (20:6-8), and concluding with a summary appeal to God: "Give *victory* to the king, O Lord." While the psalm assumes a seamless link between the temple/Zion, the anointed, and victory/salvation, it also rejects pride in military might "in the name of the Lord our God" (20:7). While Psalm 21 initially addresses God, it is not clear whether the second section speaks to God or the king (Gerstenberger 1988, 106). In either case, this psalm adds the benefits of long life and economic prosperity to military victory and dominion, while underscoring the key elements of the king's trust and God's steadfast love (*hesed*; v. 7).

Psalm 22 expresses both a sense of abandonment and trust. The initial "My God, my God, why have you forsaken me?" contrasts with the ancestors' experience of deliverance (22:4-5) and the assurance of the preceding psalms. The psalmist repeatedly speaks of being surrounded by hostile forces, which leads to calls for God to not be distant; the offer to praise God and tell of his deliverance constitutes the "vow" the psalmist commits to fulfill (22:22-24). The end of the psalm uses king language to describe YHWH rather than the anointed, reiterated in reference to God's justice (cf. Psalm 96).

▮ The Text in the Interpretive Tradition

Psalm 22 figures prominently within the New Testament portrayal of Jesus' passion. Before the addition of chapters and verses, "My God, my God, why have you forsaken me?" (22:1) functioned not only as Jesus' cry of anguish embodying the righteous sufferer but also as the incipit or effective "title" of the psalm itself (Matt. 27:46; Mays, 105).

While Augustine consistently reads the Psalms through Christ, he can speak either from an exalted position or from within the human condition; in effect, "Christ can speak *to* or *as* his body, the church" (Thompson, 56–57). Thus, for Augustine, Psalm 22 could be seen as either Christ himself or "Christ the body" speaking (Gillingham, 39).

Where Luther's "prophetic and Christocentric approach" saw Psalms 22 and 23 speaking directly of Christ, Calvin argued that—since Jesus *did* die—Psalm 22 was best understood in light of David and only secondarily of Christ or the individual Christian. Similarly, Calvin believed that Psalms 18 and 23 represented "types" that foreshadowed rather than predicted Christ (Gillingham, 144–45).

▊ THE TEXT IN CONTEMPORARY DISCUSSION

Whereas some have contrasted Christianity as a religion of peace with other traditions as inherently violent and some such as the "new atheists" have linked religion itself to violence, the potential for both peace and violence lies within the biblical tradition itself (see Psalm 149). While the Psalms generally insist on a divine monopoly on violence, the king's role as God's earthly representative provides the most notable exception (Firth, 3). In this sense, Psalm 18 provides a precedent that links divine support to military victory, a logic historically used by Christian leaders to legitimate political, national, and military interests.

To accept a mandate for human violence, however, assumes a direct correlation between a specific contemporary power and ancient Israel, sidestepping repeated biblical injunctions that victory does *not* depend on "chariots and horses" but trust in the divine (Ps. 20:7; cf. Exod. 14:13-14; Ps. 33:16-17). For Christians, such a mandate is also tempered by the New Testament's repeated transformation of a conquering messiah (Psalms 2; 18; 89a) into one who embodies suffering (Psalm 22).

In *The Prophetic Imagination*, Walter Brueggemann describes an ongoing struggle between "royal" and "prophetic" trajectories in the Bible. With this reasoning, Zion psalms seem to reflect the imperialist aspirations that the prophets (and we should) critique. Ben Ollenburger, however, has shown that Zion theology is based on God's kingship and thus places all creation and all nations, including their military might, under divine authority and God's "exclusive prerogative." Thus "the monarchical language of Zion symbolism does not legitimate 'imperial monarchy,' it prohibits it" (Ollenburger, 158–62).

Psalms 23–33: Trust in God's Steadfast Love

▊ THE TEXT IN ITS ANCIENT CONTEXT

The pastoral imagery of Psalm 23 may be the most familiar of the Psalms, speaking *about* rather than *to* God throughout. Beyond the link to David's childhood, "shepherd" was a term used for royalty in the ancient Near East, so that "the Lord is my shepherd" resonates with describing God as king (Pss. 10:16; 47:7-8; 93:1). "Setting a table" reflects hospitality and casts God as a gracious host committed to the guests' welfare (Anderson and Bishop, 183); where elsewhere enemies pursue the psalmist, here it is "goodness and mercy [*hesed*]" that do so.

Psalm 24, which begins with a cosmic description of YHWH as creator (24:1-2; cf. Psalms 74, 104), contains an entrance liturgy with a call and response among different voices (cf. Psalm 15). The psalm moves from liturgical and ethical motifs to military ones, with the concluding reference to "YHWH of hosts/armies [*yhwh tseba'oth*]" highlighting a divine-warrior motif (cf. Psalm 84). Psalm 24 also illustrates the difficulty of determining a psalm's "ancient context," with proposed settings including the ark of the covenant entering the temple during the preexilic period (Gunkel 1998, 316–17), pilgrims coming to Jerusalem for a religious festival (Sarna, 103), and worshipers approaching the Second Temple or a synagogue after exile (Gerstenberger 1988, 119).

Psalm 25 is an acrostic poem that incorporates aspects of lament alongside statements of confidence (cf. Psalms 34; 119). It declares the psalmist's *trust* in God, appeals to divine *steadfast love*, asks for God's guidance, and seeks forgiveness. In Psalm 26, the psalmist claims innocence grounded in his integrity (26:1, 11; 37:37; cf. Job 1:1, 8; 9:20-22). Oriented by God's steadfast love and truth (v. 2), the psalmist does not associate with the wicked but loves the temple (26:4-5, 8; cf. 1:1; 141).

Psalm 27 again reflects confidence and links a fulfilled life to the temple (27:4; 26:8), while also appealing for divine intervention and teaching (27:7-12). The concluding dual call to a social audience to "wait for the Lord" reaffirms the psalmist's confidence, even though the situation has not changed.

Psalm 28 begins with a lament to God that turns into thanksgiving for answered prayer addressed to a social audience. A concluding assertion of God's support for "his anointed" (*meshiho*) leading to a final appeal on behalf of the people may reflect a later broadening of material beyond an individual supplicant (cf. 3:8; Gerstenberger 1988, 129).

Psalm 29 begins by addressing the "sons of gods" (*bene 'elim*), a divine council common within ancient literature and assumed elsewhere in Scripture (82:1; Gen. 1:26; Job 1; Jer. 23:18). The sevenfold repetition of the "voice/sound of YHWH [*qol yhwh*]" punctuates the psalm and underscores the cosmic power of this deity, while the concluding description of *YHWH* as king directly counters Canaanite mythology, which used the same description for Baal. In effect, Psalm 29 redeploys language and imagery used to describe the rival storm god Baal within Canaanite mythology to affirm YHWH's sovereignty instead.

Psalm 30 again gives thanks for answered prayer, describing the psalmist's prior state, his own cry, and YHWH's response. Reference to God's anger and the psalmist's impending death suggests the psalm arises from a setting of illness (cf. Psalm 6), while the exhortation for a social audience to join the psalmist in praise reflects the public setting key to thanksgiving (cf. Psalm 116).

Psalm 31 intermingles lament and calls for respite from enemies with confident praise for answered prayer, concluding with "blessed be the Lord" and a call for broad social recognition (31:21-23). Once again, this response reflects the psalmist's "taking refuge" and *trusting* in God. The social appeal to "Love the Lord, all you his saints [*hasidayw*]" reflects the mutuality of covenant commitment (31:23; cf. 30:4), since both God and the saints/faithful ones demonstrate "steadfast love" (*hesed*). The final exhortation to "be strong" and "take courage" broadens the call familiar from Joshua to the community (see Josh. 1:6-9).

Psalm 32 begins with a description of distress, confession, and forgiveness that broadens to a social exhortation for each of the faithful to pray (v. 6). The divine voice describes God's commitment to teach and guide (32:8; cf. 25:4) before contrasting the wicked with the righteous who trust in YHWH and whom steadfast love surrounds. In effect, this psalm gives thanks for having experienced the forgiveness requested earlier (32:5; cf. Psalm 25).

Psalm 33 concludes this section with a communal hymn celebrating God's steadfast love shown in creation and to Israel, reiterating the major emphases of the preceding psalms and calling for joyful response. YHWH's role as cosmic king makes human military preparation useless (33:14-17), while the community affirms its trust and hope in God's *hesed* (33:20-22).

■ The Text in the Interpretive Tradition

Both Jewish and Christian medieval interpreters contrast the "praise of God's loud voice" in Psalm 29 with the "still, small voice" found in 1 Kgs. 19:12. However, where Rashi connects "wilderness of Kadesh" to Sinai and so sees God's voice giving torah (29:8), the *Glossa Ordinaria*, a medieval collation of biblical notations from the church fathers, identifies the same phrase with "the Jews, who do not have the sanctity of the law, that is spiritual understanding" (S. Davis, 73). Jewish interpreters Rashbam and David Kimchi link the divine voice to creation and the Messiah respectively, while Bruno de Segni ties it to inspired teaching that leads to baptism (S. Davis, 69–73).

While very different from Western or academic readings, David Adamo argues against portraying indigenous African interpretation as "fetish, magical, unchristian and uncritical." Rather, he describes how contemporary African Independent Churches recognize the "power in names" and so interpret Psalm 29 as a psalm of "protection . . . defense, liberation, healing, and success" (Adamo, 141, 135).

Jesus' final words on the cross in Luke's Gospel are: "into your hand I commit my spirit" (Ps. 31:5; Luke 23:46). While this statement contrasts with Mark and Matthew's "My God . . . why have you forsaken me?" (Ps. 22:1; Matt. 27:46; Mark 15:34), in both cases Jesus embodies the suffering of lament rather than a militaristic messiah (Psalms 2, 18, 72, 89a).

Psalm 23 has long been a liturgical resource, functioning as a "funeral psalm" alongside Psalm 22 and 116 as early as the fourth century (Gillingham, 55).

■ The Text in Contemporary Discussion

Psalms 29 and 19 draw on broader Canaanite mythology and so raise the issue of how previous traditions and understandings can be appropriately incorporated into the tradition. Missionary movements have often insisted that new adherents break from all aspects of prior culture. For instance, church-run residential schools sought to "assimilate" Native American peoples into (European) Canadian culture by systematically eliminating their indigenous language, traditions, and religious perspectives, with grave ongoing consequences. Postcolonial critics have also drawn attention to "marks of colonial hermeneutics" amid links between Christian evangelization and Western imperialism (Sugirtharajah, 61–73).

Psalms 29 and 19 reflect the ongoing dynamic of religious contextualization or syncretism whereby ancient traditions are adapted and transformed, in these cases shifting their significance to emphatically underscore that it is *YHWH's* "voice" (*not* that of Baal) that thunders (29) and *YHWH* (*not* the sun) who orients their lives through *torah* (19). This has been a long-standing issue, as attested in the "Christianization" of the winter equinox as a celebration of Jesus' birth (Christmas) and the transformation of spring fertility celebrations into a commemoration of the resurrection (Easter).

Psalms 34–41: Sickness, Enemies, and Land

■ The Text in Its Ancient Context

Psalms 34–41 reflect motifs of forgiveness, social solidarity, and wisdom. The final psalms conclude book 1 with a confident tone, ending in a doxology (41:13). This feature, the first of several in the

Psalms (72:18-19; 89:52; 106:48), was either introduced late in the composition process or provided the "pattern" for later conclusions that divide the current Psalter into five books (Mays, 13).

Psalm 34 incorporates various wisdom elements into thanksgiving for deliverance. Like Psalm 25, it has both an instructional purpose and an acrostic structure (cf. Psalm 119). The psalm employs characteristic wisdom vocabulary and motifs, including a contrast between the righteous and wicked, a "happy . . ." saying (v. 8; cf. 2:11), "turn from evil" (v. 14; Ps. 37:27; Prov. 16:6; Job 1:1), and "fear of the LORD" (v. 11; Prov. 1:7). The latter instructional motif addressed to "sons" extends beyond biological offspring to address students or apprentices as well (cf. Prov. 4:1). References to "taking refuge" in God and "servants" reflect broader motifs in the Psalms (cf. 2:11; 90:16; 102:14, 28).

Psalm 35 is an individual lament calling for divine deliverance that merges military and court language, including "fight" (v. 1); "violent witnesses" (v. 11); and pleading with God to contend (*ribah*) with his persecutors, support his cause (*rib*), and "judge" according to God's justice (*tsidqeka*) (35:1, 11, 23, 24). Since others' support has been denied to him (35:11-16), the psalmist wishes for God to dole out the same treatment that he has received (35:4-8; cf. Psalm 109). The concluding verses divide his social audience into those who "rejoice" in his plight and those who "desire my vindication [*tsidqi*]" (35:26-28; cf. 40:14-17). Psalm 36 again reflects social division and the potential for social solidarity, speaking from a setting where the wicked slander and plot (36:3, 4). The psalmist praises God's steadfast love and calls for it to continue (36:5-10), which reinforces the link between God's *hesed* and righteousness (*tsedeq*) and echoes the previous psalm's call for divine judgment (Ps. 36:10; 35:24).

Psalm 37, another acrostic wisdom poem (cf. Psalm 34), addresses the prosperity of the wicked, insisting that this is temporary and soon to be rectified; the claim that "I have not seen the righteous forsaken" seems hard to fathom (37:25). The court language found both here and in Psalm 35 resonates with the "prophetic lawsuit" tradition as well (Isa. 3:13; Hosea 2:2); *meditating* on wisdom and having "the law of their God in their hearts" also sound familiar (vv. 30-31; cf. Ps. 1:2; 19:14). The psalm's focus on land (*'erets*), which appears six times (37:3, 9, 11, 22, 29, 34), can be read in deeply contrasting ways, either as a means of legitimating the status quo or as a "utopian" vision of a future that challenges and overturns the present (Brueggemann, 243–53).

Psalm 38 assumes a link between sin and sickness, seeing YHWH as both the court of appeal and the enemy to be defended against (38:1-8; cf. 39:9-10). The psalmist also complains of social isolation and enemies (38:18-20; 41:5-9), including those who "meditate" on treachery (38:11-12; cf. 1:2; 2:1). Psalm 39 reflects on the passing nature of human mortality as a breath (*hevel*), employing the key term in Ecclesiastes often translated as "vanity" (39:5, 6, 11; Eccl. 1:2). Psalm 40 moves from public thanksgiving to reflect on God's steadfast love and truth and a call to demonstrate this once again through the psalmist's rescue; the closing distinction between opponents and supporters reflects the psalmist's self-identification with God (40:14-16; cf. 35:26-28).

Psalm 41 again links sin and sickness, with the psalmist's confession undergirding the conviction that he will be sustained through his illness. The psalmist calls out for mercy and expresses confidence rooted in his integrity (41:12; cf. 26:1, 11), while his plight is compounded by an intimate friend who has forsaken him (v. 9; cf. Psalm 55).

Psalm 41 concludes with a doxology that closes book 1: "Blessed be the LORD . . . Amen and Amen." With slight variations, similar doxologies divide the Psalter into five books (see Ps. 72:18-19; 89:52; 106:48).

THE TEXT IN THE INTERPRETIVE TRADITION

Like Psalm 45, Psalm 34 does not appear prominently within the New Testament but soon becomes a key christological psalm. Of particular interest, Clement sees Christ addressing believers with the appeal "Come, O children, listen to me," effectively portraying Jesus as divine wisdom (34:11; cf. Prov. 8:32). Later, the psalm also begins to be used within the Eucharist, building on the phrase "taste and see that the Lord is good" (34:8; Gillingham, 24–26, 52).

THE TEXT IN CONTEMPORARY DISCUSSION

The psalmists' experiences of rejection, social isolation, and stigmatization prove all too common in the contemporary world. The view of sickness as divine punishment for sin has affected responses to a wide range of contemporary issues, including HIV/AIDS, people struggling with addictions, mental health issues (see Psalm 88), and so on; Job provides a striking example of the type of social isolation such debates can prompt. An opposing tendency, perhaps particularly prominent in the West, has been to remove sickness from the spiritual arena altogether, which undercuts prayer regarding such matters.

While Psalm 37 assumes that the righteous will enjoy the land and the wicked will be cut off from it (Ps. 37:2, 22; cf. Deuteronomy 28), Brueggemann illustrates how Jesus' words in the Sermon on the Mount push this claim to a future "utopia" and so reflects a judgment of the present that does not live up to this expectation. While he points to the dispossession of small farmers at the hands of agribusiness as an example of its contemporary relevance (Brueggemann, 249–53, 257), farmers in developing nations have also repeatedly called for Western countries to halt agricultural subsidies to allow them to compete in the global market. Indigenous peoples in the Americas continue to call for the recognition of land rights, treaties, and redress for their sustained marginalization and displacement. In short, land remains a contentious issue.

The conclusions of Psalms 35 and 40 underscore the crucial social challenge such issues represent. While complex, discerning amid multiple voices remains a crucial and ongoing task of contemporary faith communities (Suderman 2012, 216).

Psalms 42–49: The Voice of the Community

THE TEXT IN ITS ANCIENT CONTEXT

Psalm 42 begins book 2 (Psalms 42–72) with this series of psalms attributed to the "sons of Korah" (42–49) as well as the "Elohistic Psalter" (42–83), which prefers to use "God" (*'elohim*) rather than YHWH, which dominates the rest of the Psalter (Anderson and Bishop, 13). This section changes from a primarily individual to an increasingly communal voice that reflects Zion theology liturgically centered on the kingship of God (cf. Psalms 93–99).

Psalms 42–43, linked by the threefold refrain "Why are you cast down, O my soul" (42:5, 11; 43:5), continue to complain against enemies epitomized in the taunt: "Where is your God?" (42:3, 10). They also introduce the tone of this section by referring to both past and future liturgical experiences related to the temple (42:4; 43:4), linking the psalmist's thirst for God with religious pilgrimage (cf. Psalm 120).

Psalm 44 provides the Psalter's first corporate cry for help (Mays, 176), not in a penitential mode but with a communal claim of innocence (44:17-22). While the first part recalls past success where God's support rather than military prowess or weaponry was the decisive element (44:4-7), the second articulates a communal lament after defeat; just as victory was linked to God's support, here defeat is seen as a sign of God's rejection (44:9-16; cf. Psalm 18). The imagery of sheep without a shepherd and being scattered among the nations builds on ancient Near Eastern royal imagery (Psalm 23) and reflects affinity with prophetic material, leading some to suggest an exilic or postexilic setting (44:11; see Isa. 53:6; Jer. 23:1-3; Mays, 178–79). "Rouse," "awake," "rise up," "my king and my God," and the concluding appeal for God's steadfast love reflect the shared vocabulary of individual and communal laments.

Identified as a "love song" in the heading, Psalm 45 reflects a royal wedding procession, with the vocabulary, imagery, and even direct address to a "daughter" proving similar to the Song of Solomon (45:10-12; see Song of Sol. 3:5-11). While the explicit voice of a "scribe" at the outset is unique (Mays, 181), links between the military, wealth, justice, and the king prove common in the Psalms (Psalms 2; 72; 89). The phrase "your throne, O God" introduces a tension into the psalm given the distinction between God and the anointed monarch in the next verse; at the same time, this phrase also resonates with the surrounding psalms' royal depiction of God (45:6-7; cf. Ps. 82). The appeal to "forget your people and your father's house" suggests the bride is a foreigner (v. 10; cf. Ruth 1:16), recalling long-standing antipathy to such unions (Deut. 7:3-4; 1 Kgs. 11:1-8; Ezra 9:12-14).

Psalms 46–48 are hymns that celebrate YHWH as cosmic king and God's intimate association with the temple and city of Jerusalem. Psalm 46 identifies God as "our refuge and strength," whose bond to the "city of God" assures its defense (46:4-5; 48:3, 10). "YHWH of hosts/armies [*yhwh tseba'oth*]" here underlines the divine role as cosmic peacemaker, who destroys military weaponry and says, "Be still and know that I am God" (46:7-11; 48:8). Psalm 47 calls on all peoples to sing to YHWH and extends God's dominion over the peoples to "us," as God's heritage (47:1-4). God reigns over nations and creation from his "holy throne" (Ps. 47:7-8; 93), with a strong military connotation both in resolving conflict and subduing others on Israel's behalf (46:9; 47:3). Psalm 48 again links God to Zion, where the city's inviolability is matched by the awe of foreign kings (48:1-8). The description of the city and temple prompts address to God and reflection on divine *hesed* as well as an invitation for pilgrims to walk around the city in awe (48:9-14); military armament and strong defenses pale in significance to the conviction that "all human affairs are under the direction and governance of God" (Sarna, 166). Strikingly, however, in these psalms, the human king has disappeared, reinforcing the basic conviction that victory is based on God's action rather than military prowess.

Psalm 49 provides a wisdom reflection, identified as a proverb and riddle addressed to a broad audience (v. 4). The frequent claim to *trust* in God" elsewhere contrasts with "those who *trust* in their wealth" here, an object lesson for the shared fate of both the "wise" and "fool" who cannot take riches with them (49:6, 10-11; cf. Eccles. 2:14). A repeated refrain underscores the mortality of humans and animals (49:12, 20).

▋ THE TEXT IN THE INTERPRETIVE TRADITION

Though not prominent in the New Testament, Psalm 45 became significant at an early stage within the Christian tradition. Like the Song of Solomon, it was interpreted as depicting the relationship between God and people and Christ and the church (Mays, 181–82). This psalm was employed in early church controversies to both argue for the divinity of Christ, reading Ps. 45:7 as addressing *Christ* as God, and to link him to the Old Testament and so counter Marcion and his followers (Gillingham, 24–26, 30).

Based on Psalm 46, Luther's anthem "A Mighty Fortress Is Our God" reflects his contentious time period, linguistic prowess, and dedication to make the Psalms accessible to a wider public (Gillingham, 140–41).

▋ THE TEXT IN CONTEMPORARY DISCUSSION

Biblical reference to the hiddenness and even absence of God has become particularly poignant in the wake of the Holocaust (44:24; cf. 13:1; 88:14; 89:46; Job 13:24). David Blumenthal identifies Psalm 44 as a "psalm of rage" expressed "at our enemies" but also "at those who betrayed us, by action and inaction. And we rage at God" (Blumenthal, 94); his multilayered reading, which draws on Elie Wiesel's *Night*, is stunning (Blumenthal, 94–110). Marvin Sweeney calls for people to recognize and reject the tendency to blame victims for their own victimization, and advocate for increased human responsibility in light of God's absence (Sweeney, 228–41; cf. Blumenthal, 108–9).

Treating the Nazi regime as an aberration too easily insulates the Christian tradition from recognizing the devastating potential of anti-Jewish interpretation and rhetoric present within it for millennia. The Holocaust forces Christians to recognize how we can and have become the very "enemies" the psalmist condemns.

Psalms 50–64: Lament and Confession

▋ THE TEXT IN ITS ANCIENT CONTEXT

The section of Psalms 50–61 begins with the first psalm attributed to Asaph (50; cf. 73–83). This section also includes the first psalms "of David" in book 2 (42–72), where contextual headings become the norm rather than the exception (cf. Psalms 3, 142).

Psalm 50 portrays a court scene where God functions as both prosecutor and judge (Mays, 194), addressing Israel as "my faithful ones [*hasidai*]" and "my people" (50:5, 7). The initial critique of liturgy does not reject sacrifice itself, but insists on God's overarching ownership of any offering (50:10-11; Mays, 196). God's concluding address articulates several charges, while thanksgiving and cries for help recognizing God's sovereignty reflect a proper liturgical stance.

Psalm 51, whose heading sets it after Nathan confronts David for his indiscretion with Bath-sheba, represents perhaps the most well-known prayer of confession in the Psalter. Following a characteristic lament structure—address, complaint, petition, and vow of praise (Anderson, 82–83)—its opening imperatives to God set the tone ("Have mercy," "blot out," "wash," and "purify" in 51:1-2), while three distinct terms for sin underscore its main theme. In the "precritical" period, the claim "Against you, you alone have I sinned" prompted significant reflection in light of the heading (v. 4); in contrast, biblical critics have frequently cited this statement as evidence that David could *not* have articulated this prayer. While hyssop reflects an ancient purification ritual (51:7; cf. Exod. 12:22; Lev. 14:51), the psalmist's appeal for a "clean heart [*leb*]" suggests improved judgment, since the heart is the site of the will in the Old Testament (see Exod. 9:7, 35; 1 Kgs. 3:9). The divine spirit/breath (*ruach*) allows the psalmist to be taught and in turn to teach other sinners to return/repent (51:10-13). The tension between God's having "no delight in sacrifice" but then the psalmist's affirming that "you *will* delight" in them (51:16, 19) has led many scholars to see the last two verses as an addition rehabilitating temple ritual, perhaps in the postexilic period (Gerstenberger 1988, 214).

Psalm 52 immediately addresses a mighty one (*gibbor*) who "boasts," "plots," and "loves evil more than good" (52:1-4). The psalmist contrasts the mighty one who trusts in wealth (49:6) with his trust in God's steadfast love (*hesed*, 52:6-9). Psalm 53 represents a minor variation of Psalm 14, with the change from YHWH to God characteristic of the Elohistic Psalter. While it does not contain a contextual heading, the initial reference to a "fool" (*nabal*) resonates with the account of David's confrontation with Nabal (1 Samuel 25). Psalm 54 calls out for divine aid, with the appeal to God's might (*gibbur*) linked to the confidence that enemies will receive their due from the divine (54:1, 5; 52:5; 53:5). This thanksgiving exemplifies the previous instruction to offer thanks and call on God (54:6; 52:9; cf. 50:14-15).

Psalm 55, which simply reads "of David," is an individual lament that addresses multiple audiences. While initially speaking to God, the turning point appears when the psalmist levels a direct accusation to someone in his social circle: "But it is *you*, my equal . . ." (v. 13; cf. Ps. 41:9). This direct accusation, similar to Nathan's strident critique of David (2 Sam. 12:7), precedes address to yet another audience *about* both the "friend" and God rather than *to* either of them. The psalm complains of both a covenant violation and seemingly innocent but in reality violent words (55:20-21); it is unclear whether v. 22 reflects what should be said or whether these are the "smooth words" of the adversary. Encouraging God's vigorous response, the psalmist ends with a claim to "trust in you."

Psalms 56–57, which the headings again place in contexts in which David was under duress, call for God and express confidence in the divine. The first centers on declarations of trust in God (56:3-4, 10-11). Where the previous psalm lamented the friend's words (*debarayw*, 55:21), here persecution aimed at the psalmist's *word/cause* elicits trust in God's *word* (56:4-5, 10); the psalmist's praise of the divine word rather than God himself proves unique and is underscored by repetition (56:10; Gerstenberger 1988, 227). Psalm 57 claims refuge in God, under the "shadow of your wings" (57:1; cf. Ps. 91:4). What begins as a lament shifts to thanksgiving for how the enemies, who are described as ravaging wild animals, have fallen into their own trap (v. 6). Here again God's steadfast love and truth ground the psalmist's confidence (57:3, 10), while a repeated refrain exalting God frames the last section (57:5, 11).

Psalm 58 depicts an inversion of justice (cf. Psalm 82), where rulers promote violence and reflect the tendencies of the "wicked." The psalmist calls for God to stop their aggression, again employing the metaphor of hostile animals (58:6-8; cf. Ps. 3:7). The conclusion underscores the basic concern of the psalm; the righteous rejoice because they "envision vengeance" as a certainty (cf. Psalm 94); vengeance is not itself the point but confirms that "there are gods judging on the earth [*yesh-'elohim shophetim ba'arets*]" (58:10-11; see Psalm 82; 94).

Psalm 59 repeats the call for deliverance from enemies, whose destruction once again provides the means for recognizing God's supremacy (59:13). Praise for God's steadfast love intermingles with the protective description of the divine as fortress, refuge, and strength (59:16-17).

Psalm 60 moves from the call of an individual beset by enemies to a communal lament by those who have suffered a military defeat. God's rejection prompts a call for victory and a reversal of God's absence from "our armies" (60:1-5, 10-12; cf. Ps. 89:39); the divine promise to which the psalmist appeals appears elsewhere as well (60:5-12; cf. Ps. 108:6-13; Gerstenberger 1988, 240). While the psalm depicts military defeat as reflecting divine anger, the solution lies not in armament but in God's victory on behalf of Israel; the claim that "he will tread down our foes" reflects the Zion theology described elsewhere (see Psalm 18).

Psalm 61, a first-person counterpart to Psalm 60, also calls for divine protection from the enemy and mentions God's dwelling (61:4; cf. 60:6). While the motif of finding refuge "under the shadow of God's wings" reappears (v. 4; cf. 57:1; 91:4), in the second part God has already "heard" the psalmist's vows. The psalm shifts to appeal for the longevity of the king, employing the language of the Davidic covenant linked to God's steadfast love and faithfulness (*'emeth*, 61:6-7; cf. Ps. 89a; 2 Sam. 7:12-16). Whether the speaker is an individual, a representative of the community, or the king himself, the appeal for the king here again reflects characteristics of Zion theology (Mays, 215).

Psalms 62–63 express trust and confidence in God. Psalm 62 twice repeats the refrain "For God alone my soul waits" that identifies God as "my rock and my salvation, my fortress" (62:1-2, 5-6). Most of the psalm speaks to a social audience, briefly addressing plural adversaries directly before speaking *about* them and finally exhorting his listeners to "trust in God" (62:3-8; cf. Ps. 55:13). The psalm underscores the motif of refuge, concluding with a brief address affirming God's divine steadfast love and expressing confidence that God will "repay all according to their work" (62:7-8, 12). Psalm 63, the last in this sequence linked to a setting in the life of David, again describes how the psalmist's soul thirsts for God and links an experience of awe in the sanctuary to his recognition of divine *hesed* (63:1-5; cf. 42:4). Here too the "shadow of your wings" appears as an image of refuge, while the final verses contrast the fate of his adversaries with that of the king (63:7, 10-11; cf. 61:4).

Psalm 64 is another lament psalm concerned primarily with the speech of the enemy. In places where the wicked's schemes and speech appear as swords and arrows aimed toward the psalmist, he expresses confidence in God's in-kind response (64:2-8). The psalm concludes with an exhortation for the righteous and upright to also "take refuge in him" (64:10).

▌ THE TEXT IN THE INTERPRETIVE TRADITION

Within the Christian tradition, Psalm 51 has been the most prominent of seven traditional "penitential psalms" (6; 32; 38; 51; 102; 130; 143), used heavily from the early church fathers to the present. It has been prominent within liturgy, monastic traditions, and private devotion. For Luther, the penitential psalms were particularly significant, since they provided the means for individual Christians to approach God directly through Christ and so bypass the system of indulgences he opposed (Gillingham, 52–53, 138).

■ THE TEXT IN CONTEMPORARY DISCUSSION

Psalms 50–64 illustrate the complex issue of "voice" so central to the Psalms. How should the community of faith respond when an abused party, such as David surrounded by his enemies, becomes an abuser, epitomized in his covetous action with Bathsheba and murderous cover-up of Uriah? Comparable issues arise at both individual and group levels, where a past victim of abuse goes on to abuse others, or where an oppressed or marginalized group gains the upper hand and employs its newfound power to subordinate, persecute, and oppress others.

In contemporary parlance, Psalm 51 reflects the voice of a (purportedly) penitent "offender," while lament psalms represent the cries of (purported) "victims." While reading the Psalms in an age of "terror," intergroup conflict, and xenophobia can reinforce the assumption that "enemies" are necessarily foreign and external, Psalm 55 reminds us that they may also be "intimate enemies" such as a close associate or even family member (Sheppard, 70); elsewhere Ulrike Bail has demonstrated the potential of reading Psalm 55 in light of domestic violence and abuse (Bail, 1998). Furthermore, reading the preposition in the heading "of David [*ledavid*]" as the also plausible "*to* David" allows the reader to hear Psalm 55 as the voice of Bathsheba—or even Uriah—confronting David, and thus complicates our understanding of the commonly employed confession in Psalm 51.

In so doing these psalms also illustrate the complexity of discerning the appropriate contemporary function of psalms material, since they simultaneously confront the social audience with both "offender" and "victim" voices. The rhetorical presence of a social audience in these psalms again underscores the role of contemporary communities to hear, evaluate, and respond to the voices they hear (Suderman 212, 216–17).

Finally, although most critical scholarship has moved away from reading psalms in light of David, such a stance isolates scholars from many lay and non-Western readings, and also from the broader history of interpretation. Just as too strong an emphasis on confession can eclipse the possibility of lament or claims of innocence, so critical scholarship can monopolize the "voice" of legitimate interpretation and so overlook the ongoing significance of "precritical" interpreters and global voices.

Psalms 65–72: Communal Praise and Thanksgiving

■ THE TEXT IN ITS ANCIENT CONTEXT

This section concludes both book 2 of the Psalter (42–72) and a David collection (see Ps. 72:20). Psalms 65–68 are identified as both a psalm (*mizmor*) and a song; though not unprecedented for psalm headings (see Psalms 30; 45; 46; 48), the latter element appears most often in book 5 to introduce the "Songs of Ascent" (Psalms 120–134).

Psalm 65 articulates communal praise and thanksgiving directly to God, describing divine response to prayer, control over the mountains and seas, and provision. God's control over creation and mention of both Zion and temple resonate with Zion theology (65:1, 4; cf. Psalm 18), while the link to fertility recalls the critique and transformation of Baal worship elsewhere (cf. Psalm 29).

Psalm 66 extends worship beyond the temple, addressing different audiences. The psalm initially addresses "all the earth," calling for a communal thanksgiving for God's action exemplified in the exodus and entering the land (66:1-8). Turning to God, the psalmist describes times of hardship as a process of testing and purification and then vows to sacrifice in the temple to express his individual thanksgiving (66:10-15). The final section, directed to "all you who fear God," recalls God's response to prayer and concludes by affirming God's steadfast love (*hesed*, 66:16-20).

Psalm 67 articulates a communal blessing that effectively transfers Aaron's blessing from the mouth of a priest to the corporate "us" of the community (67:1; cf. Num. 6:24-26; Gerstenberger 2001, 32). While it follows a similar pattern as the previous psalm by speaking *of* God, then *to* God, and finally *of* God again, here the community desires that God bless the people (67:1, 7) rather than calling on the peoples to bless God (66:8, 20). Repetition underscores the psalmist's hope that God will be recognized by those peoples beyond Israel who experience divine judgment and guidance (67:2-5).

Psalm 68 links mythological elements to the particular history of Israel to underscore the sovereignty and power of God. The initial appeal for God to "rise up" against his enemies calls upon God to enact the contrasting fate of the "righteous" and "wicked" (68:1-3; cf. 1:5-6). The psalm draws on several motifs associated with Baal, including the depiction of God as "rider on the clouds/heavens," his link to rains and fertility, and reference to the divine voice (cf. Psalm 29). The psalm also reflects competition between Mount Zion (perhaps Mount Sinai) and the mountain of Bashan as rival cultic centers (68:15-16), and corresponds directly to the ancient "Song of Deborah" (68:7-8; cf. Judg. 5:4-5; Gerstenberger 2001, 38). Reference to God as "father of orphans" places the divine in the role of a kinsman-redeemer (68:5; cf. Exod. 22:22-24), before portraying God as king entering the temple and receiving tribute from the nations (68:24-31). The repetition of divine might or power underscores God's sovereignty (68:28, 33-35).

Psalm 69 is an individual lament that cries to God for help, gives voice to extended curses or imprecations against enemies, and concludes with praise and exhortation to a social audience. The psalmist draws on water as a symbol of chaos to describe his persecution by enemies as drowning. While he grounds his appeal on God's steadfast love, truth, and mercy, drastic imprecations against enemies underscore his anguish (69:22-28; cf. Psalm 109) and precede a social exhortation to the lowly (69:32-33). The final call for God to rebuild Judah reflects a postexilic context for the present psalm, which incorporated elements of an older lament (Gerstenberger 2001, 52).

Psalm 70 calls for God's intervention, repeating almost verbatim from Ps. 40:13-17, with minor changes such as the name of God. This psalm reflects the basic social division often implicit in lament, contrasting those who "seek my life" and speak against the psalmist with those who seek God and speak accordingly.

Psalm 71, one of only six before Psalm 72 without a heading, alternates between descriptions of trouble and the psalmist's trust and hope in God (Mays, 234). References to both "my youth" and old age reflect a long-standing relationship with God, while the metaphorical depiction of God as the psalmist's midwife underscores the intimacy of this relationship (v. 6; cf. Ps. 139:13-15; Jer. 1:5). The final commitment to meditate on God's justice resonates with the depiction of the faithful elsewhere (71:24; 1:2; 19:14).

Psalm 72, whose heading is best rendered "to" or "for Solomon," describes the attributes of a righteous king who demonstrates judicial wisdom, support for the vulnerable, exercises "dominion" over a broad swath of territory, and receives service and tribute from other monarchs. Here the well-being (*shalom*) of both people and land are intimately linked to and even derive from the king (72:3, 7), while the blessing of the nations through him resonates with Abram's call (72:17; Gen. 12:3). The grammatical ambiguity of the repeated Hebrew verb form can be read as either a series of desires ("May he judge . . ." NRSV) or future action ("He shall judge . . ." KJV). Regardless, this psalm presents a portrait of an ideal king and probably emerges from a coronation liturgy (cf. Psalm 2). The initial link to Solomon illustrates the biblical ambiguity of such a depiction; renowned for wisdom, exceptional wealth, and expanding the kingdom of Israel, Solomon also embodies what a king should *not* be (1 Kgs. 3–11; Deut. 17:14-18).

Psalm 72 concludes book 2, with the marker noting the "end of the prayers of David" standing in tension with several psalms "of David" appearing later in the book (86; 101; 138). This editorial marker reflects the end of a Davidic collection that precedes the current form of the Psalter, and so witnesses to the complex compositional history of the book (see Jer. 51:64; Prov. 25:1).

▌ THE TEXT IN THE INTERPRETIVE TRADITION

Seeing Psalm 72 as fulfilled in the visit of the magi reflects an ancient interpretive tradition already present in Tertullian's *Against the Jews* in the second century and illustrated in the illuminated *St. Albans Psalter* in the twelfth (cf. 72:10-15; Matt. 2:11; Gillingham, 26, 100–101). In contrast to its prominence as a traditional "messianic" passage often employed during Advent within the Christian tradition, Psalm 72 does not appear within Jewish liturgy (cf. Psalms 2, 110; Holladay, 144).

Rashi's discussion of Psalm headings provides an intriguing counterpoint to contemporary debates. Rabbinic tradition interpreted Ps. 72:20 as "All these are the prayers of David" and so saw David as the writer of the entire Psalter, but Rashi reads this phrase as "they were concluded." However, whereas modern critical scholars point to this verse as evidence of an earlier collection, Rashi appeals to the order in which psalms were found to explain its current position. Thus, though Psalm 72 concluded David's writing, it was discovered before others attributed to David that appear later in the book (Hailperin 1963, 232–33).

New Testament writers drew on Psalm 69 to depict the life and significance of Jesus (see 69:4, 9; John 2:17; 15:25), with the passion narratives in all four Gospels describing Jesus being given a drink of sour wine on the cross (69:21). While the psalm seems striking in its vindictiveness, Romans employs Psalm 69 in its call to "build up the neighbor" (Ps. 69:9 // Rom. 15:3), after explicitly prohibiting the execution of vengeance by leaving it "for the wrath of God" (Rom. 12:18-21; cf. Psalms 109, 149).

■ THE TEXT IN CONTEMPORARY DISCUSSION

Debate over the appropriate extent and role of government continues in the contemporary world, and political advertising and propaganda abound. Psalm 72 paints a picture of an ideal king as an instrument of peace (*shalom*), a righteous judge, and a strong ruler who appears at the very center of the people's well-being; even rain and produce appear implicated in the nature of the king.

David Jobling has explored this psalm's role as royal propaganda, pointing out internal inconsistency in the psalm's transition from a "mythic" to a more "political" description of the king. He suggests that the psalm promotes a "tributary" model of production where the centralized king consumes goods and produces ideological self-justification, while those on the periphery produce goods and consume ideology (Jobling, 95, 123).

On the other hand, Walter Houston sees Psalm 72 linking the monarch to a central concern for justice. Where Psalm 82 critiques those who are supposed to judge justly but do not, this psalm provides an appeal for the king to live up to lofty ideals and so, by subordinating the monarchy to justice, "effectively demolishes the doctrine of the divine right of kings" (Houston, 360; cf. Psalm 82; Deut. 17:14-20).

Psalms 73–83: Cries from a Context of Destruction

■ THE TEXT IN ITS ANCIENT CONTEXT

Psalms 73–83 begin book 3 with a collection of Asaph psalms, shifting from an individual under duress to a community reeling from the destruction of the temple and Jerusalem. The despair of exile and destruction underlies the repeated call for God to act on Israel's behalf.

Psalm 73 is a wisdom reflection that contemplates the dissonance between the claim that God blesses the righteous and observing the prosperity of the wicked (73:3-12; cf. Ps. 1:6). While the psalmist "almost stumbled" in light of this quandary, visiting the sanctuary convinces him that this success is temporary. In effect, this psalm reframes the issue by contrasting those far from the divine with the psalmist's conviction to remain near God (73:27-28), seeing intimacy with God rather than material gain as the reward for faithfulness.

Psalm 74 is a communal lament that reflects an exilic setting in which the sanctuary has been destroyed and desecrated (74:3, 7). While the opening query asking why God has cast off his people effectively frames book 3 (Ps. 74:1; 89:38; cf. 44:10, 24), the cry "how long?" prompts a recital of God's role as saving king. Seven emphatic appearances of the pronoun "you" in five verses underscore that God gained victory over the forces of chaos and ancient Canaanite deities (sea, Leviathan, streams, the sun, 74:13-17). The psalmist calls on God to *remember* the people that God has redeemed and his dwelling in Zion, as well as the insolence of the enemy (74:2, 18, 22). The concluding appeal for God to "rise up" and "plead your case" arises from the imperative call to attend to covenant; God's role as king implies both bringing order to the cosmos and acting on behalf of this covenant people (cf. Psalm 68; 93).

Psalms 75–76 affirm and praise God's justice. A brief corporate expression of thanks to the divine introduces God's direct speech and his commitment to judge, albeit on a divine—rather than human—timetable (75:1-5). The psalm then shifts to describe God's role in judging (75:6-8). The final verses reiterate each party's commitments, with the individual vowing to praise and the divine reaffirming that the wicked will be cut off and the righteous exalted, thereby addressing the concern of Psalms 74–75 (75:10; cf. Ps. 1:5-6). While "boastful" can be read as the hubris of Babylon (see Assyria in Isa. 10:12), it also reflects a more immediate social adversary elsewhere (75:4; cf. 5:5; 52:1; 73:3); both provide cogent possibilities (Mays, 249). Psalm 76 is a hymn that again praises divine judgment and commitment to save. God's sovereignty over military forces reflects the divine-warrior motif present elsewhere (76:3, 6; cf. Exod. 15:1-3; Isa. 59:16-20).

Rather than cry to God, Psalm 77 moves from an initial description of the psalmist's distress to reflect on God's wondrous deeds. A series of rhetorical questions, beginning with "Will YHWH cast [us] off forever?" (77:7, author trans.; cf. 74:1; 89:38), question central divine attributes (steadfast love, graciousness, compassion) (77:7-9; cf. Exod. 34:6-7). Psalm 77:10 marks a shift in focus from the "I" of the early section to the divine "you" in the latter (Brueggemann, 261–67); the psalmist remembers "your way" (77:13, 19), again intermingling God's action in delivering Israel from Egypt with divine sovereignty over the chaotic waters (cf. 74; Exod. 15:1-10). Remembering God as Israel's redeemer moves beyond being God's people to God's family or next of kin (77:15; cf. Ps. 74:2; 78:35; Isa. 43:1, 14). While its economic role is more often recognized, here God also plays the role of *avenger*, who defends and metes out punishment for those who violate family members (Deut. 19:4-12).

Psalm 78 provides instruction punctuated by characteristic wisdom terminology: teaching, words, proverb, and riddles (78:1-2; cf. Prov. 1:6-8). It seeks to derive lessons from the past by contrasting God's faithful deeds with the people's repeated rebellion from the time of the exodus until that of David. While divine anger and judgment figure prominently (78:21, 31, 58-59), the psalmist also insists on God's restraint and deliverance (78:38; cf. Exod. 34:5-6; Nehemiah 9), culminating with the establishment of the temple and the Davidic line (78:67-72).

Psalms 79–80 cry out for God's response to the destruction of Jerusalem through the restoration of Israel. The graphic portrayal of the desecration of both temple and bodies prompts both the cry "how long?" and the call to shift God's anger away from Jerusalem and onto the nations (79:1-6). The appeal for God *not* to remember former sins and to show compassion reiterates elements from the previous psalm (79:8; 78:38-39), while the concluding call for vengeance leads to a vow of praise (79:10-13). Psalm 80 continues the communal appeal for God to turn from anger, calling on the divine warrior (YHWH) God of hosts/armies, to "restore us . . . that we may be saved" (80:3-4, 7, 19). While the vine also appears as a metaphor for Israel in the prophets (80:8, 14; cf. Jer. 2:21; Ezek. 19:10), this psalm calls for God's response in the aftermath of the catastrophe more than explaining why God has "broken down its walls" (80:12; cf. Isaiah 5).

In Psalm 81, God answers the previous psalms. After introductory verses, God recounts his response to the people's cry (81:6-7; cf. Exod. 2:23-25). The divine admonition centers on the beginning of the Ten Commandments, both in terms of God's identity as the one who "brought you up out of Egypt" and in terms of the commandment to not follow other gods (81:9-10; cf. 78:58; Exod. 20:1-2). The call for Israel to listen/obey provides the central motif (81:8, 11, 13; cf. Deut. 6:4); as in Deuteronomy, God's "turning" to judge the nations is here directly linked to Israel's obedience (81:14; cf. 80:14; Deut. 28:1, 15).

Psalm 82, identified by J. Clinton McCann Jr. as "the single most important text in the entire Bible" (2011), takes place within the "divine assembly" and underscores God's fundamental commitment to justice. While it appears only here in the Old Testament, this phrase has direct parallels in Ugaritic documents, where it builds on the status of El as the chief deity in the Canaanite pantheon (similar to Zeus in Greek mythology) and resonates with several Old Testament passages that also refer to a divine council (Sarna, 169; cf. Gen. 1:26; Job 1–2; Jer. 23:18). Since those charged with maintaining justice are not executing this task properly, *God* laments "How long?" (82:1-5). The psalm concludes with the psalmist's voice calling on God to judge and so fulfill the royal role others have abdicated. While the psalm depicts the failure of judges, the gods (*'elohim*) here can be understood as either humans with exalted status or "divine beings" (Sarna, 173–75). In either case, Psalm 82 emphasizes that the God of Israel is fundamentally committed to justice and willing to intervene when it is not practiced.

Psalm 83, the last linked to Asaph (cf. 50), calls on God to come to Israel's defense. A counterpart to the divine voice previously speaking of "my people" (81), here Israel's status as "your people" undergirds the psalmist's claim that its adversaries are also those of God (83:1-5). In doing so, the psalm lists traditional enemies and draws on God's past action as added motivation (83:6-12; cf. Amos 1–2). The conclusion seeks both the destruction of the enemy and their recognition of YHWH's unique status (83:16-18; cf. Exod. 14:4, 18, 25; Isa. 45:3, 6).

▌ THE TEXT IN THE INTERPRETIVE TRADITION

The use of Psalm 82 within different contentious settings proves intriguing. In John's Gospel, Jesus himself quotes from verse 6, "You are all gods," to refute a charge of blasphemy (John 10:34). Later, arguing against Marcion's proposal that the God of Jesus is different than the creator God, Tertullian insists that Ps. 82:1 reflects "other beings being judged as non-Gods" (Gillingham, 26). While Psalm 82 appeared commonly in the early church fathers, it did not receive as much attention as others in later liturgical use (Gillingham, 53).

The rabbinic *Midrash on the Psalms* (*midrash tehillim*) discusses these same verses, but with a different focus. The rabbis explain Ps. 82:1 as a "Judge among judges," referring to the apparent use of gods (*'elohim*) for human beings elsewhere (Exod. 22:8). The reference to "ye are godlike beings" and mention of *'adam* ("mortals") in the next verse led the rabbis to link the passage with Adam being driven from the Garden of Eden. The concluding verse affirms the basic conviction stated elsewhere: "Remove these mortal judges, and Thou alone be King and Judge" (Braude, 2:59–60; cf. Psalms 93–99).

▌ THE TEXT IN CONTEMPORARY DISCUSSION

The contemporary globalized world also faces significant disorientation, with protracted financial and ecological crises, as well as ongoing violence and insecurity that transcend national, ethnic, or religious boundaries. Like the psalmist, we too live in a world where we perceive the "righteous" and the "wicked," and are tempted to claim national or religious exceptionalism whereby *we* are the "righteous" by definition. While societies, governments, and religious traditions all too often claim the prerogative to function in ways they prohibit for others, these psalms insist that God is king, not just of one fiefdom but of the cosmos (see Psalms 93; 97).

In this context, several things stand out. First, the psalmist calls on the wrath of God to punish the nations, with the recognition that Israel itself has also been subject to divine judgment. Being God's people does not provide an exception to suffering, but heightens the responsibility to follow the divine will (Psalms 78; 81). Second, the call for divine judgment is grounded in God's justice, exemplified in addressing the plight of the weak, orphan, and lowly (Psalm 82); the psalms undercut the tendency to play personal piety over against social concerns. Another temptation lies in too quickly assuming the "enemies" to be other nations or entities, without recognizing the extent to which the psalmists implicate social systems (94) or even close friends (Psalm 55); more than merely about "them," it is crucial to consider when this may critique "us" or even *me*.

Finally, the psalmist's appeal for God to "save" does not represent an escapist spiritual cry uninterested in physical and social reality, but a demand for social liberation and rehabilitation in the here and now. Where contemporary thinking is often dualistic, pitting body against spirit or worldly existence with life eternal, the psalms repeatedly challenge such a dichotomy.

The destruction of Jerusalem, pillaging of the temple, and Babylonian exile represent the most traumatic but also one of the most transformative moments in the history of ancient Israel. As these psalms attest, this experience challenged the wisdom tradition's conviction that God rewards the righteous and punishes the wicked (73), contested the liturgical tradition's view of the status of the temple and Jerusalem (79), and raised profound questions about the justice, character, and presence of God (76; 82). This crisis prompted both introspection and reflection on past experience (75; 77; 78) and passionate appeals for God's intervention (80; 83).

Psalms 84–89: From Joy in the Temple to Personal and Corporate Despair

■ THE TEXT IN ITS ANCIENT CONTEXT

While references to the sons of Korah frame books 2 and 3 (Psalms 84–88; cf. 42; 44–49), Psalms 84–89 also include psalms linked to David (86) and Ethan (89), shifting from rejoicing in the temple to the agony of exile (Ps. 84; 89b). Psalm 84 also reflects a shift back to using YHWH as the dominant name for the divine, after the conclusion of the "Elohistic Psalter" (see Psalm 42).

Psalm 84 contains both a hymn and a pilgrimage song praising the temple (Gerstenberger 2001, 123–24), with its exuberance reinforced by three "Happy are . . ." sayings (84:4, 5, 12). This focus and the fourfold use of "YHWH (God) of hosts/armies," a designation consistently linked to Zion and the temple in the Psalms (24:10; 46:7, 11; 48:9; 69:6), both forms a thematic link with the preceding section and signals the shift away from God (*elohim*) as the default term for the divine (84:1, 3,

8, 12; cf. 80:4, 7, 14, 19). The psalm refers to both "your anointed/messiah [*meshihekah*]" and God as a shield (84:9, 11), introducing the royal motif that dominates Psalm 89 and frames this section.

Psalm 85 recalls when YHWH forgave in the past and calls for God to do the same in the present, articulating its existential anguish with the query "Will you be angry with us forever?" (85:1-7; cf. 79:5). The fourfold use of the Hebrew term *shub* connects how YHWH had previously *restored* Jacob and *turned* from anger to the contemporary call to *restore* and *revive* again (85:1-6). Wrath and anger reflect language typically linked to exile and imply an exilic setting (85:3, 5; cf. 2 Kgs. 17:18; 23:26; Isa. 12:1; Jer. 4:8, 26; Ezek. 7:12-14). The final section expresses confidence in God's response and describes a hopeful future. Where the psalmist calls for divine steadfast love, God will speak peace (*shalom*) to his faithful (85:8); "steadfast love and faithfulness/truth will meet; justice and *peace* will kiss" (85:10).

Psalm 86, the only one attributed to David in book 3, draws on characteristic phrases and motifs from lament and thanksgiving psalms in an "anthological style." The relationship between a servant and "my Lord," terms appearing three and seven times respectively, reflects the dominant motif that both provides a paradigm for prayer and links to the royal depiction of David in Psalm 89a (Mays, 278–79). To do so, the psalmist again draws directly on the depiction of YHWH as "merciful and gracious . . ." found in Exodus 34 (Pss. 86:15; 103:8; Exod. 34:6-7; Joel 2:13; Jon. 4:2).

Psalm 87 extols Zion and even addresses it directly as the "city of God," a hymnic feature with ancient Near Eastern parallels (87:3, Gerstenberger 2001, 139). Rather than focusing on the temple and its connection to Israel, however, this psalm links foreign nations to God, even describing traditional enemies as being born in Zion, an oddity reiterated by YHWH (87:4-6). Where Psalm 83 called for the destruction of traditional enemies, here foreign nations are incorporated into the liturgical center of Israel. While unusual, a radical opening to the nations appears elsewhere as well (see Isa. 19:24-25, 66:20-21; Amos 9:7).

Psalm 88, identified with both the "sons of Korah" and "Heman the Ezrahite," provides an unusual yet powerful individual lament. The psalm emphatically addresses God throughout, who functions as both the court of appeal and the enemy; God has put him in the depths (88:6), divine wrath confronts him (88:7, 16), God has prompted the psalmist's utter social isolation (88:8, 18), and has "cast me off" (88:14; cf. 74:1; 77:7; 89:38). The description of repeatedly calling on God leads to rhetorical questions about God's steadfast love, faithfulness, and righteousness, precisely those elements praised elsewhere (88:9-12; cf. 85:9-11; 86:13, 15; 89:1-2). Where individual laments typically conclude with a statement of confidence or vow of praise, this psalm contains no hopeful emotional turn or shift in tone; what begins with a cry to the "God of my salvation" ends in despair.

Psalm 89, consisting of two strongly contrasting sections (89:1-37, 38-52), centers on the reliability of God. Psalm 89a immediately introduces the key terms *steadfast love* and *faithfulness*, which appear repeatedly and often in parallel (89:1, 2, 24, 33, 49). The psalmist first speaks to God and then quotes the divine, a pattern that repeats itself throughout the first section of the psalm; the divine voice reiterates God's covenant with David and so introduces its dominant motif (89:3; 2 Sam. 7:16). The psalmist then praises YHWH's control over the mythological forces of chaos (89:6-12; cf. Psalms 74; 104) and then quotes a vision (cf. Isa. 1:1; Dan. 8:1). Here God speaks again to underscore God's intimate relationship with the king and weave him into the very fabric of the cosmos, such that he controls not only his enemies but even the sea and rivers (89:19-25). God again reaffirms the covenant with David, reiterating the king's status as God's son and the eternal inviolability of the covenant (89:26-37; cf. 2 Sam. 7:12-16; Ps. 2:7). Thus the psalmist links God's *faithfulness* reflected in control over creation to divine *steadfast love* embodied in a divine commitment to the Davidic king.

"But *you*" marks a dramatic shift to the second section of the psalm. Where in Psalm 89a this emphatic pronoun had been used six times to underscore God's control over creation (89:9-12, 17), in 89b the psalmist directly accuses God of betraying the covenant with David—the very subject of previous praise (89:38; cf. 89:34). He bemoans the realities of exile: the crown lies in the dust, the scepter has been removed, and the throne is discarded. Finally, the psalm moves from accusatory description to a call for action and a shift in focus from the singular "servant" to "servants" (89:3, 20, 39, 50). A dual "how long?" coupled with two calls for God to "remember!" urge God to act, and surround the climactic question that reflects the existential crisis of the psalm: "Lord, where is your *steadfast love* of old, which by your *faithfulness* you swore to David?" (89:46-51). Thus Psalm 89 reflects the basis for the expectation of an ideal, future "messiah"; the Babylonian exile coupled with the Davidic covenant provides the context for a *future* king who would restore the monarchy.

While the final verse of Psalm 89 forms an editorial closing for book 3, its muted praise in comparison to other parallel elements reflects the tone at the end of this section (cf. 41:13; 72:18-19; 106:48); Psalm 89 ends in despair over the plight of the king that parallels the depressed tone at the end of Psalm 88. A chasm has opened between the divine promise and Israel's experience, where the overthrow of the Davidic king reflects nothing less than God's violation of covenant (89:39).

THE TEXT IN THE INTERPRETIVE TRADITION

Psalms 88–89 illustrate the debates over psalm superscriptions and their implications. Jerome reads *mahalath le'annoth*] in the heading of Psalm 88 as "the *mysterium* of the Church gathered together" to praise God and proceeds to read the psalm as Christ speaking. Abandoned by his disciples, Jerome links "you have made me a thing of horror to them" to the Jews shouting "Crucify him!" (88:8). Rashi, in contrast, reads *mahalat* as "sickness" and relates the entire poem to the collective Israel that "is now suffering the hardships of exile." For him, the psalm represents the voice of "the entire Jewish people . . . 'whom the nations once respected but now despise'" (Shereshevsky 1982, 125).

Rashi also considers the attribution of these psalms, agreeing with the superscription that Psalm 89 was composed by Ethan against a rabbinic tradition linking it to Abraham. He explains the dual superscription of Psalm 88 by suggesting that Heman is the musician and performer of a psalm that was written by the sons of Korah (Hailperin, 234; cf. Psalm 72).

THE TEXT IN CONTEMPORARY DISCUSSION

Where lament psalms "have been largely purged from the life and liturgy of the church," this represents a "costly loss" since limiting appropriate religious speech to praise and thanksgiving does not adequately reckon with the struggles of lived experience (Brueggemann, 44, 98–110). The deep despair of Psalm 88 reflects the experience of many who deal with depression and forms of mental illness, overwhelmed and perceiving no way out of a negative situation. This psalm has the potential to be a powerful resource that both provides a "voice" for those who are struggling and a call for empathetic response from others. The struggle with profound social isolation reflected in Psalm 88 challenges contemporary faith communities to support and hold onto hope for those who cannot do so themselves.

Psalm 89 also proves significant. On the one hand, it cautions against simply claiming God's promises and treating the divine as a mechanistic force to be controlled. On the other hand, it also reflects the profound disorientation of having a bedrock understanding (i.e., God's commitment to the Davidic monarchy) fundamentally challenged by experience. However, this tension does not prompt a turn *away* from but rather a turn *to* God; where contemporary "new atheism" has found a receptive audience, Psalms 88–89 and biblical lament more generally reject such a move. Though its strident tone may be unnerving, Psalm 89 reflects the audacity to call for YHWH to live up to covenant responsibilities, and thus the intimacy of the underlying relationship.

Psalms 90–100: YHWH Reigns

■ THE TEXT IN ITS ANCIENT CONTEXT

The move from book 3 to book 4 marks a significant shift from despair to hope. While the placement of royal psalms at the "seams" of books 1–3 (2; 72; 89) underscores the failure of the monarchy, book 4 (90–106) responds to the call for God to reestablish the Davidic king by reiterating God's steadfast love and faithfulness but shifts the focus to YHWH-as-king rather than a mortal monarch (Psalms 93; 95–99; Wilson 209–14, 217).

Psalm 90, identified as a prayer (*tefillah*), provides a communal plea for God to turn from anger and wrath. The only one attributed to Moses, this psalm fulfills his role of interceding on behalf of the people in a moment of crisis (see Exod. 17:1-7; 32:7-14). Where humans are called to repent, the psalmist acknowledges sin (90:3, 8) and then calls on YHWH to turn and demonstrate divine compassion and steadfast love (90:13-14; cf. 86:15; Exod. 34:6-7; Joel 2:13; Jon. 4:2). While Psalm 90 picks up several motifs (anger, the short time span of life, "how long?") and continues the shift from servant to servants noted in the previous psalm, it does not mention the "anointed," David, or the Davidic covenant. Even as it reiterates a call for God's steadfast love, the final appeal for God to uphold the work of *our* hands provides a striking contrast to the previous focus on the king (90:14; cf. 89:49-51).

Psalm 91 depicts divine protection for those who trust in God, culminating in a series of promises spoken in the first-person voice of God. Shelter, shade, and the metaphor of a bird with her brood under her wings provide images of divine protection (90:1-4; cf. Ruth 2:12; 3:9); claiming God as "my refuge" appears most frequently in the Psalms, with prayer seeming to be the epitome of seeking refuge in YHWH (e.g., Ps. 2:12; 7:1; 11:1). Military imagery, ranging from large, corporate elements to individual ones enhances the depiction of divine protection from a litany of dangers. Both military and natural imagery prove defensive, so that even though the "wicked" will receive their recompense, the recipient of the promise looks on as a bystander rather than enacting it himself

(91:8; Exod. 14:13-14; cf. Psalms 18; 149). Final promises appear in the voice of God: "I will deliver . . . protect . . . answer . . . be with them . . . rescue . . . satisfy . . . and show them my salvation" (91:14-16). Reference to those "who love me," a term used elsewhere both for God's love for Israel and in contexts of marriage, underscores the intimacy of this relationship (Gen. 34:8; Deut. 7:7; 21:11).

Psalm 92, which the heading associates with the Sabbath, provides a liturgical hymn that declares God's steadfast love and faithfulness, and so responds to the query at the end of book 3 (89:49). The psalm shifts to praise YHWH directly, reiterating the temporary nature of the current prosperity of the wicked (92:7-9; cf. Psalm 73). The concluding depiction of the righteous as a flourishing palm tree recalls Psalm 1, here linked to the temple rather than the torah (92:12-15; cf. 1:2-4).

Psalm 93 introduces the "YHWH reigns" motif, which dominates book 4 (96:10; 97:1; 98:6; 99:1). While it shares vocabulary and characteristics with royal psalms (Psalms 2; 72; 89), here these attributes are directly tied to God rather than an earthly king: YHWH reigns, wears royal robes, is established and enthroned. The sound/voice (*qol*) of the rivers and "mighty waters" provide the backdrop for heightening YHWH's majesty (93:3-4; cf. Psalms 29; 104). Some scholars have linked Psalms 93 and 95–99 to an "enthronement festival" celebrating YHWH's kingship in preexilic Israel (Mowinckel, 1:106–13). In its current setting following the description of the fall of the monarchy in Psalm 89, however, Psalm 93 addresses the crisis of exile through *divine* rule rather than reestablishing the Davidic line, meeting concerns voiced earlier in an unexpected way (see Ps. 89:49).

Psalm 94 begins with the strident call,

> O LORD, you God of vengeance,
>   you God of vengeance, shine forth!

While at first glance out of place amid assurance, praise, and "YHWH reigns" psalms, this cry reflects the logical implications of the former: as king, God's royal responsibility is to ensure the proper functioning of justice (cf. Psalms 72; 82). The cry for vengeance reflects the lament "How long?" arising from the litany of abuses of society's most vulnerable (94:1-6). Justice is the fundamental issue at play; where the wicked assume God to be inert (94:7), vengeance here "is not an arbitrary or vindictive act, but a judicial intervention against the guilty" (Sarna, 192). The lack of immediate comeuppance for the wicked underlies the angst of the psalm (cf. Psalm 73). Nonetheless, the repeated final conviction that God "will wipe them out" expresses confidence that the current situation will be rectified, and corresponds to the double calls for vengeance and the cries "How long?" at the outset (94:23; see vv. 1, 3).

Psalm 95 opens with a hymn of praise and thanksgiving to YHWH, whose identification as a "great king above all gods" highlights the polytheistic context this section assumes (95:1-3). Depicting the people as God's flock (cf. Ps. 80:1) and exhorting them to hear *his* voice provides an implicit caution against following the voices of others (the floods, Ps. 93:3-4; the enemy, 55:3; charmers, 58:5). God's voice concludes the psalm, sounding a note of caution by recalling past disobedience in the wilderness.

Psalms 96–99 continue the motif of YHWH as king. Psalm 96, linked elsewhere to Asaph and celebrating David bringing the ark of the covenant into Jerusalem (1 Chron. 16:23-33), calls for public praise and recognition of YHWH and depicts all rivals as idols (96:4-5; cf. 97:9). While it briefly mentions the sanctuary, the listeners are to declare "among the nations 'YHWH reigns'" (96:10, author trans.). This royal status, underscored by a litany of adjectives concerning God's majesty, is exemplified in divine mastery over creation and establishing justice. This in turn forms the basis for the variations to come.

> He will judge the world with righteousness [*tsedeq*],
>> and the peoples with his truth [or faithfulness, *'emunatho*]. (96:13)

Psalm 97 again asserts that "YHWH reigns" (97:1; cf. Ps. 93:1; 99:1), with the divine throne based on righteousness and justice. Third-person description shifts momentarily to directly address YHWH, where "your judgments" provide the reason for rejoicing and the implicit basis for being exalted above other gods; here again YHWH's commitment to justice differentiates this God from other would-be deities (97:8-9; cf. 82). The concluding verses directly exhort those who "love YHWH" to hate evil and give thanks, confirming God's commitment to the faithful and righteous (97:10-12); God's people are also to embody the divine characteristics described at the outset.

Psalm 98 praises God's marvelous deeds and celebrates God's *yeshu'ah*, a key term variously rendered as "victory," "salvation," "liberation," and "deliverance" (98:1-3). This effusive praise again responds to the despairing question at the end of Psalm 89, reiterating that God "has remembered his steadfast love and faithfulness" (98:3; cf. 89:49), but linking this commitment to the "house of Israel" rather than the "house of David." The psalmist calls for the earth, including the sea and floods, to praise YHWH; the last verse reiterates God's role as judge.

Psalm 99, again beginning with "YHWH reigns" (99:1, cf. 93:1; 97:1) and praising God's justice, links this claim to divine holiness and the status of the temple and Zion. Being "enthroned upon the cherubim," which generally refers to the ark of the covenant (99:1; Exod. 37:7-9; 2 Sam. 6:2), proves unusual in the Psalms. While the other contexts where the term *cherubim* appears depict God as a divine warrior who fights on behalf of the people (Ps. 18:10; 80:1), this psalm does not mention enemies but immediately links the term to Zion, later referred to as God's "holy mountain" (99:2, 9). Similarly, the communal designation "YHWH our God," which appears sparingly in the Psalter but four times in this psalm, resonates with Deuteronomic language and corresponds to the key role of Moses, Aaron, and Samuel as intermediaries (99:6).

Psalm 100 is an exuberant communal entrance liturgy, presumably to a service in the temple (100:4), that calls on all of the earth to praise YHWH. The imperative to worship (*'ibdu*, 100:2; cf. 2:11) could also be translated as "serve," with the corresponding noun "servant" (*'ebed*; cf. 89:50; 90:13, 16) providing an implicit contrast with those who *serve* other gods or idols (cf. 97:7). Both the depiction of God as shepherd (v. 3, cf. Psalm 23) and the confirmation of YHWH's steadfast love and faithfulness are familiar, and again respond to the despairing question discussed earlier (100:5; 98:3; cf. 89:49).

■ THE TEXT IN THE INTERPRETIVE TRADITION

The *Midrash on Psalms* resolves the dilemma of "orphan psalms" here by extending the attribution of Moses in Psalm 90 to this whole section (90–100), matching these eleven Psalms with Moses' blessing of the eleven tribes (Deut. 33:6-26; Braude, 2:87–88). Psalms 90–93 are also recited in both Sabbath and festival services (Holladay, 142).

From early on in the Christian tradition, these psalms were interpreted christologically. For instance, Justin Martyr sees Psalm 96 as a prediction of Christ's rule after resurrection (Holladay, 163–64). Psalms 96 and 98 continue to be used in the Advent season, with the former showing that "Christ has come, and will come again" and the latter providing the inspiration for Isaac Watts's hymn "Joy to the World" (Mays, 309–10, 312).

The basic conviction that "YHWH reigns" undergirds central prayers in both Jewish and Christian traditions: "Blessed are you, YHWH our God, *eternal king/king of the universe*" and "*Thy kingdom* come, thy will be done on earth as it is in heaven."

THE TEXT IN CONTEMPORARY DISCUSSION

The intimate connection between "YHWH reigns" and justice cannot be overemphasized. As Nahum Sarna notes, in Psalm 94, God's "people" are those being oppressed, while the "wicked" are the "corrupt, privileged upper classes" who "control the levers of power," including the legal system itself (Sarna, 195, 202). Where "lady justice" is often portrayed blindfolded with balance scales in one hand and a sword in the other, projecting an image of unbiased objectivity and the right to punish, in this psalm justice is neither blind nor disinterested, but rather *for* the widow, stranger, and orphan. As the divine king, God accepts the responsibility to function as the defender of the outcast who will also return to "judge the earth" in the future, which acts as both hope and warning for life in the present.

This recognition undercuts the tendency to think in dualistic categories, separating spiritual "salvation" from physical or social "liberation"; the term *yeshu'ah* (and the derivative name Jesus) hold these together. Similarly, though "justice" is often treated as a social phenomenon and "righteousness" related to personal piety, both commonly translate the term *tsedeq*. Claiming YHWH as king cuts through such artificial divisions and pushes adherents to recognize physical and spiritual, social and individual realms as inseparably under the rule of God.

Finally, while Psalm 91 is commonly used as a "call to worship" in Christian liturgy, the devil also quotes it to tempt Jesus to claim special messianic protection: "If you are the Son of God . . ." (Matt. 4:5-6; Luke 4:9-11; cf. Ps. 91:11-12). While people may gravitate toward psalms of comfort and assurance rather than the strident language of lament, Jesus' temptation demonstrates that the former are not immune from misuse either but reflects the hermeneutical wrestling with Scripture central to both Jewish and Christian traditions.

Psalms 101–106: Praise to God and Social Warning

THE TEXT IN ITS ANCIENT CONTEXT

Psalm 101, the first of two attributed to David in book 4 (see also 103), reflects a royal inauguration or celebration (Mays, 321). Beginning by singing of steadfast love and justice, the psalm centers on the king's commitment to blamelessness and integrity (101:2-3; cf. 18:23-25). The psalmist's commitment to turn away from and root out slander, deceit, wickedness, and evil parallels his dedication to the "faithful" and the blameless, while the dual promise to destroy reflects the royal role of responding to evil (101:5-8; cf. 94:23; 18:40). While the close association between God and king implies that enemies of one are also adversaries of the other (cf. 139:21-22), in the Psalms such violence is generally reserved exclusively for YHWH or the king as God's representative (Firth, 3).

Psalm 102, immediately identified as a prayer, moves from a typical invocation to a description of distress reflecting physical torment and derision from "enemies." The extended introduction leads to God's "indignation and anger" as the main culprit, so that God is both the court of appeal and the source of affliction (102:10; cf. Ps. 38:1-3; 88; 106:32). "But you" marks a shift from the transitory nature of human life to the eternal nature of God, and from a focus on the individual to plural "servants" (102:12-14). God's response to the prayer of the downtrodden emerges from divine kingship and the restoration of Zion (Mays, 325). Recording the prayer also provides an opportunity for future generations to move from lament to praise (102:1, 17, 21). The psalm concludes by contrasting the ephemeral nature of the psalmist with God's role as creator and confidence about the future of "your servants' children."

Psalm 103, again "of David" (cf. 101), "blesses" YHWH as divine king. The opening call to "not forget" initiates a string of participles that describe God's attributes and actions on behalf of "my soul" (forgiver, healer, redeemer), culminating in the description of YHWH quoted from Exodus that effectively links God's commitment to justice with the characteristics of steadfast love and compassion (103:8; cf. Exod. 34:6-7). Like the previous, this psalm contrasts the transitional nature of humanity with the eternal steadfast love of the divine, creator king (103:15-19) with the conclusion calling on the entire heavenly court to join the psalmist to "bless YHWH."

Psalm 104, another hymn beginning with "bless YHWH" (104:1; cf. 103:1), focuses on the cosmic scale even as it is framed by personal references to "my God" (104:1, 33). While alternating between third-person description of God and momentary direct address to YHWH has led some to argue for a composite nature or different voices present in the psalm (Gerstenberger 2001, 222), the overriding motif is clear: YHWH is the creator, sustainer, and provider of the cosmos. Although the created elements and God's role in setting limits prove similar to the creation account in Genesis 1 (104:8-9), here humanity does not represent its climax (104:23; cf. Psalm 8). The next section praises YHWH directly, both grounding creation in wisdom (cf. Prov. 8:22) and reiterating divine control over the cosmos, including the mythological elements of the sea and Leviathan (104:24-26; cf. 74:12-17). The psalmist's final call for the destruction of sinners and the wicked underscores that the God of creation also remains committed to justice on the social plane.

Psalm 105 calls for people to give thanks and remember (*zikru*) YHWH's "wonderful works" (105:5), centered on the Abrahamic covenant of land (Mays, 337). It illustrates how God has remembered his covenant with Abraham and ties it to torah obedience (105:8, 42-45). The psalm identifies Abraham, Moses, and the people as God's servant(s), rather than the Davidic king (cf. 89:3, 20, 39); even the term "anointed/messiah" refers to the patriarchs rather than the monarch here (105:15; cf. 89:38, 51).

Psalm 106 provides a counterpoint to the previous, again rehearsing Israel's story from the exodus until living in the land, only this time concentrating on the rebellion of the people (cf. Psalm

78). The initial call to give thanks to YHWH "for his steadfast love endures forever" reflects a liturgical refrain (106:1; cf. Psalm 136), while those who embody God's concern with justice and righteousness are described as "happy" (106:3; cf. 99:4; 103:6). While the psalmist's appeal for YHWH to remember him links this psalm to the previous (106:4-5; cf. 105:42-44), a communal declaration of sin introduces its main subject. Where God acted to save and redeem, the people forgot, disobeyed, and prostituted themselves, leading to divine discipline and anger. Even so, the final verses reiterate the thrust of the psalm: while the people sin and rebel, God repeatedly delivers by hearing their cry, remembering covenant, and showing steadfast love (106:43-46; cf. Exod. 2:23-25). The communal call to "save us" shifts to address God once again and corresponds to the psalmist's initial request to experience salvation (106:4, 47), while the call to "gather us from the nations" reflects an exilic context (106:47; cf. Deut. 30:1-4; Isa. 56:3-8; 66:18).

The final verse provides an editorial conclusion to book 4, similar to the previous (v. 48; cf. Ps. 41:7; 72:18-19; 89:52).

■ THE TEXT IN THE INTERPRETIVE TRADITION

As one of seven traditional "penitential psalms" (cf. Psalm 51), Psalm 102 has functioned liturgically in various settings. Along with the Songs of Ascent (120–34), the penitential psalms have been used to pray for the souls of deceased individuals in the "Office for the Dead," which became an official rite in the fifteenth century. As early as the fourteenth century, the penitential psalms, along with many other psalms, were also included in booklets called "Prymers," or "first prayers," that functioned both as devotional resources and reading instruction (Gillingham, 55, 103).

■ THE TEXT IN CONTEMPORARY DISCUSSION

Environmental and ecological issues continue to prompt significant debate. As a hymn praising God's work and role in creation, Psalm 104 is striking in part because here humanity appears as part of creation but not as its culmination or climax (104:23; cf. Genesis 1–2; Psalms 8; 72). Also, rather than concentrate on the act of creation, here God continues to be at work, limiting, sustaining, and providing.

While in the West, the type of mythological perspective underlying Psalm 74 or 104 may seem like a relic of the distant past, the conviction that this particular God controls elements that others worship can still be readily witnessed in animistic traditions today. Nonetheless, if one considers idolatry as treating something created as the Creator or mistaking the finite for the infinite, it is worth pondering what populates our own pantheon in the West. For instance, might our modern "gods" include giving free rein to the market and its "forces" as the arbiter of worth; pursuing military campaigns in support of ambiguous "national interests," acting as a contemporary version of sacrificing our sons and daughters (Ps. 106:37-38); pushing for productivity such that it becomes a contemporary fertility "god" or our own version of Baal, which refuses to recognize limits? At what point does humanity's modification of climate systems, destruction of species, and attempts to modify and even control ecological systems take "dominion" too far (cf. Gen. 1:26; Ps. 8:6)?

Ellen Davis notes that Psalm 104 proves unusual in that it does not reflect "a primordial struggle with chaos monsters" prevalent in ancient Near Eastern literature; even the sea and Leviathan, elements that elsewhere embody chaos and seem to work against the divine, are here dependent on God for their ongoing nourishment (104:25-26; cf. 74:12-17). Indeed, only the last verse and its mention of humanity suggest the possibility of opposition to God's creative and sustaining action (E. Davis, 63). In effect, perhaps humans can also represent rebellious forces of chaos that need to be limited for the good of creation (104:6-9). A critical rereading of the Bible that recognizes "the present fact of Creation" and places humanity within creation rather than outside or above it has become a crucial task (Berry, 94–95). What may at first glance appear as an ancient, superstitious relic holds contemporary significance after all.

Psalms 107–112: Imprecation and Assurance

▌ THE TEXT IN ITS ANCIENT CONTEXT

Psalm 107 begins book 5 with the same liturgical thanksgiving refrain as the previous psalm: "for his steadfast love endures forever" (107:1; 106:1; cf. 136). Where the previous called on God to "gather" Israel from the nations, here the psalmist calls on the "redeemed of YHWH" who *have been* gathered to give thanks (Ps. 106:47; 107:3). The psalm then provides four examples reflecting the same pattern: an initial portrayal of distress, a refrain describing how each "cried to YHWH," God's liberating response, and a refrain calling on them to give thanks in recognition of God's steadfast love. The final section links God's sustenance of creation to divine concern for those in distress (107:33-43), while the final appeal to the "wise" reinforces the instructional purpose of the psalm and reiterates YHWH's steadfast love as its core teaching. In contrast to Psalms 105–106, the focus here lies on God's response to the cry of those in distress without reference to Israelite history.

Psalm 108, attributed to David and drawn directly from parts of two previous psalms, links individual praise with a communal call for divine support of military victory (Pss. 57:7-11; 60:5-12; cf. 18). In its present form and setting, this psalm addresses God to reiterate frustration for having been cast off (108:11; cf. 89:38). While reference to "us" can be read as the broader community, in light of the heading and royal expectations elsewhere this could also be heard as the voice of Davidic descendants, would-be claimants to the throne (Psalms 2; 18; 89). In either case, the psalm reflects a postexilic setting and yearning for divine aid.

Psalm 109, attributed to David, is the first lament in book 5. Calling out from a setting of persecution and hateful speech, debate continues on whether the unusually extensive middle curse section reflects the words of these adversaries, as suggested by the NRSV's addition of "they say" (109:6), or those of the psalmist himself (109:6-19; Gerstenberger 2001, 258–59). In either case, the psalmist affirms these words against his accusers (v. 20), and so we cannot avoid these drastic imprecations as expressing the desires of the psalmist. The adversaries here are identified as *satan*, a Hebrew term that most frequently depicts people rather than supernatural beings in the Old Testament (109:6, 20; cf. 1 Kgs. 11:14, 23, 25). Here it appears as "accuser" or perhaps prosecuting attorney in a courtlike setting, which roughly corresponds to the role of "the *satan*" in the heavenly court in Job 1–2. The crisis in the psalm arises from a lack of *hesed* understood as "social solidarity," which leads to a direct appeal for God's *hesed* to fill this void (109:12, 16, 21, 26; Brueggemann, 275–80). The shift from curses to direct address to YHWH, emphatically marked by "but *you*" (109:21), introduces the appeal for God to rectify the situation that leads to praise and the confident assertion of God's alignment with the "poor and needy."

Psalm 110 provides reassurance based on two statements in divine first-person speech. The introductory phrase "YHWH says [*ne'um yhwh*]," which appears only here in the Psalter, typically introduces oracles in prophetic books (110:1; cf. Isa. 43:10, 12; Jer. 1:8, 15, 19; Amos 4:6, 8-11). The invitation to "my Lord" to "sit at my right hand" probably derives from an enthronement ceremony, whereby the king was recognized as divinely empowered and appointed to act as God's representative (Mays, 351–52); as elsewhere, kingship is here linked with Zion and ruling over enemies (cf. Psalm 2). A divine oath formula (*nishba' yhwh*) introduces another divine statement that adds a priestly role to the king (110:4); in its only other occurrence in the Psalms, this phrase reiterates God's commitment to the Davidic king (Ps. 132:11). The concluding verses portray "my YHWH" as a conquering king and universal judge on his day of wrath (cf. Ps. 2:8-9; 18:34-40).

Psalms 111–112 function together to describe YHWH and the benefits for those who fear him. Both begin with *halelu yah* (111:1; 112:1; cf. 146–150) and then follow a twenty-two-line acrostic pattern, where each begins with the subsequent letter of the Hebrew alphabet (cf. 119). The final verse of Psalm 111 and the first of 112 hinge the psalms together, with wisdom reflection on the "fear of the Lord [YHWH]" (111:10; cf. Prov. 1:7; 9:10) leading to "Happy is the one who fears YHWH"; similarly, "all those who do *them*" (111:10) anticipates delighting in "his commandments" (112:1; cf. 1:2), linking "fear of YHWH" to torah observance (cf. 19:9; 119). These psalms portray those who "fear YHWH" as mirroring divine attributes, including righteousness (111:3; 112:3, 9), graciousness and mercy (111:4; 112:4), justice (111:7; 112:5); uprightness (111:8; 112:2, 4), and enduring forever (111:3, 10; 112:3, 9). Finally, those who fear YHWH trust in God (112:7) and reflect divine concern for the poor (112:9; cf. 82:4; Mays, 359–60). These psalms end with the prominent wisdom motif contrasting the righteous and wicked, though here the "desire of the wicked" perishes rather than the wicked themselves (112:10; cf. 1:6).

▍ The Text in the Interpretive Tradition

Psalm 110 is the most cited psalm in the New Testament; the Gospels depict Jesus using it to problematize the idea of the anointed (*christos* in Greek, *messiah* in Hebrew): "The Lord says to my lord, 'Sit at my right hand until I make your enemies your footstool'" (Ps. 110:1). Jesus argues that, since David refers to "my Lord," "how can he be his [David's] son?" (Matt. 22:45; Luke 20:44).

Psalm 110 remained significant within the Christian tradition, in part because it explained the interim period between Jesus' death and resurrection and his return in the eschatological future (Acts 2:32-36; Heb. 1:3-4, 13; 1 Pet. 3:22; cf. Psalm 8). This psalm also reflects the repeated divine forbearance in the Psalms, where the success of the wicked and suffering of the righteous represent a temporary hiatus awaiting divine intervention to set things right (cf. Psalms 73; 94; 102).

In contrast to its significance in the Christian tradition, Psalm 110 does not appear within Jewish liturgy (cf. Psalms 2; 72; Holladay, 144).

Psalm 109, with its drastic imprecations against enemies, was cited in Jesus' passion accounts and provided the opportunity for anti-Jewish rhetoric from the early church on. For instance, Luther paints this with a broad brush as a "psalm David composed about Christ, who pronounces 'terrible curses' upon Judas and 'everyone of Judas's ilk,' including 'Judaism as a whole' as well as 'all schismatics and persecutors of the Word of Christ.'" Building on his "two kingdoms" theology, Luther suggests "it is permissible to curse on account of the Word of God; but it is wrong to curse on your own account for personal vengeance or some other personal end" (Thompson, 55, 59–60, 63).

THE TEXT IN CONTEMPORARY DISCUSSION

Cursing or imprecatory psalms such as Psalm 109 continue to generate much debate. While lament psalms have largely fallen out of use in liturgical contexts, Brueggemann (102–7) has argued for their ongoing significance for giving voice to the voiceless and challenging the status quo. Some have argued for the cathartic effect of imprecation, where voicing the desire for vengeance constitutes handing over responsibility for executing it, and thus "surrendering retribution" to God (Firth). In contrast, Amy Cottrill believes that Psalm 109 represents a "revenge fantasy" that contemporary readers must resist on the grounds not only that it may prompt violence but also that the language in itself is violent (Cottrill, 147–56).

While Cottrill helpfully warns of the potential for using imprecations to justify violence, the "satanic" reading of Psalm 91 in the Gospel accounts of Jesus' temptation reminds us that the abuse of psalms to obscure God's will rather than discover it is not unique to lament, but can be found in psalms of comfort and praise as well. Lament psalms—including those with strident curses against the enemy—hold the potential to promote empathetic understandings and responses, perhaps especially when we step away from the role as "speaker" and into that of their social audience in order to attend to the voice(s) of others in distress. This possibility underscores the vital role of contemporary communities committed to hear and discern such speech (Suderman 2012, 212–16; see Psalm 137). In so doing, we may even move from being the "hero" of the psalm to identifying with the "enemy" who needs to repent and turn from wrongdoing (see Psalm 141).

In relation to New Testament material and the broader Christian tradition, Psalm 110 raises a related issue. David Firth has argued that the perpetration of violence in "I" psalms is restricted to God, with the only exception being that of the king as God's representative (Firth, 3). While Psalm 110 illustrates this exception (110:5-6; cf. Ps. 2:9), its use in the New Testament corresponds to the general trend that does not reject the possibility of vengeance but restricts its implementation. Jesus' call for his followers to forego retribution and pursue love of enemies (Matt. 5:38-48) does not make the New Testament immune from calls for vengeance; indeed, the lament "how long?" and accompanying cry for vengeance from martyrs under the divine throne challenges common notions of "heaven" (Rev. 6:10; cf. 79:10). Once again, however, God's response reflects divine forbearance; while the "cry" is recognized as legitimate and the outcome assured, God does not act immediately. Similarly, also faced with a context of persecution, Paul instructs his listeners to "pursue (*diokontes*) the love of strangers, and bless those who persecute (*diokontas*) you" and to "never avenge yourselves, but leave room for the wrath of God" (Rom. 12:13-14, 18-19). The last verse, with its quotation from Deuteronomy, underscores the point: "For it is written: 'Vengeance is mine, *I* will repay,' says the LORD" (Rom. 12:19; cf. Deut. 32:35; Ps. 94:1). While the desire for vengeance does not disappear in the New Testament, it is clear that meting this out reflects a divine and not human prerogative.

Christian history has seen the repeated religious justification of human violence, a tendency that remains a persistent temptation. Mays points to the persistent prophetic critique of the monarchy and the eschatological way in which Psalm 110 points to God's coming kingdom as two important qualifications that guard against its use as contemporary political propaganda (Mays, 353; cf. Psalm 72).

Psalms 113–119: Praise of the Cosmic God, Giver of Torah

■ THE TEXT IN ITS ANCIENT CONTEXT

Beginning with *halelu yah*, Psalm 113 calls on the "servants of YHWH" to praise God. It portrays God in cosmic terms as "on high" and "above the heavens," but without mention of temple or Zion (113:4). God's commitment to reverse the fortunes of the poor and needy and the "barren woman" illustrate YHWH's concern for those on the margins.

Psalm 114 is a hymn of praise, unusual in that it neither addresses the divine nor recounts YHWH's deeds directly (Mays, 364). Rhetorical questions addressed to the sea, Jordan, mountains, and hills introduce YHWH's presence as the key element of the psalm. Economical in its use of words, this psalm again links God's action in Israel's particular experience with divine control over mythological forces (cf. Psalm 74).

Psalm 115 is a communal hymn centered on the issue of "trust." Briefly addressing God to affirm divine steadfast love and truth, the remainder of the psalm responds to the taunt of the nations: "where is your God?" (cf. Ps. 79:10; Isa. 36:18-20). It also critiques those who worship idols they have made, which reflects a temptation in the postexilic period (cf. 106:36, 38; Isa. 44:9-20). Whereas others *trust* in idols, the psalmist exhorts Israel, the priesthood, and those "who fear YHWH" to *trust* in God; in return, YHWH will be "their help and shield" and will bless them (115:9-13). The ending reciprocates divine blessing, with the people committing to bless YHWH forever; *halelu yah*!

Psalm 116, which is divided into two in Greek and Latin Bibles, gives thanks for deliverance from distress. The opening "I love YHWH" proves unique in the Psalms (Mays, 370) and links to the main motif of the previous, since "love" moves beyond emotional attachment to connote strong loyalty (Gen. 25:28; Exod. 20:6). The psalm follows a clear thanksgiving pattern with an opening, a description of distress and divine response, and a commitment to praise and fulfill a vow. The death of the faithful is "costly" or "grievous" to YHWH, since death eliminates their praise (116:15, Mays, 370; Ps. 115:17). The final reference to the congregation and temple underscores that thanksgiving reflects a public testimony meant to inspire and exhort the broader community, while *halelu yah* provides an opportunity for others to join the psalmist's thanksgiving (116:17-19).

Psalm 117 exemplifies the basic elements of a hymn: a call, this time for all peoples, to "praise YHWH" and an affirmation of the steadfast love and truth/faithfulness of YHWH.

Psalm 118 combines hymnic elements with others derived from individual thanksgiving. The initial verses again underscore divine steadfast love with an antiphonal call consisting of a familiar liturgical element of thanksgiving to the same groups identified in Psalm 115 (118:1-4; cf. 106:1; 107:1; 136). The psalm then shifts to a tightly structured song in which an individual voice gives thanks for deliverance from enemies, leading to the rhetorical query: "what can mortals do to me?" (v. 6; cf. 56:11). The psalmist illustrates the motif of divine help by contrasting "taking refuge" in God and trusting in mortals, "cutting off" (literally "circumcising") the surrounding threat (118:7-13). The psalmist's emphatic repetition of "the right hand of YHWH" and verbatim repetition of the praise from the "Song of the Sea" in Exodus 15 underscores a connection to the exodus (118:14; Exod. 15:2; cf. Isa. 12:2). The remainder of the psalm reflects a liturgical setting with several speakers, including an entrance appeal and response (cf. Ps. 24:7-10), individual thanksgiving and communal response, a communal blessing linked to a procession, and a declaration of thankful intimacy (118:19-29). The return to the same thanksgiving refrain frames the psalm with God's steadfast love (cf. vv. 1-4; Mays, 374).

Psalm 119, the longest chapter in the Bible, is an extended hymn that praises God and declares loyalty to law (*torah*). This third torah psalm (cf. Psalms 1; 19) is an elaborate acrostic poem structured in eight-verse blocks, with each section corresponding to consecutive letters of the Hebrew alphabet; 22 letters and 8 verses per letter result in 176 verses of poetic text. The psalm repeatedly employs seven terms related to torah: "decrees," "statutes," "commandments," "ordinances," "word," "precepts," and "promise/saying"; with few exceptions, at least one of these terms appears in each verse of the poem. Just as it employs motifs and vocabulary from each genre of the Psalms, Psalm 119 also draws on material from other scriptural books. After initial "happy are . . ." sayings (119:1-3), the remainder of the psalm addresses God, continually emphasizing commitment to *your* law, *your* decrees, *your* statutes; a momentary shift to directly address evildoers underscores this basic pattern (119:115; cf. 6:6). The psalmist's stance as God's "servant," a term that appears fifteen times, is not restricted to a Davidic king (89:3, 20, 39) or exceptional figure such as Abraham (105:6, 42) or Moses (105:26), but anyone committed to following God's torah. Though individual in form, Psalm 119 serves a didactic function to instruct its listeners (Gerstenberger 2001, 316).

▌ THE TEXT IN THE INTERPRETIVE TRADITION

Psalms 113–118, referred to as *hallel* or "praise," became a significant liturgical unit used during the Passover in early Judaism (Gerstenberger 2001, 280) that continued to be recited during the home Passover seder meal as well as in the daily liturgy for all three major pilgrim festivals: Passover, Feast of Weeks (Pentecost), and Feast of Booths (Holladay, 143).

The New Testament already draws on Psalm 118 to portray Jesus and his passion, referring to the builder's rejection of the cornerstone and the crowd using the phrase "blessed is he who comes in the name of the Lord" as Jesus enters Jerusalem (118:22, 26). Psalm 118 was later one of Luther's favorites. Reading Israel as "the elect children of God," Luther emphasizes the central motif of trust, while also tying the psalmist's setting of being surrounded to his own conflict with "the pope and his vermin"; interestingly, Luther also reinterprets "cutting them off," saying that "we Christians crush the heathen through our prayers" (118:10-14). Luther read "I shall not die" as referring to "eternal life," the "gates" as the parish, Jesus Christ as the king of Palm Sunday and the rejected "cornerstone . . . , and the builders who reject him are the Jewish and papal leadership who fail to recognize God's marvelously free grace" (Hals 1983, 278–82).

■ THE TEXT IN CONTEMPORARY DISCUSSION

As addressed repeatedly, the psalmists cry out from social—as well as physical—distress. Therefore, Psalms 116 and 118 prove significant in that they reflect structured moments of public and social rehabilitation and reentry (Jacobson, 133). While this is sometimes practiced in our day when overcoming sickness, within the criminal justice system the opposite is often the case. Whereas North American society thrives on social shame and stigmatization in criminal justice proceedings, it lacks an equivalent to transform an individual's status or symbolically reintegrate former offenders into their communities, a complex issue that relates to earlier discussions on confession and abuse (cf. Psalms 51; 55).

Finally, the postexilic setting of this section and its role in identity formation proves striking. As Psalm 119 reflects, the gift of torah is to be celebrated and cherished, and comes with the expectation of obedience; far from an unbearable burden or impossibility, Psalm 119 revels in the law as God's blueprint for abundant life (cf. Deut. 30:11-20). Counterintuitively, it was the temple's destruction and the Babylonian exile (587 BCE) that gave rise to the birth of the synagogue, a transformation that helped Judaism to survive the second temple's destruction. To this day "the Talmud" refers to the *Babylonian* rather than the Jerusalem Talmud as the more authoritative collection in the Oral Torah, which witnesses to Babylon's vital significance as a center of Jewish learning well into the Common Era.

Psalms 120–134: Pilgrimage "Songs of Ascent"

■ THE TEXT IN ITS ANCIENT CONTEXT

Psalms 120–134 are a series of short psalms identified in their headings as "Song(s) of Ascent." The latter Hebrew term appears in reference to "going up" to Jerusalem (122:4) and relates to an offering associated with temple liturgy. While different genres of psalms appear in this section, their liturgical language and frequent references to Jerusalem and Zion reflect a connection to pilgrimage (Mays, 385–86).

Psalm 120 is an individual lament calling for YHWH to rescue the psalmist from malicious speech. The final verses express frustration about living with one who "hates peace," reflecting the social aspect of this term as well-being or good relationships and suggesting physical conflict: "I [am] *peace*, but when(ever) I speak, they [are] for war" (120:6-7). Here the psalmist claims a direct link to or even embodiment of *shalom* that the NRSV's "I am *for* peace" does not capture.

Psalm 121 is a poem of assurance directed to a social audience that moves from an initial rhetorical question to a declaration of confidence that unites cosmic and intimate aspects of the divine, seeing YHWH both as creator and "my help" (121:1-2; cf. 40:17; 70:5). The response, presumably spoken to the initial speaker by a liturgical leader or functionary (Gerstenberger, 2001, 324), focuses on YHWH's role as "your *keeper*"; indeed, the Hebrew root "keep" (*shamar*) appears six times (121:3-8). Both in theme and vocabulary, this psalm proves reminiscent of other psalms of assurance (cf. Psalm 91).

Psalm 122, the first of three ascent songs attributed to David (see also Psalms 124; 131), exemplifies a pilgrimage song. Reference to being "within your gates" and rejoicing in the opportunity to "*go up*" to Jerusalem and enter the temple suggest it functioned as a "song of arrival" for pilgrims (122:1-4). Reference to the thrones "of justice" and "of the house of David" may refer to dispute mechanisms initiated by David and carried into the postexilic context (122:5, cf. 2 Sam. 8:15; 15:1-6; Mays, 392–93). Wishes for the peace of Jerusalem for the temple's sake illustrate its liturgical significance within pilgrimage traditions (cf. 120:6-7).

Psalm 123 calls for mercy and shifts from the previous speech about God to address YHWH directly. The metaphors of a male and female servant underscore both the expectancy and subordinate position of the psalmist. The double call for mercy or favor corresponds to the negative doublets in the final verses; they "have had more than enough of contempt" (123:3-4). The move from the voice of an individual to a communal "we" suggests the individual functions as a representative or spokesperson for a larger group.

Psalm 124, a second ascent song "of David" (cf. 122), articulates communal thanksgiving that builds on the motif of YHWH, maker of heaven and earth, as "help" (124:8; cf. 121:1-2). Initial repetition underscores that this has been experienced as YHWH's being "on our side" (literally "for" or "of" us; cf. Josh. 5:13-15). Though water imagery is used, the primary concern here concerns when "men (*'adam*) rose over us" (124:2, author trans.). The threefold repetition of "our souls" (124:4, 5, 7) emphasizes that their whole being was threatened; whereas "soul" implies a distinction from the body, the Hebrew *nefesh* reflects one's whole being or self. The liturgical "blessed be YHWH" introduces the metaphor of an escaping bird, which describes the fulfillment of a wish elsewhere (124:6-7; cf. 11:1; 55:6; 102:7).

Psalm 125 employs the physical attributes of Zion to depict the eternal stability of "those who trust in the LORD." Where elsewhere the psalmist complains of being surrounded by enemies or the wicked, here the hills around Jerusalem illustrate how YHWH "surrounds his people" (125:2; cf. 34:7). The "the staff of wickedness," which appears only here in the Old Testament, may refer to the external threat of foreign domination or to the internal one of injustice (Mays, 398). The concluding verse reiterates the psalm's focus on the people: "Peace be upon Israel" (cf. 128:6); by extending the *shalom* of Jerusalem and the temple to those who trust in YHWH (125:1; cf. Ps. 122:6-7), the psalm provides a poignant affirmation for pilgrims from beyond the city walls.

Psalm 126 speaks of the restoration of Zion and looks forward to an even more complete restoration of the people. The phrase "the LORD turned the captivity of Zion" applies characteristic language from the prophets to Zion itself (cf. Deut. 30:3; Jer. 29:14; Amos 9:14). The restoration most probably refers to the restoration of the temple in the postexilic period, though the New

Jewish Publication Society translation renders the entire psalm as a hope for the future. The symmetry of the psalm emerges from several repetitions ("restore," 126:1, 3; "then," twice in 126:2) that moves from a broader recognition of what YHWH has done "for them" to a corporate recognition of God's action "for us," and then an appeal for a future, more complete restoration (126:2-4). The metaphor of a wadi or seasonal stream underscores the need for restoration, while the images of sowing and reaping build on ancient Near Eastern motifs that reflect current difficulty and anticipated joy (Mays, 400).

Psalm 127, one of two psalms linked to Solomon (see also Psalm 72), employs "house" in two different ways to highlight YHWH's central significance. The initial depiction of building, guarding, and work without God as empty (127:1-2) plays on Solomon's reputation as a house-builder and this motif within wisdom literature (cf. 1 Kgs. 6:1; 7:1; Prov. 9:1; 14:1). The second section uses "house" as family or offspring (cf. 2 Sam. 7:5, 11) and "inheritance" to refer to children (literally "sons") rather than possessions or land (cf. Deut. 4:21; 26:1). The parent is "happy" in part because offspring will be able to speak "in the gate," the traditional place of adjudication and decision (cf. Ruth 4:1-6; Job 5:4; Prov. 31:23, 31).

Psalm 128 declares "happy" those who "fear YHWH," which the parallel phrase "walk in his ways" links to torah obedience (128:1, 4; cf. 112:1), because they will enjoy blessings of produce, wife, and children. While the last "blessing" of witnessing the well-being of Jerusalem and long life has a singular verb form and so addresses everyone who "fears YHWH," the final "peace be upon Israel" extends this blessing to the larger people (cf. 125:5). The psalm also emphasizes Zion's special status as the site from which divine blessing comes.

Psalm 129 extends the form of individual thanksgiving to the community (129:1-2; cf. 124:1-2). Withstanding extended abuse from enemies leads to a confident affirmation of YHWH's righteousness and initiates a series of imprecations against "all who hate Zion," which again reflects the close identification of the psalmist and the holy hill (129:5-8).

Psalm 130, the sixth "penitential prayer" in the Psalter (see Psalm 51), employs the form of an individual lament to exhort Israel to hope in YHWH. An initial invocation, cry, and reflection on sin and the possibility of forgiveness address God directly. The remainder describes how "my entire being (*naphshi*)" hopes and waits for YHWH, which is then reiterated in the exhortation to Israel. The psalm affirms God's steadfast love as the key element for addressing sin and, like the previous, concludes by moving from the individual to focus on the community, Israel.

Psalm 131, another "psalm of David" (cf. 124), continues the motif of hope by emphasizing the psalmist's patient rather than haughty stance. The metaphor of a weaned child provides the emotional draw of the psalm, while the call for Israel to "hope in YHWH" repeats the conclusion of the former (131:3; 130:7).

Psalm 132 reiterates God's commitment to the Davidic covenant and reasserts the intimate connection between Zion and the messiah. It alternates between the voice of the psalmist and direct quotations of the vows of, first, David (132:1-5; cf. 2 Samuel 6–7; Gerstenberger 2001, 363) and then YHWH (132:11-12; cf. 2 Sam. 7:12-16; 1 Kgs. 2:4; 11:38-39). The final section provides God's affirmative response and commitment to act on behalf of the priests, the faithful, and David "my anointed/messiah" (132:14-18). The psalm reasserts the link between the dominant Davidic king as servant and anointed (132:10, 17; cf. Ps. 89:4) and the divine warrior, represented by the ark and might of YHWH. Where book 4 downplayed the Davidic messiah in favor of YHWH as king, here this figure reappears in familiar style (cf. Psalms 2; 89a).

Psalms 133–134 together close the Songs of Ascent. Psalm 133 describes in glowing terms the harmony when "kindred [literally "brothers"] live together in unity" (133:1), affirming the pilgrims' communal experience. The dual images of oil running down Aaron's head and beard and dew on Mount Hermon witness to divine anointing and abundance. Psalm 134 concludes the Songs of Ascent with a blessing, addressed to "all you servants/worshipers of YHWH" (134:1). Lifting arms in the night paints a picture of ancient worship, perhaps the liturgical conclusion of a pilgrimage festival. In any case, "the psalm now stands in a literary rather than a liturgical location" (Mays, 415). It concludes in symmetry that embodies the intimacy between God and people: just as God's servants *bless* YHWH, the psalm concludes with "May YHWH . . . bless you." The divine depiction as "maker of heaven and earth," a phrase unique to book 5 of the Psalter (134:3; cf. Ps. 115:15; 121:2; 124:8; 146:5), reiterates the one being worshiped as the source of blessing.

■ THE TEXT IN THE INTERPRETIVE TRADITION

The Songs of Ascent (120–134) have continued to function liturgically, having been used to pray for the souls of deceased individuals in the "Office for the Dead," during Easter, and in medieval "Prymers" or "first prayers" (Gillingham, 55, 103; see Psalm 102).

Psalm 126 illustrates the flexibility of such material, having been used as a reading for thanksgiving, advent, and lent. In the first case references to sowing and reaping function in a straightforward sense, while the latter builds more figuratively on its rich language. The description of kindred/brothers "living together in unity" has prompted the use of Psalm 133 as a reading for the Lord's Supper, and already Augustine pointed to this psalm as significant for founding monastic communities (Mays, 400, 414).

■ THE TEXT IN CONTEMPORARY DISCUSSION

The Songs of Ascent witness to the significance of pilgrimage and place, with consistent reference to Jerusalem and Zion underscoring their special status. The connection between adoration and place, however, has been a mixed blessing. Within the Christian tradition it was the special status of the "Holy Land" that prompted Christian crusaders to "go up" to Jerusalem, also as a form of pilgrimage.

The link between pilgrimage and communal identity is further underscored in the contemporary setting, where some Jews refer to moving to Israel as "making *aliyah*" or "going up," adopting pilgrimage language to speak of permanent relocation. At the same time, within contemporary Israel and Palestine, there are interweaving narratives of historic injustice and tragedy, victimhood and victimization, strength and weakness, hope and despair, identity and land. With this context in mind, the opening "Psalm of Ascent" proves particularly striking.

> Too long have I had my dwelling among those who hate *peace* (*shalom*).
> I am *peace*, but when I speak they are for war. (120:6-7)

The psalm speaks of deep-rooted animosity and suspicion, with a sense of victimization that is raw and urgent. While the issue here seems intractable, Psalm 120 also functions as an invitation to begin to "go up."

A contemporary challenge lies in attending to the many contemporary and discordant voices within Israel and Palestine, and empathetically discerning what we hear (Psalms 44; 55; 137). The call to "pray for the peace of Jerusalem" and the possibility of pervasive well-being remains both suggestive and elusive (122:6). We pray for the day when Jewish, Muslim, and Christian inhabitants of these lands may say together: "How very good and pleasant it is when kindred live together in unity!" (Ps. 133:1).

Psalms 135–145: From Distress to Praise

■ THE TEXT IN ITS ANCIENT CONTEXT

In addition to reflecting a wide range of emotions, settings, and genres, Psalms 135–145 include the final Davidic collection of the Psalter, which frames book 5 (138–145; cf. 108–110).

Psalm 135 is a hymn celebrating the sovereignty of YHWH, whose opening and conclusion reflect a liturgical call and response that invites different groups to "praise" and then "bless" YHWH (135:1-4, 19-21). The psalm shifts to first person to describe YHWH's status "above all gods," reflected in God's control over creation and mythological forces as well as the nations (cf. Ps. 74:12-17; 104:24-26; Psalm 105); the God of the cosmos is also the one who has acted on behalf of Israel in the exodus and provided the gift of land. Momentary address to YHWH introduces confidence in God's judgment and compassion (v. 13), a telling contrast to the inaction of idols (cf. Ps. 115:4-8; Isa. 44:18). The servants of Pharaoh and those who make and trust in idols provide the negative foil for the servants of YHWH and so reinforce the close identification of YHWH with "his people" Israel.

Psalm 136 represents another antiphonal hymn, where a leading voice speaks the initial lines and the gathered assembly responds with the chorus: "for his steadfast love endures forever." In doing so, the psalm recounts and celebrates God's role in creation, the exodus, and providing the land (cf. Psalm 105).

Psalm 137, a communal lament for Jerusalem, stands in stark contrast to the previous psalms. Set in Babylon, Zion exists as a memory rather than a lived reality. The prior conviction of Zion's inviolability adds salt to the wound when captors ask for a "song of Zion" (137:3-4; cf. 48:8-14; 132:13-18), while reference to a "foreign (*nekar*) land" implicitly links Babylon to the idolatry condemned elsewhere (Ps. 135:15-18; cf. Deut. 31:16; Josh. 24:20-23; Prov. 7:5). While direct address to "daughter Babylon" mirrors the earlier speech to Jerusalem, here the psalmist articulates drastic, vengeful wishes that shock contemporary readers: "Happy is the one who seizes and dashes your children against the rock" (137:9). While a few passages in the Old Testament refer to such harsh treatment in military contexts (e.g., 2 Kgs. 8:12; Hosea 10:14; Nah. 3:10), this passage reflects a desire for Babylon to be paid back in kind rather than personal vengeance. Memory is a key element here: the captives remember Zion and curse themselves if they "do not remember" Jerusalem (137:1,

5-6), which then grounds the imperative plea for YHWH to also remember. This psalm implicitly questions whether God will remember the covenant with Zion and David voiced in earlier psalms (89a, 132), or whether divine steadfast love will not prove trustworthy. The vengeful wishes here should not lead the reader to disregard the existential crisis it reflects (see section below).

Psalm 138 begins the final "of David" collection (138–145) with thanksgiving, shifting back and forth between direct address to and speech about YHWH. The initial vow to "give you thanks . . . before the gods (*'elohim*)," rendered "angels" in the Septuagint, suggests a polytheistic context (cf. Psalm 82); "your holy temple" contrasts with the Babylonian context, during which the temple lay in ruins. This psalm returns to praise God's steadfast love and truth/faithfulness (cf. Ps. 25:10; 86:15) for responding to the psalmist's distress, and sees his own praise as anticipating that of the "kings of the earth" (138:2-4). The "height" of YHWH draws attention to divine attention to the lowly, while the psalmist enjoys divine protection from enemies. The final praise for God's steadfast love reflects a liturgical formula used elsewhere and prompts an appeal for it to be sustained (138:8; Ps. 136).

Psalm 139, a second psalm "of David" that addresses God throughout, portrays YHWH's intimate knowledge and care for the psalmist. An initial description leads to a series of rhetorical questions confirming the pervasive divine presence; Jonah provides a case in point for one attempting to flee from God's presence (139:7; Jon. 1:3). "You knit me together in my mother's womb" introduces the next part of the psalm, leading to what at first glance seems a dramatic shift in tone from meditating on God's thoughts to calling for the destruction of the wicked (139:17-22). However, the strident imprecations here reflect the logic of the psalm, extending the shared intimacy between God and the psalmist to claim that God's enemies are those of the psalmist as well (cf. Ps. 26:5; 31:6). The concluding call for God to "search me" reflects a commitment to introspection and self-critique that proves significant after such strident self-identification with God.

Psalm 140, another "psalm of David," is an individual lament that calls on YHWH for deliverance from violent men. The psalmist intermingles statements of confidence with pleas for help, before calling for the destruction of the enemy by allowing the adversaries' designs to fall on themselves (140:6-10; 69:22). The psalm concludes with a confident assertion addressed to a social audience regarding divine justice for the poor and needy, and anticipates thanksgiving from the righteous.

Psalm 141, yet another "psalm of David," inverts the usual language of individual lament to ask God to preserve the psalmist himself from evil. An initial invocation calling on YHWH to come quickly moves to an appeal for the psalmist's prayer and liturgical gestures to be counted as sacrifices. The psalmist then appeals to God to guard him from joining forces or even becoming one of the "evildoers" (131:3-4; cf. 6:8). While "guard my mouth" addresses the persistent issue of malicious speech, the psalmist also asks God to keep him from evil, wickedness, and evildoers. Although the translation of 141:5-7 proves elusive, the motif continues since the psalmist's commitment to "delightful" words contrasts with his wicked potential, further underscored by the resonance between "my mouth" and the "mouth of Sheol" (141:3, 7). The psalmist looks to YHWH for orientation and to seek refuge (141:8), reiterating a key theme from early in the Psalter (Ps. 2:12; 7:1; 11:1; cf. 144:2). The final appeal to "guard me" transforms the trap described elsewhere as the vindictive attack of the enemies to the seductive allure of joining forces with "evildoers" (141:9; cf. 140:5).

Psalm 142, set as David "in the cave" by a contextual heading (cf. 1 Sam. 22:1; 24:3-4; Psalms 3; 51), is an unusual individual lament that begins by describing an appeal to YHWH in the third person rather than an invocation directed to God. Three consecutive imperatives to "attend," "rescue," and "bring me out" exemplify the psalmist's stance of taking refuge in God (142:5-7). The concluding vow to praise describes recognition and social rehabilitation among the righteous (cf. Psalm 88).

Psalm 143, the third consecutive prayer/lament (*tefillah*) of David (v. 1; cf. 141:2; 142:1), employs characteristic vocabulary to call directly on God for help from enemies. Following an invocation appealing to "your faithfulness" and "your righteousness," the beleaguered psalmist's loss of spirit prompts him to "remember" and "meditate" on God's past action, so that his entire being (*nephesh*) thirsts for God (143:1-6). Appeals for YHWH to "answer," "not hide your face," "rescue," and "teach me" are grounded in divine steadfast love and the psalmist's trust (143:7-10). This in turn leads to the final appeal for God's righteousness and steadfast love to manifest themselves by preserving the psalmist on one hand and dealing harshly with the enemies on the other.

While literary dependence is difficult to demonstrate, Psalm 144 combines vocabulary and motifs from previous psalms to address a new setting (Gerstenberger 2001, 427). The initial description of God, including that he "trains my hands for war," and the high depiction of humans resonate elsewhere (Ps. 144:1-7; cf. Ps. 8:4; 18:1-2, 9, 34). The psalm calls on the cosmic YHWH to respond to the psalmist's plight, brought on him by foreigners and their emptiness (144:7-8, 11; cf. 137:4; 139:20). The commitment to "sing a new song," linked to God's rescuing "his servant David" from enemies, resonates with royal psalms (144:9-11; cf. Ps. 18:1; 89:4, 21; 132:10). The concluding wishes for the well-being of the community (144:12-14; cf. 128:1-3) and happiness for "the people whose God is the LORD" (144:15; cf. 33:12) suggest that here again the well-being of the people is intimately tied with that of the Davidic king (cf. Psalm 72).

Psalm 145 is an acrostic hymn that provides the "climax" for book 5 and introduces the praise that closes the Psalter as a whole (Wilson, 225). The only psalm whose heading reads a "*praise* (*tehillah*) of David*," it alternates back and forth between praises to God and descriptions about the divine. Heard as the voice of David, the opening proves particularly striking since it highlights *God* as king, and so reiterates the major motif from book 4 (145:1; 93:1; 97:1; 99:1). The initial praise culminates in the quotation of the description of YHWH from Exodus, acclaiming God's compassion and steadfast love (145:8; cf. Exod. 34:6; Ps. 86:15; 103:8), which in turn leads to the emphatic insistence that "the LORD is good to *all*, and his *compassion* is over *all* that he has made." From this point on, the word "every/all" (*kol*) appears fourteen more times (seventeen in total in this psalm), which gives the psalm a breathless "comprehensiveness" as it underscores the divine-king motif and insists on God's concern for the lowly and those who cry out (145:11-19; Mays, 437–38). The psalmist reiterates the basic conviction from the outset of the Psalter that YHWH "watches over *all* who love him (the 'righteous'), but *all* the wicked he will destroy" (145:20; 1:6). This double "all" asserts comprehensive surety, despite the counterevidence in the intervening psalms themselves. The final intention to praise YHWH and claim that "*all* flesh will bless his holy name" serves a double purpose, forming an inclusio with the first verse of this psalm and introducing the central motif of the final section (146–150; Wilson, 225–26).

■ THE TEXT IN THE INTERPRETIVE TRADITION

Within Jewish liturgy, Psalm 137 is significant in that it is used daily in the "blessing after meals" on weekdays, and so links the home meal to remembering the "altar of the sacrifice in the temple" and the "loss of the temple in Jerusalem" (Holladay, 145).

While Babylon and Jerusalem already begin to function symbolically within the New Testament, the early church fathers tend to interpret this psalm allegorically. In a particularly striking example, Augustine provides an allegorical interpretation that builds on Origen and Jerome to interpret the children of Babylon as "newly-born evil desires" that his listeners should eliminate by dashing them against the "rock," which is Christ, before they become deep-rooted habits. For Augustine, this psalm also represents an ecclesial lament that recalls the church's persecution by its adversaries that predicts rather than advocates for divine judgment, with the goal of repentance (Thompson, 57–58).

■ THE TEXT IN CONTEMPORARY DISCUSSION

The drastic imprecations of Psalm 137 illustrate the vital significance of attending to "voice" for interpreting psalms. While this psalm can be interpreted as vindictive and hopelessly violent, its utter disorientation and despair also provides an opportunity for empathy with the millions of contemporary people who have been ravaged and displaced by war. Where dealing with imprecations in the psalms can be treated as an abstract philosophical problem—or even a reason to dismiss or even functionally eliminate offending biblical material—an empathetic hearing of Psalm 137 as an expression of posttraumatic stress moves beyond a justification of violence or call for militant action by those seeking to inflict it on others; the same words can have a very different function and significance when spoken by a traumatized refugee rather than a president or (para)military commander. The issue becomes particularly complex when these people may be one and the same (cf. Psalm 55). Unfortunately, in many contemporary settings, people do not suffer from *post*traumatic stress, since their distress is ongoing. Psalm 137 does not call on God to give the psalmist or his community the strength or skill to enact vengeance, even as it dramatically evokes the anger and despair of displacement (cf. Ps. 18:34, 47; 149:6-9; see Psalm 109).

Psalm 141 proves particularly significant in this regard. Where the psalmists repeatedly cry out to YHWH to free them from the vicious speech and wicked actions of the enemy, this psalm reflects how tempting it can be to collude with these "doers of evil." Psalm 141 should give us pause, since it reflects the possibility of becoming one of the wicked and so challenges the tendency to always see ourselves on the side of right, justice, and equity (see Psalm 44). Within the Christian tradition, the request here resonates with the familiar phrase from the Lord's Prayer: "Lead us not into temptation"; the concluding introspection following the imprecation of Psalm 139 points in a similar direction.

Psalms 146–150: Praise YHWH—Hallelujah!

■ THE TEXT IN ITS ANCIENT CONTEXT

Psalms 146–150 enact the concluding call of the previous psalm for all flesh to bless YHWH (Ps. 145:21). Each psalm begins and ends with *halelu yah* ("praise YHWH!"), calling for praise in ever-broadening circles: from an individual voice (David, 146), to Israel and Jerusalem (147), the angels and creation (148), and finally "all flesh" (150; Wilson, 193–94). Rather than an isolated section or summary of book 5, these psalms function as a doxological conclusion to the Psalter as a whole.

Psalm 146 fulfills the individual praise promised earlier (145:21). The psalmist begins with direct address to "my soul" and a vow to lifelong praise before addressing a social audience, exhorting his listeners to not trust in princes, whose spirit is temporary (147:1-4); again, this motif proves particularly striking if heard as the voice of David (cf. 145:21; Wilson, 226). The wisdom saying "happy are those . . ." emphasizes hope in God as "maker of heavens and earth," "doer of justice," and "giver of food" (146:5-7), which lead to a series of emphatic statements: "*YHWH* sets . . . *YHWH* opens." The fivefold repetition of the divine name and use of participles emphasizes that *this* God is active, with a strong focus on liberation and the plight of the socially marginal. The final verse extends the previous claim into the future, so that "YHWH reigns" (93:1; 97:1; 99:1) here becomes "YHWH will [continue to] reign *forever*" (v. 10). *Halelu yah*!

Psalm 147 elicits communal praise for YHWH, reiterating God's care for the downtrodden and stance against the wicked. Again the psalmist describes YHWH with a string of participles focused on divine social commitments and God's role as creator. God does not delight in military might (the "strength of the horse") but in those who "fear him" and hope in divine steadfast love (147:10-11), just as those whose delight lies in YHWH's torah are "happy" (Psalm 1:2). The LXX takes the subsequent *halelu yah*, a call to Jerusalem and Zion themselves to "praise YHWH," as the beginning of a new psalm, and divides it here (147:12; Gerstenberger 2001, 444). In any case, the peace of the city derives from YHWH and no one else (147:14). Where the prince's spirit is fleeting, God's spirit and word act together (146:3-4; 147:18); Israel is distinct not by its own merits but because it alone has received this word. While the term *torah* does not appear, word, statutes, and ordinances all relate to this term elsewhere (cf. Deut. 4:5-8; Psalm 119). The gift of torah is yet another reason for praise: *Halelu yah*!

Psalm 148 expands the praise still further, with six consecutive imperative calls to heavens, angels, hosts, and the cosmos to "praise him!" (148:1-4). The sequence and all-encompassing call to creation, including the mythological elements of sea monsters and the deeps, recalls the Genesis creation account and underscores God's sovereignty and control (148:7; Gen. 1:21 cf. Psalms 74; 104). The final call to all of humanity underscores the special status of "his people," "his faithful ones," and "the children of Israel." *Halelu yah*!

Psalm 149 builds on the previous psalm, but concentrates on the faithful (149:2, 5, 9; 148:14). The initial call to praise invites listeners into the company of the faithful, linking the children of Zion with YHWH as king, who "takes pleasure in his people" (149:4; cf. Ps. 93:1; 147:11). Where elsewhere vengeance is reserved for God or the Davidic king (18:47; 79:10; 94:1; 99:8), this psalm calls on the people themselves as agents for vengeance and judgment in a highly unusual fashion. Given the ambiguity of the Hebrew verb forms here, it is unclear whether this section should be read as a wish ("Let . . .") or future ("The high praises of God will be . . ."), and so scholars debate whether this passage is best seen in light of a historical link to "theologically sanctioned violence" or as referring to an eschatological future (149:5-9; Gerstenberger 2001, 454–55; cf. Psalm 72). In either case, the focus here lies in the judgment of ruling and socioeconomic elites and salvation for the humble (149:4; Brueggemann, 125); the tables are turned so those formerly bound are liberated, while those who acted with impunity are bound (146:7; 149:8; cf. 2:3). *Halelu yah!*

Psalm 150 concludes the Psalter with a resounding call to "praise," repeating the imperative *halelu* twelve times in its six verses. The psalm moves from describing YHWH to a picture of liturgical worship (150:1-5); the blowing of the shofar (ram's horn) was used as a summons in liturgical and military contexts (150:3; see Lev. 25:9; Josh. 6:8-9; Judg. 6:34). The concluding call to praise for "anything that breathes" summarizes not only the concluding "Hallelu" psalms (146–150) but also the entire Psalter, rearticulating the previous call (150:6; see Ps. 145:21; Wilson, 194). *Halelu yah!*

▌ THE TEXT IN THE INTERPRETIVE TRADITION

While the *Midrash on the Psalms* describes the reason for vengeance in Psalm 149 as the nations' treatment of Israel, it also limits this to foreign kings rather than the "common people" (149:8; cf. 2:2). Further, it draws on other passages to transform this psalm's unusual call for the "faithful . . . to execute vengeance on the nations" into God's vengeance, an interpretive move similar to Paul in Romans 12 (see Ps. 109; also "Contemporary Discussion" below, p. 597; cf. Deut. 32:43; Nah. 1:2; Braude 2:384).

Similarly, the exceedingly rare phrase in the Greek Bible of "two-edged" (literally "two-mouthed") sword links this passage to the "son of man" in Revelation (cf. Ps. 149:6 LXX; cf. Sir. 21:3; Rev. 1:16; 2:12), where it is both limited to Christ and transformed into his speech (cf. Heb. 4:12). In a similar vein, within Revelation the conquering "lion of Judah" is revealed as the slaughtered lamb, while the people tread a path of martyrdom rather than vengeance (Rev. 5:5-6; 6:10-11).

Where Christians may assume that the psalmist's call for God's vengeance represents an Old Testament problem (Ps. 75; 83; 94), the setting of oppression and persecution prompts similar language in the New Testament as well (cf. Ps. 79:10; Rev. 6:10). The key shift in the New Testament lies not in the absence of God's judgment, but in the conviction that it is *God's* role to execute vengeance and not that of the believing community (cf. Psalm 18; Matt. 5:38-45; 25:31-46; Rom. 12:17-21; Rev. 6:11).

▌ THE TEXT IN CONTEMPORARY DISCUSSION

The Psalms' concluding call to praise YHWH is based on who God is; humans join in as one part of the larger creation, a cosmic chorus praising its maker. This hymnic language does not eclipse the deeply personal and emotional language of much of the Psalter, but rather provides its grounding and orientation.

We may wonder why Psalm 149 ruins such a wonderful litany of praise. Rather than sidestep this psalm, perhaps it too can be a significant hermeneutical irritant for our time. In an "age of terror," it is important for Jews and Christians alike to recognize calls for religiously based violence within our own traditions rather than merely critiquing those beyond them. For communities of faith dedicated to following Jesus Christ as Lord—and not Caesar(s), ancient or contemporary—such calls to become instruments of divine vengeance represent a temptation rather than fulfillment of the divine will. Once again, the dilemma represented by this passage lies not so much in the presence of such words in Scripture as in the orientation and basic commitments of the community dedicated to interpret it (see discussion of Psalm 109). Indeed, while there are many historical examples where biblical violence has been employed to legitimate or sanction their own, to treat such a passage in this way in the Christian tradition fails to recognize the transformation of vengeance reflected in the New Testament.

At the same time, Psalm 149 underscores that the anticipated praise of YHWH by all nations, peoples, and rulers has yet to become a reality. We live with the ongoing tension of a promise and conviction yet to be fulfilled. Against persistent appearances to the contrary, the Psalms challenge contemporary listeners to declare that God does watch over his people, and that injustice and oppression will not have the last word. As we join in the resounding praise, we also do so aware that we may be part of the systems and powers that God opposes and will bring to judgment (Psalm 141). Rather than triumphant imperialism or smug self-satisfaction, the cacophony of praise at the end of the Psalms prompts ongoing introspection (cf. Psalm 139), whereby we evaluate whether we are indeed abandoning ourselves in the radical trust of God (Brueggemann, 126–29).

Works Cited

Adamo, David Tuesday. 2009. "Psalm 29 in Africa Indigenous Churches in Nigeria." In *Psalm 29 Through Time and Tradition*, edited by Lowell K. Handy, 126–43. Princeton Theological Monograph Series 110. Eugene, OR: Pickwick.

Alter, Robert. 1985. *The Art of Biblical Poetry*. New York: Basic.

Anderson, Bernhard W., and Steven Bishop. 2000. *Out of the Depths: The Psalms Speak for Us Today*. 3rd ed. Louisville: Westminster John Knox.

Bail, Ulrike. 1998. "'O God, Hear My Prayer': Psalm 55 and Violence Against Women." In *Wisdom and Psalms: A Feminist Companion to the Bible*, edited by Athalya Brenner and Carole R. Fontaine, 242–63. Sheffield: Sheffield Academic Press.

Berry, Wendell. 1993. "Christianity and the Survival of Creation." In *Sex, Economy, Freedom and Community: Eight Essays*, 93–116. New York: Pantheon.

Blumenthal, David R. 1993. *Facing the Abusing God: A Theology of Protest*. Louisville: Westminster John Knox.

Bonhoeffer, Dietrich. 2005. *Prayerbook of the Bible: An Introduction to the Psalms*. In *Life Together and Prayerbook of the Bible*, edited by Geffrey B. Kelly, 141–81. Translated by Daniel W. Bloesch and James H. Burtness. Dietrich Bonhoeffer Works 5. Minneapolis: Fortress Press.

Braude, William G., trans. 1959. *The Midrash on Psalms*, 2 vols. Yale Judaica Series 13. New Haven: Yale University Press.

Brueggemann, Walter. 1995. *The Psalms and the Life of Faith*. Edited by Patrick D. Miller. Minneapolis: Fortress Press.

Childs, Brevard S. 1971. "Psalm Titles and Midrashic Exegesis." *JSS* 16, no. 2:137–50.

Cottrill, Amy C. 2008. *Language, Power, and Identity in the Lament Psalms of the Individual*. LHB/OTS 493. New York: T&T Clark.

Davis, Ellen F. 2008. *Scripture, Culture, and Agriculture: An Agrarian Reading of the Bible*. Cambridge: Cambridge University Press.

Davis, Stacy. 2009. "Not Elijah's God: Medieval Jewish and Christian Interpretation of Psalm 29." In *Psalm 29 Through Time and Tradition*, edited by Lowell K. Handy, 69–78. Princeton Theological Monograph Series 110. Eugene, OR: Pickwick.

Firth, David G. 2005. *Surrendering Retribution in the Psalms: Responses to Violence in Individual Complaints*. Waynesboro, GA: Paternoster.

Gerstenberger, Erhard S. 1988. *Psalms, Part 1: With an Introduction to Cultic Poetry*. FOTL 14. Grand Rapids: Eerdmans.

———. 2001. *Psalms, Part 2, and Lamentations*. FOTL 15. Grand Rapids: Eerdmans.

Gillingham, S. E. 2012. *Psalms Through the Centuries*. Vol. 1. Oxford: Wiley-Blackwell.

Gunkel, Hermann; Joachim Begrich. 1998. *Introduction to Psalms: The Genres of the Religious Lyric of Israel*, Translated by James D. Nogalski. Mercer Library of Biblical Studies. Macon, GA: Mercer University Press.

Gunkel, Hermann. 1967. *The Psalms: A Form-Critical Introduction*. Second Edition. Trans. Thomas M. Horner. Biblical Series 19. Philadelphia: Fortress Press. Translated from vol. 1 of the second edition of *Die Religion in Geschichte und Gegenwart* (Tubingen: J.C.B. Mohr [Paul Siebeck], 1930).

Hailperin, Herman. 1963. *Rashi and the Christian Scholars*. Pittsburgh: University of Pittsburgh Press.

Hals, Ronald M. 1983. "Psalm 118." *Int* 37, no. 3:277–83.

Holladay, William Lee. 1993. *The Psalms through Three Thousand Years: Prayerbook of a Cloud of Witnesses*. Minneapolis: Fortress Press.

Houston, Walter J. 1999. "The King's Preferential Option for the Poor: Rhetoric, Ideology and Ethics in Psalm 72." *BibInt* 7, no. 4:341–67.

Jacobson, Rolf A. 2004. *"Many Are Saying": The Function of Direct Discourse in the Hebrew Psalter*. LHB/OTS 397. New York: T&T Clark.

Jobling, David. 1992. "Deconstruction and the Political Analysis of Biblical Texts: A Jamesonian Reading of Psalm 72." *Semeia* 59:95–127.

Mays, James Luther. 1994. *Psalms*. IBC. Louisville: John Knox Press.

McCann, J. Clinton, Jr. 2011. "The Single Most Important Text in the Entire Bible: Toward a Theology of the Psalms." In *Soundings in the Theology of Psalms: Perspectives and Methods in Contemporary Scholarship*, edited by Rolf A. Jacobson, 63–75. Minneapolis: Fortress Press.

Mowinckel, Sigmund. *The Psalms in Israel's Worship*, vol. 1 and 2. The Biblical Resource Series. Translated by D.R. Ap-Thomas. Grand Rapids: Eerdmans, 2004.

Ollenburger, Ben C. 1987. *Zion, the City of the Great King: A Theological Symbol of the Jerusalem Cult*. JSOTSup 41. Sheffield: JSOT Press.

Sarna, Nahum M. 1995. *On the Book of Psalms: Exploring the Prayers of Ancient Israel*. New York: Schocken.

Sheppard, Gerald T. 1991. "'Enemies' and the Politics of Prayer in the Book of Psalms." In *The Bible and the Politics of Exegesis: Essays in Honor of Norman K. Gottwald on His Sixty-Fifth Birthday*, edited by David Jobling, Peggy Lynne Day, and Gerald T. Sheppard, 61–82. Cleveland: Pilgrim.

Shereshevsky, Esra. 1982. *Rashi, the Man and His World*. New York: Sepher-Hermon Press.

Suderman, W. Derek. 2010. "Are Individual Complaint Psalms Really Prayers? Recognizing Social Address as Characteristic of Individual Complaints." In *The Bible as a Human Witness to Divine Revelation: Hearing the Word of God through Historically Dissimilar Traditions*, edited by Randall Heskett and Brian Irwin, 153–70. LHB/OTS 469. New York: T&T Clark.

———. 2012. "The Cost of Losing Lament for the Community of Faith: On Brueggemann, Ecclesiology, and the Social Audience of Prayer." *JTI* 6, no. 2:201–18.

Sugirtharajah, R. S. 2001. *The Bible and the Third World: Precolonial, Colonial, and Postcolonial Encounters*. Cambridge: Cambridge University Press.

Sweeney, Marvin A. 2008. *Reading the Hebrew Bible after the Shoah: Engaging Holocaust Theology*. Minneapolis: Fortress Press.

Thompson, John Lee. 2007. *Reading the Bible with the Dead: What You Can Learn from the History of Exegesis That You Can't Learn from Exegesis Alone*. Grand Rapids: Eerdmans.

Westermann, Claus. 1981. *Praise and Lament in the Psalms*. Translated by Keith R. Crim and Richard N. Soulen. Atlanta: John Knox.

Wilson, Gerald H. 1985. *The Editing of the Hebrew Psalter*. SBLDS 76. Chico, CA: Scholars Press.

Zenger, Erich. 1996. *A God of Vengeance? Understanding the Psalms of Divine Wrath*. Louisville: Westminster John Knox.

PROVERBS

Carole R. Fontaine

Introduction

Proverbs is a composite text, like so many others in the Bible, woven of discrete blocks of material drawn from different times and places. Some individual proverbs probably began as oral compositions in the towns and villages of Israel and Judah as early as the Iron I period of settlement (c. 1200–1000 BCE). Like all Wisdom literature, the book reflects an international awareness because of its scribal origin as a product of the bureaucracies of teachers, counselors, administrators, and scribes of indigenous monarchies (1 Sam. 8:15-18; 20:23-26; 1 Kgs. 4:1-6). Later, the sages in the Second Temple period maintained administrative contacts with the empires that colonized them (Perdue, 105–7). The final editing of Proverbs probably can be placed within the late Persian or early Ptolemaic periods, with a final point for dating the collection before the persecution of the Jews by the Seleucid monarch Antiochus IV Epiphanes in 175 BCE.

Individual proverbs are composed in parallelism, the primary feature of Hebrew poetry, where the second line of a verse restates the first in some way (synonymous = basic identity; antithetic = contrast; or synthetic/formal = second part advances the first). Most proverbs are composed as two-line verses, but longer compositions (especially in 1-9 and 30:1—31:31) pile up parallelisms, creating much longer compositions. In general, the sages favor antithetic parallelism because they present options between what is good and approved and what is not. By adopting this rhetorical form, they invite hearers to make correct decisions. The poetry of Proverbs also uses syntactical variations: uncommon word order, omission of verbs, or distributive use of adjectives so that they refer to elements in both lines of the verse, and so forth. These features require the hearer—often fancied to be a student of the sage—to puzzle over meanings, thereby enhancing his or her growth as an astute user of purposeful language.

Given the diversity of content and social circumstances, it is no coincidence that early Christian missionaries often began their work by translating Proverbs into local dialects, since in traditional societies such forms represent hallowed knowledge. The use of proverbs—biblical or otherwise—globally in modern development work and as measures of psychological and cognitive competence connects these ancient oral forms to modern endeavors.

The book will be divided into "sense units" as follows:

Proverbs 1:1-33: Wisdom Introduced
Proverbs 2:1—6:35: Instructions by the Sage Parent
Proverbs 7:1—9:18: A Triad of Females: Wisdom, Folly, and Strange Woman
Proverbs 10–15: Antithetic Teachings Collection
Proverbs 16:1—22:16: The Royal Collection
Proverbs 22:17—24:22: The Egyptian Teachings
Proverbs 24:23-34: More Sayings of the Wise
Proverbs 25:1—29:27: More Sayings of Solomon
Proverbs 30:1—30:33: Teachings and Numerical Sayings
Proverbs 31:1-9: A Mother's Instruction
Proverbs 31:10-31: Acrostic on the Strong Woman

Proverbs 1:1-33: Wisdom Introduced

THE TEXT IN ITS ANCIENT CONTEXT

Proverbs 1:1-7: A Course in Wisdom

Proverbs begins with a theological syllabus from the Second Temple period, introducing Solomonic authorship (1 Kgs. 4:29-34; cf. ascriptions in Prov. 1:1; 10:1; Eccles. 1:1; Song of Sol. 1:1; Psalms 72; 127). Solomon's legendary knowledge made him the envy of surrounding peoples (1 Kings 10). Solomon could not have been the author of the whole books of Proverbs, Qoheleth, or Song of Songs, since some sections are in late Biblical Hebrew. The Solomonic ascription protects these often secular, not particularly religious or "Israelite," wisdom books from being disqualified from the canon. In that sense, Solomon has indeed "authored" the appearance of wisdom within the biblical tradition.

Jews—especially the elite, learned class of the postexilic period—found themselves living in a more cosmopolitan world as provinces of Persian or Hellenistic empires. Traditions of Greek philosophy were known, which called for a new articulation of the source of Jewish knowledge, the Torah. In highlighting Solomon's legendary wisdom, sages and students found a secure, Jewish base for their work and daily ethics.

The opening treatise offers an organic approach to study: Wisdom teaches moral and ethical values (not simply facts), and the "course" will use a literary method, teaching the skillful use of language as well as mastery of social skills (wise dealing, etc.). Whether a son leaving the family to take up a scribal post at the court, or an already learned sage, all can "hear and gain in learning."

Willingness to accept correction, regardless of age or status, is a key feature of wisdom. Understanding hidden meanings of riddles and metaphorical turns of phrase helps develop cognitive skills, and "cultural competence" is learned through interpreting complex, multilayered speech as proverbs and "enigmas" (NRSV "figure," 1:6).

The passage ends with the "motto" (Fox 2000, 67–71) in 1:7: "'fear of the Lord' is the beginning of wisdom." This fear is a key term for the religion of ancient Israel *and* a way of being that roots all thought and action in a creaturely relationship before God. This is *the* prerequisite for learning and having "wisdom." Fools who reject wisdom and reproof are not simply untutored or stupid; they make an existential *choice* that distances them from God and wisdom.

Proverbs 1:8-19: The Father's Instruction

A section of "instructions of the father" (sage) to the youth (student) begins—a form familiar from Egyptian literature (the *sebayit*; see below, Prov. 22:17—24:22). Instructions incorporate proverbs and miscellaneous forms to make longer poetic units. The sage inhabits the role of the patriarchal father, the final authority for the socioeconomic unit (*bet 'ab*) of the extended family. Probably composed after the proverb collections, this section of the book probably reflects a more educational or professional context of scribal training as the real "life setting" (Perdue, 86–89).

Egyptian parallels appear: a "garland" reflects the headdress symbolizing status and excellence; "pendants" are signature seals indicating scribal office and personal name (1:9; cf. 3:3; 4:9; 7:3; allusions in Deut. 6:6-9; Sir. 6:29-31; Prov. 6:21; 3:22). In 1:11-14, the deceptive speech of temptation is used by the "father" to depict the wicked path of sinners of Ps. 1:1. Such behavior ends in death in the form of Sheol/the Pit (1:12). Evil acts inevitably bring about their own punishment, at least in Proverbs—a theory known by modern interpreters as the act-consequence relationship, and a concept dear to the hearts of educators of every time and place ("What goes around comes around").

The "Torah of the Mother," equal to the father's, appears as a source of knowledge to which the child/scribe must attend with all seriousness (1:8; 4:3; 6:20; cf. 31:1-9, 26). Women were important household managers and first teachers to children, but this may also refer to their social roles under later empires (Fontaine 2002). This instruction ends with irony: the wicked intend a bloody fate for innocents, but finally, the blood shed is *their own*, and their fate is in Sheol! A nature proverb in 1:17 highlights act and outcome: even birds will avoid a net when they see it, but the sinners of 1:10-19 don't.

Proverbs 1:20-33: Wisdom Calls

Woman Wisdom's poem ends this unit. She is a personified Scold, knowing mother, cosmic goddess figure, or good Israelite prophet. The prophets echo in her speech: she makes known thoughts and words (1:23-24; cf. Isa. 65:2, 12; 66:4; Jer. 7:13, 24-27) leading to life or death. This composite figure is the male sage's counterpart. She speaks frequently in chapters 1–9. In fact, she is the most talkative female in the entire Bible. She is the subject of admonitions (imperative proverbs) to young men; poems of praise for her by the sage are intermixed with her self-praise ("aretalogies") in Proverbs 1–9. These are often juxtaposed with warnings against her "evil twin," the negative female

(2:16-19; 5:1-23; 6:20-35; 7:1-27). In fact, both are hybrid characters—part goddess figures, part real women—and serve as inverted "mirror" images of each other (Yoder 2001, 73–74).

■ The Text in the Interpretive Tradition

Proverbs 1:1-7: Solomon, a Wise Sinner

Solomon is almost a folklore character by the time we reach New Testament times, appearing in sayings of Jesus in the Gospels (Matt. 1:6-7; 6:28-29; Luke 12:27), and in the apocryphal Wisdom of Solomon as Wisdom's royal lover (Murphy 1988; Wis. 6:12; 7:10; 8:9). Qumran also reworks this material (4Q525). Church fathers revere Solomon as a scriptural king in Jesus' lineage, thus promoting an explanation of why Christians may learn rhetoric or science from foreign philosophers (Jerome, *Letter to Magnus*; Clement of Alexandria, *Strom.* 1, 3, 5). Language skills count, since the "true" gospel meaning of Hebrew texts might be a hidden riddle that Christians must solve. Magical Solomon appears in the Pseudepigrapha (*The Testament of Solomon*), the Qur'an ("The Ant" sura), Christian Ethiopia (*Kebra Nagast*), Jewish (*Tg. Esther Sheni*), and Islamic folklore (Fontaine 2002).

Proverbs 1:8-19: The Father's Instruction

All later authorities agree that it is the duty of fathers to teach their sons the ways of righteousness, and to take the father's instructions at face value. Ideas here inform Heb. 12:5-6, and subsequently the idea of harsh discipline of children as "love" becomes standard for both Christians and Jews, but for different reasons: Jews because they must teach the hard truths of surviving persecutions (*b. Sanh.* 101a; *Gen. Rab.* 42:1), Christians because they must be ready to emulate Christ's suffering (Clement of Alexandria, *Strom.* 3.18).

Proverbs 1:20-33

By the time of Paul's writings, Jesus Christ is the "Sophia" of God, in a way that both nods to the Hebrew tradition, but also normalizes the tricky issue of such an exalted, preexistent female figure (1 Cor. 1:24; see discussion of Prov. 8:1-36) by providing a link to Jesus as wisdom/*logos* in John's prologue (1:1-18). Jews and Christians begin to part ways: Wisdom's female voice can be read as identical to the Torah's, God's, Christ's, or the Gospel's. The Torah is referenced in Wis. 9:18, Sir. 15:1, and *Pirqe Aboth* 6. For Christians, Christ is the true referent in speech by or about Wisdom (Gregory of Nyssa, *Against Eunomius* 3.2). Wisdom's cry and human lack of response applies to any situation the writers find worthy of their concern or scorn. Martin Luther explains, using 1:28: God does not hear the prayers of "Jews, heretics, and schismatics," because proud minds preclude knowledge of God (Luther, *Lectures on Romans* 10).

■ The Text in Contemporary Discussion

Proverbs 1:1-7

In the developing world, the use of proverbs still flourishes for purposes of teaching or deciding legal matters (Fontaine 1982; Oha, 21). Child-rearing proverbs are frequent: "Treat a son like a *raja* for the first five years, like a slave for the next ten, and like a friend thereafter" (from North India, White, 16); "Children are not dogs; their parents are not gods" (Haiti); and "A child is a certain worry, but an uncertain joy" (Old English). A brief survey of "proverbs" in professional databases shows that, worldwide, proverbs are taken as an index of cultural values (Healey and Sybertz, 34–35), and the ability to interpret these figurative speech acts is often used to assess both cognitive and psychological states (Katz and Ferretti).

Proverbs 1:8-19

Adopting the voice of an eternal Wisdom linked to fear of the Lord, Solomon's authority, or the father's authority is a strategy for control. What the text *actually* conveys is cultural content such as customs, values, and other very much time-bound views. Similarly, content is also heavily conditioned by gender, ethnicity, and social status, along with the political and historical circumstances of its authors' worlds. By speaking as the authority, the text takes on a power it might not have otherwise, dripping with grave implications of cosmic punishments. But who is *really* speaking in the instructions and poems of Proverbs 1–9, and why should we listen? Audiences are taking it "on faith" that what the author tells us is true—though subject peoples like women, the poor, and colonized peoples might well beg to disagree. Yet, even in the ethico-moral realm, the sages present us with truths that hold in their own time, place, and status: we dispute elements of their program, but we cannot doubt their sincerity.

Proverbs 1:20-33

The mother may be the best clue to understanding Prov. 31:10-32, but Woman Wisdom (Hebrew *hokmah*; Greek *sophia*) is a goddess-like figure (see note on Proverbs 8), familiar from surrounding cultures as well. Ordinary mothers rarely appear shouting from the tops of the town or the marketplace (1:20-21), telling their erring children "what's what"! Wisdom's words, harsh and scolding, show her as a direct distributor of "the fear of the Lord," using language as her method, by way of her counsel, knowledge, and reproof (1:23-25, 29-33). She intends to mock and scoff when disaster strikes fools.

Ignoring advice and refusing correction are foolish choices, both then *and* now. The authoritative voice of Gaia, in the form of global warming, melting glaciers, and ice caps, flammable drinking water, mass extinctions, and polluted atmosphere, is today speaking loudly to her human children, without much response. Ecological interpretations of the figure of Woman Wisdom abound, making this passage especially relevant in ecotheology. Is Wisdom the personified "self-revelation of creation," always paired with divine self-revelation teaching mortals the ways of God and earth (Rad, 149–62)? Ecotheologians claim she is the voice of Earth—the evangelist of the interdependent web of creation who teaches us deep ecology (Habel and the Earth Bible team, 23–34; Wurst, 48–64). Both her anger here and industry as the wife in Proverbs 31 point to a wisdom of attentiveness to what is actually before us. Wisdom suggests a biblical way to authorize a repentant, deeply "local" attention to the economic and environmental practices that have global impact. Immediate action is required, though like the thieves of 1:8-19, the powerful tell us there will be no consequences, so like the stubborn children of 1:20-30, we refuse Mother Earth's reproof. We must wait to see if humanity is capable of hearing what Earth Wisdom cries out to us from her vantage point on the heights of our cities and from the corruptions of our market-driven world: perhaps it is not too late if we do not scorn her insights and repent.

Proverbs 2:1—6:35: Instructions of the Sage Parent

■ THE TEXT IN ITS ANCIENT CONTEXT

A number of instructions by the father/sage appear together in these chapters (2:3-22; 3:1-12; 3:27-33; 4:1-27; 5:1-23; 6:1-35). Long passages about Wisdom (2:1-15; 3:13-18, 19-26; 4:1-19) and her protection against undesirable women (2:16-19; 5:1-23; 6:20-35) form an alternating antithesis in the instructions. We also see embedded proverbs (3:32-33, 35; 5:21), *'ashrey* ("happy" or "blessed") sayings (3:13), nature wisdom (6:6-11), admonitions (positive or negative commands, 3:5, 9, 11, 27-31), and numerical sayings (6:16-19; see entry below on 30:1-33, 30:14-31; Amos 1:3-2:8), common in Ugaritic literature, following the pattern of x and $x + 1$.

Ostensibly, the father addresses the youth using the formula "my child" (lit. "my son") in 2:1; 3:1, 11, 21; 4:1 (plural), 10, 20, forming a marker for the boundaries of different instructions (5:1-6, 7-23; 6:1-5, 20-35). Favorite topics occur: wisdom as intellectual pursuit (2:1-11; 3:5-7), personification (3:13-20; 4:5-13), with the latter now flanked by negative females (Hebrew "strange woman" [*'ishah zarah*]; NRSV "loose woman," 2:16a; 5:3-23), "foreign woman" (*nokriyah*; NRSV "adulteress," 2:16b-19), "adulteress" (*'eshet ra'*, "evil woman," 6:24-35), and prostitute (*zonah*, 6:26). All of these variations of sexually dangerous women stand in antithetic contrast to the fine figure of Woman Wisdom and her earthly variation, one's own wife (5:18-20). At the same time, they flesh out the portrait of female wickedness to complement the descriptions of male wickedness, forming a nice synonymous topic.

Proverbs 5 begins an ongoing discourse on the "wrong woman." Egyptian instructions often counsel the young would-be scribe or diplomat not to approach women in their professional work. In Israel, professional ethics says the same, but adds much more personal descriptions of the harm, based on biblical law and the difficult inheritance problems for Second Temple communities after return from exile. This may be why the "strange woman" (that is, "not known") and the "foreign woman" are more dangerous than prostitutes. Mythology of goddesses who descend to the underworld or kill their partners also contributes to the warnings (2:16-19; 6:26; 7:22-27; 9:18).

The wicked of both sexes display similar traits: "perverse or scornful, deceptive speech" (2:12, 16; 3:34), a negative "way" (2:12, 15; 4:14-15, 19), pleasure in their wicked acts (2:14; 4:16-17), and final punishments (2:22; 3:25, 32-33). Wicked/fool and righteous/wise (2:20-21; 3:27-35; 4:18) form a key topical antithetic pair. The same is true of the contrast between Woman Wisdom and negative females (cf. 2:16-19 to 3:13-18; 4:6, 8-9, 13). The "path" or "way" of each side of either pair is illustrated by their deeds and traits (2:8, 12-15, 18-19, 20; 3:8, 17, 23, 31; 4:11-12, 14-15, 18-19, 26-27).

Other key themes are: wisdom's cosmic origin (2:6-9, 3:19-20), and the image of a Tree of Life (3:18). Egyptian goddesses influence imagery: Ma'at, patroness of scribes, is usually shown with the *ankh* (life) and a symbol of wealth in either hand; Isis and Hathor appear as sacred trees, as does Canaan's own mother goddess, Asherah, who was worshiped in the Jerusalem temple (Murphy 1998). "Fear of the Lord" gets its standard treatment (2:5; 3:7). In 6:20-35, the mother's torah (v.

20b) once again urges memory, respect, and reproof, acting just like light illuminating darkness (13:9; cf. Ps. 119:105).

◼ THE TEXT IN THE INTERPRETIVE TRADITION

Positive statements about wisdom inform the later traditions: torah, Tree of Life, cosmic genealogy, rich benefits, and wisdom's role in history all appear in later Jewish writings (4Q525 2 ii + 3; Wis. 3:10-11; 7:8-13; 10:15-21; Sir. 1:26-27; *1 En.* 32:6). A favorite observation in 3:11-12, "the Lord reproves the one he loves," citing a father's discipline of the child, is well used (Clement of Alexandria, *Strom.* 1.5; to Luther, *Letter to Elector John of Saxony*), but it is *not* to be considered an evil end dealt out to sinners. The "strange" woman is expanded at Qumran in the so-called Wiles of the Wicked Woman (4Q184; cf. 4Q525, frg. 15). The strange woman could be an allusion to wicked Hellenistic culture (Clement of Alexandria, *Strom.* 1.5).

◼ THE TEXT IN CONTEMPORARY DISCUSSION

Sages share a strongly biased, patriarchal view of the world. The adolescent males they teach must submit to self-control and often violent authority in order to one day join in the social control of inferiors. After all, if God "himself" punishes *his* loved sons as a father does, then oppressive control is divinely authorized by the plain sense of the text. Negative females represent the ultimate expression of male fear of loss of control projected onto the mythological plane of the dark underworld. Warnings against her suppress many levels of male causality; her oily words are usually effective. Patriarchal bad faith is at work here: Is there a recognition that women in ancient society, owned and denied rights or choices, might actually *not* be all that accepting of the situation?

Studies of proverbs in Africa show a similar trend (see Schipper). Obododimma Oha, writing of female devaluation in Igbo proverbs, demonstrates that these units of folklore are far from neutral. A continual attempt is made rhetorically by male speech and literary forms to portray women as intellectually and morally inferior, all presented as a cultural truth that none can contest. The Igbo say that "proverbs are the palm-oil with which words are eaten." Students of masculinized rhetoric make clear that the oil, in the case of proverbs, is rancid indeed (Oha, 87–102). But perhaps our sages are correct: women released from men's control will indeed be the death of them, as the patriarchal ceilings of male heavens fall, as this proverb from Africa notes: "When sleeping women wake, mountains move" (www.worldofproverbs.com).

Proverbs 7:1—9:18: A Triad of Females—Wisdom, Folly, and Strange Woman

◼ THE TEXT IN ITS ANCIENT CONTEXT

Proverbs 7:1-27: Warning against Woman Stranger

Another teaching on the strange woman begins with a description of commandments as law (Deut. 6:6-9) held close to the body (cf. Prov. 3:1-3). Wisdom is here called "sister" and "friend" in lover-like language familiar from Egypt and the Song of Songs (Prov. 7:4; Song of Sol. 4:9-12). Only she can force out the delicious temptations of the strange woman's words.

A view from the sage's window showing the strange woman stalking her youthful victim is constructed like an eyewitness account. Archaeological tableaux from the ancient Near East repeatedly show women—prostitute, goddess, or queen—looking out of a window (Brenner and van Dijk-Hemmes, 120), so perhaps the sage's mother could be the speaker here. Certainly, mothers are concerned with their son's choice of mate (Gen. 27:46) and involved in the making of marriages (Judg. 14:2-4).

Twilight is a dangerous time of mistaken identities, when the Sumerian demoness Ardat-Lili (Lilith in later traditions) lurked at crossroads looking for male victims, just as the strange woman, now "decked like a prostitute" (7:10), does. Body language is telling: she is loud-voiced, direct, brazen, and bold in presentation of her desire. Seduction is primarily verbal: rich, absent husband, a lush bed invoking fertility and luxury. Lusty males descend to the level of trapped animal or slaughtered beast (7:22-23). She is the embodiment of the crooked path (7:25-27) leading to a mythological death.

Proverbs 8:1-36: The Cosmic Genealogy of Wisdom

Woman Wisdom speaks in self-praise, similar to the *Aretalogies of Isis* in Egypt (8:17). The setting in 8:1-5 directly recalls 1:18-22 but is less scornful. Open and affirming, this exalted figure addresses the untutored with her splendid offers: learning, life, and success (8:5-6, 14-19, 21, 35-36). Fear of the Lord and the emphasis on language recur in 8:13, 6-9. Excellence in counsel (8:14-16) makes her the *real* reason leaders succeed. The origin of her exceptional nature in 8:22-31 is cosmic: she is the firstborn of the Lord's creation, saw it all, and perhaps even assisted as a "master craftswoman" (8:30a), or perhaps a beloved royal child, constantly in God's company, frolicking in joy at YHWH's work (8:30b; the meaning of *'amon* in 30a is disputed).

The Hebrew text bristles with ambiguities. "Created" in 8:22 could be translated as "acquired," with the latter including an aspect of sexual creation (Gen. 4:1b). "God acquired me first" *before* starting creation suggests a preexistent entity that YHWH engages for his creation project. If God created Wisdom in a sexual way as the very first thing done in creation (Egyptian mythology of Ma'at may be of influence here, Fontaine 2002), this is hardly a better reading for patriarchal theology's relentless rejection of all things female. In 8:24, the phrase "I was brought forth" refers to the female's labor in giving birth (literally "I was given birth to"), not a male god "begetting." This strengthens the image of a darling daughter found later in 8:30. Who is the mother here? YHWH is the only possible referent for the act. Once born, baby girl Wisdom delights in the diversity of the entire created world, including humanity (8:30-31), a laughing link between heaven and earth (Wurst, 48–64). The way of Wisdom is linked to the power of primal knowledge, God's power to create and order—she has seen it all, and participated. Who wouldn't make her their choice, and thrive?

Proverbs 9:1-18: Invitations to Wise and Foolish Banquets

The conclusion to Proverbs 1–9 ends with significant metaphorical ambiguity, as audiences discover once again just how similar are the words of personified Folly and Wisdom, if one does not take into account the differing outcomes of their offers. The two banquets (9:1-5, 13-18) could not be more different, although the invitations sound exactly the same. Verses 1–6 present Wisdom inviting the untutored (9:4, cf. 8:5) inside her house, offering bread and spiced wine. The seven pillars in 9:1 may refer to the folk idea that seven mountain pillars held up the firmament over the earth, or other sets of seven (cf. 1 Kgs. 7:17; Prov. 26:16; Clifford, 105). Whatever the case, spacious luxury is indicated, for "seven" carries the meaning of completion. Wisdom's feast might echo a dedicatory celebration of a finished temple or palace (1 Kgs. 8:1-5), a scene from Ugaritic epics about Baal's new palace (*KTU* 1.4.6; *ANET* 134).

Mixed wine has a place in ancient practice, whether watered (John 2:10) or spiced (Song of Sol. 8:2). "Bread," meaning any staple food, refers to Wisdom's spiritual teachings (cf. Isa. 55:1; Sir. 15:3). Openly searching, she calls in 9:3 from places in town where she cannot be ignored (8:2; 9:14; cf. 1:20-22, busy roads and city gates where business happens), but we note that she has a female staff in 9:3 (cf. Prov. 31:15). Her offerings (the sages' teachings) sate the deepest hunger and thirst. Wisdom, the hostess with the mostest, offers life to her guests, something other goddesses seldom do (Ugaritic Anat kills those who rebuff her; *ANET* 151).

Proverbs 9:7-12 inserts a number of wisdom sayings, thus interrupting the immediate juxta-position of wise and foolish banquets. Many scholars move these verses to the end of Proverbs 9. Scoffers and evildoers have a ready and cynical answer—or even violent action—to every reproof. The helpful sage may be the one who suffers (Prov. 22:10). The entire teaching of Proverbs 1–9 is summarized in verse 10: the fear of the Lord is the beginning of wisdom, leading to a long and successful life (9:11-12).

We conclude with Woman Folly's banquet (9:13-18). Like the would-be adulteress of Prov. 7:11a, Woman Folly (but "foolish woman," Fox 2000, 253–62) is painted in negative images. Since *'eshet-kesilut*—"woman/wife of foolishnesses" (pl.)—occurs only here in the Hebrew Bible, perhaps we should contrast her also with the wife of substance (*'eshet-hayil*) in Prov. 31:10, and understand her as a "wife of fools" (see note 31:10). Traits from the adulteress are reassigned (cf. 2:16-19; 5; 6:20-35; 7), depicting a disruptive, active female persona. Inhabiting high places (where wealthy homes and palaces are located), she calls to the gullible outside like a sideshow barker at her door. Her invitation has deep meaning—it *does* encapsulate truth, but should one embrace the ethical gray zone it highlights? (The sages would answer no.) Instead of Wisdom's transparency, Folly sug-gests stolen water (intercourse? cf. 5:15-20) is sweeter than one's own; illicit bread spices consump-tion with secret pleasure. Like the fertility goddesses who invited kings or champions to marital banquets only to slay them and take their power, or punish their rebuffs (Clifford, 107), Folly's menfolk are the walking dead in the sages' eyes.

▌ THE TEXT IN THE INTERPRETIVE TRADITION

Proverbs 7:1-27

Here the strange woman is clearly designated as someone's wife, so all strictures concerning adul-tery apply (Deut. 22:22-25; *b. Sotah*), though if she is married to a foreigner, other laws than Isra-elite ones would be in force. Here, the Qumran expansions of the mythological filth and death are extreme in their misogyny (4Q184; cf. 4Q525, frg. 15). The Talmud comments on the connection to demons and twilight in 7:9 (*b. Ber. 3b*). Warnings about the strange woman are taken to refer to attractive Christian heresy and governments in *t. Hul.* 2:22-24. Adultery is particularly heinous for women, reflecting inappropriate agency in one meant to be fully subject, even in body, to her husband (Eph. 5:22-24). Paul (1 Corinthians 7) and the Christian fathers may not be enthusiastic about marriage compared to virginity, but a Christian wife is *far* less dangerous than the liaison presented here (Jerome, *Pammachius* 47).

Proverbs 8:1-36

Assorted themes are carried forward in Sir. 1:4, *Ahiqar*, the *Odes Sol.* 33:5; 41:9; *2 En.* 24; 25:4, 26; 28:4; 30:8; and the *T. Sim.* 5:2. The most important tradition developed concerning Wisdom's genealogy is in the prologue to the Gospel of John, where the Second Temple Jewish *Sophia* of our sages is transmuted into Greco-Roman *logos* of Stoic philosophers and Christian theologians. Proverbs 8 sparks Paul's thinking (1 Cor. 1:24; Col. 1:15-17; Heb. 1:2-3, 6a, 8-10), and the Christian fathers follow. By the time of the fourth century CE, Proverbs 8 becomes critical for the debate over whether Christ was created by or coexistent with the Father (Arians versus Nicenes). Gregory of Nyssa (*Against Eunomius* 3.2) extensively harmonizes female Wisdom with the Christ-Wisdom of the Gospels and Letters—warning the prudent in his audience *not* to take the texts' meaning literally, "absolutely and without examination" at first reading—something seldom said of masculine metaphors! Luther follows the trend (*Commentary on Romans* 1:2): it is the glorious Gospel that has been set up for humanity before creation. Wisdom becomes a cover symbol for the Word, extending the Logos theology of the New Testament.

Proverbs 9:1-18

The image of Wisdom, the life-giving hostess, appears in the New Testament and late wisdom (Sir. 15:3; 24:21; John 6:35-40). The seven-pillared house finds expansive interpretation in Jewish and Christian interpretation: seven firmaments (*Midrash Proverbs*), days of creation (*b. San.* 18a), seven sacraments, gifts of the Holy Spirit, and so on (Fox 2000, 297–98). Byzantine liturgies read this passage for Holy Thursday; the West used 9:1-5 for feasts of the Virgin Mary. Hippolytus of Rome glosses Wisdom's house as the Virgin's pregnancy, producing the bodily incarnation itself (*On Proverbs*, frg. 2).

▮ THE TEXT IN CONTEMPORARY DISCUSSION

Proverbs 7:1-27

Biblical scholars have struggled much to separate the composite wicked woman into her various aspects: an in-group or out-group woman married to another (adulteress); a prostitute, often of foreign descent (Rahab, Delilah); a strange woman—someone not from the speaker's own ethnicity; a woman worshiping in a cult that is forbidden in Israel (7:14-20); and/or a reference to foreign goddesses like Inanna, Ishtar, or others who are noted for either descending to the underworld or killing their human partners (Inarash, Aphrodite, etc.). Translations that blur these distinctions are not especially helpful for discussions of biblical sexuality. Whichever aspect of the "bad girl" paradigm we might find emphasized in different texts, it is clear that only Wisdom or the woman of substance could counteract her dreaded influence.

Male fears of adultery in the past (and some modern traditional cultures) stem from the reality of arranged patriarchal marriages: young women often found themselves given for life—without choice or consent—as glorified property to a much older man, to be used functionally for his bed, hearth, and comfort. Prostitutes were equally at risk under patriarchy: supposedly, only dire family economics could account for it, and daughters sold as debt slaves were at the sexual mercy of their owners (Exod. 21:7-8; Lev. 19:29; Neh. 5:5). Foreign women as wives represented a major threat to the transfer of property, and might promote participation in or tolerance of foreign cults.

Today, adultery can still carry broad economic and violent consequences, but is not so likely to be mythologized, though the trope of the "divorced wife" and "cuckolded husband" are used as a figure of fun or torment in male culture. Where an ideology of romantic love exists, "cheating" can create a radical rupture for the innocent partner, creating a sense of loss, betrayal, and descent to the depths. Divorces caused by adultery can be rancorous and costly, economically and psychologically. Considered a moral and ethical rift in a committed relationship, adultery today is different from times in the past because wives currently have more recourse and choices in how they might deal with male infidelity.

The exact nature of Lady Folly is complex too: she could be a degraded foreign goddess, an adulteress, a foreigner, idolater, or any combination thereof. She and Wisdom speak in similar language in Prov. 9:1-18; Wisdom/Folly function as a gendered pair expressing a *single* male ideology of the female other. Texts dependent on Proverbs 7–9, such as the Wiles of the Wicked Woman at Qumran (4Q525 15; 5Q16; 4Q184 1), easily portray the negative archetypes from 7:1—9:18 in ways that suggest fear of the goddess, the witch, the faithless or murderous midwife of neighboring mythologies. On the positive pole of the female other archetype, Wisdom of Solomon (8:9; 7:28; 8:16) depicts a goddess-bride Wisdom who ennobles her king, as though she were the Greco-Roman Isis rising from the wave, loving those who love her (Apuleius, *The Golden Ass*).

Proverbs 8:1-31.

Happy are those who find Wisdom! For biblical theologians and feminists, the figure of Lady Wisdom/wife of substance and her negative variations—multifaceted Lady Folly and the unfortunate wives appearing in Proverbs—are a source of fascination and speculation. First mother who is made manifest by her child Jesus, or cosmic sender of whom he is *the* prophet par excellence, Wisdom has been located in the earliest Jesus movement (see Schüssler Fiorenza). Other scholars posit a gnostic "myth" of Sophia, come down from heaven to guide men, as a basic trope for the equation of Jesus/Christ with Sophia. In the Nag Hammadi gnostic texts, some see Wisdom as the precursor of the paradoxical speaker in the disturbing "The Thunder, Perfect Mind" (McGuire 1994, 39–54), where a list of extreme juxtapositions (Madonna-whore, life-death, etc.) proclaimed by a single female character lend credence to Wisdom/Folly as a *single* entity, bifurcated into positive or negative forces. By highlighting Wisdom's genealogy and activities, modern scholarship has accounted for reasons why she morphed into certain aspects of the Messiah or Holy Spirit for Christians or Torah, the Shekinah, or Kabbalistic Tree of Life for Jews.

For believing women, so often excluded from the "salvation history" of call, covenant, election, and redemption, Wisdom suggests new ways to relate to the biblical traditions. Her connection with Jesus Christ in subsequent texts gives welcome relief from the imagery and theologies of male-only religion, as in the "Re-Imagining" movement in Christology of the late twentieth century (see Cole, Ronan, and Taussig). Indeed, happy are women and men who find themselves able to return to the tradition, enhanced and enlarged by Wisdom, who supports their varied aspirations.

Proverbs 9:1-18

Banquets, good and bad, continue to function as powerful images of social interaction, exchanges of power, and ultimately redemption from the trials of poverty and disgrace. Perhaps representing philosophical symposia of Hellenistic philosophy as their key referent (Fox 2000, 303–6), or as scenes rooted in the everyday life of families, villages, and cities, feasts were important. Some took place at seasonal, religious, or socially critical times of change (births, marriages, death; Matt. 22:1-14; 25:10; Mark 6:21; 12:39). Other banquets in New Testament Gospels (Luke 5:29-32; 12:35-38; 14:7-24; 20:46) harmonize with Wisdom's in Proverbs 9. Other banquets could become scenes for disgrace (see the banquets in Esther), with unanticipated, and deadly, outcomes.

Folly's invitation to a banquet of wickedness can be related to the world of globalized economies and corporate control of resources. In the face of world poverty and despair, lavish gluttony of "the good life" is enshrined everywhere ("competitive eating" competitions, corporate retreats, political fundraising, etc.). "Stolen water is sweet, and bread eaten in secret is pleasant," remarks Folly truth-fully out of *her* wisdom, and the same is true today. How sweet are the corporate profits from buying up potable water in the developing world and then selling it back at a profit. The secret profits of global banking industries or wholly arbitrary, outrageous health-care fees levied on ordinary people by big corporations for profit are sweet to those who benefit. Global manipulation of currencies in developing companies creates debt that allows outsiders to capitalize on the subsequent disasters ("disaster capitalism"). These are common examples of the secret doings that keep the rich getting richer in games rigged to their advantage. African proverbs used at the United Nations with NGOs in Western countries, in Somalia, and in other African contexts express the dynamics of rich/poor: "When elephants fight, the grass gets hurt" (Healey and Sybertz, 36–37).

Proverbs 10–15: Antithetic Teachings Collection

◼ The Text in Its Ancient Context

Ascription to Solomon (*mishlay*, "proverbs-of"; cf. commentary on 1:1-7) may reflect the presence of significantly older material in the collections of Proverbs 10–30. Since the meanings of proverbs are "decoded" by their application in social settings, whether oral or literary (Fontaine 1982), it has been said that "a proverb in a collection is dead." While scholars are limited with respect to social use, sound observations may still be made. The antithetic collection uses antithetic proverbs to the virtual exclusion of all other forms. Antithetic word pairs build up these divergent observations, pressing for the affirmation of one and renunciation of the other as a matter of "common sense." The "way of wisdom," introduced in Proverbs 1–9, is given flesh and sinew by the piling up of so many keenly examined examples, but "faith statements" play their part as well, contradicting what even casual observers of life know to be true: the righteous *do* fail occasionally; the wicked often live long and prosper.

The cast of characters from Proverbs 1–9 reappears in this collection, as they pursue their "way" to found their "house," neatly tying up Wisdom's teachings and object lessons from her cosmic vantage point with everyday examples in the human realm. Fathers (10:1; 13:1; 15:5) and mothers (10:1; 15:20) appear together. Sons (translation mine)—lazy or diligent, attentive to education or not, corporally punished for their own good, secure into the following generations—are found in 10:1, 5; 13:1, 22, 24; 14:26; 15:11 ("son of *'adam*" = mortal), 20, but daughters appear not at all. This is a serious lacuna in the sages' ideology of worthy females: Are there no intelligent, pious daughters who could benefit from the sages' teachings? Is it useful to urge a morality on young men if young women are not also indoctrinated to uphold it? Good wives were critical to any successful household (11:16, 22; 12:4; 14:1). Where are the proverbs that teach young women about their duties? The mother was thought to instruct her daughters in all they needed to know, but the sages' blindness to this educational task underscores the gendered nature of their teachings. The "house" motif, the domestic sphere in which women hold paramount power, occurs in 11:29; 12:7; 14:1, 11; 15:6, 25, 27, where men who leave daily decisions to the industrious wife or servant are contrasted with fools who constantly interfere without cause. Perhaps this reflects a mother sage's point of view in keys to selecting a good mate: at home, fools make tiresome partners.

The wise/righteous person is shown with a good understanding of the role of speech, a favorite wisdom theme (10:6, 11, 13a, 14, 18-21, 31-32; 11:9, 12, 13; 12:6, 13, 14, 17-19, 22; 13:1-3, 5; 14:3, 5, 7, 25; 15:1-2, 4, 7, 14), compared to the fool or wicked, who delights in lies, strife, slander, scoffing, and other deceptive or ignorant linguistic behaviors. The poor are a topic as well: although some poverty results from laziness (10:4), the sages call out the unfair advantage of the rich in their dealings with others, suggesting that poverty may be a consequence of a stacked deck or a well-placed bribe (10:15; 13:7-8, 23; 14:20-21, 31; 15:15). Compassion to the poor neighbor renders one "happy" (blessed) in 14:21; God prefers such behavior (14:31). All the days of the poor are hard, but better that than living with hate or without knowledge of God (15:15-17).

Faith statements that contradict common observations usually invoke God or following sage advice as the guarantor of a final good outcome in 10:3, 22, 27, 29; 12:2-3; 14:27; 15:3, 25, 29.

■ THE TEXT IN THE INTERPRETIVE TRADITION

The sayings of Solomon are received by the tradition as true and worthy of transmission and obedience—whether taken literally or metaphorically—by both Christian and Jewish authors. Ben Sira repeats many of the antithetic sayings with some slight variation or elaboration (cf. Sir. 7:17 with Prov. 10:27; Sir. 3:17-24 with Prov. 11:2; 15:33). In Sir. 20:5-8, the saying in Prov. 15:23 is further amplified: the wise wait to use a "word in season" (Prov. 15:23, "How good!"), whereas fools never manage it, because they are talkative but have nothing truthful to say (Sir. 20:5-8a). The pseude-pigraphical work of *Ahiqar*, among others, also reuses sayings from this section (see, e.g., v. 156 = Prov. 10:32; v. 168 = 11:11; 14:11). Proverbs 11:24 undergirds 2 Cor. 9:6; Acts 13:10 references the straight path of Prov. 10:9. Proverbs 10:12 becomes the kernel of a beloved passage on love in 1 Cor. 13:1-8a, and finds its way into 1 Pet. 4:8. Rabbinic stories like those of Rabbi Akiba's long-suffering wife show Prov. 12:10 in narrative use vindicating the woman's view over her neighbor's (*b. Ketub.* 62b). The church fathers also appeal to the wisdom of these proverbs (e.g., Clement, *Strom.* 1.6, 10; 2.7, 11, 13, 18; Jerome, *Against Rufinus* 3.43; *Pelagians* 1.33; 2.1), assuming their truth content to be self-evident and useful.

THE TEXT IN CONTEMPORARY DISCUSSION

Modern observers of action and its relationship to the character of the actor often reject the stark contrasts of the antithetical sayings: black-and-white characterizations like those of the sages have yielded to a modern world of many shades of gray. This rejection of hard-and-fast rules is hardly modern, however: in Job and Qoheleth, we find serious questions about the reliability of retribution. Modern sayings suggest instead: "No good deed goes unpunished"; "Nice guys finish last"; "The cockroach knows well how to dance in the sun, but the fat chicken prevents him" (Africa); or "Keep your head down and your mouth shut." As always, context determines how much "truth" is ascribed to the proverb/saying, and whether it should be understood literally (see Katz and Ferretti).

Proverbs 16:1—22:16: The Royal Collection

THE TEXT IN ITS ANCIENT CONTEXT

Dating is more certain here: the monarchy of Judah ended in the Babylonian exile of 587/586 BCE. Many scholars date "royal sayings" about kings and counselors ("the wise") before that time. Regional wisdom texts from times of the biblical monarchies show similarities to the themes in this collection: warnings against taking part in or even witnessing angry disputes are common. Calm, deliberative speech and careful listening are the hallmarks of the sage and the wisdom ideal, foster-ing the goal of patient, generous responses in a heated moment. A diplomat must know better than to befriend hot-headed, ill-tempered, loud-mouthed fools who often stir up strife by slander and gossip just because they can.

Earlier wisdom themes appear, but in many, features used to describe sages or the righteous *now* describe the (ideal) king (16:10, 12, 13, 15; 20:8; 21:1), whom sages manage with persuasive speech at times of quick anger, or petulant use of power (19:12; 20:2). Differences between wise and mali-cious speech dominate this collection (16:1, 10, 13, 21, 23-24, 27-28; 17:4, 5, 7, 14, 20, 27-28; 18:2, 4, 6-8, 13, 17, 20-21, 23; 19:5, 9, 22, 28; 20:19-20; 21:6, 28; 22:10-12, 14). This is the case because the profession of court counselor relies on influential speech to achieve goals (16:13; 18:20-21). Other elements of life at court come in for comment: bribes appear in 17:8, 23; 18:16; 19:6; 21:14 but show a range of evaluations that characterize the more nuanced proverbs of the Royal Collec-tion. When neutrally appraised, they are effective "gifts" that work almost magically to open doors

(17:8; 18:16; 19:6). In Prov. 21:14, the gift becomes an outright "bribe," which averts retribution, and in 17:23, bribes lead to perversion of justice by the wicked who accept them. Wives are a "good thing," a sign of God's favor (18:22); wise wives are "from the Lord" (19:14). "Better-than" sayings heighten contrasts (17:12; 19:1), or suggest, counterintuitively, that sometimes "less is more" (21:9). The sages recommend poverty and integrity over wealth and pride (16:8, 19). Bread and water with quiet calm trump a fractious feast (17:1). A mere corner of an exposed rooftop is preferable to a house with a fretful wife (21:9, cf. 19:13); better a deserted island than a miserable wife (21:19).

Court experience puts a worldly twist on the more simplistic faith affirmations of Proverbs 10–15. Things do *not* always work out as people expect, even thoughtful plans (16:1, 7, 9; 19:21), one's "way" (16:2, 9; 20:24), outcomes (16:3, 33), speech (16:1b), or observed events (16:25; 21:31). Actually, human circumstances are determined finally by God who alone knows inner reality and final outcome. Even wisdom cannot prevail against the Lord (21:30). How can a mortal ever understand God's ways (20:24) under such circumstances? Still, following wisdom's general program of behavior is the best strategy available (22:4).

◼ The Text in the Interpretive Tradition

Fourth Ezra 3:34, *Pss. Sol.* 5:16, *2 Bar.* 38:1, *2 En.* 50:5, Clement of Alexandria (*Paed.* 2.10; *Strom.* 2.18), Jerome, and many others use content, form and vocabulary of the Royal Collection as they evaluate local rulers. Jerome considers "contentious wives" (Prov. 21:9, 19) enough to cancel out all wifely virtues, even their origin from God (Prov. 18:22; 19:14; *Against Jovinianus* 1.28), recommending virginity as the only safe path. *Pirqe Aboth* 1 and 2 discuss the ideal of silence and wise words, but find wives deleterious to their achievement. In *b. Ber.* 19b, Prov. 21:30 provides a "rule" (God may confound wisdom or rabbinic logic) that helps resolve contradictions in texts, interpretations, or common practice.

◼ The Text in Contemporary Discussion

The sages in this collection show a keen attention to "what works": in their role as counselors to the great, they suggest appeasement of the powerful (16:13); refusal to rescue a violent person, since it is pointless (19:19); refusal to guarantee a neighbor's loan (17:18); hiding from danger (22:3), and refusing friendship to gossips (20:19). While these worldly tips betray the weary cynicism of "don't get involved," they are also balanced with a recognition of how persuasive language can positively affect a situation (e.g., 16:13, 21, 23-24; 17:10), just as malicious, lying speech destroys harmony (e.g., 16:27-28; 17:4; 18:6-8; 19:28).

The power of language seen in 18:21, "Death and life are in the power of the tongue," is nicely demonstrated by the Teacher from Galilee. In Luke 10:30-37 and Matt. 22:15-22, Jesus manages to follow *all* of wisdom's rules, but twists them to critique power relations without incriminating himself. Lawyers, Pharisaic disciples, and Herodian spies all try to draw Jesus into a quarrel, but he answers softly, crafting wisdom speech (the parable or saying) to raise subversive interpretations. In Luke 10, he presents a Samaritan who violates wisdom's goal of noninvolvement in dicey situations and surpasses the Jewish elites' righteousness, thereby enlarging the vision of the "neighbor" across boundary lines. In Matt. 22:15-22 (cf. Mark 12:13-17; Luke 20:20-26), Jesus sidesteps an explosive question with a question and response of his own: pay feudal taxes to the one who owns everything; but for the devout Jew, Caesar owns nothing, creates nothing but misery, so pay *him* nothing! "God is the All-Provider, not Caesar" becomes the message for the poor in the crowd around this sage. Jesus refuses the quarrel but reframes the encounter, and gives it a double-sided "takeaway" lesson: "Render unto Caesar what is Caesar's."

Proverbs 22:17—24:22: The Egyptian Teachings

■ THE TEXT IN ITS ANCIENT CONTEXT

Here monarchic and colonial sages make use of a twelfth-century-BCE instruction from Egypt, that of the sage Amenemope. Returning to the format of instructions in Proverbs 1–9, the title "The Words of the Wise" (22:17a) is followed by admonitions, "Incline . . . hear . . ." with a motivation: what follows is "pleasant," lip-ready, and generates trust in YHWH (22:19-21). Aramaisms throughout this section reflect the international character of diplomatic and bureaucratic training. Features found in the Egyptian forerunner of Prov. 22:17—24:22 have provided explanations for some textual difficulties in the biblical text, allowing for better translations (Fox 2009, 709–12).

Standard themes are featured in 22:17—24:22: good and bad speech (22:24-25; 23:9; 24:7-9, 28-29), treatment of the poor (22:22-23, 23:10-11), work ethic and riches (22:29; 23:4-5; 23:19-21; 29-34; 24:10), court manners and good sense (22:26-27, 23:1-3; 23:6-8), the blessings of wisdom (23:12-16, 22-25; 24:3-6; 24:13-14), prostitutes and adulteresses (23:26-28). Students are to refrain from envy, avoid the bad and emulate the good, making their parents very happy indeed (23:15-16, 22-25).

■ THE TEXT IN THE INTERPRETIVE TRADITION

The New Testament endorses the general tone and teachings of this section of Proverbs: the admonition against too much wine and strong drink (23:19-21, 29-35) underlies Eph. 5:18. The repayment for all one's deeds in 24:12 undergirds statements about Christ's judgment in Matt. 16:27; Rom. 2:6; 2 Tim. 4:14-15; and 1 Pet. 1:17. God and emperor/king (24:21-22) viewed as objects of reverence and obedience ("fear") are found in 1 Pet. 2:17. Many of this collection's themes are also echoed in the *Syr. Men.*, Clement, Ambrose, John Cassian, and Athanasius.

■ THE TEXT IN CONTEMPORARY DISCUSSION

It is remarkable to observe how easily an Egyptian text from the world of the polytheistic occasional enemy Egypt fits in with the biblical messages from Proverbs. Often, interpreters stress a radical discontinuity between Israel and the world of the "other," as though Israel had a totally unique vision of ethics, right behaviors, or the role of the divine in securing justice or punishing wickedness. The earlier Egyptian text corresponds closely to that of Prov. 22:17—24:22, with respect to attitude toward life, duty, and the role of the divine in assuring justice. This suggests that the "us/them" antithesis—at least between wisdom teachings from various cultures—has been overdrawn by later writers.

Second, there is a compelling statement here of an ancient cross-cultural ethic of duty to the innocent, poor, and disenfranchised. Amenemope rehearses this theme, with emphasis on land tenure, in the form of honoring boundary markers of inherited fields (Amenemope 6:13—9:9), and this is repeated in Prov. 22:28; 23:10-11. Both texts give the same reason: the divine Creator is the advocate of the poor, the widow, the disabled, and the stranger, and punishes those who abuse them (Prov. 22:23; Amenemope 21:5-6; 24:11-14; 25:9-6). Such universally held sentiments by the sages of the region provide evidence that can serve to inspire a global interfaith ethic: *everyone* now is our neighbor, and we have duties of rescue (intervention) toward them. Ignorance is *no excuse* in Prov. 24:12. The judgment scene in Matt. 25:31-46 endorses this very ethic for the followers of Jesus.

Proverbs 24:23-34: More Sayings of the Wise

■ THE TEXT IN ITS ANCIENT CONTEXT

A title (24:23a) begins this small collection of lengthy admonitions, ended by an extended vignette ("example story") on laziness (24:30-34). Proper judgments, industriousness, false witness, revenge, and poverty are all covered here. The strong emphasis on working the land (24:27, 30-34) continues a hallowed biblical fixation: without land, there is no life (Ezra 5). Family inheritance must be worked properly and not become the property of outsiders (Ruth 4:1-10), for it represents the well-being of future generations.

Proverbs 24:29, simply put, "*Don't* do unto others as they have done to you," is a precept critical to Jewish and Christian teachings as a "Golden Rule," and is based on the basic community ethics of Jewish law. Revenge is forbidden, reserved *only* for God (Deut. 32:39-42), for punishment is certain, even if delayed. Leviticus 19, the "heart" of the Holiness Code, entwines duty to land, the poor, and fair judgment with laws forbidding vengeance, false witness, slander, taunting the handicapped, bearing a grudge, and hatred of the neighbor (Lev. 19:9-18), for "you shall love your neighbor as yourself" (Lev.19:18b). Ultimately, even the land/field/vineyard has "standing" before God, and can charge humans with misuse (Job 31:38-40).

■ THE TEXT IN THE INTERPRETIVE TRADITION

Second Enoch 50:4 counsels avoiding vengeance. Sirach 10:30 counsels work as an antidote to want. Jesus' teachings focus on lessons learned in working fields, fishing, and observing nature (Matt. 6:28-30; 12:33; 13:3-9, 18-33, 36-40, 47-49; John 4:34-38). In James 5:4, the cries of defrauded harvest workers are heard by God. The scholars' work—studying the Torah—is the fields and vineyards that must be worked diligently in the Babylonian Talmud (*Mas. Eruvin* 21b:28-31).

■ THE TEXT IN CONTEMPORARY DISCUSSION

Interpreters debate whether the ethics of the sages tilt toward the elite, but proverb collections show considerable nuance: one must be impartial, but the scale tilts on the side of advocacy for the poor. The sages of Proverbs are well aware of the tendencies by the avaricious "haves," which put economic justice at risk for the "have-nots." From their administrative vantage point, kings and administrators have the job of carefully monitoring the behavior of the wealthy for such unfair practices.

Proverbs 25:1—29:27: More Sayings of Solomon

■ THE TEXT IN ITS ANCIENT CONTEXT

Two collections of "other proverbs of Solomon" for the court professionals in training, 25:1—26:28 and 27:1—29:27, are bound together here under one title (25:1), ascribed to the "officials of King Hezekiah" (715–687 BCE), who collected them together. Kings, counselors, messengers, and military leaders figure in stories of Hezekiah's clashes with invading Assyrians, showing each side using proverbial speech (2 Kgs. 18:21: Egypt is a "broken reed"; 2 Kgs. 19:3b, a mother unable to give birth easily). Proverbial sayings in this unit share similar sharply crafted images to convey meaning, perhaps deliberately arranged to instruct court officials (Van Leeuwen).

Proverbs 25:1—26:28

Typical wisdom themes unite the sections, but there are also differences: Proverbs 25–26 does not show the strong antithetic character of Proverbs 10–15, but makes use of sharply crafted similes. Parallels to the Egyptian instructions are evident as well. Professional duties are the most important topics in Proverbs 25: Well-timed, reasoned persuasion is likened to rich or desirable items: gold apples in silver setting (25:11), gold jewelry (25:12), and soft words convince—and break bones (25:15)! Cold weather or water, so precious and welcome in a hot climate, are compared to faithful messengers (25:13) and good news from afar (25:25). Less desirable similes (comparisons to rain-less clouds [25:14], implements of war [25:18], rotting teeth and lame feet [25:19], vinegar in a cut, along with moths and worms [25:20], muddied water sources [25:26]) lend color to sayings about negative items. Proverbs 26 has less striking language, but uses stark juxtapositions to raise issues of ambiguity: Does every context not call for its own application of wisdom theories or language (26:4-5), just as different sorts of people require different responses (26:1, 3, 23-26)? Honor for a fool is like bad weather during agricultural seasons or setting a stone in a slingshot (26:1, 8); those who use fools for messengers might as well cut themselves or drink poison (26:6), for fools whom one hires are like archers who shoot friend and foe alike (26:10). Worst, perhaps, is the fool's use of language: proverbs told at the wrong time hang useless like crippled legs (26:7) or a thorn in the hand of a drunk (26:9), making it difficult to judge whether to indulge their folly with wise answers (26:4-5). The retribution for a "sin" may be inherent and congruent in verse 27: a pit might swallow its digger; a stone might fall back on its mover (cf. Ps. 7:16; Eccles. 10:8-9).

Proverbs 27–29

Antithetic sayings return as the colorful language of Proverbs 25–26 takes a back seat. Proverbs 29 uses an acrostic (alphabetic) form to signal its unity: 29:1 begins with *'aleph*, the first letter of the alphabet, and 29:27 begins with a *tav*, the final. Standard wisdom themes are reviewed but show less coherence, and YHWH sayings are less frequent here than elsewhere.

In Proverbs 27, fools and their havoc appear in 27:3, 22, along with unseemly praise, boasting (27:1-2), contentious wives (27:15-16), jealous, envious enemies, and inappropriate friends or kin throughout the chapter. The chapter ends with nature wisdom advising good practices on the land (27:23-27). The world can be uncertain (27:1, 20), filled with paradox: a friend may wound by truth-telling; an enemy is all kisses (27:6); a close neighbor might be better than faraway kin (27:10b).

Proverbs 28 and 29 concern public governance, based on whether righteous, wise leaders are in power or hasty (28:20, 22), wicked (28:3, 15), cheating fools who are a danger to everyone. The two types form antitheses in 28:2, 4, 5, 7, 8, 10, 12, 28, and throughout: people flourish under the former, but hide or cry out under the latter. "Torah" appears in 28:4, where it may refer to the teachings of this collection that uphold Mosaic laws, which institutionalize care for the poor, the widow, orphan, and stranger (see Leviticus 18–20). It is clear that a "preferential option" and God's blessing are aimed at the welfare of the poor: rulers who understand the rights of the poor and take action to guard them win God's favor (28:4-5, 8, 25, 27; 29:2, 7, 13-14, 26), whereas wicked rulers who raise taxes and gouge the poor are fools who will bring about rebellion eventually (28:2-4, 12, 15-16, 29:2, 4, 7, 16, 27). The sages criticize those who put profit first (28:8; 29:4), using the proverbial image of a growling lion, familiar in antiquity in reference to kings, heightening the portrait of predatory behavior by wicked elites (28:15; cf. Ezek. 32:2, Prov. 19:12; 20:2; 30:29-31). Ultimately, it is the Lord who made both the rich and the poor; elites do not deserve more than their fair share. The marked differences between the righteous and the wicked, the unjust and the upright, make them into each other's worst nightmare, "abominations," in 29:27.

THE TEXT IN THE INTERPRETIVE TRADITION

The book of Tobit puts Prov. 25:2 into the mouth of the angel Gabriel, but with a twist: in Prov. 25:2, God's glory is to conceal; the king's glory is to search out hidden things (injustice, plots, etc.). In Tobit 12:7, 11b, it is "good" to conceal a king's doings, but it is good to reveal the "works of God," acknowledging God's honor and glory. The rabbis of *b. Shab.* 30b worry about 26:4-5: Is a sage to answer a fool, or not? They resolve the dilemma by specifying that 26:5 refers to improper readings of the Torah: *that* foolishness *must* be corrected! Proverbs 29:24 seems to be based on Leviticus 5: witnesses must come forward, or they are accessories to the crime. The most important legacy is in 25:21-22: students are advised to "love their enemies" in very concrete ways by providing sustenance. This may provoke a change of heart (?), but even should it not, it pleases God. Romans 12:17-21 is based on these verses. Proverbs 26:11, the fool who commits his idiocies repeatedly, like a dog who returns to its vomit, is found in 2 Pet. 2:22, where it is used of those who fall away from the true faith, and linked to a nonbiblical proverb about swine.

THE TEXT IN CONTEMPORARY DISCUSSION

The sages join the rural Hebrew prophets (Amos, Micah) and the Teacher from Galilee in offering scathing analyses of elite profit-taking and rigging the system in the favor of the "haves." Astute observations of what the way of the wicked looks like "on the ground" is thoroughly explored here; obedience is not simply a matter of "right" (monotheistic) theology and pure cultic worship. The denunciation goes much deeper in Proverbs, to the heart of the worldview that secures the sages' ethical practice: one must *choose* to be good. Bearing witness to economic cheating, corrupt court processes, trumped-up quarrels used to distract, and the power of wicked propaganda against the innocent is obligatory. The humility of the sages is their protection: they may hold themselves in high esteem, but they have learned not to trust in themselves and their own wisdom (26:12, perhaps a comment on 26:4b and 5b; cf. Prov. 3:5, 7). YHWH has made *all* citizens of the planet (even the flocks and fields), and cares about them all, not just successful elites.

Romans 12:17-21 is nested in a longer discussion, but vengeance is forbidden, not just for legal reasons but also because it fractures a community and makes reconciliation among kin unlikely. Our proverb as applied in Romans goes a step further: no hope of future gain should motivate those who follow Christ. They must opt for love over all else, even the natural human desire to settle scores with enemies in their own coin—an eye for an eye! Evil must be fought with good, not passivity where the righteous give way to the wicked (Prov. 25:26). The enemies may not turn to friends, but God's pleasure is assured—and the enemies *may* succumb to God's peace after all (16:7). "In the end, love wins."

This deep insight into the way that Christians, and before them, Jews, must think and act their way out of the trap of retributive violence is the basis of nonviolent resistance to worldly wickedness. Taking a cue from the life of Jesus (among others), great visionaries like Mahatma Gandhi, Martin Luther King Jr., and Bishop Desmond Tutu, along with Tibetan Dalai Lamas, have demonstrated that this text is not dead, but deeply influential—for some, even extending down into daily diet in a refusal to take part in the suffering of animals, also creatures of worth. Those who would be good and wise may never just "pass by on the other side" or keep silent when justice is at stake, even if attempting to correct a wicked fool may seem doomed to failure.

Proverbs 30:1-33: Teachings and Numerical Sayings

▋ THE TEXT IN ITS ANCIENT CONTEXT

Another discrete section opens here consisting of extended passages (30:1b-4, 5-6, 7-9, 11-14, 15-16, 18-19, 21-23, 24-28, 29-31, 32-33) incorporating admonitions (30:6, 10, 32b), individual sayings (30:5, 15, 17, 20, 33), and numerical sayings incorporating nature wisdom (30:15-16, 18-19, 21-23, 24-28, 29-31). The title "The Words of Agur" (30:1) may refer to authorship, collection, or patronage, and some scholars read the NRSV's "an oracle" as a place name, meaning "from/of Massa" in northern Arabia. If the latter is correct, then Agur was not an Israelite, lending another piece of evidence to the international nature of wisdom teachings.

The world-weariness of verses 30:1b-4 is not without antecedents: the Egyptian Dialogue of a Man with His Soul and other cynical or "contest" dialogues often express ennui and despair at humanity's inability to know the "whole story," as does Qoheleth (e.g., Eccles. 1:2-11). The rhetorical questions in 30:4 have many echoes in Job's dialogues and recall YHWH as Creator in Job 38–42, questioning his upstart worshiper on cosmic subjects. The extended units here often sound like a riddling contest, inviting the audience to puzzle over what unites the items listed. Items in 30:15-16 are all ones thought to be insatiable, and unite to identify "greed" as the topic; "inexplicable movement" is the referent that binds 30:18-19; "crushing weight" is the topic of 30:21-23; in 30:24-28, "size doesn't matter" is illustrated by the unclean critters that still have a valuable lesson to teach; "swaggering movement" is the answer in 30:29-31.

THE TEXT IN THE INTERPRETIVE TRADITION

The speaker in 30:4 raises weary questions, based in cosmic, natural, or intimate sources of knowledge: Who can go between heaven and earth, wrap up water, or discern identities? While some traditions claim Enoch went up and down between heaven and earth (*1 En.* 72–82), the questions here, and their echo in Job 38:4-30, 34-38 and 39:4, make clear only the Lord has or could do these things. Humans, even sages, are deeply limited creatures! Nature wisdom featured in 30:15-16, 24-28, and 29-31 reminds us that the world of field, flock, and wilderness are also players in God's drama of creation, and the choice of animals considered unclean underscores that *all* of nature has something to teach. These creatures can illustrate interpreters' own personal views. Jerome (*Against Jovinianus* 1.28) uses the sucking leech in verses 15-16 (the "daughters" are the two prongs at either end that suck blood) as a condemnation of all *women* by reading "women's love" for "barren womb," and linking it further to the unloved woman and uppity maid of 30:23. Reading this with all of Proverbs' previous negative sayings about wives, Jerome concludes that *any* wife is a dreadful choice, since woman's love is "the grave . . . the parched earth, and . . . fire" (Schaff 1995).

THE TEXT IN CONTEMPORARY DISCUSSION

The collection of things that look different on the surface but share a hidden connection (at least as the sage views them) suggests both the encyclopedic knowledge essential for those in the "education and counsel" business, but also a form of intelligence that is holistic and contextual. Categories are at work here that the sages' forms unlock for the student: What similar features do "small" things (30:24-28) share? Can these function as a lesson for students about aspects of wisdom (providing food for winter, 30:25; managing one's environment, 30:26; ability to work together without oversight, 30:27; ability to change venues, 30:28)? Yes, of course, they can, in the hands of masterful teachers: understanding the hidden connections in nature (30:15-16, 18-19, 21-23, 24-28, 29-31) serves to illuminate *human* categories of behavior (women under patriarchy searching for personhood via motherhood, 30:16, 23; male-female relations, 30:19; changes in status, 30:22-23; and the self-aggrandizement of leaders, 30:31b). The sage of Proverbs 30 reminds us that the "little" folk of lower status or size in these numerical sayings *also* have worthy or surprising things to teach. The author's own pleasures in knowledge when its grasps "things too wonderful [that is, unexpected and difficult to understand] for me" (30:18) is palpable.

Proverbs 31:1-9: A Mother's Instruction

THE TEXT IN ITS ANCIENT CONTEXT

This "royal" instruction reminiscent of Egyptian instructions aimed at monarchs (Fox 2009, 883; 2000, 82–83) gives us finally an instruction purportedly composed by an unnamed mother for her son, Lemuel, thus providing examples of the mother's torah featured elsewhere (1:8; 6:20; 31:26). As the father's voice in instruction, coupled with cosmic Lady Wisdom's speech, opened the whole book, here at the end, Proverbs 31 balances the ending with a mother's instruction (31:1-9), followed by a look at Lady Wisdom at home in 31:10-31 as the woman of substance. This forms a deliberate inclusion of parental teaching paired with an appearance of female Wisdom. Clearly, this is a sign of editorial decisions at work.

While no "Lemuel" (= Solomon?) is known in the Bible, we find a second mention of Massa (see note on "oracle" in 30:1ab), a region in northern Arabia. The queen mother regards her son as exceedingly dear (31: 2), a "son of my womb," and so her prohibitions take on an especially urgent tone. She warns against too much engagement with women (harem politics, perhaps), which can undercut effective leadership (cf. the courtly riddle contest in 1 Esd. 4:13-32). Wine is also called out as a potential danger, but the queen is attentive to wisdom's theme of the "right season/time": kings *shouldn't* drink, but condemned criminals and the destitute *should* be given wine to numb the pain of their condition (31:6-7). Kings must *never* forget their duties (31:4-5), but those at the far end of the status continuum ought to be allowed to forget (31:6-7. cf. 1 Esd. 3:18-24 for wine's strength). The ultimate duty of a king, then, is not to abuse the pleasures or resources of his status, but to raise his voice for the voiceless (31:8-9) in judgment and in governance.

Proverbs 20:1 already commented on the effects of intoxicants that "lead astray," and it is followed directly by the "dread anger" of a king in 20:2. Proverbs 20:8 speaks of a king's unimpaired judgment as he "winnows" evil (sifts the evidence). Similarly, in Prov. 28:15-16 and 29:14 we have associations seen in the queen mother's teaching: angry kings who oppress the poor are swept away. The secret to a long, successful rule is knowledge of the rights of the poor and enforcing them. Lemuel's mother is speaking authoritatively here, blind neither to the tendencies of kings nor the faults of members of her sex.

◼ The Text in the Interpretive Tradition

The Talmud (*b. Sanh.* 43a:18-19) offers intriguing comments on 31:5-7 in the context of executions of proven criminals: judges and witnesses should *not* drink, for it impairs judgment, but the condemned *should* be given drink to "benumb" their minds. The rabbis report that the women of Jerusalem provided the condemned with wine into which frankincense had been mixed as they were taken to the place of execution, giving compassionate care for the moment of death. They even went so far as to provide the money for the wine and drug out of their own pockets, suggesting that they took the sentiments of Lemuel's mother to heart. These practices illuminate the ministries women provided to Jesus during the passion event: Mark 14:3 (= Matt. 26:6-7) speaks of a woman giving "final care" to Jesus (Matt. 26:10-12; Zaentz). She anoints him with an expensive natural analgesic (unspecified in Matthew 26, but probably "myrrh" [Mark 15:23], used in treatment of leprosy, as was frankincense), perhaps already available in the host's, Simon the Leper's, household. The wines given to Jesus during his agonizing execution may also be part of the Jerusalem women's service to the condemned: women ("daughters of Jerusalem" in Luke 23:27-28) were among the crowd looking on (Matt. 27:55-56), and the wines offered to Jesus are "mixed" with palliative drugs ("gall" in Matt. 27:34, 48; Mark 15:36; Luke 23:36; John 19:29 specifies hyssop, also a fumigant and analgesic). It is easy to imagine one of them commissioning a bribe that facilitated the provision of their medicaments to Jesus.

THE TEXT IN CONTEMPORARY DISCUSSION

The advice offered by Lemuel's royal mother is precious, not only for its example of motherly concern about the right use of life's pleasures and their impact on essential duties, but also because of the balance her instruction provides to the father's voice and all the negative proverbs found throughout the book. In Prov. 31:1-9, we finally hear a female voice, one endowed with worldly experience, knowledge of legal proceedings, and compassion for the destitute and condemned. The words of this woman offer sound advice, insightful conclusions, and a finely tuned sense of how situational ambiguity moderates individual precepts. Her advice ranges from her most intimate relationship ("son of my womb") to the greatest possible extent—the huge mass of the poor and needy who require the voice of another to give words to their distress. One of the voices that performs this noble task is that of the mother.

Proverbs 31:10-31: Acrostic on the Strong Woman

THE TEXT IN ITS ANCIENT CONTEXT

The crowning achievement of an unknown editor's defense of woman occurs in Prov. 31:10-31, an acrostic poem in praise of the strong woman or woman of substance. Designed with each successive letter of the Hebrew alphabet beginning a new line, its use as an exercise for students is highly likely, and its content fits with that goal. There have been many warnings about the attractions of the "wrong" (= exogamous) woman, but now they are balanced out by a portrait of the woman the sages *do* recommend. The Hebrew term that describes this affluent, industrious, and wise woman, *hayil*, when used of men, describes full adult strength and capacities (power and courage), but may also refer to wealth (e.g., Gen. 34:29; Num. 31:9; 1 Sam. 14:48; Job 20:18). The portrait of her wealth and industry in a variety of household, financial, and market venues suggests that this woman is not merely a "good wife": instead, she is a "strong woman," or better, given the sociological setting of the Persian and Hellenistic periods, "woman of substance" (Yoder 2001, 77).

This wife and mother is one with many resources: her bride price and her dowry speak of wealth (31:11-12), and her access to female staff, fields, profits from her textile work, provisions of exotic imports for her family, her real estate and its usufruct all betoken great luxury, suggesting a daughter of a wealthy elite who brings economic advantages into her marriage. Like Woman Wisdom, she is the making of her man (31:16, 18, 20-24), offering many of Woman Wisdom's gifts. Wealth and honor (3:15; 8:11; 31:10), a luxurious house and staff (9:1, 3; 31:15, 21, 27), and a secure future are hers to bestow. Both figures appear at gates (1:21; 8:3; 31:31); both are hard to acquire (1:28; 8:17; 31:10); both reward their men with good things (3:16; 4:8; 8:18, 21; 31:11-12) and fine reputations (3:4, 16; 31:23). Both are able to "laugh" at the future (1:26; 8:30; 31:25), since both exemplify the teachings of wisdom and their benefits. Equally as important as their wealth, they both teach compassionate care for others (1:24; 4:6; 31:20, 27). In verse 26, we learn that when this wise woman speaks, it is with the "torah of kindness" (*torath-hesed*) on her tongue, invoking the "covenant love" (*hesed*) that God supplies in abundance to those who are part of the covenant community. She is indeed, as her husband and children attest, "a woman who fears the Lord" (31:30).

■ THE TEXT IN THE INTERPRETIVE TRADITION

Proverbs 12:4 taught that an *'eshet-hayil*, the "woman of substance" like the one we see in 31:10-31, is a "crown for her husband," and Proverbs 31 amplifies this with examples. Later interpreters had qualms about the merits of marriage, often castigating woman as bringer of sin and death (1 Tim. 2:11-15; cf. Sir. 25:24; 42:13-14). Sirach 26:1-4 makes clear that if one *must* have dealings with women, the "good wife" of Proverbs 31 is the best and most desirable of the lot. Even Clement of Alexandria (*Paed.* 3.11), while excoriating harmless adornments of women (based on 1 Tim. 2:9; 1 Pet. 3:1-4), finds that the industry and piety of the wife of 31:10-31 make her a "store of excellence" worthy of his blessing.

■ THE TEXT IN CONTEMPORARY DISCUSSION

The "woman of substance" is no mirage, but a composite of the economic activities of elite women in the complex, vibrant colonial economies supervised by elites during the Persian and Hellenistic Empires, though her activities have precursors in the monarchic period that gave us Abigail, Jezebel, and other powerful wives. As Christine Elizabeth Yoder points out, this is "women's work" raised to a level of theological validation as an outcome of "fear of the Lord" (Yoder 2001, 108–9). While that is better than venomous proverbs, this wife is still objectified and viewed from a male perspective as both an acquisition of and means to men's material gratification—just as Woman Wisdom is to the sages who praise and seek her, as YHWH did before them in 8:22-31. The woman of substance presents a largely unattainable model for real women (not unlike a "virgin mother"), because she reflects the activity of *many advantaged* women, not just one. While she is naturally viewed from a male author's point of view—all authors speak out of their own subject position at some level—her description also reveals the biases of the elite class of sages.

"Wisdom is good with an inheritance!" (Eccles. 7:11a, RSV). What a difference status makes! This is no average woman, as details and contrasts reveal. Boasting of the future is usually forbidden (27:1), but not for her (31:21, 25). Yes, she works hard—but not on tedious cleaning or childcare; she has staff to take care of that. Moving around the city, vocally bartering with merchants, wearing fine clothes or jewelry—all these activities are discouraged by the sages when lesser women are involved, but in this woman, they are exemplary. Strong woman has no need to nag a lazy, drunken, quarrelsome, violent fool of a husband: *she* has her *own* resources, which *she* manages to the welfare of those for whom *she* cares. After all, how much trouble can her fortunate man cause the household, while sitting in the city gates, basking in the glow of her wealth?

Poor women, then and now, are not so lucky.

Works Cited

Brenner, Athalya, and F. van Dijk-Hemmes. 1996. *On Gendering Texts: Female and Male Voices in the Hebrew Bible*. Leiden: Brill.

Clifford, Richard. 1999. *Proverbs: A Commentary*. OTL. Louisville: Westminster John Knox.

Cole Susan, Marian Ronan, and Hal Taussig. 1997. *Wisdom's Feast: Sophia in Study and Celebration*. Kansas City: Sheed & Ward.

Fontaine, Carole R. 1982. *Traditional Sayings in the Old Testament: A Contextual Study*. The Bible and Literature 5. Sheffield: Almond.

———. 2002. *Smooth Words: Women, Proverbs and Performance in Biblical Wisdom*. Sheffield: Sheffield Academic.

Fox, Michael V. 2000. *Proverbs 1–9: A New Translation with Introduction and Commentary*. AB. New York: Doubleday.

———. 2009. *Proverbs 10–31: A New Translation with Introduction and Commentary*. AYB. New Haven: Yale University Press.

Habel, Norman C. 2000. *Readings from the Perspective of Earth*. Earth Bible 1. Cleveland: Pilgrim.

———. 2003. "The Implications of God Discovering Wisdom in Earth." In *Job 28: Cognition in Context*, edited by Ellen van Wolde, 281–97. Leiden: Brill.

Habel, Norman C., and the Earth Bible Team. 2001. "Where Is the Voice of Earth in Wisdom Literature?" In *The Earth Story in Wisdom Traditions*, edited by Norman C. Habel and Shirley Wurst. Earth Bible 3. Sheffield: Sheffield Academic.

Healey, Joseph, and Donald Sybertz. 1996. *Towards an African Narrative Theology*. Maryknoll, NY: Orbis.

Katz, Albert N., and Todd R. Ferretti. 2003. "Reading Proverbs in Context: The Role of Explicit Markers." *Discourse Processes* 36, no. 1:19–46.

McGuire, Anne. 1994. "The Thunder, Perfect Mind." In Searching the Scriptures, Vol. II: A Feminist Commentary, edited by Elisabeth Schüssler Fiorenza, 39–54. New York: Crossroad.

Murphy, Roland E. 1988. "Wisdom and Eros in Proverbs 1–9." *CBQ* 50:600–603.

———. 1998. *Proverbs*. WBC. Nashville: Thomas Nelson.

Newsom, Carol A. 1989. "Woman and the Discourse of Patriarchal Wisdom: A Study of Proverbs 1–9." In *Gender and Difference in Ancient Israel*, edited by Peggy L. Day, 142–60. Minneapolis: Fortress Press.

Oha, Obododimma. 1998. "The Semantics of Female Devaluation in Igbo Proverbs." *African Study Monographs* 19, no. 2:87–102.

Perdue, Leo G. 2008. *The Sword and the Stylus: An Introduction to Wisdom in the Age of Empires*. Grand Rapids: Eerdmans.

Perkins, John. 2005. *Confessions of an Economic Hit Man*. New York: Plume.

———. 2008. *The Secret History of the American Empire: The Truth About Economic Hit Men, Jackals, and How to Change the World*. New York: Plume.

Rad, Gerhard von. 1972. *Wisdom in Israel*. Translated by J. D. Martin. London: SCM.

Schaff, Philip, trans. 1995. The Nicene and Post-Nicene Fathers, Second Series, Vol. 6: Jerome: Letters and Select Works. Hendrickson Publishing (www.ccel.org/schaff/npnf206.vi.vi.I.html, accessed 3/15/2004).

Schipper, Mineke. 1991. *Source of All Evil: African Proverbs and Sayings on Women*. Ivan R. Dee.

Schüssler Fiorenza, Elisabeth. 1994. *Jesus: Miriam's Child, Sophia's Prophet*. London: Continuum.

Van Leeuwen, Raymond. 1988. *Context and Meaning in Proverbs 25–27*. SBLDS 96. Atlanta: Society of Biblical Literature.

White, Sarah C. 2009. "Men, Masculinities, and the Politics of Development." *Gender and Development* 5, no. 2:14–22.

Weber, Elke U., Christopher K. Hsee, and Joanna Sokolowska. 1998. "What Folklore Tells Us about Risk and Risk Taking: Cross-Cultural Comparisons of American, German, and Chinese Proverbs." *Organizational Behavior and Human Decision Processes* 75, no. 2:170–86.

Wurst, Shirley. 2001. "Woman Wisdom's Way: Ecokinship." In *The Earth Story in Wisdom Traditions*, edited by Norman C. Habel and Shirley Wurst, 48–64. Earth Bible 3. Sheffield: Sheffield Academic.

Yoder, Christine Elizabeth. 2001. *Wisdom as a Woman of Substance: A Socioeconomic Reading of Proverbs 1–9 and 31:10–31*. Berlin: de Gruyter.

———. 2009. *Proverbs*. Nashville: Abingdon.

Zaentz, Paula Rendino. 2008. "Matthew 26 and Mark 14: Spikenard and Women's Healing Ministries to Jesus." Unpublished paper.

ECCLESIASTES

Micah D. Kiel

Introduction

The author of Ecclesiastes weaves a web of dicta, reflections, and wisdom aphorisms shaped by tradition, experience, and context. The book squirms beneath difficult questions about the relationship between God, experience, and justice: Do people get what they deserve? Does God act in predictable ways? What is the nature of life, and how are we to live? The questions are timeless; the answers, however, assert an epistemological skepticism that have long left Ecclesiastes marginal to some.

Ecclesiastes is attributed to "the son of David" (meaning Solomon), although the name Solomon is never used. Solomon is associated with much of the Wisdom literature, so such an ascription here is not surprising. Solomon did not write Ecclesiastes, however. Linguistic analysis proves that it was written during the Persian period, probably sometime between 450 and 325 BCE. The author also is referred to as Qoheleth, which in Hebrew most literally means "gatherer." This word is commonly used as a proper name for the author of the work.

The book makes no discernible references to historical places, figures, or events. Details suggest that a Palestinian origin is most likely. Historical research about the Persian period—especially its economics—illuminates Qoheleth's words. Taxation was widespread and highly organized. Coins were minted in unprecedented numbers and became the basis of economic activity. Inscriptions of this period portray concern about economic issues. Ecclesiastes reveals a similar preoccupation. Qoheleth's opening reflection on meaninglessness is immediately made concrete in the economic realm: accumulated wealth and all of its accoutrements (houses, vineyards, herds, and silver) are nothing but a chasing after the wind (2:1-8).

The economic system under the Persians was marked by mobility. There was opportunity to move up or down the economic ladder, often rapidly. At the same time, excessive debt was rampant. Many borrowed money to feed their families. People were forced to work in prisons to pay off debt.

There is even evidence that rich individuals owned their own prisons in which they could hold those unable to pay back their debts (Seow, 31).

Ecclesiastes also appropriates language similar to that used in the dissemination of land grants (Seow, 24). These grants were distributed rather arbitrarily, often at the whim of rulers or other elites. The land also was not inherited by offspring. The prospects of wealth accumulation or, the opposite, rapid descent into destitution, provide a crisp backdrop against which Qoheleth's message can be understood. At times, Qoheleth despairs at the capricious economic context, observes indeterminacy, and recommends nothing other than mirth (8:15; 9:7). At the same time, many of the book's idioms, and even its very depiction of God, are analogies that come from this economic context. Thus God is depicted as capricious, a deity whose future actions are unknowable (3:16-22). Qoheleth evinces an epistemological uncertainty that parallels the relationship between Persian leadership and rapid economic change.

One must also have a sense of Qoheleth's canonical and theological contexts in order to understand the edge to his words. Qoheleth interacts with a specific theological ideology that claims there is a close connection between actions and consequences. This formulation is given expression in Deuteronomy: "If you will only obey the LORD your God . . . all these blessings shall come upon you" (28:1-2). The opposite is also true: "But if you will not obey the LORD your God . . . then all these curses shall come upon you" (28:15). This ideology, sometimes called "Deuteronomistic" because of its source in Deuteronomy, is a perspective that has influenced large portions of the Old Testament.

This close connection between act and consequence finds a particular formulation in Israel's Wisdom literature: "Those who listen to me will be secure and will live at ease" (Prov. 1:33). Later Wisdom literature reaffirms this rigid connection between act and consequence: "You who fear the Lord, trust in him, and your reward will not be lost" (Sir. 2:8). If the Wisdom literature gives us any access to life among ruling elites and their education system, then such a tidy formula—that God repays according to action—might serve their ruling interests well: by offering a clear definition of God; by claiming to know how and why God acts; and, most importantly of all, by ordering obedience.

In such a context, Ecclesiastes stands out. Contrary to a doctrine of close connection between actions and consequences, Qoheleth recommends a pursuit of pleasure, because life's events contradict such a tidy theological formulation: "There are righteous people who perish in their righteousness, and there are wicked people who prolong their life in their evildoing" (7:15). Experience contradicts the theological party line: "the same fate comes to all, to the righteous and the wicked, to the good and the evil, to the clean and the unclean" (9:2). Qoheleth, like the author of Job, offers life's experiences as a rebuttal to the widely held theological dictum that God treats people according to their actions. Ecclesiastes, then, is situated not only in a specific historical context of rapidly shifting economic opportunities. It also interacts with conventional theological formulations, often refusing to accept them wholesale.

Ecclesiastes 1:1-11: Philosophical Musings of a Teacher

■ THE TEXT IN ITS ANCIENT CONTEXT

The book opens with the repetition of the Hebrew word *hevel*, which evokes a puff of smoke or a vapor. *Hevel*'s connotations—something brief, fleeting, and indeterminate—are hard to convey in English. Most translations, following the Septuagint and Vulgate, use "vanity" or "meaningless." Starting with *hevel* sets an immediate agenda: when scrutinized, life appears to be little more than an abridged vapor.

In Eccles. 1:4-11, Qoheleth attempts to prove that all is *hevel* by contemplating the created order. Such contemplation is common in Wisdom literature. The regularity of creation is often used to support the idea that God is in control of the universe (Sir. 16:26-30). It can also be used to judge deviations from its regularity (*1 En.* 80–81). In Job, God brags about creation's workings in order to make Job's complaints seem minuscule in comparison. Qoheleth's response to creation is quizzical. The sun rockets around the earth. Streams flow, do not fill, yet do not run dry. The wind blows and returns. Scrutiny of such things is deemed "wearisome; more than one can express" (1:8). The experience of creation is too magnificent to be summarized, yet too vexing to comprehend.

The poetry is skillfully constructed so as to support this conclusion. Pronouns are avoided. Instead, the nouns themselves (generation, sun, sea, wind) are repeated. The poetry thus embodies the very idea that life is repetitive, that there indeed is "nothing new under the sun" (1:9).

The ultimate metaphor in which all of these reflections are grounded, however, is economic. The Hebrew word *yitron*, meaning "advantage" or "profit," is used ten times in Ecclesiastes, and it reinforces the idea that economics (both real and metaphorical) are central in the thought of the author. The word conveys a sense of surplus, an amount beyond what is necessary. Given what we know about the economics of the day—it was a "lively economic environment" (Seow, 22)—such an operative analogy throughout the text should not be surprising. Qoheleth assumes that his audience is shrewd enough to understand the concept of *yitron*: if an activity does not produce a surplus, he deems it a waste of time.

■ THE TEXT IN THE INTERPRETIVE TRADITION

In Rom. 8:20, Paul uses the Greek word *mataiotēs* ("futility"), which is the Septuagint's translation of *hevel* in Eccles. 1:2. The confluence of this word with Paul's broader reflection in chapter 8 about creation suggests that Paul may intentionally be interacting with Ecclesiastes. For Qoheleth, the vapor-like quality of life came from monotony, regularity, and a sense that nothing has changed. Paul also connects creation with futility. Because of his apocalyptic worldview, he concludes that the futility is not God's doing, nor the fault of creation itself, but is instead something that has been imposed on it. Because life is *hevel*, Qoheleth will eventually advocate the pursuit of happiness because nothing is assured and everything is meaningless. Paul, however, looks forward to a day when the futility of creation will be fixed though liberation, it will be "set free from its bondage"

(Rom. 8:21). Thus Qoheleth and Paul both sense a futility in the created order, but their respective points of view lead to drastically different responses to that basic observation.

In a completely different context, Ephrem the Syrian (d. 373 CE) finds the image of the unfillable sea (Eccles. 1:7) as a type of Christ. In an acrostic hymn, Jesus, as the sea, is the one into whom the endless Jewish symbols, similes, and typologies flow: "Since it [i.e., Jesus/sea] is a wondrous gulf, all creatures cannot fill it. . . . Therefore, the sea is Christ Who is able to receive the sources and springs and rivers and streams that flow forth from within scripture" (McVey, 302–3). While the supersessionism of such a perspective is unpalatable, Ephrem's reading here is remarkable in its subtle appropriation of the image from Ecclesiastes.

■ THE TEXT IN CONTEMPORARY DISCUSSION

While much of the discussion of creation in the Bible demonstrates differences between the ancients and ourselves, here in Ecclesiastes, one might find Qoheleth's contemplation of the created order relevant. Science and all of its learning has not removed the basic experience of being flummoxed by nature. The most learned of our astrophysicists, observing colliding particles and getting brief glimpses of the origins of the universe at the quantum level, are continually surprised by what they find. We best not have God enter at the point where science, for the moment, cannot explain something. Qoheleth here offers a different way: a quizzical reaction to the mysteries of the world's working. We want to know more; the eye is not satisfied with seeing, nor the ear with hearing (1:8). This speculation, for Qoheleth, leads ultimately to pessimism. The regularity of the created order suggests that things have never changed, that there is nothing new anywhere.

Ecclesiastes 1:12—2:26: Uselessness of Seeking Wisdom

■ THE TEXT IN ITS ANCIENT CONTEXT

We might think of the next section in Qoheleth as the reflections of a workaholic. No matter how hard one works, what is crooked will stay crooked. Qoheleth, using the ancient literary form of a fictional royal biography, lists accomplishments and things acquired: great deeds, houses, vineyards, flocks, and so on. Qoheleth's employment of this biography, however, is ironic. None of this allows one to corral the vapor that is life.

Even pursuit of wisdom is nothing more than a chasing of the wind, for "in much wisdom is much vexation" (1:18). All is still *hevel* ("vanity" or "meaningless") because a life of wisdom provides no discernible advantage—the wise one dies just like the fool; one fate befalls everyone. Qoheleth goes one step further: pursuing wisdom may actually make it worse! Increased wisdom only brings increased pain and vexation (1:18). Ignorance is bliss.

■ THE TEXT IN THE INTERPRETIVE TRADITION

Martin Luther has an extended treatise, "Notes on Ecclesiastes," in which he attempts to tackle the problems that Qoheleth presents. He does so obliquely, however, by changing God's role, thereby blunting the force of Qoheleth's skeptical theological suppositions. For example, in 1:15 Qoheleth proclaims that what is crooked cannot be made straight. From this observation, Luther argues that what Qoheleth says is true for human beings. Luther says that anyone who claims his or her life "has gone at all times just as he had proposed" should be accused of lying. The solution, Luther says, is "to commit everything to God" (Luther, 26–27). This does not face the critique head-on because Qoheleth suggests that even God cannot be observed to fix such problems.

THE TEXT IN CONTEMPORARY DISCUSSION

Qoheleth here offers a deeply skeptical view of the human condition. To those in a Christian context, one might jump to the afterlife to avoid his skepticism: Why despair over a terrestrial end when something better awaits? Qoheleth had no such luxury. For most of the Hebrew Bible, the afterlife as a place of ongoing reward or punishment was not a part of the belief system. The conspicuous lack of an afterlife, however, does not make Qoheleth's thoughts irrelevant. Such reflections should force the reader to linger on the questions of existential angst one finds here. Who has not, after a long and frustrating day, asked "What's it all for?" Who has not laid awake at night, anxious about the future? Even at night, our hearts are not at rest (see 2:23). At the very least, Qoheleth gives honest expression to what it is often like to be a human.

Ecclesiastes 3:1-15: A Time for Everything, Yet Undesignated

THE TEXT IN ITS ANCIENT CONTEXT

The poem in the third chapter of Ecclesiastes proceeds with paired opposites: birth/death, plant/pluck, weep/laugh. The paired phrases are not given grammatical subjects; they tumble forward in infinitival constructions governed only by prepositions and the noun for "time," *'eth*. The poetry obfuscates who acts. This suggests that God is the actor, making the poem "an invitation to embrace God's grace and to have faith that situations will change" (Tamez, 58).

The prose section that follows the poem is built on the same theological foundation. He *knows* that it is good to be happy (3:12) and that God's work endures forever (3:14). This is Qoheleth at his most optimistic and faithful. God is in control of history, God appoints times and seasons for everything, and that which God does should induce awe (3:14). Problems arise, however, because humans can discern little about the actual big picture. Verse 11 summarizes the vexing situation in which humans find themselves: God has made a time suitable for everything and given humans a sense of time—a past and a future—yet what God has actually done in the past and what God will do in the future are beyond human ken. In his own words: "that which is, already has been; that which is to be, already is" (3:15). It is as if Qoheleth has a pile of puzzle pieces in front of him, but no idea what the picture looks like, and thus no idea where to start putting it all together.

THE TEXT IN THE INTERPRETIVE TRADITION

The specific pairing in the poem of a time to be born and a time to die is used frequently in early Christian authors with reference to baptism. The language and imagery is similar to that of Paul in Rom. 6:3-4. Cyril of Jerusalem, for example, in his second lecture on the mysteries addressed to those preparing for baptism, says: "What Solomon said in another context is applicable to you: 'A time for giving birth, a time for dying,' although for you, contrariwise, it is a case of 'a time for dying and a time for being born'" (Cyril of Jerusalem, 165).

■ THE TEXT IN CONTEMPORARY DISCUSSION

One cannot read Ecclesiastes 3 without hearing jangly 1960s pop music in the background. The song "Turn! Turn! Turn! (To Everything There Is a Season)," written by Pete Seeger and made popular by The Byrds, has made this text one of the most recognized in the Bible.

Peace advocates often use Eccles. 3:8 ("a time for peace") to claim that *now* (in whatever context they may be situated) is the time for peace. This problematically ignores the fact that verses 9-15 suggest we will not know when any of these times are. God is the one who decided when a time is suitable (3:11). Humans are blessed with a sense of past, present, and future, but yet are cursed with an inability to discern completely God's actions: "yet they cannot find out what God has done from the beginning to the end" (3:11).

Ecclesiastes 3:16—4:8: Epistemological Nihilism

■ THE TEXT IN ITS ANCIENT CONTEXT

In 3:16-22, Qoheleth reinforces the epistemological skepticism from the previous section. He begins with a simple observation: wickedness and righteousness often do not have their rightful places. Then Qoheleth lets the reader in on his own inner dialogue ("I said in my heart . . ."), which attempts to resolve the tension in the distortion of justice on the earth. The first option is that God will judge the righteous and the wicked (3:17), for there is a time appointed for everything. This idea, which echoes 3:1-15, is not developed.

Qoheleth whispers another option to himself (3:18): what is perceived as lack of justice is little more than God testing humans. The concept of testing finds a natural home in the wisdom tradition. In a pedagogical setting, trouble and problems in life are seen as God testing the individual, who, if successful, will emerge better and stronger on the other side (e.g., Sir. 2:1; 4:17), like gold that has been tested in fire. The trial burns off impurities, leaving behind a stronger, purer original (Prov. 27:21). This is not where Qoheleth takes the idea of testing, however. The test instead is meant to show humans that they are but animals. Animals and humans share the same fate: death and decomposition. The reflection culminates with the phrase: "Who knows?" (3:21), a stark contrast to 3:12 and 14, when Qoheleth happily claimed, "I know." Upon further reflection, things have changed.

Modern Bibles start Ecclesiastes 4 in the middle of what is really a continuation of the flow of thought until 4:8. In 4:1-3, Qoheleth's gaze turns to the oppressed. He does not specify the nature of the oppression, but it is broad and systematic. The oppressors oppress the oppressed (the word is used in a similarly repetitious way in Hebrew), and there is no one to comfort them. Conspicuously absent is the sentiment of texts such as Ps. 69:33 and Sir. 4:16 that God will hear the cry of the poor or oppressed. Because of this, the dead are better off than the living, because they no longer have to see such injustice. Better yet, however, are those who have never been born because they have never seen the oppression at all. Again, for Qoheleth, ignorance is bliss (cf. 1:18).

▮ THE TEXT IN THE INTERPRETIVE TRADITION

Much of the history of the interpretation of this portion of Ecclesiastes has been spent trying to make it say something other than what it actually says. Ambrose of Milan (d. 397), in his treatise *Death as a Good*, struggles to explain Qoheleth's statement that death is preferable to life (4:2). Death is not bad for one who is pious, of course, because of the Christian belief in the afterlife, but the death of one who is impious will lead to hell. Ambrose proceeds to say that death is preferable for the impious as well, because at least he or she will cease to sin. Such a reading, of course, is done through the lens of later Christian eschatology, and does not accurately explicate Qoheleth's intentions.

▮ THE TEXT IN CONTEMPORARY DISCUSSION

One might not immediately associate Ecclesiastes with the pervasive biblical concern for social justice, but this text suggests that the concern may be close to Qoheleth's heart. Noticing and calling out oppression and oppressors puts Qoheleth in a long line of biblical texts that do the same with similar vocabulary, such as Exodus and Amos. Amos, for instance, insists that God rushes to alleviate the plight of the oppressed. In Exodus, God hears the cry of the Israelites in slavery and decides to fight on their behalf (2:23-25). Wisdom literature tends to focus on the oppressed with a more pedagogical goal, that proper care of the oppressed is a way of honoring God (e.g., Prov. 14:31). In Ecclesiastes 4, however, God is conspicuously absent. One comes away rather frustrated. God is not isolated as the champion of the oppressed, nor are humans given a directive to change their treatment of the same. Despite his clear exposition of the problem of oppression, it is ultimately not clear what Qoheleth would want us to do.

Ecclesiastes 4:9—5:20: Contemplating the Oppressed

▮ THE TEXT IN ITS ANCIENT CONTEXT

In 5:8-9, Qoheleth returns to oppression, a topic already mentioned in 3:16-17 and 4:1-3. Here, however, the oppressed are defined as the poor, framing the issue in a specifically socioeconomic way. The oppression of the poor stems from economic structures, layers of bureaucracy, and unchecked power. Most scholars see here a reference to the system of satraps in the Persian world (Seow), or the political world of Ptolemaic Egypt (Tamez). In either scenario, one finds a series of powerful individuals who looked out for the power of each other to the detriment of the poor.

Striking, again, is Qoheleth's response to the poor and oppressed. God is absent. There is not even a strong condemnation of those who are aggressively oppressing. In 5:13, it seems clear that even riches are fleeting, but this is far from a vision of social justice. The action he does prescribe is enjoyment. Qoheleth notes that everything is temporal, picking up the theme from the opening chapter. Individuals should hope that God gives something good, and when it arrives, enjoy it. Such a directive makes sense in the unstable economic conditions of the Persian context.

■ The Text in the Interpretive Tradition

Whether Qoheleth's original intentions or not, Eccles. 4:9-16 has, across the centuries, been read to emphasize the importance of community. Qoheleth's example of a "threefold cord" (4:12) is an evocative metaphor for finding strength in numbers in a spiritual group. Gregory of Nyssa uses Ecclesiastes to support the idea that an individual committing to a life of celibacy should not do so alone, but should have a spiritual guide, because two are better than one (Wright, 237; Gregory of Nyssa, 70).

■ The Text in Contemporary Discussion

Qoheleth here offers a powerful condemnation of an economy based on greed and backroom collaboration. Evil is not just personal but also structural. The challenge lies in the fact that the solutions to such problems are not personal, individual ones. Structural evil will not be solved by simply changing ourselves. Solutions require collective action, engaged communities, and most importantly, a comprehensive revaluation of what is good. Qoheleth seems to give voice to this very idea in 5:10-20—that those who love money and riches will never be satisfied and that they provide no real benefit to life.

Ecclesiastes 6:1—7:14: Who Knows What Is Good?

■ The Text in Its Ancient Context

In 5:18-20, Qoheleth says to enjoy while you can, but at the beginning of Ecclesiastes 6, Qoheleth claims that God will prevent an individual from enjoying possessions because the things God gives a family are suddenly enjoyed by a stranger. It's almost as if, in juxtaposing these two suppositions, Qoheleth wants to represent the paradox that is life. Given the capricious economic context in the Persian period, it would make sense that there could be some anxiety over a family actually retaining their possessions (Seow, 210).

In Eccles. 6:12, Qoheleth asks, "who knows what is good?" This is a typical question for the author (e.g., "who knows?" in 3:21). The "better than" sayings in chapter 7 purport to answer the question of 6:12. What Qoheleth deems to be "better" comes as a shock. Mourning, sorrow, rebuke, and sadness are "better" than laughter, feasting, and songs. Although in the form of proverbial wisdom, Qoheleth subverts expectations. The episode ends with Qoheleth saying that God makes both good and bad so that humans have no idea what will happen (7:14).

■ The Text in the Interpretive Tradition

Midrash Qoheleth offers an extensive reflection on 7:1, trying to explain the text's claim that the day of death is better than the day of birth. The midrash suggests that at birth, one's station in life is not yet known, while at death, it is. Thus one can rejoice at death if good deeds have led to a good life, while rejoicing at birth would be premature. The midrash uses the analogy of two ships, one leaving the harbor and the other arriving. Although everyone rejoices as one leaves, a wise person holds the opposite view: "there is not cause to rejoice over the ship which is leaving the harbor because nobody knows what will be its plight . . . but when [a ship] enters the harbor all have occasion to rejoice since it has come in safely" (as cited in Christianson, 190). This metaphor does not stray far from Qoheleth's main intention, that for epistemological reasons (i.e., that humans do not know what will happen to them) or for anthropological ones (i.e., humans have no ability to influence the outcome of their lives), humans need to rethink the causes and occasions for both joy and sorrow.

THE TEXT IN CONTEMPORARY DISCUSSION

I was shocked recently to find out that the crib my wife and I had purchased five years earlier had been deemed "illegal" because it no longer cohered to the most recent safety standards. Our society spends a lot of time, money, and energy in order to prolong life. I do not suggest we abdicate the civic responsibility of safety standards. When it comes to life, however, we often value quantity over quality. Much of the focus of our health-care system is designed to prolong life (a noble pursuit, to be sure); but does this ignore the importance of quality of life? Qoheleth's words challenge our society. Even if someone lives to be two thousand years old, he says, it would be better to be a stillborn child if there is no enjoyment during those years (6:4-9).

Vexing, however, are Qoheleth's collateral statements suggesting that enjoyment itself is difficult, if not impossible. The things given in life for enjoyment may be taken and given to another (6:2). The appetite is never satisfied (6:7). Humans are not even given the ability to dispute their lot in life, because "the more words, the more vanity" (6:11). Everything, as Qoheleth has already said, is but a chasing of the wind.

Ecclesiastes 7:15-29: An Accounting of Everyday Life

THE TEXT IN ITS ANCIENT CONTEXT

In 7:15, Qoheleth enters fully into a critique of the conceptual underpinnings of much of Israel's Wisdom literature. Texts such as Deuteronomy (e.g., 4:40; 28:1-2, 15) and Proverbs (e.g., 3:1-2, 24-26) avow a connection between act and consequence. With one experiential observation, Qoheleth undermines such simplistic theological formulations: he has seen "everything"—one righteous sufferer or prosperous sinner fractures the formula.

Qoheleth's responses to a lack of justice vary; here he recommends moderation. This raises certain questions, however. How can he recommend that one not be too righteous (7:16)? Likewise, saying the opposite: "Do not be too wicked" suggests that a moderate amount of wickedness is appropriate. Some have suggested that Qoheleth here is being sarcastic, or that he speaks against an overly confident wisdom. This may be a point where scholars overthink the problem: in a book that often uses hyperbole (e.g., the preferred status of a stillborn baby in 6:4-6), his point here is simple. The observation in 7:15 obliterates the traditional "Deuteronomistic" formula. In 7:16-18, we find absurdity, a parody of attempts to express a tidy formula that can efficiently encapsulate the totality of humanity's interactions with God. If his formula seems ridiculous, that is exactly the point: any tidy formula will wilt in the face of the human condition; life and experience are too complex.

■ The Text in the Interpretive Tradition

In 7:26, Qoheleth refers to a woman who is a trap and more bitter than death. Similar sentiment about women is extant in other Wisdom literature (e.g., Prov. 25:24; Sir. 9:1-9; 25:16-26), and so we should not be surprised to find it here. Many early Christian commentators laud "Solomon" for such words and often use them as a resource to explain the benefits of celibacy or virginity. For example, Pseudo-Clement of Rome (third century CE) warns consecrated men from consorting with women with "much silliness, without fear of God" (Wright, 256).

Although scholars argue about whether Qoheleth was misogynistic, there is an unfortunate legacy stemming from 7:26. Qoheleth's description of the "bitter woman" finds its way into what has been described as "one of the most malignant and destructive texts of Western culture," the *Malleus Maleficarum*, a treatise written to help identify witches in the fifteenth century (Christianson, 39). It explains that a woman is more bitter than death because death only kills the body, but "the sin which arose from woman destroys the soul" (as cited in Christianson, 40).

■ The Text in Contemporary Discussion

Feminist critics of Scripture have rightly balked at Qoheleth's words in 7:26-29. Such words force modern interpreters to confront the social, cultural, and religious differences between the time of the text and our own. The exegetical details are always important, however. Qoheleth may not have intended to repudiate all women everywhere (as some across the centuries have interpreted the text). In its literary context, he may simply be trying to contrast the personified woman, Wisdom, with another personified woman, Folly (see Seow, 270–73). Nevertheless, there are legitimate reasons to be skeptical of a text from a patriarchal culture that evinces misogynistic language. Texts have the power to promulgate a hierarchical relationship between genders, and modern interpreters should have their ears attuned to such readings of texts.

Ecclesiastes 8:1—9:18: Eat, Drink, and Be Merry

■ The Text in Its Ancient Context

These two chapters build on and offer some similar observations to the central themes at play throughout the book. Qoheleth's reflections on life lead to one conclusion: enjoy yourself while you can; as the poet Robert Herrick says, "Gather ye rosebuds while you may." Qoheleth's observations go beyond just the inevitability of death, but that while alive there is no way to predict people's fates. The basic observation in 8:14 could summarize much of Ecclesiastes: the righteous are treated like the wicked, and the wicked are treated like the righteous. This leads to the conclusion that all is vanity. Qoheleth expands on this observation in 9:1-8, making it more explicit by pairing opposite groups of people (righteous/wicked, good/evil, clean/unclean, good/sinners) to whom the "same fate" comes (9:3).

◼ The Text in the Interpretive Tradition

Gregory the Great (d. 604 CE) coordinates Eccles. 8:14 with the theology of Job. The fact that justice is not apparent in the world, he says, has no doubt been ordained by God. Gregory comes to this conclusion because of two contextual factors. First is his belief in an afterlife, which was not necessarily operative in Qoheleth's own theological tool kit. From Gregory's afterlife-influenced point of view, those doing the evil are "hastening onward to those torments that are without end" (as cited by Wright, 261). Second, Gregory conflates the situation in Job, in which the prologue describes God's role in the genesis of Job's ordeal, with the situation in Ecclesiastes, where the point seems to be the opposite: God's conspicuous absence.

◼ The Text in Contemporary Discussion

Qoheleth, one might say, is preoccupied with death. In this way, he shows some similarities to modern philosophy. The existentialist philosopher Martin Heidegger speaks of "being-towards-death." He says that the experience of life always leaves one with a sense that there is "constantly something still to be settled," that we all die (Heidegger, 279). For Heidegger, there is a "not yet" that belongs to individuals, as long as they exist, which is a "coming-to-its-end" (286). The connection between being and death is part of the experience of existence itself: "death is a way to be" (289), which an individual assumes as soon as he or she comes into existence. He quotes German poet von Tepl: "As soon as man comes to life, he is at once old enough to die" (*Der Ackermann aus Böhmen*). Authentic living, for Heidegger, must exist toward the inevitability of death "without fleeing it or covering it up" (305).

Qoheleth agrees with these sentiments. He similarly suggests that death needs to be part of our very self-understanding (e.g., 9:2-3, 5). The inevitability of death must be part of our lived experience: "no one can anticipate the time of disaster" (9:12). Death is the great equalizer and reveals nothing about how a person has lived her or his life (contrary to Sir. 11:28). For Qoheleth, the experience of "being-towards-death" should influence not only our theological formulations but also how we live our lives: "Go, eat your bread with enjoyment, and drink your wine with a merry heart" (9:7).

The critique that might be leveled against Heidegger and Qoheleth is their individuality. Qoheleth's observations about the lack of justice in the world are, for the most part, personal reflections, not indictments of structural injustice. Likewise, Heidegger insists that an individual's "ownmost possibility," by which he means death, is "non-relational" (308). This is part of his existentialism, just as the individual-based reflections of Qoheleth are in keeping with the approach of the wisdom tradition. One might ask them: "Where is 'the other'?" Qoheleth's sober realization of death's inevitability could be directed outward, recommending solidarity with those around the world who live a truly contingent existence, where, because of war or extreme poverty, death is a daily reality.

Ecclesiastes 10:1—11:6: A World Gone Awry

▊ THE TEXT IN ITS ANCIENT CONTEXT

Chapters 10–11 depict a world on the brink of chaos. One cannot trust in governmental officials (10:5-6; 16-17). Rulers and slaves have traded places (10:7). One can again see the historical context—marked by economic turmoil—as the impetus behind such reflections. Evidence suggests regular turnover among the rulers and elusive economic security (Seow, 23–26, 325) because of such rapid changes and the policies correlated with them. Qoheleth presses this point by moving from words about kings and rulers to quotidian, agrarian situations. Camouflaged pits with nets suddenly trap those who dug them (10:8). Woodworkers will be threatened by their craft (10:9). The world has gone askew.

The call to "send out your bread upon the waters" (11:1) and to "divide your means" (11:32) are often thought to advocate foreign and diversified investments in order to avoid any vicissitudes that might threaten economic viability. On the other hand, there is nothing here specifically about profit, as one might expect from economic advice. All Qoheleth says is that "you will get it back" (11:1). Seow coordinates the saying in 11:1 with the Egyptian Instruction of Anksheshonq, which says: "Do a good deed and throw it in the water; when it dries you will find it" (Seow, 342). Perhaps Qoheleth advocates doing a good deed without expecting anything in return. This fits Qoheleth's overall observations, that human actions in no way guarantee any kind of commensurate response; the "consequences of human actions are often contrary to expectations" (Seow, 343).

▊ THE TEXT IN THE INTERPRETIVE TRADITION

Interpreters have long recognized 11:1-2 as Qoheleth's clearest call for charity and concern for others. *Midrash Qoheleth*, later Christina interpreters, and modern authors such as Louise Erdrich all recognize "the passage's implicit and poetic urging of generosity" (Christianson, 219–20).

Authors as early as Alcuin (d. 803) allegorize this text and conflate it with New Testament imagery of the sowing of seeds. This turns it into a call for evangelization. This interpretation remains prevalent today in Christian evangelical contexts. The Internet is replete with sermons connecting Eccles. 11:1 with evangelization, often asserting that if one casts bread (i.e., sows), then one will reap a harvest of believing souls.

▊ THE TEXT IN CONTEMPORARY DISCUSSION

Richard Wilbur's 2010 poem offers what one interpreter called a "midrash" on Ecclesiastes 11:1.

> We must *cast our bread*
> *Upon the waters*, as the
> Ancient preacher said,
>
> Trusting that it may
> Amply be restored to us
> *After many a day.*

That old metaphor,
Drawn from rice farming on the
River's flooded shore,

Helps us to believe
That it's no great sin to give,
Hoping to receive.

Therefore I shall throw
Broken bread, this sullen day
Out across the snow,

Betting crust and crumb
That birds will gather, and that
One more spring will come. (see Works Cited, p. 641)

This poem is constructed of Haiku in which the first and last lines of each stanza rhyme. It recapitulates the image of Qoheleth into a different context, but seems to retain the central idea of hope for a future, although one more selfish and less focused on charity.

Ecclesiastes 11:7—12:14: The End of All Things

■ THE TEXT IN ITS ANCIENT CONTEXT

The consensus suggests that 11:7—12:8 is a reflection on youth and old age. Many scholars argue that the text was originally intended to be an allegory. Some elements work well allegorically: dimly lit windows represent poor eyesight (12:3); women who cease to grind represent a lack of teeth (12:3). Other elements, such as terrors in the road or being afraid of heights (12:5), do not. Choon-Leong Seow (376–82) suggests that Qoheleth combines the imagery of old age with eschatological language so as to depict the end of humanity itself. Qoheleth's talk of death, to this point in the book, has remained abstract. Here at the end, a "cosmic doom" that depicts "the end of human existence" (379) forcefully imposes on the reader "the finality of death" (380).

A short epilogue concludes the book in the third person, not Qoheleth's customary first person. Based on such observations, most scholars consider the epilogue extraneous to the core of the book because it came from the hand of a different author. The final two verses show the widest variance: "Fear God, and keep his commandments; for that is the whole duty of everyone. For God will bring every deed into judgment." Most conspicuous here is the mention of the commandments, an emphasis lacking in Qoheleth's reflections throughout the book. Qoheleth sporadically refers to judgment, but does not generally refer to God. We have, at the very end, the intrusion of a later redactor into the text of Ecclesiastes.

■ THE TEXT IN THE INTERPRETIVE TRADITION

Medieval French Talmudist Samuel ben Meir (d. 1158) was the first to attribute the end of Ecclesiastes to an editor (Christianson, 249). Those who avoid this observation, however, have tended to find in the text's final two verses a powerful way of framing the skepticism of most of Qoheleth's message. Thus St. Bonaventure says that it cannot be properly understood without reading all of it (Christianson, 253). While some suggest that a "faithful" ending may have helped such a skeptical book become canonized in both the Jewish and Christian traditions, no direct evidence supports such a conclusion.

■ THE TEXT IN CONTEMPORARY DISCUSSION

Endings matter, especially in Ecclesiastes. Some say that the "conservative" ending is an intrusion into Qoheleth's intentions and unfairly frames his original intent. It is worth noting, however, that recommending the commandments (Eccles. 12:13) does not necessarily contradict any of Qoheleth's teachings or observations. The final words could be read as an appropriate response to Qoheleth's skepticism that one must eventually arrive at a more faithful belief. On the other hand, such a view might give too much weight to the ending and simultaneously must ignore the possibility of redactional activity.

Should we be so flummoxed, however, to find diverse traditions within a biblical text? All of Scripture is the product of tradition; it does not fall into our laps straight from the lips of God. Sometimes traditions are woven together to constitute whole biblical texts. At other times, changes and emendations are made after the time of the "original author" (to the extent that such a thing can even be discussed). Scripture is diverse. To find diversity within a specific book only demonstrates the diversity of the canon. No book embodies that diversity better than Qoheleth, whose observations, brash honesty, and bold recommendations push faith communities to rethink and reexamine the most sacredly held truths and ideals. In a way, whether original or not, the final two verses show Qoheleth considering that which we thought he had rejected, which is the very posture his readers must adopt in order to read his words with open hearts and minds.

Works Cited

Basil of Caesarea. 1950. *Ascetical Works*. Translated by Monica Wagner, CSC. FC 9. Washington, DC: Catholic University of America Press.

Christianson, Eric S. 2007. *Ecclesiastes through the Centuries*. Oxford: Blackwell.

Cyril of Jerusalem. 1969. *The Works of Saint Cyril of Jerusalem*. Vol. 2. Translated by Leo P. McCauley, SJ. FC 64. Washington, DC: Catholic University of America Press.

Davis, Ellen F. 2000. *Proverbs, Ecclesiastes, and the Song of Songs*. Louisville: Westminster John Knox.

Gregory of Nyssa. 1967. *Ascetical Works*. Translated by Virginia Woods Callahan. FC 58. Washington, DC: Catholic University of America Press.

Heidegger, Martin. 1962. *Being and Time*. Translated by John Macquarrie and Edward Robinson. San Francisco: Harper & Row.

Limburg, James. 2006. *Encountering Ecclesiastes: A Book for Our Time*. Grand Rapids: Eerdmans.

Luther, Martin. 1972. *Ecclesiastes, Song of Solomon, 2 Samuel 23:1–7*. Translated by Jaroslav Pelikan. Luther's Works 15. St. Louis: Concordia.

McVey, Kathleen E., trans. 1989. *Ephrem the Syrian: Hymns*. Mahwah, NJ: Paulist Press.

Seow, Choon-Leong. 1997. *Ecclesiastes: A New Translation with Introduction and Commentary.* AB 18C. New York: Doubleday.

Tamez, Elsa. 2000. *When the Horizons Close: Rereading Ecclesiastes.* Translated by Margaret Wilde. Eugene, OR: Wipf & Stock.

Wilbur, Richard. 2010. "Ecclesiastes 11:1" from *Anterooms: New Poems and Translations.* Copyright © 2010 by Richard Wilbur. Reprinted by permission of Houghton Mifflin Harcourt. All rights reserved. Reprinted by permission of The Waywiser Press (http://waywiser-press.com). UK and Commonwealth rights reserved.

Wright, J. Robert, ed. 2005. *Proverbs, Ecclesiastes, Song of Solomon.* Ancient Christian Commentary on Scripture: Old Testament 9. Downers Grove, IL: InterVarsity Press.

SONG OF SONGS

Hugh R. Page Jr.

The Song of Songs is a song (Heb. *šîr*) purportedly composed by or making specific reference to Solomon (1:1). It is, in reality, a pseudonymous work. The interpretive literature on the book is vast, and accessible summaries can be found in the more recent commentaries of Tremper Longman III (2001) and J. Cheryl Exum (2005). Scholarly agreement is far from uniform, even among more contemporary commentators, about its content and structure. Some, like Longman, treat it as a poetic "anthology" (Longman, 48). Others are convinced that it is a unified composition with a coherent organizing theme. Exum attempted early on in her engagement of the book to employ a hybrid strategy, synthesizing both of the aforementioned approaches, but eventually abandoned this in favor of reading it as a literary "whole" (Exum, 37). Marvin Pope in his now classic magisterial treatment in the Anchor Bible Commentary series argues that "characterization of the Song as an Anthology is not especially helpful" (Pope, 37). Evidence can be marshaled in favor of either position, so this is an issue about which there is likely to be healthy disagreement among interpreters well into the future.

Insofar as it treats love—in its concrete and ethereal dimensions—as a topic for serious intellectual and spiritual musing, a solid case can be made for its inclusion in the Bible's corpus of Wisdom literature. While not a new suggestion, it is worthy of consideration because within the Song, the taxonomy and lexical inventory used to talk about love (e.g., Heb. *dôd*, *'āhēb*, *ra'yāt*, and *'ahăbâ*) are crucial didactic elements—as crucial as the words used with reference to prudent behavior and its religious underpinnings in Proverbs, Ecclesiastes, and other exemplars of the wisdom genre. In pedagogical contexts, I have found it useful to follow those who see the Song of Songs as a libretto or script for a ritual performance. From my vantage point, one finds in it at least four main voices: (1) a male voice, (2) a female voice, (3) a narrator (or chorus), and (4) Love (Heb. *'ahăbâ*).

The latter of these voices, Love, invites readers to ponder its mysterious calling and to yield themselves to its urgings. In some respects the Song of Songs is reminiscent of the Sumerian cycle of poetry focused on the gods Inanna and Dumuzi (Wolkstein and Kramer) as well as the *hieros gamos* ("sacred marriage") tradition preserved in the Ugaritic tale (CAT 1.23) describing the conception and birth of Dawn and Dusk (Coogan and Smith, 155–66). Resonances to love poetry in ancient Egypt, Canaan, and Mesopotamia have also been noted (Longman, 49–54). It is possible that the liturgical function of what we have in the Song of Songs is to explain the divine etiology of love. Its internal rhetoric emphasizes that the locus of human meaning is found in the unquenchable desire for, and the process of seeking union with, one's beloved, and in recognizing the transcendent moments that are part of the quest that such a quest generates.

From a form-critical standpoint, the *Sitz im Leben* ("life setting") and date of the book are virtually impossible to discern from internal data. Certain linguistic features suggest that the book is either relatively late in composition or hails from an Israelite provenance in which lexical archaisms were prevalent. For example, one particular grammatical element recurring in the text—the use of the prefixed Hebrew particle *šin* as a relative pronoun—could be indicative of either an early or late date. It also contains a number of words that appear only once in the entirety of the Hebrew Bible (see Pope, 33–34). Such a specialized lexicon suggests that the book had a didactic thrust not unlike other works within the biblical wisdom corpus. It views the cosmos as an *esoteric* landscape in which the beloved is at once an archetypal concept and a palpable presence in the human realm. It asserts that the concrete and infinite are part of a single cosmic reality. The physical textures of life are honored through fulsome descriptions of the natural world, the spectrum of human emotions, and the template of the human body. Love occupies a central place in the book, but also poses the ultimate paradox. Giving oneself and one's possessions to pursue and seek communion with it will make one an object of contempt (Heb. *bûz*). Thus 8:6-7 can be said to provide the *axis* around which it and indeed life itself revolves. The quest for and union with one's beloved are those essential features of a terrestrial pilgrimage leading to the *šalhebetyâ* (8:6)—the ineffable flame—in whose presence light, peace, and wholeness are found.

1:1—3:11: Voices of Love and Nocturnal Visions

■ THE TEXT IN ITS ANCIENT CONTEXT

The first three chapters of the Song of Songs model a structural pattern discernible throughout the book: juxtaposition of poetic monologues by what appear to be representative male, female, and unidentified voices. A woman speaks in 1:1-3, inviting an unnamed suitor, perhaps a monarch, to shower her with kisses and to spirit her away (1:4a). A scene shift immediately follows to a royal abode. In the remainder of verse 4, we have an invitation given to a host of young women present (1:3)—or perhaps to a chorus—to celebrate and remember.

> Let us rejoice because of you.
> Let us keep your love always in mind.
> Those who are just love you far more than wine. (1:4)

Soliloquies celebrating the attractiveness of the two lovers follow in the remainder of chapter 1 and in chapter 2. Pastoral imagery abounds (1:7-8, 17) as the comely features of the lovers and the natural surroundings in which their attachment to one another deepens are described in evocative detail. Throughout, one senses that the similarity of nature's rhythms to those of human love is a secret this section is intended to reveal. The agony of unfulfilled longing (3:1-3) and the joy of union with one's beloved (3:4) are revealed in a night vision, the timelessness of which is expressed antiphonally here and later on in the book: "Don't rouse or push Love until the time is right" (2:7; 3:5; 8:4).

THE TEXT IN THE INTERPRETIVE TRADITION

Jewish and Christian expositors have made innumerable interpretive forays into the Song of Songs. Pope offers a selective summary of this rich tradition and notes the presence of Jewish allegorists who see the Song as expressive of YHWH's relationship with Israel, Christian allegorists for whom it is emblematic of the bond between "Christ and the church," and later Jewish mystical traditions that see reflected in the Song "the union of active and passive aspects of the intellect" (Pope, 89). One can readily imagine the rich interpretive possibilities that emerge from applying such paradigms to Song of Songs 1–3.

THE TEXT IN CONTEMPORARY DISCUSSION

Love maintains much of its allure as modern trope and mystery in twenty-first-century life. However, there is reticence to discuss, particularly in faith communities, love and relationships using evocative imagery like that found in the Song. In the West, there remain, at times, strong unspoken taboos that prevent frank discussion about longing and the consummation of desire, even within the parameters of committed long-term partnerships. The Song certainly urges modern readers to "push the envelope" and be more daring in claiming ownership of our emotions and our bodies. We also have to be cognizant of the patriarchal milieu from which the Song comes, the relatively narrow understanding it has of the human gender binary (male/female), and the heteronormative paradigm it reifies. Interpretive readings that reach beyond these cultural signifiers toward the book's core message about love will be better able to deploy it in support of theologies that nurture inclusive communities of conscience.

4:1—8:4: Awakening and Being Intoxicated by Love

THE TEXT IN ITS ANCIENT CONTEXT

How does one comprehend—at a deeper level—the rationale for and implications of the baroque language in this section's evocative monologues? Moreover, what are we to make of the following recommendation in 5:1?

> Friends, Lovers:
> Eat, drink, become inebriated!

Exum's intriguing suggestion about "conjuring" in the Song offers important insight: "The Song casts a spell with words: through seductively beautiful poetry the lovers materialize and dematerialize in a continual play of seeking and finding" (Exum, 6). This raises the possibility of seeing the

Song, in its entirety, as a literary talisman—a *conjurational* implement of power—capable of making the Love that can "stand toe to toe" with Death a reality (8:6). Therefore, the final command in 5:1 (Heb. *wĕšikrû*) could be translated, in context, "be spellbound." It is a directive that should perhaps shape one's approach to this second section in its entirety. As Exum suggests, the Song "invites us to become lovers too" (7).

THE TEXT IN THE INTERPRETIVE TRADITION

Strikingly, Ambrose of Milan sees in Song. 5:1 allusions to Christ communing with the faithful and encouraging them toward greater perfection. A host of other early Christian commentators have noted elements in this section of the Song with important dimensions of the church and the life of faith. Some of the more interesting are Gregory of Nyssa's identification of the frankincense in Song. 4:13-15 with Christ's divinity and his comment on the absence of the beloved in 5:6 as emblematic of the transcendence of Christ; Theodoret of Cyr's reading of Song of Songs 6:5 as a reference to the God's ineffable light; and Ambrose of Milan's suggestion that the nursing-breast imagery in 8:1 alludes to Christian baptism (for the aforementioned references, see Wright, 339–62).

THE TEXT IN CONTEMPORARY DISCUSSION

The strength of interpretive paradigms developed after the Enlightenment is that they stress the value of empirical evidence. When applied to biblical studies, evidence-based approaches treat the Bible purely as an ancient artifact from which information can be mined using scientific methodologies. It becomes an object subject to scholarly and ecclesial gaze—an ossified recipient of our querying. To subject a book like the Song to such treatment deprives it of the vitality it was intended to have. Jewish and Christian allegorists allowed the Song to fire their imaginations. We too should take Exum's lead and allow the evocative poetry in 4:1—8:4 to conjure the lovers in the text as well as the courage we need to love in our generation and live with the consequences—not always salutary—of a life guided by its dictates.

8:6-14: Love Gives Voice to Life's Greatest Paradox

THE TEXT IN ITS ANCIENT CONTEXT

It is in this final section that the Song of Songs most displays the traits of a classical treatise in the genre of speculative wisdom, albeit with a haunting resonance to Canaanite mythology. Love (Heb. *'ahăbâ*) speaks of its vitality and boasts of its power. Both make it a worthy opponent for two forces most emblematic of the life cycle in the ancient Syro-Palestinian imagination: waters and death. To place it as a "seal" on one's thoughts ("heart") and actions ("arm") is to become its devotee and to be warmed by its powerful "divine fire"—the meaning of Hebrew *šalhebetyâ* (8:6). This unquenchable inferno is the iconic hypostasis of the celestial force made manifest in the human longing, the drive to seek the ineffable, and the physical consummation of desire between lovers. One detects unmistakable reminiscences of Ugaritic myth—that is, of the cosmic battle between Ba'lu, the Canaanite storm god, and Yammu, the deification of the sea, whose sobriquets are "Prince Sea" and "Judge

River." One also detects resonances of the story of the continuous battle between Ba'lu and Môtu, the personification of death.

> They fight each other like heroes
> Môtu is strong, as is Ba'lu
> Like raging bulls, they go head to head
> Môtu is strong, as is Ba'lu
> They bite one another like serpents
> Môtu is strong, as is Ba'lu
> Like animals, they beat each other to a pulp
> Môtu falls, Ba'lu collapses. (CAT 1.6.6.16–22)

The protagonists fight to a virtual draw, both falling exhausted from a contest in which neither can claim absolute supremacy. The implication here, and in the Song of Songs, is that Love and Death are engaged in a timeless battle, which is ongoing in the celestial and terrestrial realms. While neither can claim victory, Love's ability to hold its own against its fearsome foe is reason for hope in the divine and human realms.

Nonetheless, the author—or perhaps an editor—of the Song of Songs wonders aloud why it is that in spite of the undeniable truth of Love's remarkable power, those who yield themselves to its inspiration are fated to be misunderstood and shunned by others (8:7). The scene then shifts, perhaps intentionally, to present a parallax view of how the all-encompassing essence of love is made known in the preparation of an earthly lover for the arrival of her beloved (8:8-9) and the feeling of all-encompassing wholeness (Heb. *šālôm*) that her visage engenders (8:10).

■ THE TEXT IN THE INTERPRETIVE TRADITION

Both the Pauline Letters (e.g., Rom. 12:10; 1 Corinthians 13) and the Johannine corpus (e.g., John 13:34; 1 John 14:18) in the New Testament celebrate the centrality, transformational power, and mystery of love (1 John 4:8, 16, 18). In the Fourth Gospel, it is the focus of Jesus' "new commandment" to love one another as Jesus has loved them (John 13:34; 15:12, 17). It is tempting to imagine here and elsewhere that early Christian tradition is in conversation with the tradition of love in Song. 8:6-7. Although editors of the most recent edition of the Greek New Testament (Aland et al., 887–901) identify no quotations or allusions to the Song of Songs in the Gospels, Acts, epistolary texts, or the Apocalypse, it is hard to imagine that a passage like 1 Cor. 13:8, "Love [*agapē*] does not fall," is neither in conversation with nor alluding to Song. 8:6. Among early Christian expositors on this text are Ambrose of Milan, for whom the "seal" in 8:6 is Christ; Augustine of Hippo, who opines on the soteriological impact of love; and Cyril of Jerusalem, who uses Song. 8:7 as a proof text for the actions of the women who came to anoint the body of Jesus after his death (for the aforementioned and additional citations from other early Christian exegetes see Wright, 364–66).

■ THE TEXT IN CONTEMPORARY DISCUSSION

The mystery of love and its transformational power have long been celebrated in music, literature, and art. Moreover, certain musical genres such as blues, rhythm and blues, and soul explore its physical, emotional, social, political, and spiritual dimensions. It is perhaps the late twentieth century's failure to realize the teleological goals expressed in this musical tradition that gave rise to hip-hop culture, whose countercultural thrust offers a strong critique of an older generation that failed either to create Martin Luther King Jr.'s "Beloved Community," or to board the "Love Train" of which the 1970s soul ensemble The Spinners so movingly sings. Nonetheless, today's Bible readers and interpreters have a remarkable opportunity to retrieve the Song of Songs from its place in the archive of potentially scandalous and incredibly difficult biblical texts to which it is often relegated.

The impetus for this reclamation can and should be Song. 8:6-7, which has the ability to function as a window onto a long series of conversations in the ancient world about love. This same text can also be the starting point for a radical reorientation of traditional approaches to Scripture reading. Rather than beginning with the Gospels or taking a yearlong blended (combination of readings from the Old Testament, New Testament, and Psalter) book-by-book approach such as that advocated by the Center for Biblical Studies' "Bible Challenge" (see http://thecenterforbiblicalstudies.org and related links), one could imagine using Song. 8:6-7 as an eschatological antiphon with which to begin and end *lectio divina* or to supplement other strategies of engagement. At a time when the comparative study of Scriptures is not just an activity localized in the academy, but an essential activity in the promotion of interfaith relations as well, texts like Song. 8:6-7 allow clergy and laity to focus on larger—at times intractable—life issues and ponder ways that an appropriate array of texts, biblical and other, can be brought into an illuminating and empowering dialogue with one another. Such a process would certainly eliminate some long-standing barriers standing in the way of our being advocates for a vision of love and loving as all-encompassing and fully embodied acts of solidarity linking the hearts and minds of those willing to risk the "disdain" (Song. 8:7) of others and sit before the *šalhebetyâ* (8:6).

Works Cited

Aland, Barbara, Kurt Aland, Johannes Karavidopoulos, Carlo M. Martini, and Bruce M. Metzger, eds. 2005. *The Greek New Testament*. 4th ed. Stuttgart: Deutsche Bibelgesellschaft/United Bible Societies.

Coogan, Michael D., and Mark S. Smith. 2012. *Stories from Ancient Canaan*. 2nd ed. Louisville: Westminster John Knox.

Exum, J. Cheryl. (2005). *Song of Songs: A Commentary*. OTL. Louisville: Westminster John Knox.

Longman, Tremper I., III. 2001. *Song of Songs*. Grand Rapids: Eerdmans.

Pope, Marvin H. 1977. *Song of Songs: A New Translation with Introduction and Commentary*. AB. Garden City, NY: Doubleday.

Wolkstein, Diane, and Samuel Noah Kramer. 1983. *Inanna: Queen of Heaven and Earth*. New York: Harper & Row.

Wright, J. Robert, ed. 2005. *Proverbs, Ecclesiastes, Song of Solomon*. Ancient Christian Commentary on Scripture, Old Testament, 9. Downers Grove, IL: InterVarsity Press.